Our Need for Others
and its
Roots in Infancy

Our Need for Others and its Roots in Infancy

JOSEPHINE KLEIN

London and New York

First published 1987
by Tavistock Publications Ltd

Reprinted 1993 (twice), 1994, 1995
by Routledge
11 New Fetter Lane, London EC4P 4EE
29 West 35th Street, New York, NY 10001

© 1987 Josephine Klein

Printed and bound in Great Britain by Clays Ltd, St Ives plc

British Library Cataloguing in Publication Data
A catalogue record for this book is available from the British Library

Library of Congress Cataloguing in Publication Data
A catalogue record for this book is available from the Library of Congress

ISBN 0-415-05879-1

Contents

xii

Acknowledgements

The author and the publishers would like to thank the following copyright holders for permission to reproduce material:

Harper & Row, Publishers Inc. for *Figures 5, 6, 7,* and *8.*
Professor Donald O. Hebb for *Figures 9, 13, 14, 15* and *16.*
Century Hutchinson Ltd for *Figure 19.*
Penguin Books Ltd for *Figures 20* and *21.*
Professor George A. Miller for *Figure 22.*
Macmillan Publishing Company for *Figures 25* and *26.*
Aqualac (Spring Waters) Limited for *Figure 47.*

'Prayer Before Birth' is reprinted by permission of Faber and Faber Ltd from *The Collected Poems of Louis MacNeice.*
The lines from 'Missing Dates' by William Empson are reprinted by permission of the author's literary estate and Chatto & Windus: The Hogarth Press; and New Directions Publishing Corporation in the USA.
'the great advantage of being alive' by e. e. cummings is reprinted from *Complete Poems 1913–1962* by permission of Grafton Books (Collins Publishing Group) and Harcourt Brace Jovanovich in the USA.
'The Fall of Rome' by W. H. Auden is reprinted from *Collected Poems* by permission of Faber & Faber Ltd and Random House, Inc. in the USA and Canada.
The author and publishers have made every effort to obtain

permission to reproduce copyright material throughout this book. If any proper acknowledgement has not been made, or permission not received, we would invite any copyright holder to inform us of this oversight.

Preamble

Our need for others has its roots in our earliest experiences and is bound up with our deepest feelings. This may be obvious, and yet a hundred years of otherwise creditable psychological thinking took it for granted that we begin life as individuals, who somehow at some later stage get into relationships with each other. In the last fifty years, however, psychology has begun to catch up with common knowledge, and all kinds of evidence have been accumulating to suggest that relationships are at least as basic as individuals. Indeed, I shall argue that there may be many people who never get to be very highly individuated, and that being an individual may not be such a big prize anyway.

The field of psychodynamic theory, on which the practice of psycho-analysis is built, also started at a very individualistic extreme. It relied on theories which considered instinctual drives to be the basic forces which moved individuals about, towards food or sex or other goals, and hence, incidentally, towards other people. More recently, however, a new way of thinking has been gaining ground, with which the name 'object-relations theory' has been associated.

Object-relations theories are about our relations to the 'objects' – the people and things – to which we are attached and which give meaning to our lives. These are theories about what goes on between you and me, and between us and them, and about how these relationships govern our lives. In this book I have tried to sketch out an account of what has been written about the origins of such relationships, and about some of the developments to which they are subject. My focus will be, 'What was life like in those early days when we began?' There will be two subplots. (1) 'Suppose that is what life was like in the early days, when we were cared for by others. What implications does this have for our later years, when we can no longer call on others in quite the same way to take care of the baby which still survives in us?' (2) 'Suppose that is what life was like in the early days. What does this tell us about the help which psychothera-pists and psycho-analysts can give if, in later years, we find we are compulsively recreating the relationships which were first developed between the baby-self and the parent adult?'

A surprising amount is known about all this, though in piecemeal form. I have tried to fit the pieces together in a loosely arranged overall account. Loosely arranged they have had to be: in the present state of knowledge, if we are too precise and treat these ideas as though they were as solid as pieces of a jigsaw puzzle which can fit in only one way to make a true picture, then we are bound either to be disappointed or to cheat. It is important to remember that we are dealing with what are, after all, only tentative hypotheses. To get different tentative hypoth-eses to fit tightly together is the vain ambition of obsessionals: a slight difference made by a new finding – even a change in the language used to describe a finding – could change the whole thing.

This is the more true the more intangible the field. The only tangible evidence in this kind of field is provided by test results like 'Four out of five babies exactly 6 weeks old smile when their feet are tickled' (I do not know if this is true). We cannot know what such a result means, what brings about the smile in the four babies, what inhibits it in the fifth, what grimace is a smile, whether it also happens in Siam, or was prevalent in the sixteenth century. So if someone else comes along and says, 'Two out of three babies exactly 5 weeks old gurgle when their feet are tickled', there is no point in opposing this finding to the other. We have to work towards an account of baby-life in which both findings have a place.

There are many problems of this kind: how do we know for sure that a baby is angry? How do we know for sure that a baby grieves? What do we mean when we say a baby understands, or remembers? There are useful answers suggested by various people to each of these questions, and I shall mention some. I am making a case for not fighting each other when the answers do not tally. Our knowledge is not sufficiently advanced for that.

There are also problems presented by the fact that different authors are interested in different aspects of the same phenomenon, and have different sensitivities about the same developmental processes. For instance, Kernberg's interests ranged from the cultural differences between societies to details about the way the brain works. So he gives us a version of early mental processes which lets us take a great range of contemporary ideas into account. Kohut had fine intuitions about the pride which mothers take in their small children, and he provides some very attractive ideas about the role of parental admiration. Both writers make major contributions to our imaginative understanding of the baby-mind and of the adult's in regression. Yet they may be presented to the student mainly with reference to a controversy about the roots of aggression. They differ deeply and interestingly on this issue, but it would be a pity to allow it to obscure the many other useful ideas each contributes.

For these and many other reasons, the present book is not intended to be a scholarly exposition of all that has been written about early experiences, although it is based on much scholarly work to which reference is duly made. Since I started writing, an admirable scholarly account of object-relations theories has been written by J. R. Greenberg and S. A. Mitchell (1984), and perhaps there are others. But I believe there is room for an easily read version which brings together a variety of ideas, some of which have been in the air for decades, and some of which are more recent. These ideas have tended to be presented in isolation from one another, embedded in arguments which take attention away from the common ground out of which further knowledge may grow. It is common ground this book looks for.

I have tried to write a book for intelligent lay people, while at the same time hoping to interest my colleagues in the way I have come to hold the views I am advocating, and also paying due respect to the work of those others from whom my own ideas derive. I have to confess that I have not been able to read or include all the relevant literature. Where does it end? There are always problems of time and space. Then, too, some ideas were couched in language which aroused in me an unconquerable aversion – to these I make no further reference. But there are also more controversial gaps in my account. The most serious of these is my disregard of much contemporary empirical child psychology, a fascinating and relevant field, but I felt that I lacked the expertise to evaluate it all, and anyway, the book is quite long enough as it is. I intend no disrespect to that research, however, which often appears to me to give substance to my guesswork. I have also left out Margaret Mahler and her co-workers, for lack of time and space, and because of problems in identifying the particular cultural settings of the mothers and children she studied. Others may wonder at my scant references to Sigmund Freud. He is, of course, relevant, but others have already covered that ground very adequately. For much the same reason I hardly allude to Anna Freud and to Melanie Klein.

I have taken liberties with even my favourite authors. When first drafting my chapters I wrote in a conscientious and properly scholarly manner: I quoted my sources in full to give substance to my points and to make acknowledgement of the origins of my ideas. Even my best friends refused to enjoy this. Accordingly I changed my approach. I now have passages which paraphrase other writers, and in the quotations I have sometimes omitted words or sentences which were irrelevant to my purpose; I have, I hope, been careful to give references at the end of all such passages. This approach has given greater style and unity to the book, and I hope it has not been at too great an expense of fidelity to the overall contributions made by the authors I have used as sources. My emphasis is sometimes different, and I have left out large chunks, especially when I disagreed with them. Readers primarily interested in a particular writer, rather than in the argument for which this book is designed, must therefore go to the original text for a properly balanced picture. Indeed, I hope that my efforts will encourage many readers to do so.

·1·
Introduction and overview

'I have no name;
I am but two days old.'
  (William Blake, *Songs of Innocence and Experience*)

How mysterious a baby is, its personality still largely potential, and how helpless. Yet how powerfully it reaches out to us and touches the heart – for sustenance and for the relief of its distresses, but also for recognition.

'What shall I call thee?
"I happy am,
 Joy is my name".'

A baby seems to reach out for validation and confirmation that it is already a person. And we respond.

'Thou dost smile;
I sing the while,
Sweet joy befall thee!

Pretty joy!
Sweet joy, but two days old;
Sweet joy I call thee.'

Sweet joy *I* call *thee* – we respond and recognize and validate. Blake celebrates the lovely and loving side of infant and adult.

1

But he also knows of the despairing, devastated, hating, and envying side of the relationship.

'Oh rose thou art sick.
The invisible worm
That flies in the night
In the howling storm:

Has found out thy bed
Of crimson joy;
And his dark secret love
Does thy life destroy.'

(*The Sick Rose*)

Joy, but also fear, pain, loss, and hate, may be a baby's everyday experiences. How can it manage such feelings, helpless as it is? It cannot — that is what the adult is for. The fortunate infant has adults whose care goes beyond managing its appetites and distresses. Such a baby will still be subject to misery and terror — we all are — but it will meet them in a context of love and acceptance. Its pains and rages will be surrounded, contained, and modified by memories of joy and bliss, and by expectations of more happiness to come. Indeed, I shall argue that memories of bliss are converted into expectations of bliss, as also, alas, memories of distress turn into expectations of more grief. Good memories give a baby a better chance of continuing to feel appealing and acceptable in all circumstances, in sorrow as well as joy, when it is bad as well as when it is good.

The infant is helpless. It is the adult who mainly provides the context of its experiences. For a context within which the infant can hold on to its experiences and not be devastated by them when they are bad, the infant needs adults who, consciously or unconsciously, understand how the baby feels. Adults who recognize the depths of their baby's feelings, good and bad, give solidity to that baby's experience of itself. Such recognition helps consolidate the baby's integrity and sense of self: its identity. Joyous recognition will encourage a joyous identity.

I shall be suggesting that there is a strong connection between the way adults see a child, and behave toward it, and the child's identity (that is the way the child sees itself and feels about itself), and the basic structures of its personality. The very structures of the personality are determined by early experiences. Differences between adults, differences in the nature of our feelings, and in our need for others, and in our relationships with others, have roots in the different ways in which our minds are structured.

If the mind is a structure, what is it a structure of? There are answers to this question at different levels of complexity; in order of increasing complexity, there will be answers in Chapters 2, 3, 4, 8, 10, 14, and 18.

I shall argue that there is more than one good way of being an integrated person with a unique identity, self-image, and personality-structure. For instance, we often tend, in our culture, to think of ourselves as rather like a computer or a motor car, with the parts organized so that they fit together to do some work, or calculate something, or take us somewhere. In this phantasy we may include a driver to keep the motor car moving towards our objective, or we may think of our machine as self-starting and self-motivated but, essentially, we assume that there is a point in being what we are and that we should be organized around that point. However, as far as some of us are concerned, our experience of ourselves may be much more like a landscape, a stormy and volcanic one or a quiet one with hills, hedges, meadows, rivers, roads, and settlements – many varied features in specific relationships with one another, and integrated, but not organized in any obvious or purposeful way.

Our love and recognition of a child may also lean more to one or other of these models. Is the child a motor car to us or a landscape? The child's experience of itself – its self-image and indeed the very structure of its personality – will be affected accordingly (though not necessarily in ways we intend).

In all these processes and influences, words are unimportant. What happens between adult and infant is not primarily conversational or intellectual. The foundations of our personality are not composed of words, and do not derive from conversational or intellectual apprehensions. How poor we would be if we needed words to appreciate a landscape! And how hard it is to put our appreciation into words.

The non-verbal nature of infant experience is similarly hard to apprehend and put into words. This makes it easy to neglect the non-verbal elements from which our personality is built up. In

order to carry conviction when writing of our non-verbal life, I
have had to lay some solid foundations. The book's first part, its
Conceptual foundations, contains three chapters on non-verbal,
and indeed barely psychological, processes. In the fascinating
area of neurophysiology, we can find the elements which will
eventually combine into the more recognizable psychological
structures which we call thoughts, words, feelings, images,
symbols, emotions, motives. Each of these is a structure of more
basic elements, and we shall see them built into more complex
organizations at different points in the book.

The part which follows, *The e-merging of self from (m)other*, is
also preparatory to the main narrative of this book, though a
little less remote from human experience. One chapter is mainly
on the infant handicapped by being born into a world which its
neurophysiology cannot cope with; one is mainly on the infancy
of animals whose species seem destined never to be conscious
and verbal; and one is on the human infant in the very moment
of its individuation and separation from the mother.

The human infant is, relatively speaking, quite sophisticated
and complex by the time it experiences itself as separate from
others.

> 'The baby new to earth and sky,
>   What time his tender palm is prest
>   Against the circle of the breast,
> Has never thought that "this is I".
>
> But as he grows he gathers much,
>   And learns the use of "I" and "me",
>   And finds "I am not what I see
> And other than the things I touch".
>
> So rounds he to a separate mind
>   From when clear memory may begin,
>   As thro' the frame that binds him in
> His isolation grows defined.'
>
>   (Tennyson, *In Memoriam A. H.* xlv)

The third group of chapters, on *The relation of self to others*, looks
at this individuation in more detail. The neurophysiological
elements reviewed in the earlier chapters are now elaborated into
true psychological structures, in the course of which some

interesting questions are considered: How are we to think of human experience? What are its basic units? What is an integrated person? What is it that integrates? How are we to describe the difference between the integrity of a motor car and the integrity of a landscape? What does it means to be an individual? When is differentiaton mere lack of integration and when is it accurate and useful individuation?

Once this is clarified, our focus can finally come to rest on recognizable adult experiences, albeit on those adult experiences in which the effects of our childhood are very apparent. We are now in the second half of the book, and moving toward conclusions which help us understand new things about ourselves and our need for others. A fourth section looks at our *Sources of strength*, and in particular at the parent–child relationships associated with a durable sense of well-being and an integrated optimistic identity. Wordsworth described these good feelings with wonderful accuracy in his *Ode on Intimations of Immortality from Recollections of Early Childhood*, though he attributes them to memories of our time with God (before we were born) rather than to memories of our early life with loving adults:

'There was a time when meadow, grove, and stream,
The earth, and every common sight,
    To me did seem
    Apparell'd in celestial light
The glory and the freshness of a dream.'

This sunny section is necessarily followed by one which looks at *Splits*, at the sources of weakness, at what can go wrong and cause breakdown and disintegration. Where does it come from, the invisible worm that flies in the night and gnaws at our capacity for joy? It is here that our motor car versus landscape analogy of personality-structure comes back into the argument. People operating on the model of a machine, a model in which we are organized around some point, have a somewhat easier time when feeling disturbed or unwell: if the car will not go, there must be something wrong with it – find the part that has gone wrong and mend or replace it. But landscapes cannot go wrong in quite the same way. And what will make them feel better? In this section, which takes the landscape as its model of personality-structure, an attempt is made both to list some ideas about the various lines along which a person may fall apart, and to contribute to a theory of personality-structure in which these ideas can find convenient lodging.

The argument, which has been slowly building up from chapter to chapter, reaches its culmination in the final part, on *Holding and healing*. Here the influences are examined which make for integration, and either prevent splits or go some way toward mending them. Some conclusions are drawn which may seem obvious in the light of what has gone before, about caring for ourselves and others, about the use of the intellect (called 'ego-functioning' in this book), and about the nature of psychotherapy.

I shall argue that, in the course of development, there is a transfer of functions from the adult to the child. Care and nurture must be the adult response to the tiny helpless infant if it is to survive at all: if this is done with joy, so much the better — there will be joy at the heart of that person's identity. A little later, adults can lend encouragement and support to the busy crawling baby who is beginning to communicate in words, and to the toddler trying for intellectual understanding. Not much later, some mutual consideration and recognition of the other's needs becomes possible. A little later yet, adult and child can begin to share responsibility for setting goals, the adult giving support when control is needed to sustain the pursuit of a chosen goal. All these things are first brought to the relationship by the adult. That is the origin of our need for others. But in the course of development, the fortunate child begins to want to do for itself the things which were first done for it by loving and competent adults. In this way we learn how to care for, and how to take care of, ourselves and others. We do this, for good or for ill, in the manner and in the spirit we learnt from others. We do as we were done to.

What, then, of the children who took over the functioning of unloving and incompetent adults? Can later relationships help them? Later teachers, friends, and lovers may indeed be able to stir buried memories of good functioning into life: there may be seeds from which hopeful expectations for the future may spring. But early insufficiencies can leave structural weaknesses which lead people to experience themselves as fragmented, liable

to fall apart, not really alive, only pretending to be people. They
need holding before they can be healed. They need a considerable period of very secure attachment. They need to experience
some limit to their feelings of endless disconnectedness and lack
of direction. It is not often possible for others to do this in the
normal course of living, at least for the very long time that may
be needed. And they may be further hindered because sometimes people's capacity to learn, to have friends and use them,
and to relate in love, has not developed or has a destructive
invisible worm at its core. Then professional help has to be
looked for.

Yet until recently this kind of help did not fall within the
sphere normally allotted to psychotherapists, psycho-analysts,
or counsellors: their help was more directed toward helping
people to understand themselves in their world, to accept
themselves as they are and perhaps as they might become. But the
people we are now considering cannot be helped by this, any
more than a baby who has had a bad fall can be helped by being
made to understand itself. From the point of view of the person
giving help, there is no point in aiming at the capacity to
understand intellectually (because it is not there). More is
therefore required of the professional help than in the otherwise
often excellent ways of listening and talking currently taught to
students training to be analysts, counsellors, or therapists. Of
course, in practice many of these do more than they were
formally taught to do. They recognize intuitively that, since the
elements which went into the construction of the personality
were so largely non-verbal and non-intellectual, the damage
wrought in those early days cannot be mended by purely
intellectual understanding. But there are many gaps in the
theories which might back them up.

In this book I have tried to add further substance to such
intuitions. The parallels I draw in the final chapters, between
what good parents do and what good psychotherapists do, may
be obvious. I hope the conclusions drawn there will seem equally
obvious when the reader gets to them. Yet it seems to me that at
present we do not give them the place they should have, either in
theory or in practice. However, our understanding of psycho-
therapeutics, evolving over a hundred years, is being perfected
all the time. Though it is a slow process, the trend continues

towards understanding and achieving the relationships which will help us integrate and live well when our capacity for joy has been damaged at the core.

PART 1

CONCEPTUAL FOUNDATIONS

THE PHYSICAL PERSPECTIVE

THE FORMATION OF CONCEPTS

INTENTIONAL BEHAVIOUR

Whether we are structured more like motor cars or more like landscapes, we are composed of discernibly different parts or aspects. How can these become integrated into a more or less unified composition? And how can we conceptualize the relationships between them which would integrate them in this way? The concept of 'networks' brings us very nearly to a complete answer. Networks may be organized with a centre to them, or without a centre, or with more than one centre. So may we. Networks may operate simultaneously at different levels of complexity. So may we. In the three chapters which follow, networks of nerve-cells are shown to build up into organizations of great complexity and power.

The reader who likes to begin with the more immediately human implications of an argument, may prefer to skip this section and start at p. 75 with the three chapters of Part 2, *The e-merging of self from (m)other*. But the section after that, which includes chapters on the basic units of experience, the emergence of painful relationships, and the language of 'splits', will be heavy going unless the present section has at least been glanced at.

·2·
The physical perspective

The simplest neurophysiological facts

As far as we know, without processes in the nervous system, there are no psychological processes. This suggests that we should, if we can, try to theorize in conformity with what is thought to be characteristic of the human nervous system; this should set some limits to our speculations on how the mind works. To start with, we need to agree some brief definitions of basic words.

The nervous system is made up of *nerve-cells often called neurons*. A nerve-cell has various parts to it (see *Figure 1*). The *cell*

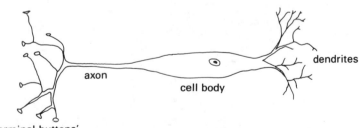

Figure 1 A nerve-cell

11

body contains the nucleus and much else that provides for the life-processes of the cell. The *axon* is the part of the cell which divides and branches into *dendrites*. 'Dendron' is the Greek word for tree, and the dendrites look like tiny branching trees. At the end of each of the twigs is a little knob called the *terminal button* or *synaptic knob*.

Nerve-cells converse with one another; the dendrites (and sometimes points on the skin of the cell body) receive these neural messages. The axon carries the messages from the cell body to the terminal buttons. The messages from nerve-cell to nerve-cell pass across a *synapse*, which joins the terminal buttons of the transmitting cell to points on the cell body or to the dendrites of the receiving cell, as illustrated in *Figure 2*.

Messages are electrical in nature but they are not carried along the cells in the way a message travels down a telephone wire. They are transmitted by means of complex changes in the skin of the axon, which result in exchanges of various chemical consti-tuents of the fluids inside and outside the axon. These exchanges produce alterations in electrical currents, and it is these which excite the cells into transmitting messages down the line.[1]

The terminal buttons of the axon have the special function, when a message is passed down the axon, of secreting a chemical – *the transmitter substance*. There are various transmitter sub-stances, used by different kinds of nerve cells, some excitatory some inhibitory. Transmitter substances are picked up by the receiving cell and produce effects there, either to excite or to

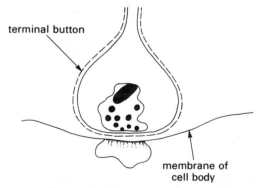

Figure 2 A synapse of a terminal button on the membrane of a cell body

inhibit transmission. These effects will play a part in determining whether messages will be sent on further down the line.[1]

Neurons can connect with other neurons in long chains or in
more sophisticated ways. A simple (imaginary and unrealistic)
illustration of the principle would be as shown in *Figure 3*, or
thus:

(a)   chains of neurons excited by the stimulus of stripes

(b)   chains of neurons excited by the stimulus of dots

(c)   chains of neurons excited by the stimulus of black

(d)   chains of neurons excited by the stimulus of stipples

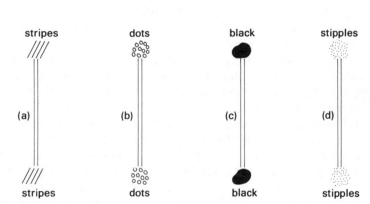

Figure 3

Figure 4 shows how these can then be combined:

$$a + c = \text{black stripes}$$
$$a + d = \text{stippled stripes}$$
$$b + c = \text{dotted black thing}$$
$$b + d = \text{dotted and stippled thing}$$
$$a + b + c = \text{black dotted stripes}$$

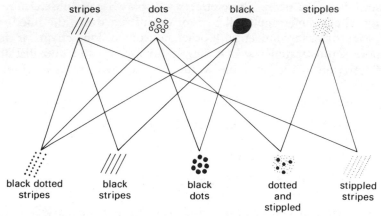

Figure 4

Figures 3 and *4* foreshadow, in very diagrammatic form, how quite complex experiences may come to be organized, through the simultaneous transmission of separate messages which get combined somewhere along the line. So Turkish Delight can come to smell, look, feel, *and* taste delicious (at least to those of us who like it) all at the same time. Interlinked messages produce a sorting or coding or editing of stimuli.

Figures 3 and *4* are just explanatory drawings showing the relational principles. But *Figure 5* shows part of the retina at the back of the eye, a structure which is thought to work on these same principles. On the left are shown the receptor cells, which receive the messages of the image to be perceived. (There are some 130 million of these in the retina of each eye!) Some analysis of an image occurs as the receptors transmit messages to the retinal ganglion cells via the bipolar cells. (Ganglion cells are groups of nerve-cell bodies located outside the Central Nervous System, that is outside the brain.) Bipolar cells, gathering messages from a number of cells and sending them on are sometimes called 'internuncial', that is, between messages, as in the quotation on p. 19. Groups of receptors funnel into a particular ganglion cell, as indicated by the shading; each group forms that ganglion cell's receptive field. Inasmuch as the fields of several ganglion cells overlap, one receptor may send messages to several.

Next, more complex, but still amazingly more simplified than

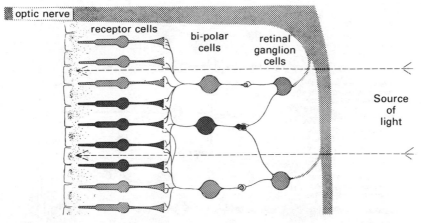

Figure 5
Source: Hubel, D. H. (1963) The Visual Cortex of the Brain. In N. Chalmers, R. Crawley, and S. P. R. Rose (eds.: 1971) *The Biological Bases of Behaviour*. Milton Keynes: Open University.

in real life, *Figure 6* shows a section cut through the retina of a mammal, first tidied into diagrammatic form, then as actually revealed by silver impregnation.

A single message from a single neuron to a second one is unlikely to excite it. It needs more than a minimum number within a given time-span. Together, these will cause a message to be transmitted which does excite the receiving cell, which then passes the messages further up the line. This is achieved in at least two ways. Messages from one neuron to another can follow in rapid succession within a short time, thus amplifying their effectiveness. Also, messages may reach a neuron from more than one other neuron at a time, and these messages can combine to reach the threshold for being excited. *Figure 7* shows the terminal buttons from many neurons more or less covering a cell body, which is thus likely to be a very excitable one.

The process by which simultaneous transmissions from a large number of cells, and/or a large number of transmissions from the same cells, finally reach a level which excites another cell, is called *summation*. This summation can be reached in a variety of ways. Simplifying to illustrate the principle: suppose a cell is excited whenever it has received ten transmissions within a

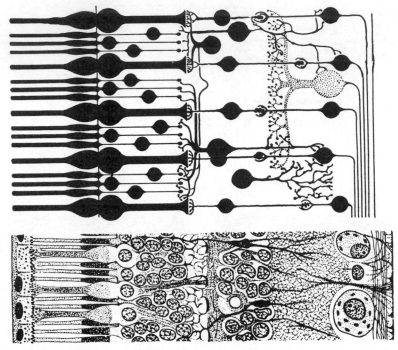

Figure 6
Source: This drawing is by Walls, partly after Polyak. From Romer, A. S. (1970) The Eye. In N. Chalmers, R. Crawley, and S. P. R. Rose (eds.: 1971) *The Biological Bases of Behaviour.* Milton Keynes: Open University.

given time-span. Suppose it is in touch with 100 other cells. Then any ten together can excite it. Or any five firing twice within the given time-span can fire it. Or any six, of which four fire a second time within the time-span. Or ... etc., etc. So there is great flexibility. And great complexity.

We have therefore a system by which a number of excited cells are required to excite another cell, and this cell may, through its many terminal buttons, take part in exciting yet another set of cells, not on its own but in conjunction with other excited cells. So there is quite a communication network among neurons.

Figure 8 shows a microphotograph which gives us some visual

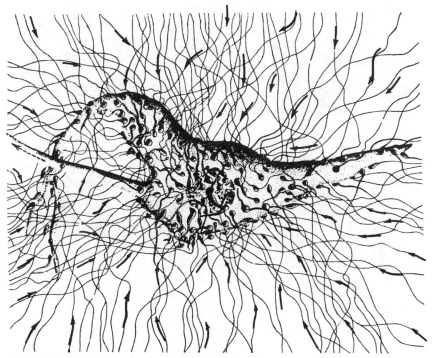

Synaptic knobs. The terminals of axons from other
nerve cells cover the surface of a motoneuron cell body and its
processes except for the axon (on the right).

Figure 7 Synaptic knobs
Source: Katz, B. (1961) How Cells Communicate. In N. Chalmers, R.
Crawley, and S. P. R. Rose (eds: 1971) *The Biological Bases of Behaviour.*
Milton Keynes: Open University.

impression of this complexity. It is a section through the sensori-
motor cortex of a cat, enlarged some 150 diameters: fewer than
20 per cent of the cell bodies and dendrites actually present are
stained and shown here! The axons do not show up at all with
this staining method.

Now that we have some impression of the immensely complex
ways in which interconnections can be made, we can take
another tentative look at the fact that the interlinking of
messages can produce a sorting or coding or editing of sensory
experiences. D. O. Hebb produces an imaginary diagram of how

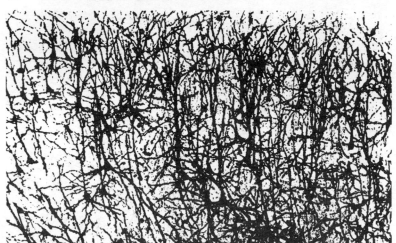

Figure 8
Source: The photograph was made by the late D. A. School of University College London, and is cited by Katz, B. (1961) How Cells Communicate. In N. Chalmers, R. Crawley, and S.P.R. Rose (eds: 1971) *The Biological Bases of Behaviour*. Milton Keynes: Open University.

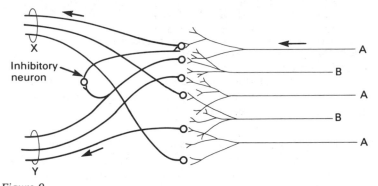

Figure 9
Source: Hebb, D. O. (1958) *A Textbook of Psychology*. Philadelphia and London: W. B. Sanders.

sensory coding might work (see *Figure 9*):

'A and B are neurons leading toward the Central Nervous System. A has a lower threshold for firing than B; a weak stimulus fires A only; a strong one fires A at a higher rate and also fires B. At the next synaptic level, internuncial neuron X may have a lower threshold than Y, or respond more readily to a lower frequency of firing. With low-level activity in A alone, X will fire and Y tend to be inactive. When the level of stimulation goes up, however, Y begins to fire and inhibits X (for clarity, only one inhibitory neuron is pictured).

More concretely, and involving three effects: A weak acid on the tongue (which tastes sour) produces firing in three sets of neurons, A, B, and C. Salt solution fires set A plus set B; quinine, which is bitter, fires set A plus set C. Despite having a common activity in neurons A, these three processes produce effects at higher levels that are quite distinct from each other. (Sour, salt, and bitter, together with sweet – for which less physiological information is available – constitute the four primary taste qualities.)

Activity on line A, therefore, may contribute to any one of three different awarenesses (considered as neural awarenesses in the cerebrum), depending on the total pattern of activity: A–B–C one central process, A–B another, A–C a third.

Another example is found in the perception of temperature. Steady warmth and steady cold have a considerable overlap in their use of connections, but warmth produces a slow, irregular firing (of the neurons), cold a faster and regular firing. Ultimately these messages get completely sorted out, at some point in the Central Nervous System. They must, since they determine quite different responses.

It is not difficult to see how the sorting out might be achieved, although the synaptic mechanisms are not known specifically. In taste, A and B fibres may produce summation and fire cells that A and C do not (these cells in turn inhibiting any others that happen to be excited by A alone). As for warmth and cold and differences of temporal pattern, we have seen that some cells may have a low threshold for impulses of one frequency, other cells a low threshold for another frequency, and this may be a factor in sorting out the "warm" message from the "cold" message.'

(Hebb 1958: 99–100)

Feelings

Laboratory experiments have tended mainly to use examples from the visual and cognitive side of human experience (and from the behavioural side of animal experience), yet messages about feelings are also continually coming in, and form an element of many experiences. It is therefore worth looking in a little more detail at the neurophysiology of emotional experience.

In some respects, feelings are registered just like sights, sounds, and smells. What are commonly called the senses – vision, hearing, taste, smell, touch, and so on – depend on specialized sensory nerve-cells, often concentrated at one end in an organ like the eye or the ear. The cells become active when something from outside the animal produces the stimulus which activates that particular kind of sensory cell. These cells and their immediately following cells are called 'exteroceptors' (*extero* for outside, *ceptor* for receptor).

We know more about ourselves and about the world than the exteroceptors convey. There are specialized nerve-cells, related not to external stimuli but to something internal. We know, for instance, whether we are standing on one leg or two, whether our fist is clenched or not. We know this from other specialized nerve-cells called 'interoceptors' and 'proprioceptors', which give information, not about the world but about such things as the amount of tension in a muscle or the amount of a hormone in the blood. Partly through these, we know 'how we feel': tense or relaxed, alert or sleepy, joyous or sad, satisfied or uncomfortable. There is of course more to feelings than this, and we will look at it in greater detail in later chapters – here we are just looking at the neurophysiological processes involved.

Freud postulates two basic feelings, *Lust* and *Unlust* – pleasure and distress – mirror images of each other. This seems to reflect something in our common thinking. Neurophysiologically, however, they belong to very different bodily systems. Although in our culture we think of them as opposites, both systems can contribute simultaneously to our experience, and indeed, often do. Both systems are very complex and wide-branching, so there need be no difficulty in imagining that these experiences, of pleasure and of pain, can also be connected with other experiences, and organized together, just as 'black' and 'stripes' are organized in purely visual material.

Some messages register as 'pain'.

'There is general agreement that there are nerve endings which generate the messages which are ultimately interpreted as pain. These sensory nerve endings are found in the skin, in the sheath surrounding muscles, in the internal organs, and in the membrane surrounding bones. . . . Just about any kind of manipulation that causes tissue damage will cause pain, and thus most investigators believe that pain receptors are chemically stimulated by substances liberated by damaged tissues.'

(Carlson 1977: 99–100)

The experience of pain is like our experience of 'black' or 'bitter' or other information brought in by the senses, in that there are various specialized sensory nerve-endings which can be activated and which in due course produce the experience 'pain'. There are different kinds of pain, with different kinds of nerve-endings concerned with each.[2] There are chemical substances, drugs, which can alter the way messages register because a cell's receptivity can be affected by chemical substances in the bloodstream – in effect such drugs relieve the perception of pain or change our perception of how unbearable it is.[3] There is also evidence now that the body can itself produce morphine-like substances to regulate the registration of pain – endorphins.[4]

Some messages register as 'pleasure'. The experience of pleasure seems much more diffuse than the experience of pain, and does not depend on sensory nerve-endings as pain does. On the other hand, distinct areas of the brain are again concerned. Experiments with animals have made it clear that there is an area in the medial forebrain, which can be called a 'pleasure-centre'. If stimulated electrically, it produces an effect which the animal seeks to repeat.

'Routenberg and Lindy (1965) trained rats to press two levers – one delivered rewarding electrical brain stimulation (ESB), the other one produced food pellets. The animals were allowed to press the levers for only one hour each day, and some of them spent so much time at the bar that delivered ESB that they starved to death. When food and ESB are continuously available, however, rats will alternately eat, press the lever for ESB, and sleep; they will not remain at the lever for ESB to the exclusion of other activities (Valenstein and Beer 1964).'

(Carlson 1977: 474)

What excites a pleasure-centre in normal circumstances (that is not because of an electrode implanted in the brain by an experimenter) is not yet clear. But neural messages must be involved, and that must mean that the experience of pleasure is available to be organized with other experiences, just as a sound is, or a touch or a smell or a pain.

Carlson, from whom much of this material is quoted, also cites evidence suggesting that when the pleasure-centre is stimulated, this tends to arouse the biological drives, so that animals who have access to increased pleasure-stimulation also explore more, eat more, drink more, copulate more (Carlson 1977: 474). Pleasure is thus a general arouser of activity – an anti-depressant!

Aggression and fear can also be produced in the laboratory. Flynn and some colleagues report a study in which cats could be induced to attack a rat or flee from a cage in response to electrical stimulation of the brain.[5] Various hormone-like chemicals, some sex-linked, increase or decrease the amount of aggression shown by animals in the laboratory. The psychiatrist has at his or her disposal a whole range of chemicals which alter the amount of aggression or fear which might otherwise be produced or experienced by a person.

For our purpose we do not need to understand the details. We need only to notice that just as information is available to the nervous system about where our limbs are or our head, so there is information available about the amount of pain or pain-inhibition, or aggression, or fear, or pleasure, or sexual stimulus, floating in our bloodstream, contracting a muscle, or distending a vessel.

Feelings and other neurophysiological events

Hebb (1949: 147), in one of his occasional informal moments, writes of the place of feelings in scientific and pre-scientific thought:

'The original idea of emotion was probably a reference to the demons that now and then disturb ordinary behaviour. Demons or no, let it be observed that this was an inference from *behaviour*, demons not being easily seen by most people.

Very much later a quite different idea appeared, and is still current. Emotion is now generally thought of as an awareness, a distinctive conscious process that is quite separate from intellectual processes. This notion has led to a good deal of confusion, for it has gradually become clear that no such distinct kind of awareness exists.'

In the same way, it may have been a hindrance to the development of our understanding, that traditional psychology and traditional neurophysiology discuss perception and emotion in different chapters. This is not surprising or wrong, since they originate in such very different systems, but it does impede the imagination.

Never mind where sight originates anatomically or physiologically! Never mind what hormones and what patch of brain-tissue is required for aggression! The Central Nervous System is sufficiently complex to have vision and aggression going on at the same time, and room to spare. Just as 'black' and 'striped', coming from two sets of nerve cells originally yet arriving simultaneously at some central point, give the experience of 'black stripes', just in the same way 'nice' and 'black' can be experienced simultaneously although the messages come from very different sources (see *Figure 10*).

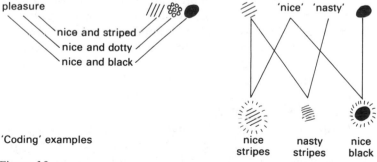

'Coding' examples

Figure 10

Whatever their origins, messages of feelings can be organized along with other messages. In some corners of the thinking world this is an obvious statement. But not everywhere. There is, lurking in the thoughts of many, a conviction that feelings are a special kind of psychological phenomenon, different from other phenomena in being intangible, coming from nowhere, unpredictable. That may be how we usually experience feelings, but it does not make them inaccessible to systematic study. We do well to heed John Bowlby's warning:

'Although affects, feelings, and emotions are commonly treated as though they were discrete entities, it is quite inappropriate so to treat them. To speak of "an affect", "a feeling", or "an emotion", as though it were an atom or an orange, is as inadmissible as it would be to speak of "a redness" or "a squareness". Instead, feeling is to be regarded as a property that certain processes connected with behaviour from time to time come to possess.'

(Bowlby 1969: 139)

Feeling is not a thing but a process experienced or studied from a particular point of view, Bowlby goes on to say.

'The viewpoint adopted here, with the diffidence necessary in a field so strewn with boulders, is well expressed in Langer's recent book on the subject (1967). Langer takes her cue from some reflections of a neurologist concerned to understand voluntary control of muscle. "It will be with feeling that we shall be largely concerned", writes Gooddy (1949), "for sensory symptoms so commonly are a complaint of patients with dysfunction of voluntary movement. 'My hand feels funny when I try and move it'". Pondering on this, Gooddy notes that "the natural use of the words 'feel', 'seems', 'numb', 'clumsy', 'heavy', 'helpless', 'stiff', is to describe what turns out to be motor dysfunction". Gooddy then asks the troublesome question of how it is that events neurophysiological can "break through to feeling".

At this point, Langer notes that "feel" is a verb. To say that what is felt is "a feeling" may well be deceptive: "the phenomenon usually described as 'a feeling' is really that an organism feels something, ie that something is felt. What is felt is a process ... within the organism". This leads on to Langer's main proposition: *"Being felt"*, she concludes, *"is a phase of the process itself"*.

By "phase" Langer means one of the many modes in which something may appear without anything having meanwhile been added to or subtracted from it. As an illustration she considers the heating and cooling of iron:

"When iron is heated to a critical degree it becomes red; yet its redness is not a new entity which must have gone somewhere else when it is no longer in the iron. It was a phase of the iron itself, at high temperature.

As soon as feeling is regarded as a phase of a physiological process instead of a product of it – namely a new entity metaphysically different from it – the paradox of the physical and the psychical disappears".

Thus, continues Langer, the question is no longer one of "how a physical process can be transformed into something non-physical in a physical system, but how the phase of being felt is attained, and how the process may pass into unfelt phases again".'

(ibid. Bowlby's italics)

· 3 ·

The formation of concepts

Sensory messages combine into concepts

Messages, about variations in light, sound, temperature, or whatever, are sent from the peripheral sensory nerve-cells to other nerve-cells not directly responsive to stimuli from outside the body.

Messages are also sent from various parts of the body when bones and muscles change position, giving information about posture and movement.

Messages are sent from yet other parts of the body about hormonal secretions or other chemicals in the blood and elsewhere, and this has to do with the emotions then being experienced.

Messages about all these situations – and others less easily briefly alluded to – can interlink, and thus we get ever more complex organizations of messages.

Messages can start anywhere, but in their interlinking they can home in on particular cells which thereby gain an organizing or coding or sorting function. These cells are conventionally spoken of as more central, that is nearer the brain which is being thought of as a centre of the body. Most *central* are the cells in the appropriately named 'association areas' of the brain. These can be contrasted with the more *peripheral* sensory cells, which are only affected by the particular stimuli they are constructed to be affected by, not by other nerve-cells.

Figure 4 showed how, starting with the stimulus of something black, or dotted, or striped, or stippled, we could in principle arrive at new categories of a more specific kind: black stripes, black dots, striped stipples, and so on. In that greatly simplified scheme, we built on the known fact that there are nerve-cells whose function is to discern black and nothing else, and other groups of cells which between them convey a dotted impression, and yet others whose functions could be to discern vertical or horizontal lines, and so on.

Going now a step away from the sensory periphery, we can extend that diagram, suggesting how, from some very specific events like the sight of black stipples or dots in stripes, we can arrive at abstract concepts: 'blackness', 'stippling', 'stripes in general'. These abstractions cannot be *perceived* by the senses, they have to be *conceived* by central processes – they are concepts. According to the *Shorter Oxford English Dictionary*, *concept* has meant *an idea of a class of objects* or *a general notion* since 1663, and is worth keeping. There are many, many words for the processes now to be discussed: patterns, schemata, symbols, configurations, meanings, *Gestalten*, generalizations, classifications, (higher-order) abstractions, structures, attitudes, sentiments, complexes even. *Concept* is the word I shall use in general, employing the other words when common speech, euphony, or context require it. The type of process will be the same.

Figure 11 is *Figure 4* put on its side, as it were. *Figure 12* shows a 'higher-order' process. In *Figure 12*, although a perceptual process is going on, no *peripheral* sensory nerve-cells are involved. It all happens *centrally* in the association-areas of the brain. It is estimated that there are around 100,000,000,000 (10^{11}) cells in the brain, and many of them can combine with many others, so there is plenty of room for patterns to be able to form.

We cannot see 'blackness', only a black this or a black that. 'Blackness' is a concept which may be excited when a top hat is perceived, or Pat's kitten, or ink, or whatever. *And* the appropriate mood and the effect of rain clouds (in minds that speak the English language at least). *And* certain colours of the earth, which painters show us aren't black at all, etc., etc. And for each of these, while the concept 'blackness' is evoked, so are a large

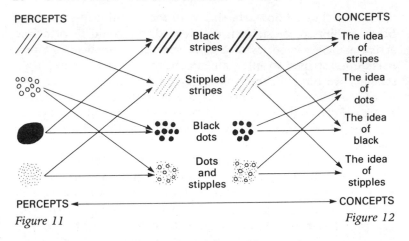

Figure 11   Figure 12

number of other concepts which share nothing else in common. 'Blackness' just happens to be the common factor among the examples I have chosen.

The processes involved in achieving the concept 'triangle'

We can now form a tentative notion of how perceptions get organized into concepts. Concepts, it will be remembered from the previous chapter, can carry feeling as well as cognitive components. We now take two more steps in imagination. One is to imagine how movement, and hence action (and hence 'drives' and 'motivation' and other such) can be built in at this level of the most elementary detail of our cerebral organization. The other takes us into a deeper understanding of concept-formation: on the one hand a concept is built up from component perceptions, on the other hand the components get their meaning from the concept to which they contribute – they make a *Gestalt*.

From this point, the present chapter owes much to D. O. Hebb's seminal book, *The Organization of Behaviour* (1949). Crucial to the discussion is Hebb's account of how a triangle comes to be perceived as such.

In *Figure 13* A, B, and C are angles of a triangle. We may use

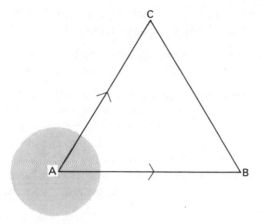

Figure 13
Source: Hebb, D. O. (1949) *The Organisation of Behaviour*. New York: Wiley, p. 85.

the small letters *a*, *b*, and *c*, or the non-verbal symbols ∠, ⅄, and ∧, to represent the effects in those nerve-cells which are excited when the eyes focus on A, B, or C. Angle A excites *a*, angle B excites *b*, and angle C excites *c*. Hebb postulates a process by which 'perceptual activity in *a* facilitates the arousal of both *b* and *c with appropriate eye-movements*' (1949: 86). He is referring to the fact that when we focus our eyes on one angle, say A, there is a field of focus (represented by the grey area on Hebb's diagram), such that angles B and C can be seen from the corner of the eye. Within this field of focus there is a certain amount of sensory stimulus coming in from B and C. The eye is so constructed that this peripheral stimulation also excites muscle-responses, *and so* the muscles move the eye from focusing on A to focusing on B or C. In due course, for the same reason, the eye moves again.

The eye runs a neural path over and over again between angles A, B, and C, until finally, at the level of *a*, *b*, and *c*, there is an integrated structure of neurons which we might call *abc*, but which Hebb calls *t* (for 'triangle'); reasons for this become clear when we use the non-verbal symbols. Then we can imagine the eye running between A, B, and C, until finally, at the level of the three symbols ∠, ⅄, and ∧, there is an integrated structure of neurons which could be represented by a triangle. Let us imagine it in symbol-form, though we have to say it in words:

a-b-c-b-c-a-c-b-a-t-a-c-b-c-t-b-t-a-c-t-b-c-a-c-b-t-a

∠ ⟍∧⟍∧∠∧⟍∠▲∠∧⟍/▲⟍∠/▲⟍∧∠∧⟍▲∠

We are here concerned with a simple idea that is difficult to put across. I have used algebraic-looking letters, and I have used non-verbal geometric-looking symbols to help it across. Really I should use pre-verbal, pre-conceptual, pre-anything means to communicate with: we learnt to read about triangles a good few years after we formed most of our concepts. But how can I, in a book? Here is another attempt, suggested by a poet of my acquaintance:

snuffle-suck-yum-grope-sniff-gulp-yum-teat-gulp-suck-
teat-yum-sniff-snuffle-teat

Muscle-movements and other perceptions (for example the perception of angles) activate one another, round and round, and back and forth, until the concept ('triangle') joins the chase.

In effect, achieving the concept 'triangle' – achieving any concept, making sense of anything – involves sequences of nerve-cells such that sensory input and motor input are mutually stimulating. *By the time the simplest concept has been established, movement and behaviour are already built in.* In this way, Hebb does away with the question of the relation between cognition and conation: *motor behaviour is involved from the start, and so is perception.*

Concepts as symbols

Hebb was unwilling to use the letters *abc* for the structures resulting from the facilitated pathways between *a*, *b*, and *c*. He wanted the notation *t* because that would show that something new had come into being. He writes of the new structure *t* as

'the assembly of cells whose activity, in the schema, is the perception of the triangle as a distinctive whole. As Gestalt writers would say, that is something other than the sum of its parts.'

(1949: 97)

So we have the concept *t*. Hebb emphasizes that concepts do not replace perceptions. Sometimes the concept 'triangle' is in focus, sometimes it is not, but then one or more of the component parts of the triangle are in focus. Thus concepts come to give additional meaning to perceptions.

On this very simplified foundation I propose to construct, bit by bit, in succeeding chapters, everything that has to do with the inner life: concepts, symbols, internal objects, relationships. For the way the concept 'triangle' is arrived at illuminates not only how people come to see a particular triangle as a triangle, but also how people begin to recognize triangles wherever they occur, whatever their angles. It is, even, how people begin the process which will lead them to think of triangles when they see an angle, so that an angle can 'stand for' or 'mean' a triangle and a triangle can 'stand for' or 'mean' an angle.

stands for = means = symbolizes

In the same way, the nipple may stand for other, for mother, for pleasure, for particular sensory experiences; the mother may symbolize sensory pleasures, and so on.

When one aspect of something stands for the whole, the whole may be activated although the person registers only the one aspect. A phobia would be an unpleasant example of this. Goodness knows what a spider 'stands for' for different people.

Learning takes time

Even the simplest meanings have to be learned. The recognition of a triangle as a triangle is an achievement. It means that percepts have acquired meaning, have contributed to concepts. We tend to take our ability to do this for granted. But it is important to realize that people who are born blind take a long time to learn to recognize even simple shapes if they have the good fortune to be given their sight in more mature years.

'Investigators are unanimous in reporting that the perception of a square, circle or triangle, or of sphere or cube, is very poor. To see one of these as a whole object, with distinctive characteristics immediately evident, is not possible for a long period. The most intelligent and best-motivated patient has to seek corners painstakingly even to distinguish a triangle from a circle. The newly seeing patient can frequently find a difference between two such figures shown together . . . but the differences are not remembered. There is for weeks a practically zero capacity to learn names for such figures, even when tactual recognition is prompt and complete.'

(Hebb 1949: 28–9)

It also takes time to learn to generalize as sighted people do.

'When the patient first gets to the point of being able to name a simple object promptly, recognition is completely destroyed if the object is slightly changed or put into a new setting. The patient who had learned to name a ring showed no recognition of a slightly different ring; having learned to name a square made of white cardboard, could not name it when its colour was changed to yellow by turning the cardboard over; and so on. These reports consistently indicate that the perceived whole at first vision is simultaneously unified and amorphous. There is not a single instance given in which the congenitally blind after operation had trouble in learning colour names; but a great number in which perception of identity in a simple figure was poor indeed.'

(Hebb 1949, quoting Senden 1932: 135–41)

This may be hard for a sighted person to imagine, but many of us do still have to count the corners to tell an octagon from a hexagon, and many of us remember how hard it was to learn to read music. As Jerome Bruner and his colleagues so tellingly write at the beginning of their chapter on concept attainment:

'It is curiously difficult to recapture pre-conceptual inno- cence. Having learned a new language, it is almost imposs- ible to recall the undifferentiated flow of voiced sounds that one heard before one learned to sort the flow into words and phrases. Having mastered the distinction between odd and even numbers, it is a feat to remember what it was like in a mental world where there was no such distinction. It is as if the mastery of a conceptual distinction were able to mask the pre-conceptual memory of the thing now distinguished. Moreover, the transition experience between "not having" the distinction and "having it" seems to be without experien-

tial content. . . . Concept attainment seems almost an intrinsically unanalysable process from an experiential point of view.
Now I understand the distinction; before there was nothing,
and in between there was only a moment of illumination.'
                    (Bruner, Goodnow, and Austin 1956: 51)

I think this is a point worth making much of, when writing for
people whose main interest has been therapeutic psychodynamic
theory. It illuminates the danger of assuming, from the therapists' or from the patients' memories, that we 'always had' some
of our subjective experiences – that we 'always had', for
instance, envy or a primitive ego, or whatever feels basic. I am
presenting an alternative point of view, in which each of these
experiences is an achievement.

Hebb concludes his section on the slow learning of the newly
sighted with a warning. We are not used to thinking of simple
perceptions as slowly and painfully learned. Hebb thought that
the slowness of such learning, and the frequent instances of
failure to learn at all in periods as long as a year following the
operations, would seem 'extraordinary and incredible' had they
not been confirmed by evidence such as that provided by animal
psychologists. Riesen (1947), for instance, worked with chimpanzees, some of which he reared in total darkness. Perpetually in
the dark, they were highly motivated by hunger and by
loneliness, poor apes, to cling to their attendant when – still in
the dark – they were made to leave their familiar cages. Yet when
they were finally brought into the light, there was no sign that
either hunger or the desire to cling could teach them, in 40 or 50
hours of visual experience, to recognize their white-clad attendant as more important than any other feature of their environment. Astonishing as it may seem, the chimpanzees appeared not
to be able to see, or not to be able to use what they saw. They
could not conceptualize. Another experiment (equally unjustifi-
able in my view) showed that even a dozen bad experiences did
not help them avoid a large and easily visible object which gave
them electric shocks when they touched it. Yet normally reared
animals would go nowhere near it after one shock (Hebb 1949:
112). Hebb concluded that this slowness to learn new things is
due to the very complexity of which primate thinking is in fact
capable. It is the more primitive animals who catch on fast, if

they catch on at all; less primitive animals are far more capable of conceptual learning, but it comes later in their development.

Defining 'facilitation', 'reverberation', and 'following'

Facilitation is the process which happens when the axon of a cell *a* is near enough to excite cell *b* and repeatedly takes part in firing it. Some growth process or metabolic change takes place in one or both cells such that *a*'s efficiency, in being one of the cells that can fire *b*, is increased (Hebb 1949: 62).

Since a number of cells are simultaneously involved, in a pattern, facilitation means that a pattern of cells firing frequently in such a process, becomes in some sense a stronger structure. Hebb calls such stronger structures 'cell-assemblies'. The hypothesis of a more permanent change, a structural change, is crucial to most writers in this field. It is this permanence which is made to account for learning, that is for the fact that previous experiences can affect subsequent experiences.

Cell-assemblies have the interesting property that they may be able to prolong their period of excitation – and hence their capacity to excite other cells – by a process called *reverberation*:

> 'A repeated stimulation of specific receptors will lead slowly to the formation of an assembly of association-area cells which can act briefly as a closed system after stimulation has ceased; this prolongs the time during which the structural changes of learning can occur, and constitutes the simplest instance of a representative process (image or ideas).'
>
> (Hebb 1949: 60)

Hebb drew a diagram to show how such an assembly might be organized (see *Figure 14*).

> 'Arrows represent a simple assembly of neural pathways firing in sequence. Pathway (1, 4) fires on the first and the fourth occasion. Pathway (2, 14) fires on the second occasion and the fourteenth, and so on, illustrating the possibilities of an 'alternating' reverberation which would not extinguish as a simple closed circuit.'
>
> (Hebb 1949: 73)

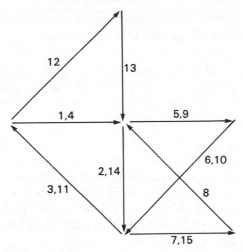

Figure 14
Source: Hebb, D. O. (1949) *The Organisation of Behaviour.* New York: Wiley.

The process of reverberation is important for at least two reasons. (1) A set of stimuli – or any interconnected set of concepts – can be kept buzzing in the head long enough to affect the patterning of messages which come in thereafter. (2) A set of stimuli kept going in this way increases the chances that a permanent structural change will occur.

Hayek, to whom Chapter 4 is much indebted, uses the notion of facilitation to understand the conceptualizing or, as he calls it, the 'classifying' function of the nervous system, and his way of looking at things introduces the valuable notion of the *following* of a stimulus. Because of the processes of facilitation and reverberation,

'a system of connexions is formed which will record the relative frequency with which, in the history of the organism, different groups of internal and external stimuli have acted together. Each individual impulse will, on its occurrence, have evoked other impulses which correspond to the other stimuli, which have in the past usually accompanied its occurrence. We shall call this bundle of secondary impulses which a primary impulse sets up through these acquired connexions, the *following* of the primary impulse.'

(Hayek 1952: 3. 34)

There is continual working and reworking in this process. Some connections between particular neurons will strengthen with experience; others will weaken. An accumulation of tiny changes will have major effects in the long run.

'Some units capable at first of synchronising with others in the system, would no longer be able to do so and would drop out: "fractionation". Others, at first incompatible, would be recruited. With perceptual development there would thus be a slow growth in the assembly, understanding by "growth" not necessarily an increase in the number of constituent cells, but a change.'

(Hebb 1949: 76, 77)

This kind of change can make possible a development of the utmost psychological significance: the formation of concepts not based on any particular perceptions.

'There is no reason why such connexions as we have been considering would be formed only between primary sensory impulses. ... Any impulse which occurs as part of the following of other impulses will, on each of those occasions, acquire or strengthen connexions with other impulses forming part of the same following. Connexions of this kind will therefore also be formed between impulses which, as primary impulses, rarely if ever occur at the same time.'

(Hayek, 1952: 3. 52)

Forming concepts (and symbols and meanings) without sensory input

'Adult learning is a changed relationship between the central effects of separate stimulations.'

(Hebb 1949: 127–28)

Hebb draws a diagram which illustrates how two sets of events, which were separately experienced on two unconnected occasions, can become associated (see *Figure 15*). Concretely, and

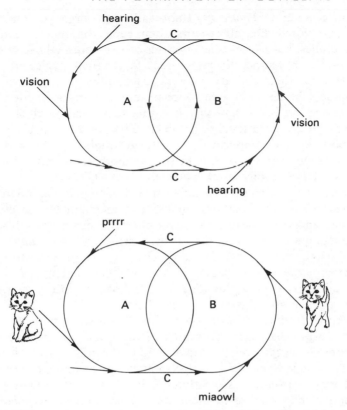

Figure 15

going further than Hebb did, *Figure 15* makes it possible to begin to imagine how one might learn to recognize, for instance a cat, either through seeing and touching it, or through hearing it. In *Figure 15* the cycles A and B represent two conceptual organizations. Each is a circular cell-assembly capable of reverberation, as in *Figure 14*. Cycle A was originally put together by auditory, tactual, and visual stimulation (that is it involved assemblies in each of these modes); Cycle B was put together by visual and tactual stimulation only. The lines C represent possible connections between A and B. Connections such as represented by the lines C can be reinforced through reverberation, again as in *Figure 14*. Hebb calls these organizations 'not simple closed neural circuits, nor even the more complex assemblies, but *phase-cycles*: systems of assemblies whose several activities are temporally integrated'. When these cycles are well organized, their activity may be excited by just part of the original stimulation. Cycle A, for instance, might be excited just from hearing *or* touch *or* vision, rather than needing all three to reach the required level to get excited. Or, and this is the other important new implication, Cycle A might be excited by stimulation from Cycle B, once the processes represented by the lines C have become established (Hebb 1949: 126).

In this way, Hebb has made new learning independent of direct sensory stimulation: the association might be set up by vision, and yet be manifested later purely from hearing a sound, or feeling a touch. Any element can 'stand for' the whole, and the whole can 'stand for' any element, as in the story of achieving the concept 'triangle'. We catch here a glimpse of what is called conceptual learning or symbolic learning; learning through the use of words and symbols.

Figure 16 illustrates the possibility that a subsystem, C, may act as a link between two systems (conceptual structures). One concept is represented by A_1, A_2, and C; the other by B_1, B_2, and C. The two systems have a subsystem in C in common, to provide a basis of prompt association (Hebb 1949: 130). Thus, *two concepts may acquire a latent association without ever having occurred together in the subject's past experience* (132).

And so the experience of seeing something can be associated with something heard, or a word that is read may be associated with a picture or a sound. These can all stand for or mean each other. The process of 'thinking' must be rather like this – a sequence of central events which starts when one central activity is a stimulus for the next, without needing the intervention of a sensory stimulus.

Simple and complex conceptual structures

What Hebb calls environmental or sensory control is the first great achievement of the young animal. Before it is established, the young being's behaviour, like a plant's, is just the outcome of

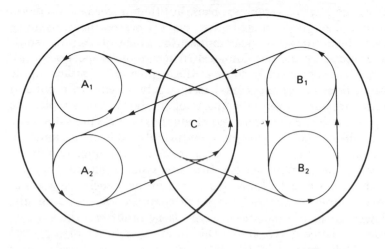

Source: Hebb, D. O. (1949) *The Organisation of Behaviour*. New York: Wiley.

A person fears apple-picking and window-cleaning because these are associated with going up steps, and this is associated with some danger connected with being in an upstairs room.

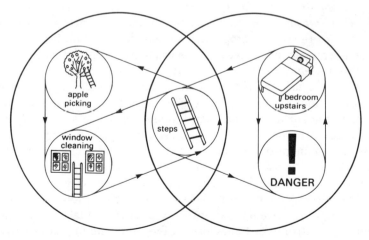

Figure 16

its simple physiological responses. But then it learns to do more: to recognize good things and to move towards them, to move away from the bad. The extent to which it can do so is determined by the physiological structure of its species.

Hebb sees primary learning as the acquisition of rather simple connections between events, based largely on sensory input and simple messages from other parts of the body. The simpler the organism, the more simply and easily these connections are made – the faster, too, and the more enduringly. Mature learning, on the other hand, depends a great deal on meaning, that is on relating the current sensory input to what is already known. And what is already known is stored in the association areas in very complex ways. So, the more complex the organism, the slower the incorporation of new sensory input into the existing frame or context. We know this from other forms of organization. How hard it is to get some change introduced into a bureaucracy, and how hard it is for us outsiders to talk to those inside – insiders like to talk to each other.

Only the higher animals have the capacity to learn through the use of concepts and symbols. '*The first learning of primates is extremely slow, and very different from that at maturity.*' Hebb doesn't just print this in italics; he has it in capital letters, and he goes on to give the interesting evidence from people born blind, and from the poor chimpanzees raised in darkness, to which reference was made on p. 33. He sees human slowness in learning as due to the very complexity of which our thinking is ultimately capable: primitive animals learn fast; complex, patterned, configurational learning comes later and takes longer.

To appreciate the nature of more central functioning, it now becomes important to distinguish between two parts of the cortex (the surface of the brain). Some cells here are connected directly with the sensory nerve-cells bringing messages about the environment or the state of the body; other cells are mainly connected with each other; this is the distinction between the sensory cortex and the association cortex, respectively.

The distinction between sensory and association cortex enables Hebb to speculate about how environmental, peripheral, sensory control over behaviour differs from the higher achievements of some animals: more central controls over behaviour, even amounting to purposive behaviour.

Facilitation and the shift from peripheral to more central control

Two kinds of changes affect the neural pathways. One kind is the momentary electrochemical change which is the physical means by which impulses travel along the nerves. This change depends on *stimulation*: when the stimuli cease, so do the processes. This is how the environment – the source of many stimuli – controls the behaviour of the organism. The other kind of change has to do with what happens at the synapse of neurons which frequently activate another. With use, more permanent structural changes take place which enable impulses to travel more easily through these synapses than through others: *facilitation*. It is now generally believed that there are these two kinds of effects. Hebb makes the distinction; so does Hayek. Pribram, on whose work we shall draw in the next chapter, made the distinction the basis of his book on *Languages of the Brain* (1971) and very interestingly points out in another book (Pribram and Gill 1976) that Freud, as early as 1895, near the very beginning of his career which he after all started as a neurologist, postulated a similar difference for which at that time there was no experimental evidence. He distinguished between what he called *Phi* elements which were concerned with momentary discharges, and *Psi* elements which bind nervous energy on a more permanent basis ('cathexis').

This difference, between fleeting and more enduring changes in the nervous system, makes it possible for more central dominance to emerge. Central dominance, from this perspective, accounts for the relatively slight effect made by fleeting changes – particular messages being sent along at any moment of perception – on the more enduring structures which are slowly being built up in the course of facilitation, and confirmed by reverberation. This is how the organism controls its own behaviour, instead of being controlled by environmental stimuli only.

Enduring changes in the pathways affect the reception and organization of subsequent messages, more than these later messages affect the existing organization. As on p. 37, we are saying that the connection C can become so enduring and can cause such reverberations that *whenever* a particular sensation is

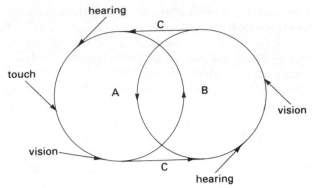

Figure 17

registered in Cycle A, say touch, this reverberates not only through the entire Cycle A but also through Cycle B (*Figure 17*).

To establish more central control is a victory of the organism over the environment, enabling the individual to adapt the environment in its own interest. Past memories can then be drawn upon to evaluate current events, giving individuals the benefit of past experience before they need to take action.

Meaning, attention, expectation, and central direction

We have now begun to look at a characteristic whose development markedly distinguishes the human from other animals – our greater ability to steer behaviour in a particular direction. The potential for this is to some extent built in; that is why it was worth while studying in such detail the process of learning to recognize a triangle. That process is the prototype for all direction-giving processes.

Simplifying grossly, we may say that because of the way the eye is constructed, its attention travels between angles until the structure 'triangle' is registered. When this has happened very often, a more permanent structure is established: the concept *t* for triangle. Once this has happened, the concept 'triangle' sometimes comes to mind when angles are perceived. We begin sometimes to think 'triangle' *before* we have counted the corners. Here is a kind of system where the perception of two angles (or sometimes just one) can call forth the concept 'triangle', and where the concept 'triangle' calls forth the activity of looking for angles. 'Looking for' (formally called expectancy) is a direction-giving process, closely related to attention-giving. Referring to the reciprocal facilitations which operate when looking at the triangle in *Figure 13*, Hebb defines expectancy and attention.

'When the animal looks at B after looking at A, the assembly *b* is excited in two ways: centrally by the facilitation from *a* and from the motor activity; and sensorily by B itself. In these circumstances, the two facilitations would just about coincide in time. "Expectancy" implies that the central facilitation definitely precedes the sensory, so it would be better to speak here of *attention*.'

(Hebb 1949: 87n)

Attention is the central reinforcement of a sensory process.

'But the same process is called *expectancy* when the sensory reinforcement is delayed.'

(ibid.)

I shall usually call this process 'expectation'. Seeing an angle, the eye is drawn along a line to the adjacent angle. This is the influence of the past. It can however become the influence of the future. Because the eye is drawn along, there is an element of action. A neural organization can come into being, which involves both an expectation of what will happen next, and an impulse to do the next thing. A pretty example, at a somewhat higher level of organization, is given by the behaviour of the shrew described on p. 58 of Chapter 4.

To sum up so far, structural changes produce enduring concepts, and perhaps quite elaborate structures of ideas and feelings which give meaning to much that happens. One consequence of such structures is to make it possible for us to expect events to happen which have not happened yet. Expectations can cause a message to get organized in a more powerful way than the message would warrant if the structures had not already become established, and in a more powerful way than other messages coming in at the same time. Expectations give meaning to current events. So much so that, in the next example (*Figure 18*), expectation is often the same as meaning.

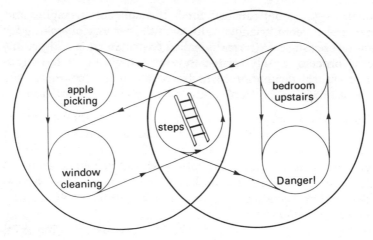

Figure 18

If the central 'steps' assembly reverberates easily and is a relatively enduring structure, then a great variety of messages about height can evoke a sense of danger – height will come to stand for danger; height will bring with it the expectation that something dangerous is about to happen. This sense of danger will have come from the person's anticipation that he or she is about to remember the painful experience associated with the upstairs room. This anticipation is called *signal anxiety*: the present situation is a signal (symbol) that something else will happen next, in this case, something undesirable.

The central processes which lead to expectancy and meaning can also act selectively so that certain stimuli are sought for – 'selected'.

Selective perception by means of more central processes

For Hebb, an attitude is an expectation, an 'enduring selectivity in central action' which, because of its enduring quality, can steer the organism in directions which experience has determined to be in the animal's interest. There is 'central reinforcement of sensory processes':

'It seems that there can be no explanation of learning and problem-solving in any mammal without reference to the persisting central neural influence that sustains activity in one particular direction. Even in the rat, learning continually shows this selective responsiveness to one aspect or part of the environment. In higher forms, where expectancy has been most clearly demonstrated, it seems often to be organized by an expectancy of a particular reward or goal. This is clearly not sensory but a conceptual process (to which, however, sensation must continually contribute).'

(Hebb 1949: 141–42)

'Persisting central neural influence' well defines what attention is. Established conceptual structures can, through reverberation, cause certain messages to have particular impact, more than others: the attention has been directed.

Abercrombie (1960) provides an amusing example of a central organization which is so strong that we attend only to what we expect to see – we do not attend to what we do not expect to see. There is something wrong with the three statements in the triangles in *Figure 19*, but it is hard to find it. (The puzzled reader

Figure 19
Source: Abercrombie, M. L. J. (1960) *The Anatomy of Judgment*. London: Hutchinson.

is requested to read the statements aloud.) Incidentally this is a good example of not seeing something which is there to see, without there being any repression – a point which will become important in later chapters.

In the higher animals, expectancy = meaning, and meaning can refer to the process by which an enduring structure causes us to expect and search for (that is give our attention to) particular events in otherwise ambiguous stimulus situations.

How many triangles can the reader recognize in *Figure 20*? In identifying triangles for the purpose of counting them, we have to focus on lines which but a moment ago we had to ignore. We have to stop the eye from travelling more than halfway along

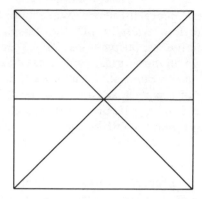

Figure 20
Source: McKellar, P. (1968) *Experience and Behaviour*. Harmondsworth: Pelican.

lines which but a moment ago the eye pursued to the end. Lines can be organized into figures in one way, or in another way, or not at all. We may draw the conclusion (1) that something in us creates the perception of triangles out of what is not immediately apparent as a collection of triangles, or, to put this in different language, that something in us makes concepts apparent to us where these are not immediately obvious; and (2) that we select, search for, attend to certain things we have set ourselves to pay attention to. The exercise also helps us to realize how much percepts and concepts slip and slide into one another. (Incidentally, I counted fourteen triangles.)

Another exercise of the same kind: looking again at *Figure 20*, can the reader see the letter X? The letters E? N? Z? How many other letters can the reader see in the figure? If we think of each letter as a different concept, we can see that concepts are less tidy, less clearly bounded, less neatly separable from each other, more overlapping, more blurry, than we let ourselves think sometimes. And if concepts are, then symbols are, and if symbols are, then inner objects and relationships are. This will also become very important later in our narrative.

One more example, to demonstrate just how powerful the steering, directing, and motivating aspect of central functioning can be. *Figure 21* shows a reversible figure which can be seen as a smart young woman in a fur collar and a plumed hat, or as an old

Figure 21
Source: McKellar, P. (1968) *Experience and Behaviour*. Harmondsworth: Pelican.

crone with a bent nose and a head-scarf. To make the meaning change from the one to the other, we make ourselves attend to (focus on) a bit of the picture which we know to belong to the meaning we want to evoke – this activates a system of associated structures and the whole reverses itself (McKellar 1968: 44).

No wonder that this propensity of the human mind is used to systematize tests for differences in personality or mood. The subject is presented with simple pictures or inkblots and required to make up stories about them.

'The stimulus materials tend to be interpreted differently by different individuals and thus reflect their learning history, personality traits, and emotional preoccupations. In short the responses given by the subject reveal the sets [i.e. attitudes] he has built up during his life history, and the influences these have on his present perceptions. Under the heading of words like "values", "interests" and "expectancies" we encounter the influences of set upon selective perceiving.'

(McKellar 1968: 49)

This is not exactly the way psycho-analytically minded people tend to approach a person's reactions. They tend on the whole to think of symbols as acquired through a process of 'internalization'. To this we return in later chapters.

We have construed a perceptual and conceptual apparatus which can direct behaviour. We must now look more closely at the directing process. 'Values', 'interests', and 'expectancies' point the way – we must look for yet higher levels of organization and yet more central functions.

·4·
Intentional behaviour

While Hebb was working out his ideas in Canada, Hayek was theorizing towards similar ends in Britain, from very different psychological and philosophical traditions. *The Sensory Order* (1952), the book we draw on in this chapter, is subtitled *An Enquiry into the Foundation of Theoretical Psychology*. It was an interesting excursus for the author – his world-wide reputation was built on such works as *Monetary Theory and the Trade Cycle*, *Profits, Interests and Investments*, and *The Pure Theory of Capital*. Hayek used his economist's interest in building theories on the basis of relatively few data to construct a set of hypotheses about the kind of activities and relationships we must imagine among the nerve-cells, if these are to fulfil their function of enabling us to lead our lives in an organized way. This set of hypotheses forms his theory. In the logico-mathematical tradition, he numbers each of his paragraphs, first by chapter and then by its order within the chapter. I have retained this usage for easy reference, and I have sometimes taken the liberty of simplifying or abbreviating an excerpt.

Hayek's ideas have much in common with Hebb's, though his technical terms are different and though he argues almost entirely from logic and not from neurophysiological information. Hayek starts with stimuli. Stimuli are events, sights, sounds, smells, movements, which put in motion processes of sensation and perception. Stimuli set off (neural) impulses. These impulses

49

have effects. By effects, Hayek means the activation of other (neural) impulses – usually more central ones in the language we have used so far, that is further away from the original stimulus.

Classes, concepts, and symbols

We have already seen in how many ways neurons can relate to each other in a complex network. The possibilities of such a network fascinated Hayek. It was through the classifying power of networks that he saw his way to an understanding of the mechanisms of the mind; he based his developed theory entirely on it. By 'classification' Hayek means a process by which an event has the same effect whenever it occurs. Events which produce the same effects belong to the same class (2.34).

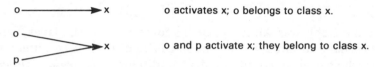

o activates x; o belongs to class x.

o and p activate x; they belong to class x.

Any impulse, therefore, which activates a subsequent impulse X thus belongs to class X. Some of these impulses may also activate a subsequent impulse Y – in that case they belong to class Y as well as class X. This can be further complicated in many ways. For instance, not only may each individual event belong to more than one class, but it may also contribute to produce different effects if (and only if) it occurs in combination with certain other events (2.39).

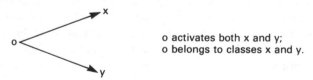

o activates both x and y;
o belongs to classes x and y.

In the terms of the previous chapter, the connection we are here looking at could be of cell-assemblies or phase-sequences or phase-cycles. These can build up into concepts. And concepts are classifying processes, classes for short. So we can write that o is part of the class (that is, the concept) X or that o is part both of the class (the concept) X and of the class (the concept) Y. Though a logician and not a neurophysiologist, Hayek has arrived at exactly Hebb's position. Below is Hayek's account of the formation of a symbol – 'a class of classes' – which may be compared with Hebb's account of the formation of the symbol *t* (for 'triangle') on pp. 28–30.

> 'The transmission of impulses from neuron to neuron within the central nervous system, which is conceived as constituting the apparatus of classification, may either take place between different neurons carrying primary impulses, or between such neurons and other ("internuncial") neurons which are not directly connected with receptor organs. In the former instance, the same event may occur either as the primary object of classification or as a "symbol" classifying some other primary impulse. All impulses, whether primary or secondary, are likely to be subject to further classification, and therefore appear both as instruments and as objects of classification.'
>
> (2. 48)

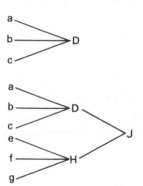

a, b, c are 'objects of classification'.
D is the 'instrument of classification'.

a, b, c contribute to class D (i.e. the concept D).
D classifies a, b, c.

D stands for a, b, c. D is a symbol for a, b, c.

Here D is both object and instrument of classification.

a, b, c contribute to concept D, and D contributes to the higher-order concept J.

So stimuli (in the external world) set off impulses, and because the patterns of stimuli affect the patterns of impulses, a subtle classification-system comes into being, with many connections and interconnections. The network of these connections will reproduce a sort of record of the past associations which any particular stimuli have had with other stimuli acting on the organism at the same time (5. 17). Hayek expresses his wonder at the subtlety with which this system can work.

> 'The word classification scarcely conveys an adequate idea of the almost infinite wealth of variety and graduation of the

discriminations which can be peformed by this apparatus. Since it is not merely a question of a particular impulse either belonging or not belonging to a particular class, but also of its belonging to it more or less "strongly", it would be more appropriate to describe these complex processes by some such term as "evaluation".'

(3. 57)

And so we have arrived by a new route at the idea of central dominance. On the relation between sensory and central dominance, Hayek, in the fifth chapter of *The Sensory Order*, branches into ideas not elaborated by Hebb. Only brief excerpts are given here, but the whole brilliant chapter is a delight to read.

Influential maps and working models

'The gradual evolution of the mental order involves thus a gradual approximation to the order which in the external world exists between stimuli evoking the impulses which "represent" them in the central nervous system.'

(5. 19)

'In discussing the relationship between a network of connexions . . . and the structure of external events which it can be said to reproduce, it will be useful sometimes to employ the simile of the *map* which, in a somewhat analogous manner, reproduces some of the relations which exist in certain parts of the physical world.'

(5. 25)

This map reflects the relationships between various events in the external world, relationships which the linkages gradually produce in the higher nervous centres (5. 26). In the terms of the previous chapter, the map consists of connections between concepts. It must not be thought of as flat and two-dimensional like a geography map, however; it is multi-dimensional, defining the relationships of everything to everything else.

At the beginning of life there is no map; it is in process of construction from incoming experiences, all new. However, as the system becomes more and more complex, and more and more firmly established, any new event is less likely to affect the general system of inerlinking concepts to any marked degree.

We must now consider the manner in which the many impulses proceeding at any one moment can mutually influence each other. The centres at which such impulses arrive are never to be found in an inactive state. As the impulses ascend to higher and higher levels, they will be less and less likely to evoke specific responses. Increasingly their function can only be to modify behaviour *in the light of the whole situation*, which is represented not only by other impulses arriving simultaneously but also by the whole retained representation of the environment (5. 33). Regarded from this point of view, *the map* will be seen as a relatively enduring structure, steering the organism *in terms of past experience.*

The patterns of information coming in at any particular moment make a sort of representation of the environment at that moment. This representation Hayek sees as *a model* of the environment, which will enable the organism to take account *of the environment at that moment.*

> 'This "model", which is formed at any moment by the momentarily active impulses, must not be confused with what we have called the "map", the semi-permanent connexions representing not the environment of the moment but the kind of events which the organism has met during its whole past.'
>
> (5. 41)

The map is a representation of all that has happened to the organism. The map is timeless. Because it is composed of memories, it is a map of past experiences. Because it is a map from which the current position (the world) can be read off, it contributes to a model of the present situation. On the map there is no sense of a flow *from* the past *to* the future *via* now. This is one of several similarities between Hayek's map and Freud's formulation of the unconscious.

By providing a model of the environment as it is now, against a background of all previous information, the organism's reactions are adjusted to those elements in the environment which are active just now (5. 37). In so far as the present model and the past experiences produce attention, the map contains at least an expectation of what the future could hold. It is therefore not fanciful to call this whole organization of map and model an instrument of orientation, like a gyroscope.

Images, plans, and feedback loops

Miller, Galanter, and Pribram offer some useful thoughts on this self-correcting gyroscopic process. They postulate an equivalent of Hayek's map, using the metaphor of imagery (1969: 17).

'The Image is all the accumulated organised knowledge that the organism has about itself and its world. . . . It includes everything that the organism has learned – values as well as facts – organised by whatever concepts, images, or relations it has been able to master.'

Images can be organized into structures they call 'plans'. A plan is any hierarchical process that can control the order in which a sequence of actions is to be performed. At its simplest a plan is just a kind of elaborate concept. It is an idea of the steps needed to get from one situation to another – from London to Liverpool, for instance. More elaborately, the steps in a plan might be: if hungry, you can get food by going to the kitchen, to the fridge, opening the door, getting out some cold chicken, and so on. The natuie of such a plan comes partly from experience (Hayek's map) and partly from current information (Hayek's model). A person may have a large repertory of plans, depending on where the starting-point is at which the situation arose, say, of being hungry. Equally, there may be a large variety of end-points, any of which would mean the satisfaction of the hunger. On p. 55 is a crude example of an Image, to give the general idea. In each case, only one alternative plan, out of a huge number of possibilities at each level, is actually written out, to keep the example on the page; the reader has to use his or her imagination to fill in all the unstated alternatives.

At each level in the sequence, information from the rest of the máp or from the rest of the model can affect this process. At each level, alternatives can be considered, and the alternative with the least objections or the most advantages (minimizing displeasure or maximizing pleasure, whatever that may mean to a particular individual) can come to the fore. For instance, the plan on p. 55

shows that the steps from level 1 to level 2 could be changed by
the knowledge that this would be the third lot of sandwiches
that day. A not very attractive image results and so that part of
the plan could be dropped and another plan, 'buy apples and
pears', substituted. Or there could be a change of plan at level 4,
because yesterday the people at the corner shop had been
rude to a customer, which has led to today's decision to buy
elsewhere.

1   Hunger can be satisfied by eating

2   I can eat sandwiches   or   all other ways of satisfying hunger

3   I can buy sandwiches   or   all other ways of getting sandwiches

4   . . . . at the corner shop   or   all other places to buy sandwiches

What can be said about the processes involved in the selec-
tion, evaluation, and correction of plans of action? Miller,
Galanter, and Pribram are interesting in that they construct a
practical version of this process, which they call the 'TOTE' –
nothing to do with the racetrack, the word is an acronym for the
sequence TEST – OPERATE – TEST – EXIT. A TOTE is a looped
sequence, a feedback organization such that when an action (an
operation) is undertaken which is not right when tested, another
action (operation) is undertaken, after which there is another
test, and if things are still not right, there is another action, and
so on, round and round in a loop (see *Figures 22* and *23*).

'The interpretation toward which the argument moves is one
that has been called the "cybernetics hypothesis", namely
that the fundamental building-block of the nervous system is
the feedback loop. . . . Action is initiated by an incongruity
between the state of the organism and the state that it is being
tested for, and the action persists until the incongruity is
removed.'

(Miller, Galanter, and Pribram 1969: 26, 25)

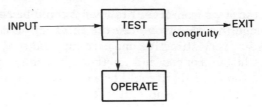

Figure 22
Source: Miller, G. A., Galanter, A., and Pribram, K. (1969) *Plans and the Structure of Behaviour*. New York: Holt.

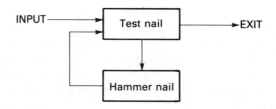

Figure 23

In words, reading from left to right, this says: a message comes in that something is happening peripherally (*input*). This message is TESTED centrally and may feel *congruous* with the map of how things should be, and that is the end of that (*exit*). But if the message does not feel congruous with the map of how things should be, something is done: an OPERATION, which when TESTED, is then *congruous* with how things should be and that is the end of it (*exit*).

It can be seen that there may be several turns round the loop. Something is happening which, when tested, feels incongruous with how things should be. So something is done which, when tested, is incongruous with how things should be. So something is done which, when tested, is incongruous with how things should be. So something is done which, when tested, is (at last) congruous with how things should be and that's the end of it – exit.

Purposive orientation and action

We have already seen that external stimuli are not necessary for central processes to be active (pp. 36–41). As networks of assemblies and phase-cycles are activated and continue their processes in semi-independence of further incoming information, we get something like 'looking ahead'.

'The pattern of impulses formed within the structure of connexions will function as an apparatus of orientation by representing both the actual state of the environment and the changes to be expected by that environment.'

(5. 51)

Here we are back to the process of 'expectancy'. Our expectations of what will happen are already on the map. Either a similar sequence of events has happened in the past and for that reason may be expected again in the future; or higher-order processes have formed an image of what can happen, on the basis of whatever information is available about what has happened in the past. Thus behaviour now is guided and directed by an expectation, just as the concept *t* (for 'triangle') could direct and guide the eye to look for angles.

'The representation or model of the environment will thus constantly tend to run ahead of the actual situation. This representation of the possible results following from the existing position will of course be constantly checked and corrected by the newly arriving sensory signals which record actual developments in the environment.'

(5. 58)

'The representations of the external environment which will guide behaviour will thus be not only representations of the actually existing environment, but also representations of the changes to be expected in that environment. We must therefore conceive of the model as constantly trying out possible developments and determining action in the light of the consequences which, from the representations of such actions, would appear to follow from it.'

(5. 59)

Preferred outcomes acting as gyroscopes

On the map are good places, and paths to good places – goals, we might say, and steps to those goals. The model is the active part of the map which shows at any moment where we are in relation to the good places on our map (and in relation to painful places as well).

The map enables us to look ahead to some extent, that is to have expectations of what can happen next. What can happen next may lead to good places eventually or to painful places. Expectations can turn into preferred or dreaded outcomes by virtue of the same processes illustrated in the previous chapter, on pp. 35 and 39.

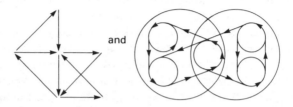

Figure 24

The image on the map which already has good feelings attached to it may be kept in mind by the processes of reverberation. It is thereby likely to steer the organism to respond selectively to further information, according to the messages' congruity with a 'good' path. The parts of the map associated with good feelings, which hold our preferences, can thus act as gyroscopes, bringing the organism back on course towards good things when it has deviated. Parts of the map associated with bad feelings may of course operate in a similar way.

The example of the shrew

Konrad Lorenz gives a captivating description of a little mammal's behaviour during map-construction, map/model-congruity-testing, action, and feedback. The path-habits of the water-shrew, he writes, are of 'a really amazing immutability'.

> 'Unless the little animal is severely frightened, it moves, in strange surroundings, only step by step, whiskering right and left all the time and following a path that is anything but straight. Its course is determined by a hundred fortuitous

factors when it walks that way for the first time. But, after a few repetitions, it is evident that the shrew recognises the locality in which it finds itself and that it repeats, with the utmost exactitude, the movements which it performed the previous time. At the same time, it is noticeable that the animal moves along much faster whenever it is repeating what it has already learned. When placed on a path which it has already traversed a few times, the shrew starts on its way slowly, carefully whiskering. Suddenly it finds known bearings, and now rushes forward a short distance, repeating exactly every step and turn which it executed on the last occasion. Then when it comes to a spot where it ceases to know its way by heart, it is reduced to whiskering again and to feeling its way step by step. Soon, another burst of speed follows and the same thing is repeated, bursts of speed alternating with very slow progress. In the beginning of this process of learning their way, the shrews move along at an extremely slow average rate and the little bursts of speed are few and far between. But gradually the little laps of the course which have been "learnt by heart" and which can be covered quickly begin to increase in length as well as in number until they fuse and the whole course can be completed in a fast unbroken rush.

   Often, when such a path-habit is almost completely formed, there still remains one particularly difficult place where the shrew always loses its bearings and has to resort to its senses of smell and touch, sniffing and whiskering vigorously to find out where the next reach of its path "joins on". Once the shrew is well settled in its path-habits it is as strictly bound to them as a railway engine to its tracks and as unable to deviate from them by even a few centimeters.'

(Lorenz 1952: 108)

What happened with the little shrew? Short sequences which had often happened in the past (its path-habits) have been mapped and guide its behaviour now. Path-habits are expectancies. Whenever it encounters an expected path, it knows where it is and 'rushes forward for a short distance'. Being only a simple shrew, these more enduring neural path-habits are established with some difficulty, and so it often has to rely on further sensory input, 'sniffing and whiskering vigorously'. This gets the reverberations going again so as to reinforce its fading purposes. The shrew is searching and attending selectively in the environment, and incidentally providing us with a nice example of central reinforcement of a sensory process.

The shrew, it is commonly assumed, runs through its paths because of rewards (good feelings) which are associated on its map with the end of the run. That is what establishes the feedback process. INPUT: 'I want water' and 'Here is a blade of grass'. TEST: 'Does my map show this blade of grass to be on a path to nice water?', that is, 'Is the model (of this blade of grass being on the right path for water) congruent with the map?' If the answer is yes – if there is no incongruity – OPERATION: carry on. If no (that is, there is incongruity) – OPERATION: quarter the area sniffing and whiskering, repeating the INPUT: 'Here is a blade of grass', and the TEST: 'Does this blade of grass have the right place on my map?', 'Or this one?', 'Or this one?' until one of them does.

Bowlby on principal systems

This way of thinking has gained a good deal of popularity, more particularly outside strictly psycho-analytic circles. But at least one psycho-analyst, John Bowlby, to whom Chapter 6 of the present book is also devoted, holds a similar viewpoint (1969: Part II). Reviewing an immense amount of literature, he too came to the conclusion that the mental apparatus was made up of a number of complex systems organized in a loosely hierarchical way with a highly complex network of communication between them. He also saw these systems as controlling and evaluative in function, though he emphasized, rather more explicitly than the authors so far quoted here, the controlling and evaluative roles played by feelings: sensations, emotions, preferences, and so on.

These systems act as 'instructions' or 'programmes', words which help to remind us that they are not static but dynamic. They are images and plans, maps and models. They act on feedback principles, so that deviations from the desired state bring warning feelings, often of anxiety, whose effect is to correct the course of action to a more desired direction.

Bowlby imagined something like a hierarchical structure, with, at the centre or at the top (depending how you draw it), one or more principal systems of this evaluating and controlling kind. One of the conveniences of this way of thinking is that it allows us to imagine different personality-structures, which is what different organizations of principal systems would be. Some might be very centralized and hierarchical (the 'motor-car' model, or, in the 'landscape' model, dominated by one city or by a sort of Massif Central). Others might have several equal systems each concerned with a major aspect of that person's life; in terms of the landscape model, this would be one with different foci of interest – towns, hills, deltas, and so on.

In the effort to understand and explain purposeful controlled behaviour, the writers I quote have tended to assume very hierarchical models of the personality. One example of such thinking appealed so much that it is quoted by Kernberg (1976: 90) as being Bowlby's comment (1969: 106–07) on an idea he attributes to Miller, Galanter, and Pribram (1969).

'In a hierarchical system of this sort, each plan and sub-plan is to be regarded as a set of instructions for action. As in the case of a military operation, the master plan gives only main objectives and general strategy; each commander down the hierarchy is then expected to make more detailed plans and to issue more detailed instructions for the execution of his part of the master plan. By leaving detail to subordinates, not only does the master plan remain simple and intelligible, but the more detailed plans can be developed and executed by those with knowledge of current local conditions. With planned hierarchy there can more easily be flexibility. The overwhelming advantage of an organisation of this sort is, of course, that the same set goal can be achieved even though circumstances vary over a wide range.'

Similarly Hayek:

'The position of the highest centres in this respect is somewhat like that of the commander of an army (or of the head of any other hierarchical organisation), who knows that his subordinates will respond to various events in a particular manner, and who will often recognise the character of what has happened as much from the response of his subordinates as from direct observation. It will also be similar in the sense that, so long as the decision taken by his subordinates in the light of their limited but perhaps more detailed observation seems appropriate in view of his more comprehensive knowledge, he will not need to interfere. Only if something known only to him but not his subordinates makes these normal responses inappropriate, will he have to overrule their decisions by issuing special orders.'

(1952: 4. 40)

I hope to show later that we do not need the very authoritarian and hierarchical assumptions underlying these models. On the contrary, we need to allow for a variety of less tightly organized personality-structures, and for multi-centred ones in particular. In the subsection below, we shall read descriptions of control from *one* centre. But actually we need not assume that this is the top hierarchical centre of centres. By the same token, although the descriptions are all in terms of motor cars driven by a driver with a purpose, the descriptions can easily be adapted to more landscape-like models.

Control from a centre

The little shrew was guided by the congruity between the information it already had (on its map) and the information which it was currently acquiring (its model). Whenever it moved, it acquired more information, on the basis of which it made its next move, which brought it yet more information.

'The sensory order is both a result and a cause of the motor activities of the body. Behaviour has to be seen in a double role: it is both input and output of the activities of the higher nervous centres. The actions which take place independently of the higher centres help to create the order of the sensory impulses arriving at that centre, while the actions directed from that centre are determined by that order.'

(Hayek 1952: 4. 38)

Map and model together steer the organism.

'The evaluations of sensory impulses arriving at the highest centres may be compared to the appreciation of events on the road observed by a person who is being driven in a car, or to the judgments of the pilot of an aeroplane which is being steered by an automatic pilot. In these instances, different observed events will lead the passenger of the car, or the pilot of the plane, to expect certain responses of the car or plane, and those events will come to "mean" particular kinds of responses of the vehicle, just as certain kinds of stimuli mean certain spontaneous responses of the body.

The sight of an oncoming car will come to mean the sensation of the car in which the person rides drawing to the side, and the sight of a red traffic light will mean the feeling of the car slowing down. Very soon what will actually be noticed will no longer be that normal response, but only its absence if it fails to occur.'

(4. 39)

to mean = to stand for = to symbolize

We have arrived at the idea that the motivation for an action is implied in the meaning of the whole situation. In simple human terms, the alarm clock rings, and that 'means' it is seven o'clock; seven o'clock means it is time to get up, which means tottering toward the coffee-machine, and so on.

Thus, within a general framework of meaning, subsystems have autonomy, provided that they do not act incongruously in relation to the more comprehensive systems to which they contribute.

Self-imagery as a central process

We have built an imaginative account of how the world may come to be represented in the nervous system of the organism. Because of this, it becomes possible to extend the imagination towards an idea of the self as also represented there, in the nervous system of the organism. We can 'put the self on the map'.

Some self-imagery is on the map to start with; we are born

with it. The cortex carries mapped representations of our bodies, often called *homunculi* (little persons). One set of nerve-endings, when traced into the brain, maps out the endings of the nerves which activate movement: these nerve-endings sketch out the *motor-homunculus*. Another set of nerve-endings delineates the nerves which transmit sensations from our skin: the *sensory homunculus*.

The *homunculi* are ourselves as experienced in our muscles, our bones, our skins, our glands. Their cortical mappings look weird because motor and sensory nerve-endings do not arrive in the cortex in the same proportions as our optical nerve-endings do when we look in the mirror.

Figures 25 and *26* were modified by Blakemore (1977) from Figures 17 and 22 of Penfield and Rasmussen (1957). The *motor homunculus (Figure 25)* was first discovered by John Hughlings Jackson. Imagine the right side of the brain, sliced through the motor cortex. The cartoon of the body shows the order of representation of the muscles (with the leg at the top of the motor strip, the face at the bottom) and the relative amount devoted to each part. The *somatic-sensory homunculus (Figure 26)* is arranged along the cortex directly behind the motor strip. It has much the same sequence of representation and exaggeration of certain features. It is here redrawn as a complete body, showing the over-representation of certain parts of the skin surface.

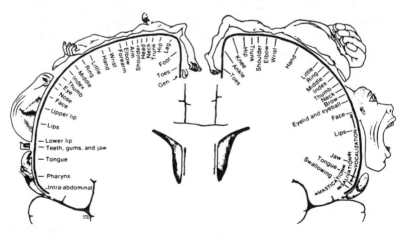

Figure 25

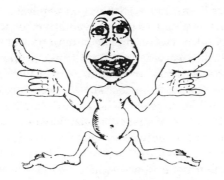

Figure 26
Note: Figures 25 and *26* are adapted with permission of Macmillan Publishing Company from *The Cerebral Cortex of Man* by Wilden Penfield and Theodore Rasmussen. Copyright © 1950 by Macmillan Publishing Company, renewed 1978 by Theodore Rasmussen.

The *homunculi* must be the basis of what Schafer (1968) had in mind when he wrote of the *self as a place* where things happen. This he contrasts with the more personal *self as an object*, which refers to those regions which carry the memories of all the messages that ever reached us about what is happening to us. We are not only recipients of experience, however. Also mapped are records of what we have done, and of the impulses to action which we have experienced. This kind of self-imagery is also built into the map-imagery, Schafer might say, of *our selves as agents*.

Our self is on the map. It is usually also represented in the model of the situation in which we find ourselves. The model, it will be remembered, is that active part of the map which at each moment accounts for where we are in relation to our world as it is, and in relation to our world as we expect it to be, and in relation to good places and bad places, allowing feedback processes to act gyroscopically. Thus our current sense of self (the model) is closely linked with the self on the map, giving a sense of identity and continuity, direction and value. The 'model' self stands out in relation to the 'map' self: 'This is myself now', 'Here I am now' in relation to 'This is the sort of person I am in general, with these experiences behind me, and with these hopes and fears about my well-being in general'.

Thus self-imagery can have an evaluative, controlling function. Our image of ourselves in the situation, and our favourite
self-imagery, influence what we do. I think of myself – 'I am a
person who gets up early' or 'I am a person who runs towards
trouble and not away from it'. This is continually confirmed
when I behave 'like myself'. The more I can do so, the more
pleased I am to think of myself in particular ways. Whenever
there is incongruity between what I am doing (which is
represented in my model of my self in the situation) and the
person I imagine myself to be, or the person I would prefer to be
(represented on the map), I am under tension to reduce the
incongruity.

So now we have a map, with imagery about the self as well as
about the world. When there is too great an incongruity between
the self on the map and the running-ahead anticipating model
self, feedback processes bring about a situation in which the
model self and the self-imagery on the map may correspond more
closely. To put this in everyday language, I steer myself
by a sense of what is 'me' and I avoid behaviour which is
'not me'.

This gives us a picture of a person with all his or her
experiences stored, including experiences of the self, meeting
new events either by adapting to them or by taking steps to
change the environment to suit the self. Here is a self that is
active, has a memory, and has direction.

> 'Once such a continuous reproduction of the environment is
> maintained in the highest centres, it becomes the main
> function of the sensory impulses to keep this apparatus of
> orientation up to date and capable of determining the re-
> sponses to particular stimuli in the light of the whole
> situation.'
>
> (5. 49)

How integrated is the self?

One of the things wrong with this picture, which is quite like the
common-sense idea we have of ourselves as human beings, is that
it may be too unified. Hayek rightly produces warnings:

'For a description of the process by which linkages will
gradually produce a map of the relations between the stimuli
acting on the organism, the simile of the map soon becomes
inadequate. . . . The classifications with which we are concerned will occur on many successive levels. We have to think
of the whole system of connexions as consisting of many
superimposed sub-systems which in some respects may operate independently of each other.

(5. 30)

Every subsystem of this kind constitutes a partial map of the
environment. Such partial maps at any level serve for the
guidance of a relatively more limited set of responses, and act at
the same time as filters or pre-selectors of information which
could be on its way to other and perhaps 'higher' centres.
Bowlby calls these 'partial selves'.

Geography books help us to a useful analogy. In an atlas there
will be a master-map of Europe. But also filed away are partial
maps which show only Britain, or only France – partial selves:
myself as student, myself as aunt. And each of these partial maps
can itself be substructured further: France in Europe, Paris in
France, the Louvre in Paris. There are also other kinds of partial
maps, whereby particular features are abstracted from the total
information on other than spatial principles. Instead of abstracting France from Europe, we can abstract annual rainfall from all
areas in Europe, or proneness to earthquakes, or density of
population or intensity of industrial output. From my map of
myself, I can abstract not only partial selves but also the number
of towns I have lived in, the illnesses I am prone to, the sort of
men I am attracted to – all kinds of subsystems.

It will become important in later chapters to keep in mind that
there may be several subsystems, each to do with a partial view
of the self, and each able to give an account of what is going on,
from the perspective of that particular partial map. If there is
little intercommunication between these subsystems, the result
would be that a person had several 'partial selves', moods, one
might say, or roles.

The concept of subsystems is also important when we think of
psychical systems as not necessarily hierarchical, but as parts of
a system in the making – of parts of the personality with some

organization but not (yet) integrated with other parts. As later chapters show, we must not think of the personality as more integrated than it is.

Nor must we think of the personality as more widely conscious than it is.

> 'While the full and detailed classification of sensory impulses, corresponding to the order of sensory qualities which we know from conscious experience, is effected mainly at the highest centres, we must assume a more limited classification on somewhat similar principles to take place already at the lower levels, where certainly no conscious experience is associated with it.'
>
> (5. 31)

Consciousness, self-consciousness, and identity

When Hayek considered the development of consciousness in the mental order, he asked himself what might be the criteria of consciousness.

> 'What are those special attributes of conscious behaviour by which we distinguish it from behaviour which also appears to be co-ordinated and purposive but of which the person is not "aware"?
>
> In conscious behaviour a person will (a) be able to "give an account" of what he is doing or has been doing, (b) be able to "take account" in his actions of other simultaneous experiences of which he is also conscious, and, (c) be guided to a large extent not only by his current perceptions but also by images . . . which might be evoked by the existing situation.'
>
> (6. 8)

This is a very attractive and easily understood idea, that we are conscious when we can tell the story of what is happening to us.

> 'When we say that a person is able to give an account of his mental processes, we mean by this that he is able to communicate them to other people by means of symbols.'
>
> (6. 9)

Symbols are concepts that can 'stand for' other concepts. The symbols we mostly learn to use to communicate with are words, and most ordinary states of consciousness depend on words for symbol-formation and symbol-use, though there are (in my view enviable) people who can also communicate to others in painting or music or dance, and there are also (in my view pitiable) people who can communicate only in these ways.

To express in symbol-form what I experience myself to be can be a lifetime's occupation. But to sum it up simply, our sense of identity comes from the imagery of ourselves that we have on our maps – selves as objects, selves as agents, selves as seen in the mirror, and so on. And we have to be able to say something about ourselves 'to give an account of ourselves' to be self-conscious. So the sense of identity, at least the way I shall think of it, requires self-consciousness, an ability to use symbols, and an ability to stand back from phenomena to some extent and see them in some way as separate from one's own stream of existence. It is, incidentally, with the latter achievement, that most of the present narrative is concerned.

The words in which we give an account of ourselves and others

In most of this book we are considering processes which take place long before verbal concepts have evolved. Still, this is the point at which it may be salutary to consider the place of words in the development of the personality. Because 'considering' is a process which is done in words, and for many related reasons, it is easy to have a rather simple unquestioning belief in the validity of the words we use. A reminder is needed that words not only symbolize but also falsify our inner experiences.

The use of words drastically affects our capacity to 'give an account' of ourselves, our consciousness, and our self-consciousness. For better, and for worse, it sets the growing child a number of problems to surmount. Consider, for instance, how a child learns to use sentences in which 'I' is used correctly to refer to itself, and 'you' to refer to others; and consider the difficulties caused by the fact that the child is addressed by others as 'you' and therefore has perhaps at first learnt to think of itself as 'you'. Objects, such as tables, chairs, and cars, are much more easily correctly labelled.

Words are given by people who mean something to the child;

this has a strong effect on the concept to which it will be attaching their verbal label. The concepts the child has constructed from experience now acquire all sorts of additional elements, based on how others use the word-labels.

Moreover, once people really start talking to the child in words, concepts can also be acquired just from what other people say – the child is no longer dependent only on experience, as animals are. The child learns 'Drinking all your milk is good' and 'Getting your feet wet is bad'. Who knows what moral ideas it gathers from this? Someone in a song is 'mighty like a rose'. What does that mean to a child? With much useful and accurate information, all kinds of nonsense enters a child's mind.

We must keep remembering that the child's concepts are not always in all respects what we think they are, though we use the same words. There must have been a time, for instance, when the child did not as yet have verbal concepts for 'milk' and for 'drinking'. In the very early days, messages directly to do with milk may come to be so inevitably associated with messages about comfort, warmth, arms, mouth, and so on, that the concept 'milk', which singles out the liquid bit, may not begin to be attained until the child has experience of it in bottle or cup. We, the observers, know that the child is 'drinking milk', but the child does not, and is indeed not doing what we unthinkingly imagine it to be doing when we say 'the child is drinking milk'.

The general culture in which the child is brought up plays an important role in our learning to use the right words for our experiences. This is particularly so when what the words refer to is not visible. The culture plays an important part in our learning to label emotional states so that they have meaning for ourselves and for others. For instance, the experience of distress is, at the beginning of life, a very undifferentiated one: not enough has happened yet for differentiation into more refined concepts. More experience (including verbal learning) has to happen before distress becomes differentiated into 'anger' or 'rage' or 'fight' or 'aggression' or 'assertion' or 'fear' or 'flight' or 'panic' or 'anxiety' or 'worry' or 'embarrassment' or 'boredom' or 'hurt', and so on. Using such words correctly is not just a matter of increased skill in identifying feelings and in naming them correctly so that others understand us. It is not just the process by which 'horsey' differentiates into 'horse', 'cow', and 'donkey'. Feelings are private. We cannot point at them, the way we can point to donkeys. If we wish, we can certainly consent to a set of rigorous criteria which we have agreed shall determine the proper use of each disputed word. But what are we in touch with at the end of that process?

The effect which language has on the way we organize our experience is most easily seen when we compare cultures, even cultures as closely similar as the various European ones. This gives a very convincing demonstration of the extent to which our emotional experiences are organized by the words we use, which we have been taught by the grown-ups in the culture. Take a German word like *fleissig*, very frequently used, and compare it with its nearest English translation 'industrious' – hardly ever met. Who ever speaks of an 'industrious child'? (There must *be* some!) In Holland, many people are *driftig*, a state of mind frequently met and accepted among the Dutch. The nearest English translation, 'hot-tempered', is very rare and seems to me (Dutch by origin) to carry a tinge of disapproval. So early in my argument I would not wish to antagonize any potential reader by turning my eye to such technical words as 'psychotic', 'narcissistic' or 'schizoid'.

PART 2

THE E-MERGING OF SELF FROM (M)OTHER

'I AM NOT YET BORN'

THE UNATTACHED INFANT

HOLDING ON TO SAFETY
VERSUS STEERING CLEAR OF DANGER

This section is almost about people. We might say it is about 'almost-people'. It is about our experiences just at the point where the infant and the mother are, from the infant's point of view, one and indistinguishable. What is life like for the tiny baby at that time? Its apparatus for experiencing life is not yet quite like ours. This section suggests that, because of this, the tiny child may be experiencing some events in ways which are very different from our adult conceptions.

· 5 ·
'I am not yet born'

Hebb's speculations, and those of Pribram and his collaborators, come from the facts of neurophysiology; Hayek's come from a liking for logical system-building. What Tustin writes scarcely feels like speculation; it is nearer poetry. She puts herself into intimate contact with small children and tries to describe how they experience their world. In the course of doing this, she arrives at words (concepts – symbols – metaphors) with which she communicates to us her sense of what is going on. Her concepts to some extent dovetail with those derived in Part 1 from thinkers who had quite other matters in mind, and this gives one a sense of confidence that all of them are writing about similar phenomena, which each conceives of and perceives from a special perspective. In this chapter we look particularly at what we can learn from autistic states of mind, which tell us something about ways in which we may experience the discovery that there are other people in the world.

The e-merging of self from (m)other

Frances Tustin, through her understanding of autistic processes, helps us to guess something of what it may feel like to be in that state of being before there has been any differentiation between 'self' and 'not self'. This state is normal after birth. She calls it 'auto-sensuous': 'a body-centred sensation-dominated state

75

which constitutes the core of the self' (1981; Chapter 1). These processes are 'of the nature of sensations arising from inbuilt dispositions which as yet do not constitute apprehension but which, given facilitating conditions, will lead on to this' (ibid.).

Tustin imagines the world of the infant before the differentiation of 'me' from 'not me'. This world is not what the observer sees. The observer sees something like *Figure 27*, and imagines the child to be experiencing, in its senses, something like a mouth filled with a nipple and pressed against a soft breast. But this takes too much for granted. The baby has not yet got to a stage where it can conceptualize its experience in this way.

The primitive self is a sensory experience, not a conceptual one. There is as yet no baby, only sensations registered in the cortex. There is as yet no (m)other, only sensations registered in the cortex. There are only neural effects. These effects make up a (m)other whom the baby experiences as part of its own body-imagery, the sensations being the baby's own bodily sensations. Tustin calls this the 'sensation-giving' or 'auto-sensuous' mother, not (yet) differentiated as 'other', but very real (ibid.).

Sensory messages are streaming into the baby's cortex. The senses create cortical effects which gradually make shapes and patterns, and some of these, if all goes well, are increasingly accurately experienced as 'me' while others are experienced as 'not me but other'. Messages about 'not me but other' go to the cortex just as messages about 'me' do. Where else? But some amount of cortical organization has to take place before these messages can find a place in the cortex *as* messages about 'the (m)other'. So at this time there is hardly any differentiation between the (m)other and the baby, or between the baby's various bodily parts, as far as the baby's experience goes. What the (m)other does is experienced in terms of those bodily zones which are just then in a state of excitement. Before differentiation, (m)other and baby are one in the baby's experience: both are embedded in the one stream of sensations. From the point of view of the baby's sensations, we might say that mother and baby are merged. Mrs Tustin (1972: 33) quotes Winnicott with approval.

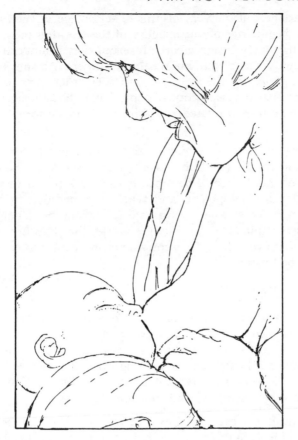

Figure 27

'Psychologically, the infant takes from a breast that is part infant, and the mother gives milk to an infant that is part of herself.'

(Winnicott 1958a: 239)

Somehow the baby has to e-merge − come out of the merge. As the baby e-merges, so does the (m)other, in the baby's experience.

We are here at the very origins of self-imagery. We find here also the beginnings of our imagery of the world of other people and things. Body-imagery is the forerunner or prototype both of self-imagery and of our knowledge of others. As suggested by the *homunculi* in the previous chapter, there are probably constitutional predispositions to particular body-imagery. Mrs Tustin entertains a related possibility, of 'innate forms'.

'These innate forms would seem to be the bodily forerunners of later thoughts and phantasies. They seem to be the flexible moulds into which experience is cast, at a primitive level of emotional development, and which are modified by the experience so cast. When an innate form seems to coincide with a correspondence in the outside world, the child has the illusion that everything is synonymous and continuous with his own body stuff.'

(1972: 29)

Unless something goes wrong, these predispositions are confirmed, refined, and elaborated by sensory messages: by the feel of cloth against skin, the feel of warmth and fullness inside, the feel of muscles flexing and stretching. Also, if things go well, the infant will feel interested and pleased when it discovers a difference between 'me' and 'not me'. However,

'the healing cleansing flow between mother and baby can seem to be broken in such a violent and catastrophic way that it cannot be recycled, transformed and made bearable by interchanges between mother and baby.'

(1982)

To some extent,

'all infants suffer the disillusionment of the "fall" from the seeming perfection of the continuous silky smoothness into the broken, gritty darkness of lack of perfect satisfaction in the exact terms which they desire.'

(ibid.)

The autistic child

Mrs Tustin's particular interest is in children who suffer from pathological autism of a psychogenic kind, who show no detectable brain damage of any kind. It may be that a too abruptly experienced encounter with the 'other' may be a precipitating factor in this kind of autism.

> 'Disturbances of primary sensuousness bring a feeling of being traumatically disconnected from the sensation-giving mother, who then becomes a "not-self" mother. This provokes a volcanic uprush of elemental feelings of rage, distress and terror, expressed as spasms of agitation, cramping tantrums, even seeming epileptic fits. . . . The baby recoils from the not-self mother with which these are associated.'
> (1981: 11–12)

In defence, the infant may attempt to preserve an illusion of fusion with the other, or to maintain some confusion of self with mother, or, as in autism, it may create a hard shell of 'encapsulation' which shuts out the not-self world as much as possible (1981: Chapter 3).

Mrs Tustin (1982) cites Louis MacNeice's *Prayer Before Birth* to help us understand.

> 'I am not yet born; O fill me
>   With strength against those who would freeze my
>   humanity, would dragoon me into a lethal automaton,
>   Would make me a cog in a machine, a thing with
>   One face, a thing, and against all those
>   who would dissipate my entirety, would
>   blow me like thistledown hither and
>   thither or hither and thither
>   like water held in the
>   hands will spill me.
>
> Let them not make me a stone and let them not spill me
> Otherwise kill me.'

'John', at the age of 3, showed many of the traits associated with autism. Dr Mildred Creak, the referring psychiatrist, wrote of him that his chief interest seemed to be

> 'to tap different surfaces, or to spin objects. He is fascinated by mechanical moving parts, and has always been quite clever at learning to move his body. Although he is sure-footed he still does not feed himself; not that he cannot – it seems as if he will not. He shows excessive anxiety at times, with days of screaming. He has no useful speech, and only communicates very tentatively by trying to use your hand.'
>
> (Tustin 1972: 13)

Mrs Tustin writes of him on his first visit to her, when he was $3\frac{1}{2}$.

> 'His face was expressionless. He went past me as if I did not exist. The one moment when this was not so occurred in the consulting room when he pulled my hand towards the humming-top which I spun for him. At this, he became very flushed and leaned forward to watch it spin. As he did so, he rotated his penis through his trousers whilst his other hand played around his mouth in circular spinning movements. This suggested to me that he made little differentiation between the movements of the top and those of his own body. He exuded a quality of passionate sensuous excitement.'
>
> (1972: 15)

Mrs Tustin worked with John for three and a half years, and she writes she would have liked more time. However, when they parted this little boy was attending a school for normal children, which reported that he was not markedly different from other children there. He was still a finicky eater, and in times of stress he was inclined to stammer and to have sleeping difficulties. But he enjoyed life, he enjoyed school, he was learning avidly, and he was making friends with other children (1972: 26).

It took much imagination, much empathy, much skill, and much determination to help John come out of his shell and relate to other people and things in a rewarding way. At first Mrs Tustin was totally responsible for establishing a relationship between herself and John, since John had neither the inclination nor the skill to do so. How she did so, how she was able to be an

unintrusive person to John and to give him the concepts in terms
of which he could experience himself and her, and reflect on
himself and her, without feeling invaded, I hope interested
readers will go to her books to find out. I also hope that as they
read on here, they will find further understanding of the process
of helpful intervention in people's lives. In this chapter we look
at what autistic states of mind may be able to teach us about the
ways in which we experience the discovery that there are others
in the world.

'I am not yet born': The 'unreadiness' hypothesis

Given the right conditions, 'sensations lead on to apprehensions'.

> 'Parental nurture provides such facilitating conditions. But
> ... the reception of nurture may be severely blocked or
> confused. ... Unable to make sufficient use of nurture, the
> child remains in, or regresses to, a sensation-dominated state.'
>
> (1972: 10)

Why should this be?

> 'According to my observations, a very common precipitating
> infantile situation ... is one in which a particularly
> vulnerable child experiences a series of shocks at a time when
> his neuro-mental apparatus is not sufficiently developed to
> stand the strain.'
>
> (1980)

When autistic children first began to be distinguished from other
handicapped children, psychologically-minded people tended to
see the mothers as responsible for their children's condition:
they were described as cold and emotionally ungiving. On the
other hand, physiologically-minded people tended to see the
cause as neurological and unavoidable. The truth seems to me to
be at once more hopeful and more tragic. The mothers are not at
fault: anyone can have an autistic child. Yet it turns out that,
with patience and some very inspired guesswork which led to a
deeper understanding of these children's condition, some can be
rescued from their handicap and come to live satisfying adult
lives well within the normal range.

Tustin (1986) is at pains to stress that there may be many possible causes of autism. However, I am going to use some of her data for a particular purpose, and entertain the hypothesis (for which there is as yet no physiological evidence I know of) that the autistic baby is born at term, apparently perfect, but with its sensory apparatus not yet ready for an out-of-womb existence. This would explain why 'the reception of nurture seems blocked or confused'. It does look as though some of the baby's senses are literally not yet registering properly. It is as though messages from the eyes, the ears, the taste-buds, and so on, are not leaving appropriate memory-traces in the cortex, which therefore cannot yet organize sensory input into dynamic concepts. This would account for such facts as that an autistic infant tends to have a weaker sucking reflex, to be later in opening its eyes, slower to focus and track movements with its eyes, more apt to lose the nipple, less apt to cuddle into the mother, less consolable in distress. Unready to meet the world, the autistic infant may experience as intolerable impingements what a more fortunate baby would placidly accept as the coming and going of hunger, bowel movements, dressing and undressing, bathing, feeding, cuddling, and so on. By the time the infant's sensory apparatus has developed the capacity to manage these experiences, it is no longer a new-born baby in the mother's eyes, and she does not handle it as such. Nor is it now treated like a more fortunate 4-day-old or 4-week-old child, for its plight and consequent strange unresponsiveness have not been understood. The mother, faced with such unfamiliar behaviour, has begun to feel inadequate or rejected. Perhaps especially with a longer delay, of weeks rather than days, the mother's confidence in her ability to be loved by her child may have been seriously undermined. This is a tragic thought, that the child should, so to speak, wake up to a mother who has been loving it fruitlessly and unnoticed for days and weeks, and who is now discouraged so that that child does not meet the love which had been waiting there all along.

Tustin does not attribute autism specifically to an under-developed sensory apparatus in the way I do here. But she seems to have understood, very sensitively, the dreadful experience which such underdeveloped infants must be undergoing when, perhaps within days and certainly within weeks, all the sensory apparatus does finally 'come to term', which is when it should have been born.

'Shapes'

In an important paper (1984), the unreadiness hypothesis seems to me to be suggested in a very striking way. Mrs Tustin there starts from the generally accepted premise that all children can experience patterns of sensations, given the appropriate stimuli. She calls these patterns (which I might call primitive concepts) 'shapes'. Tustin concentrates her attention on autistic children, but I think it possible that she has caught a very early moment of sensory/perceptual development through which we have all passed.

> 'With the younger children, the "shapes" of sound, smell, taste and sight seem to be "felt" rather than heard, smelled, tasted or seen. Such children's consciousness is very restricted because what they take in is so restricted: touch being an avenue of awareness which, in these younger autistic children, overrides other sense-perceptions.'

'Shapes' seem to be vague formations of sensations, standing out from the random flux of sensations which constitute the infant's early sense of being. 'In the first place, these "shapes" will occur without the child's intervention', writes Mrs Tustin, and this makes sense since the child is simply processing incoming stimuli. 'However, the child will soon learn that it can make some "shapes" recur by its own movements', it can reinforce the incoming stimuli and cause the sensations to prolong themselves by cortical reverberation. 'Thus, as well as arising spontaneously, they will become self-induced.'

> 'In normal development, this shape-making propensity will soon become associated with the actual shapes of objects. This will result in the formation of percepts and concepts which facilitate a working relationship with objects in the outside world which can be shared with other people. Normal sensation-shapes are the basic rudiments for emotional, aesthetic and cognitive functioning. If things go wrong here,

then dire trouble is in store. That is what happened with autistic children.'

'Shapes' are an autistic version of what I have called concepts.
Tustin gives a telling example of the primitive experience of a 'shape':

'Try a little experiment. Forget your chair. Instead, feel your seat pressing against the seat of the chair. It will make a "shape".'

(1984)

She points out that if you wiggle, the 'shape' will change. These 'shapes' are entirely personal to oneself and incommunicable to others. The autistic child's attention is on these 'shapes' more than on the chair, which it does not experience in the same immediate way. Because of its continued reliance on touch sensations rather than sight perceptions, the autistic child does not progress from experiencing 'shapes' to more sophisticated impressions of the world, which would involve sight and sound and context and meaning. It does not acquire higher-order conceptual and dynamic structures. Tustin says it keeps its world 'monotonously the same'.

Since touch is the main sense through which experiences reach the autistic child, the mere sight of objects carries little meaning for it. The autistic child does not make much sense of the things it sees – it does not have accurate expectations as to their significance and meaning. Hence they may impinge agonizingly. If you can see the corner of the table but it means nothing to you, you may walk into it and be shocked by the pain when you do.

The self as a stream needing a container

If the child's sensory apparatus is not (yet) working properly,

'it seems tenable that for the very young infant, "being" is a stream of sensations. Put in another way, in earliest days, the infant *is* the stream of sensations from which constructs emerge as nameless entities. As soon as some degree of separateness is tolerated, the infant may be said to interpret the outside world in terms of these nameless entities.'

(1972: 60)

The 'stream of sensations' which Tustin imagines the normal tiny child to be persists in the older autistic child. According to Tustin and her fellow-workers, autistic children are at times unusually interested by what is going on in pipes and tubes, those of the central heating or the plumbing for instance: here is something flowing and shapeless in the pipes! Mrs Tustin suggests that this may correspond to their body-image and/or self-representation. This is not so surprising, since our bodies are rather like tubes through which things gurgle digestively. Not only food. Many of us have at times a sense of perceptual flow — of things coming through our eyes and ears into ourselves and out again. There are times when our sensations are not processed, not digested, not organized into meaning, not metabolized — they just flow through us as 'nameless entities' — they are 'shapes'.

Could it be that autistic children sense, in their body-imagery, an affinity with pipes and tubes, containers of flowing things, sensing the flow of digestion from intake at the mouth to elimination at the lower end, and the flow of sights and sounds in, through, and out again? Could it even be that children who feel these affinities have already made some progress (through therapy or for other reasons) in that they are somehow able to sense what pipes and tubes are for? Have they progressed beyond the simple capacity for experiencing 'shapes'? Are these the ones already able to conceptualize themselves as containers, holding things? Before this relatively well-organized state of mind, might there be a stage when the child has only a sense of itself as a flux, no more organized or differentiated than water streaming out of a tap or a hose?

'The thesis which is being developed is that, at first, the "felt self" is experienced in terms of fluids and gases. This is not surprising since the newly-born infant has emerged from a fluid medium and his early food and excretions are associated with fluids and gas. As Spitz has pointed out, after birth the neonate has to adjust from being a water creature to being a dweller on dry land. This is quite a big adjustment, so that it is to be expected that sensations associated with floating in a fluid medium will linger on to become part of the early body image.'

(Tustin 1982)

Quite different writers have curiously similar metaphors. Anticipating a later more detailed treatment we may quote Balint:

> 'Birth is a trauma which upsets the equilibrium by changing the environment radically and enforcing a new form of adaptation. . . . Objects, including the ego, begin to emerge from the mix-up of substances and from the breaking up of the harmony of the limitless expanses. The objects have – in contrast to the friendlier substances – firm contours and boundaries which must henceforth be recognised and respected.'
>
> (Balint 1968: 67)

It is interesting that Hayek also thought in these terms, in a moment of dissatisfaction with the metaphor of the map.

> 'A closer parallel to our case would in some respects be provided by a system of pipes or tubes through which move columns of a pliable substance. Let us assume that at many points of interconnexion these tubes are joined by "afferent" tubes which can bring in from the outside new columns of the substance, and by "efferent" tubes which may drain such columns from the system and that at any junction the columns may divide. Supposing also that the direction of the pressure of the columns meeting at such junctions will decide in which further direction they will jointly move on. . . . It will then be the pattern which the moving columns trace within (and relative to) the pattern formed by the system of tubes, which will correspond to the pattern traced by the nervous impulses within (and relative to) the structure of connected fibres.'
>
> (Hayek 1952: 5. 47)

The mother as skin, container, and organizer of experiences

At first, the child is a stream, or the stream is a child, and the auto-sensuous mother acts as a skin might do, before the infant has developed what one might call its own skin – something to contain all its fluctuating rushes of sensation. Tustin takes up a suggestion by Bick (1968).

> 'In the early infantile stages of unintegration, the parts of the

personality which are little differentiated from bodily parts
need the experience of being held together by a "psychological skin", the infant's own experience of his skin being
important in that regard. ... This "skin" formation occurs
when the infant has internalised sufficiently soothing and
sheltering experiences with the mother.'

(1972: 57)

If the mother has not been able to do this, or the child has not
been able to receive it, the child develops something Mrs Tustin
calls a second skin, an artificial carapace, a False Self. In this
connection she cites Bick's description of an infant whose
'primary nurturing containment' was disturbed, and who
showed a 'muscular type of self-containment – a second skin
instead of a proper skin container'. It seemed clear that this
infant was attempting to do for itself what the mother would
normally do at that stage.

Freud, in *The Ego and the Id* (1923), already used the metaphor
of an enveloping skin to convey the idea of an 'ego' whose
function it is to mediate between the id-needs and wishes of the
child and the realistic facts of its environment with which it has
to come to terms. Ego-functions (that is cognitive functions like
perceiving, conceptualizing, remembering, evaluating, planning,
and so on) hold and contain bodily processes such as impulses
and reflexes. Like an enveloping skin, they hold the flow of
input steady for long enough to allow some pattern-making and
pattern-recognition, some organization and structuring, to take
place. And this is exactly what the mother does when all is well
with her and her baby.

The function of mother as skin, container, and organizer of
experiences is most clearly seen when things go wrong. And
however happily the smooth flow of the infant's life may be
arranged, there are bound to be times when it feels irritation,
frustration, deprivation, or some other distress. It has as yet
nothing as sophisticated as a memory or a time-perspective to
help it endure much – nothing to help it 'put things in
perspective'. Above a certain pitch of intensity, the distress may
become intolerable, filling the infant's whole experience. Once
this intolerable level has been reached, something seems to
become self-perpetuating at a cortical level. The baby cries and

cries and cries. Even when the cause of the distress has long been removed, even when the baby finally falls asleep exhausted, the smooth flow of life is not resumed. The experience has left its mark.

> 'Slowly the poison the whole bloodstream fills;
> The waste remains, the waste remains and kills.'
>
> (William Empson, *Missing Dates*)

As the baby's distress escalates, it may also get more and more frightened by premonitory fears of destruction – it becomes frightened at the possibility that it may become intolerably frightened – signal anxiety. Tustin imagines that this is when the child needs someone to be there

> 'to contain, to recycle and filter the child's "overflow" so that it is not allowed to become out of control, to become a "waterfall" or a "volcano". Thus processed by a caring recipient in a sane and practical way, the experience can begin to flow back to the child in a transformed and bearable form so that it begins to be able to process it for itself.'
>
> (1982)

What Tustin seems to have in mind here is an auto-sensuous precursor of processes which Melanie Klein and others have called 'projective identification'. For the baby receives, in its own body, the impact of its mother's feelings as these express themselves in looks, posture, voice, management, and so on. The mother receives, in her more sophisticated cortical structures, the impact on her of the baby's cries, posture, expressions, and so on. Tustin calls this 'flowing-over-at-one-ness' (1981).

No skin, no body-image; no body-image, no self; no self, no ego-functions

When a child does not have the use of a protective mother/skin, practically everything must feel like an impingement from an 'other'. Sights, sounds, and tactile sensations, if they are not held and contained, cannot be processed. Unprocessed, the child must necessarily experience them as sudden and meaningless, and as intrusive as a lightning flash, a bang, or a push. Similarly the child may experience its own impulses and physiological processes, its sneezes and hiccups, as alarmingly intrusive. The old-fashioned use of the word *insult* as meaning 'attack, assault, the act of leaping upon', is appropriate here — it was used in medical circles until quite recently. When we are feeling very vulnerable, all unanticipated stimuli, from whatever source and regardless of whether they are inherently painful or rewarding, are experienced as impingements. An unlucky infant may experience apparently quite harmless sensations — caused perhaps by hunger, or by an inability to shift round, or by the elusiveness of something it is trying to grasp with its little fist — as impingements which nothing and no one could stop. 'Tantrums pound through muscle and vein and cause the child to fear total annihilation' (1968: 110).

The child needs a skin. Partly this means it needs a good start for its cognitive (ego) functioning to develop. It also means that the child needs whatever a skin does to enable it to develop an accurate body-image. When its perceptual apparatus is not ready to process (that is 'contain') the sensory flow, too much impingement will impede the development of the primitive *homunculi* into more highly coherent and differentiated body-imagery. This can have dire consequences, for body-imagery is what identity — the sense of self — is based on. We can put this in terms of being contained and held together by a skin or in terms of being organized and 'integrated' by a connecting process. Both are good metaphors; Tustin uses both.

> 'We have seen that the infant's experience of his skin seems to be of primary importance in enabling him to feel that his bodily parts are held together and contained. This means that he can begin to be a "container".'
>
> (1972: 60)

'It will have become clear that in studying primary autism we are studying an embrionic "self". The inner sense of "linking" provided by satisfying experiences of encircling the nipple in the mouth, of being encircled in the mother's arms, and of being held within the ambience of the mother's caring attention seems to be a vital first step from which *integration* can begin to take place. This is integration of the various parts of the personality, and also integration of the emerging self into a situation where other "wills" exist apart from his own.'

(1972: 59)

Integration makes a structure – 'I', and inevitably this leaves other elements in the situation – 'not I'. For the more autistic child,

'integrations are likely to take place which bring the fact of bodily separateness into the focus of the infant's attention in an unacceptably sudden and incontrovertible way. This brings with it the despair about replacing something that is "gone". That which is "gone" becomes an inimical "not-me" void to be avoided by all the forces at the child's command. The fact that this avoidance creates further voids is the tragedy of pathological autism.'

(1972: 87)

Tustin surmises an autistic resistance to developing a skin: skin so inevitably differentiates self from other.

'To realise that it has a skin, the infant must accept the fact that the flow of its body-stuff can come to an end. Prior to this realisation, the infant's whole experience seems to be in terms of its own body-stuff to which an end or boundary is not conceived.'

(1972: 60–1)

Body-stuff is one of Tustin's telling words to describe what the body feels in its undifferentiated state while at one with the auto-sensuous mother – complete, perfect, unending, boundless, timeless. The autistic part of us may feel that it will be damaged by the slightest intrusion of the other – indeed by an indication that other people exist. Since this part still clings to the phantasy of unbounded body-stuff, whatever reminds us of our not being absolutely everything everywhere, makes us feel that it should not exist.

An autistic way of minimizing impingement without having to acknowledge that you have limitations and boundaries is to turn your back on threats and hurts. This gives you a feeling that they cannot reach your essential self, which most of us feel is on our front side – the back acting as a shell. We are encouraged to let insults run 'like water off a duck's back'. Strictly regarded, the back is a barrier only – it need not be an armour that surrounds and thus circumscribes the whole person. When you turn your back you do not have to acknowledge that you are circumscribed – a self among other selves, no more.

In this connection, Tustin was interested to find that many of her little patients wrapped themselves in a blanket or a rug in the playroom. She believed that we are not to think of this as though the children were burrowing inside a wrapping. The cover is only a barrier for the child – it protects the child from intrusion but it does not remind the child that it is bounded on all sides by a skin. A wrapper, on the other hand, is a container; it shows that you come to an end, are not uncontained, have a shape, an organization, a structure, however much this may hurt your pride when you want to think of yourself as unlimited.

A person able to tolerate the existence of 'other' as well as 'self' can experience *relationships* between self and not self, sharing and negotiating as well as persecuting and destroying. The autistic child (in us) is frightened of meeting the 'other' and tries to evade the encounter. Yet, tragically, encounters with others are the very events which would develop the protective and containing organization. Through them it would develop the skills and ego-functions which are a precondition for ego-development and which help the child look after itself, and to relate constructively to other people and things.

> 'Awareness of solid objects as separate from the body is a necessary prelude to moving on from a predominantly fluid "felt-self" to transitional states in which there are felt to be inner and outer structures which can contain and control the fluids which overflow and become out of control. Lacking such regulating structures, autistic children feel that they can be trodden underfoot like an insect, as in Kafka's story *Metamorphosis*, which clearly described Kafka's own terrors.'
> (1982)

Tustin (1981) notes how many autistic children avoid lumps in their food, preferring the texture of smooth paste; some are actually afraid of the hard bits in a phobic sort of way. It may be that avoiding the lumps is a way of avoiding the insult of there being an 'other'. Tustin believes that the child resists the development of any conceptual structures which would mark the e-merging of self and (m)other and would acknowledge, reflect, match, or map the intolerable gap between self and other, a gap which the autistic child experiences as a gaping hole. Instead of acknowledging and relating to the 'lumps' – the other people and things – the over-sensitive vulnerable child likes to recreate the sensations of at-one-ness in a delusional way. It concentrates its attention on 'shapes', sensations it experiences from substances held in the mouth, the nose, the bowels, the hand.

'In treatment, as the children encounter the hardness of frustration, in a sane and caring setting, and as they feel that the uncontrollable "waterfalls" and "volcanoes" of their impulsivity are received, processed and understood by another being who has sensitivity and robust common-sense, their body-image begins to feel more substantial and intact. They begin to feel that they have an inner structure and that there is an outer structure which helps them to bear what had previously been unbearable. These unbearable sensations had seemed to gush out in an uncontrollable way which had undermined their self-confidence. As these are felt to be held and contained, the children begin to develop hopefulness and a sense of purpose.'

(1982)

We see then, incidentally, that the impulsiveness of these children is not a challenging wilfulness and disobedience: it is due to their lack of 'skin', of ego-functioning.

Helps and hindrances in the development of ego-functioning: transitional and auto-sensuous objects

Many little children have, like Christopher Robin, a soft cuddly toy or, like Linus, a security blanket. They relate to it as though it had an independent existence, teaching it new things, scolding it for naughtiness, hugging it for comfort. Such things are used as a bridge between the self and the 'not self' – they are experienced as not quite 'self', but not quite 'other' either: they are transitional between the self and the other. Many autistic children also have something to hold, but it is different in one remarkable respect: it is not cuddly, it tends to be hard and clearly defined, a toy car or a key, held tightly in the hand, tight enough to leave ridges when the hand relaxes.

Tustin believes that the autistic child experiences the hardness, not in the hand – as an observer might think – but cortically as a diffused generalized hardness which is interposed between the vulnerable flow and the lumpy destructive 'not me'. The child can use the toy car, the key, the back, the door, the rug, the closed eye, the screams, as barriers to keep the vulnerable flux safe from harm. 'Shapes' may be the precursors of these things, which Mrs Tustin at first called 'autistic objects' and later, when their function became clearer, 'auto-sensuous objects'.

But such barriers inhibit the development of ego-functioning. 'Tantrums pound through muscle and vein and cause the child to fear total annihilation. To counteract this deadly terror it clutches a hard autistic object. This means it never learns to deal with bodily and mental irritation in a considered thinking way' (1981: 110). I am in touch with my own autistic processes each time I dive into a book or a crossword or my ear-phoned music to shut out the inconveniences of travel or other minor aches and pains. Such organized distractions from annoyances are my 'autistic objects'.

Recourse to autistic objects keeps the autistic child 'in a raw unnurtured state relatively unmodified by the disciplining and humanising elements of mother and infant in the nursing situation'. (1981: 109) It is at the mercy of elemental inbuilt patterns which are stereotyped and unmodified by experience. These are unregulated and have not been co-ordinated in the normal way.

Such a child will evade the 'practising' stages of normal infancy. It will expect to do everything perfectly at the first attempt, without needing practice beforehand. When it fails, it will not try again. Tustin thinks this trait an important component in the passivity and lack of confidence such a child feels. She also notes that Ricks (1975) had found that many of these children had missed the lalling and babbling stages of infancy. Her own observations concur.

'Many of them have missed the normal sucking and mouthing stage when children create a working simulation of the breast. This simulation enables them to develop a more skilful and efficient use of the actual breast when it comes.'

(1981: 104)

Such children have not learned to play, and so they have missed the great quantity of early learning which happens in play. Referring to Winnicott's work on transitional processes, Tustin notes that they have missed the 'creative work of adjusting illusions and developing phantasies which facilitate the emergence of individuality'. To this we return in later chapters.

The loss of attachment

So far we have considered the child's experience of its first encounter with the other as mainly a painful intrusion. It may also be experienced as mainly a painful absence – indeed, at a primitive level these two apparent opposites are the same experience described in two different ways. When the fact of bodily separateness eventually comes into focus in an undeniable way, it brings with it a sense of something gone, and a search for something to replace it and take away the pain of absence. In normal circumstances there is a strong enough reaching out on the part of the infant, and a strong enough response by the mother supported by her family, for the infant to be able to tolerate the absence and bridge the gap. Nevertheless, Mrs Tustin writes, there seem to remain in the depths of us all, vestiges of comfort-seeking autistic inertia, exerting a backward pull (1972: 87–8). Freud must have been referring to this when, in *Beyond the Pleasure Principle* (1920), he wrote of the pull to return to the inanimate – the Death Instinct.

When all goes well, the child emerges gradually out of a merged state of being-at-one to a state which holds a welcome sense of self and a welcome sense of the other. With this change of awareness goes a changed sense of connectedness. Throughout its life, the sense of being attached and connected need not desert the child, though the nature of the attachment changes.

The loss of attachment and connectedness must be unimaginably painful. Something that had been felt to be a part of the body is suddenly found not to be so. Tustin (1972: 52) is reminded of L. P. Hartley's *The Shrimp and the Anemone*, which describes a disastrous separation-experience. Untimely death results when Eustace, the soft-bodied shrimp, is torn from the enveloping tentacles of his sister Hilda, the anemone. From a merged state of at-one-ness, abrupt separation may be experienced as 'an explosion-producing gap between primitive illusion and actuality' (Tustin 1972: 34).

'The exploding-away is experienced as if a part is uprooted from one's own body, which then seems threatened with dissolution. The foreign body which is expelled is felt to have taken a piece of the self with it.'

(1972: 52)

Instead of the interesting and potentially constructive discovery of a relationship between 'me' and 'others' − a new kind of connectedness − there is only a messy chaos.

'Interchanges break down. The seamless robe of perfection is rent with holes: waterfalls, volcanoes and whirlpools threaten.'

(1982)

The autistic child feels that it had something of immense value which has now gone into the hostile void − gone into a hole, as one of Tustin's little patients called it. The 'hole' which the child feels, through which it feels its body-stuff to be seeping away, is the gap between the self and the mother or the object-world. So all other holes are unbearable gaps as well, through which terrible things can escape or enter. Instead of a creative 'space between', the transitional space, this distance is experienced as a destructive vortex. The orifices are not bridges to the world of objects but weak points in one's defences (1981: 135−36).

In another brilliant metaphor, also taken from a little patient, Tustin calls the thing that is needed to fill the gap, a button. A button joins two pieces of material to make one whole; a button fills a button-hole; a button can be a nipple filling a mouth (though Tustin warns against too facile a reference to nipples and mouths, as this assumes a greater sense of 'self' and 'other' than has yet been established).

'It is important to realise that the child's inability to tolerate the fact of loss comes from its having experienced excruciating distress about the seeming loss of the nursing mother, which had been felt to be part of its body.'

(1980)

Here, again, Tustin refers with appreciation to Winnicott. He distinguished between two kinds of depression. One kind, the reactive depression, is connected with the loss of a loved person. Another kind, much more severe, is 'more like the loss of one's own body-stuff'.

From here we go on quite naturally to consider John Bowlby's work. He might say that the unlucky infant experiences a hole or an explosion where it should have been experiencing an attachment.

·6·

The unattached infant

A previous chapter used some of John Bowlby's ideas on the organization of the personality. He has much more to offer – he is, in fact, one of those universally well-informed men, *homo universalis*, whose knowledge ranges over a great variety of fields: the study of engineering, cybernetics, and computer programming; the psychology of perception and cognition; the study of animals in general and as social beings. He is also a psycho-analyst; one of his books is dedicated to the patients 'who have worked hard to educate me'. From the riches of an intellectual store which holds all this, he has derived ideas on the nature of a person's attachment to other people, and on what happens when people are separated, temporarily or for ever, from those to whom they have been attached. To this we now turn.

I have used as source material the three volumes published first in hardback and then in Pelican edition: on *Attachment* (1969, 1971), on *Separation, Anxiety and Anger* (1973, 1975) and on *Loss, Sadness and Depression* (1980, 1981). In the text I shall refer to them by volume number and chapter number, as for instance (I, 1).

With Bowlby's breadth and depth goes a characteristic lack of defensiveness. He mistrusts the certainties of many adult and professional worlds. Over and over he points out that we do not take seriously enough what children say about their own feelings

97

and needs, their fears, their version of life as they experience it. He makes us wonder if we may not have encouraged the secretiveness (which misleads us) with which a child may hide its fears when parents in a temper threaten to leave home or kill themselves or throw the child out. A similar secretiveness may be encouraged when the child realizes that a loved person's death must not be talked about. The feelings surrounding separation are so painful that they tend to be denied, as is the pain many of us feel when we leave a child on its own without us. We do not care to put ourselves in the shoes of a child that feels unprotected and abandoned, and so we rather tend to claim that children feel less, or don't remember, or 'must learn' and so on. This although we know that adults have clearer time-perspectives, better self-control, more ways of compensating, and so on. We cannot bear to think what childhood can be like. Professionals too, for a variety of reasons, may help to obscure the worries of childhood.

Bowlby's readings in animal behaviour enable him to put human behaviour in interesting perspectives. Nowhere is this more apparent than in his discussion of the anxieties and worries of the young. These are often considered neurotic manifestations when they are not. In Bowlby's view they are natural to the young of a species whenever their 'attachment figure' is not available to them.

Attachment

Attachment is Bowlby's most basic concept.

> 'In the countryside in springtime there is no more familiar sight than mother animals with young. In the fields, cows and calves, mares and foals, ewes and lambs; in the ponds and rivers, ducks and ducklings, swans and cygnets. So familiar are these sights and so much do we take for granted that lamb and ewe will remain together and that a flotilla of ducklings will remain with mother duck that the questions are rarely asked: What causes these animals to remain in each other's company? What function is fulfilled by their doing so?
>
> (I, 11)

Bowlby postulates that over the millennia an instinct has evolved that enabled the species to survive, and this causes the infant animal to seek to be close to another animal – the 'attachment figure', usually the mother. Anxiety grows in intensity, the longer the attachment figure is away. This is a biological effect. Bowlby gives many charming examples of attachment behaviour from the animal world, such as this one from the life of the rhesus monkey:

> 'During the weeks after the baby first leaves the mother, if it is on the ground and she moves away, it usually follows; and even though it can barely crawl it will still attempt to follow. ... Should mother move too fast, or depart suddenly, the baby "geckers" and the mother responds by hugging it to her. ... A baby that loses its mother makes very long calls through protruded lips, and this may lead another female to pick it up. In the event of any sudden disturbance occurring when the baby is off its mother, each at once runs to the other.'
>
> (I, 11)

Bowlby quotes substantial evidence of the search of the young of many species for someone to hold on to. Harlow's experiments with the rhesus monkeys are now well known: baby monkeys removed from their mothers at birth would cling to a roughly made model of a monkey made of soft cloth, or even to wire-netting twisted into a cylinder shape if nothing else was available. In one experiment the need to cling was shown to be more urgent than the need to eat.

> 'Eight monkeys were raised with the choice of a cloth model or a wire model. Four infants were fed (on demand) from the cloth model and four from the wire model. The time the infants spent on each was measured. ... Irrespective of which model provided the food, all the infants soon came to spend most of their time with the cloth model. Some infants whose food came from the wire model managed to lean over and suck the teat whilst still maintaining a grip on the cloth model.'
>
> (I, 12)

Bowlby notes that primate apes carry their infants about until these have the strength to move on their own initiative – three or four months of constant support. The baby clings, the mother hugs. And he reminds us that in some simpler human societies, also, the baby is not put in a stationary cradle while the others go away from it. The baby is carried about while people move around. Even when put down, the others are in sight and hearing and while it is carried, it is constantly rocked by the other's movement in a way that can be both stimulating and soothing.

> 'Only in more economically developed human societies, and especially in Western ones, are infants commonly out of touch with mother for many hours a day and often during the night as well. This evolutionary shift in the balance from infant taking all the initiative in keeping contact, to mother taking all the initiative has an important consequence.'
>
> (I, 12)

It leaves us doubtful, according to Bowlby, about what is natural and what is not. It leaves us with 'a difficulty in deciding by what criteria to judge the beginning of attachment behaviour in human beings.' (246).

Bowlby argues that infants in Western-type societies are relatively isolated in their earliest days, and that because of this they are slower to display such attachment behaviour as crying when the mother leaves the room, and cooing and smiling when she returns. If this biologically normal development is delayed because the child has experiences which are not biological to the species, what other 'norms of development' may we have established, asks Bowlby, based equally mistakenly on the peculiarities of our economically developed way of life?

Crying, cooing, smiling, suckling, clinging, and trailing after the mother or other attachment figure are the kinds of activities in which attachment behaviour is manifested. When Bowlby started work, in the 1940s, he was thinking of these as instinctually determined. Later he came rather to hold the belief that the child's tie to the mother is built up from the many experiences which come from being physically close to a person. Attachment behaviour is rewarding to both participants, and thereby their tie is rewarded and confirmed (1, 14).

Nevertheless, attachment behaviour is based on biological predispositions, making loneliness and lack of support as agonizing a deprivation as hunger. Yet we live in a society where people are more likely to be economically successful if they can cultivate individual enterprise, independence, and some ability to disregard their own feelings and other people's. They, and those who have been unsuccessful in this endeavour, may have to pay quite a price for this.

Neither the family nor the social group are the convenient units they were in the days when our species evolved. Not surprisingly, in the present century loneliness and disorientation have become major psychological problems. Kierkegaard's 'dread', Sartre's 'nausea', and in my view much of 'schizophrenia', all refer to loneliness and disorientation. The norm is now that men may have to leave their family and the group they might have belonged to, for the day or perhaps for days, for years in the case of 'guest-workers', for life if there is a divorce without a remarriage. The women may be left psychologically unsupported with just small children to relate to, during the day or perhaps for days, until these too leave. The generally accepted sociological fact, that women are now responsible for most emotional and social ties within families and between people – the men relying on the women to make and maintain these connections for them – throws into stark light the extent to which we have impoverished our lives. The normal species support between people has been thinned down: there is less of it, for children, for parents, for those in the home, and for those who work outside it. The solution is not, as some suppose, to insist that women stay at home and keep their loneliness to themselves while men cultivate an unfeeling independence, but to reconsider some aspects of our lifestyle.

Bowlby summarizes his views on attachment in Chapter 3 of his final volume:

'Attachment behaviour leads to affection, and this happens not only in childhood but between adults.

Attachment is "any form of behaviour that results in a person being in proximity to some other particular person. As long as the latter – the attachment figure – remains accessible and responsive, attachment behaviour may be no more than keeping an eye on the person's whereabouts". In other circumstances, attachment behaviour shows itself in crying, following about, clinging, and so on, likely to elicit a caring response.

Attachment behaviour derives from a distinct biological motivational system (like an instinct), just as feeding does, or sex, or any other biologically rooted behaviour.

Experience through learning elaborates the biologically given behaviour; the infant may learn what leads to a better maintenance of closeness, and it may learn about the circumstances in which it is best to be close to the other, and when this is less important.

Attachment behaviour occurs in many species and works for the survival of the species.

When attachment behaviour occurs, another animal will tend to respond by giving care. Especially the attachment figure will do so.

Very intense emotions are involved. The formation of an attachment bond is described as falling in love, maintaining a bond as loving someone, and losing a partner as grieving over someone. The threat of loss arouses anxiety. Actual loss gives rise to sorrow. Loss also arouses anger. The unchallenged maintenance of a bond is experienced as a source of security, and the renewal of a bond as a source of joy.

Attachment behaviour is not neurotic but normal. And it is not mainly oral. It is more about clinging than about sucking. [There is a very useful review of psycho-analytical literature on the child's tie to the mother up to 1968, in the appendix to volume I, where the 'oral hypothesis' is evaluated in some detail.]

The patterns of affectional bonds that a person makes throughout life depend on the way in which an individual's attachment behaviour has become organized in his or her personality.

A person's experiences with his or her attachment figures during the years of immaturity – infancy, childhood, and adolescence – are the principal determinants of the pathway along which that person's attachment behaviour develops.

When things go wrong this is due to the psychological development having somehow followed a deviant pathway. It is not due to a fixation at, or a regression to, some earlier stage of development.

Disturbed patterns of attachment behaviour can be present at any age, due to a deviant development. A common form of disturbance occurs when attachment behaviour is over-readily called forth, resulting in over-anxious attachments. Another common form is the partial or total de-activation of attachment behaviour.'

Separation anxiety

In *Separation, Anxiety and Anger* (1973) Bowlby contended that early separations from the mother (or other attachment figure) cause anxiety, indeed distress if at all prolonged, and, in severe cases, permanent lack of feeling for others ('deactivation of attachment behaviour'). Besides massive evidence from the study of animals, he also cited from our growing knowledge of the distress which children feel when separated from their parents. From the late 1940s onwards, these studies, in many of which he was instrumental, began radically to alter our understanding of children's reactions to separation. In the few decades since then, for instance, most hospitals in Britain have changed, from insisting that parents should never visit their sick children 'because it upsets the children', to encouraging free visiting at all times in most children's wards: an interesting perspective on how changes in everyday practice are affected by research. Bowlby described some work which could not now be done as even the most remote researcher would recognize its inhumanity. The experiment required complete strangers to go to the homes of children between 2 and 3 years old, and take them from their mothers' side, into a strange car and away for a day's testing, while noting their reactions throughout! (Heathers 1954, quoted by Bowlby). This does not seem to have been perceived as likely to cause indefensible suffering. However, the study is one of many which did demonstrate that children do suffer when removed from their parents, and this began to be taken seriously. But even now, as those know who have an inkling of what goes on in some nursery schools, day-centres, and creches, Bowlby's warning still counts, that there are many misconceptions about the norms of behaviour to be expected of young children when left, even briefly, in a strange place with strange people.

> 'Misconceptions persist, especially among professional people. Again and again it is implied that a healthy normal child should not make a fuss when mother leaves, and that if he does so it is an indication either that mother spoils him or that he is suffering from some pathological anxiety. It is hoped that such reactions will be seen in a new and more realistic light when

the natural history and function of attachment-behaviour are understood.'

Bowlby listed the elements which in his view are typical of the young child's response to even a brief separation, when no special effort has been made to prepare and cushion the child:

'yearning and searching for the missing mother, sadness, increasing protest at her absence and growing anger with her for staying away, increased ambivalence on return home and evident fear of being separated again.'

(II, 1)

In the next chapter, he comments:

'Whenever young children who have had an opportunity to develop an attachment to a mother-figure are separated from her unwillingly, they show distress: and should they also be placed in a strange environment and cared for by strange people such distress is likely to be intense. The way they behave follows a typical sequence. At first they *protest* vigorously and try by all the means available to recover the mother. Later they seem to *despair* of recovering her but nonetheless remain preoccupied with her and vigilant for her return. Later still they seem to lose interest in the mother and to become emotionally *detached* from her.'

(II, 2)

'Each of the three main phases of the response of a young child to separation is related to one or another of the central issues of psycho-analytic theory. Thus the phase of *protest* is found to raise the problem of separation anxiety; *despair* that of grief and mourning; *detachment* that of defence.'

(II, 2)

Bowlby suggested that these three types of response are phases of a single process and need to be understood in that context. In his view the damage done by these early separations is not totally reparable, and always leaves some mark on the adult personality, in severe cases having so strong an effect as to be the main determinant of the adult's thought and feeling.

Attachment behaviour has deep biological roots, in Bowlby's view, and therefore the anxieties which attend separation from an attachment figure must also have deep biological roots. In a most interesting review of the literature (II, Appendix) he contrasted this view of one of our most basic anxieties with the currently more widely held view that the deepest anxieties concern the fear that the organized self may be disrupted when the nervous system has to handle more stimulus than it can manage at a time, so that the emerging neural structuring disintegrates. In that view, the mother's function is to take the overload and prevent disintegration. (There is, of course, no reason why there should be just one basic anxiety: it can certainly be argued that both may be aspects of the same anxiety.)

From a similarly 'biological' standpoint, Bowlby challenged Freud's view, expressed in many places but especially in *Inhibitions, Symptoms and Anxiety* (1926), that all anxieties which are not to do with what Freud (and many) think of as 'real' danger – that is danger 'which threatens a person from an external object' – are neurotic anxieties. To Bowlby, the anxiety which is felt when the attachment figure is not available – usually when mother is not there – was useful for the survival of the species and has persisted as part of our biological make-up. The phobias which puzzled Freud did not seem puzzling to Bowlby: he saw them as vestiges of the need to respond to what he called natural clues to danger.

> 'Ethologists take for granted that many of the stimulus-situations that arouse fear in animals can be regarded as naturally occurring clues to events that constitute a potential danger to the species in question. This applies especially to situations that arouse fear on the first occasion that an individual encounters them.'
>
> (II, 8)

Bowlby listed a number of these: strangeness, being unsupported on a height, being alone, having something zoom rapidly into view, and other such. None of these is intrinsically dangerous, but in the animal world they indicate the possibility of an increased risk of danger. 'A natural clue is associated as a rule with a raised degree of risk' (II, 9), and this can make a child's behaviour appear phobic when it occurs in situations which appear incomprehensible to the adult world.

In Bowlby's view, the fact that Freud did not fully appreciate the survival function which anxiety had had for the species, led him to a mistaken explanation for the origins of anxiety – an equilibrium theory according to which a person finds all stimuli disturbing to a kind of static peace. Stimulus, in Freud's view, aroused disequilibrium, which is experienced as anxiety, which motivates action to remove the painful stimulus. The person would prefer less and less stimulation till the peace of death covers all.

In marked contrast, Bowlby saw the human being as naturally equipped to relate, indeed to cling, and naturally equipped to move about and explore and seek stimulus, always providing that there was a person or a place of safety to move back to. This tension between moving outward and hanging on is the main topic of Chapter 7.

Anger at separation and loss

Bowlby and Freud also held contrasting views on the nature of anger. Much of this is not relevant to the present narrative, but anger at separation and loss is in my view so prevalent and so relevant to any consideration of social problems that a few paragraphs may be in order. Anger at the absence of an attachment figure is not like the anger which is felt when an instinctual drive is frustrated (unless we take attachment to be the frustrated instinct) and it is not like the anger felt during an experience of deprivation or persecution – two frequent sources of anger mentioned in psycho-analytic literature. Bowlby gave an example from Robertson (1952) whose film *A Two-Year-Old Goes to Hospital* was immensely influential in changing public opinion on the effects of separation.

> 'Robertson describes the angry reproaches of Laura, a child of two years and four months whom he had filmed during an eight-day stay in hospital for a minor operation. Some months after her return home Robertson was showing an early version of his film to her parents for their comments, while Laura was in bed believed asleep. As it happened, she awoke, crept into the room and witnessed the last few minutes of the film, in which she was seen on the day of her return from hospital, at

first distressed and calling for her mother, later when her
shoes are produced delighted at the prospect of going home,
and finally departing from hospital with her mother. The film
over and the lights switched up, *Laura turned away from her
mother* to be picked up by her father. Then, looking
reproachfully at her mother, she demanded "Where *was* you,
Mummy? Where *was* you?"'

(II, 17)

Bowlby then asked himself what might be the biological function
of such anger.

'The answer proposed is that whenever separation is only
temporary, which in the large majority of cases it is, anger has
two functions: first, it may assist in overcoming such obstacles
as there may be to reunion; second, it may discourage the
loved person from going away again.'

(II, 17)

Bowlby called this *coercive anger*, and thought of it as the anger
of hope.

'Angry coercive behaviour, acting in the service of an
affectional bond, is not uncommon. It is seen when a mother,
whose child has run foolishly across the road, berates and
punishes it with an anger born of fear. It is seen whenever a
sexual partner berates the other for being or seeming to be
disloyal. ... It occurs also in non-human primates. For
example, when he sights a predator, a dominant male baboon
may behave aggressively towards any wandering member of
his own group who may be at risk.'

(II, 17)

Dysfunctional anger, on the other hand, occurs whenever a
person becomes so intensely or persistently angry that the bond
of affection is weakened instead of strengthened.

'Clinical experience suggests that the situations of separation
and loss with which this work is concerned are especially
liable to result in anger that crosses the threshold of intensity
and becomes dysfunctional. Separations, especially when
prolonged or repeated, have a double effect. On the one hand,
anger is aroused; on the other, love is attenuated. Thus not

only may angry discontented behaviour alienate the attachment figure but, within the attached, a shift can occur in the
balance of feeling. Instead of a strongly rooted affection laced
occasionally with "hot displeasure", such as develops in a
child brought up by affectionate parents, there grows a deep-
running resentment, held in check only partially by an
anxious uncertain affection.'

(II, 17)

Bowlby also suggested that at this point the 'hot displeasure'
may in some circumstances become the cold malice of hatred.

Loss

Anger is often felt during bereavement and is then a part of
separation anxiety. At first sight, it appears to serve no useful
function.

'The reason that it occurs so often nonetheless, even after a
death, is that during the early phases of grieving a bereaved
person usually does not believe that the loss can really be
permanent; he therefore continues to act as though it were still
possible not only to find and recover the lost person but to
reproach him for his actions. For the lost person is not
infrequently held to be at least in part responsible for what
has happened, in fact to have deserted. As a result, anger
comes to be directed against the lost person, as well as, of
course, against others thought to have played a part in the loss
or in some way to be obstructing reunion.'

(II, 17)

Anxiety is, in Bowlby's view, a species' reaction to the absence
of the attachment figure when he or she is still needed for the
well-being of the infant (or of the infant in us all). The protest
which follows such an absence is meant to bring the needed
person back (or at least bring someone) so that there may be some
protection from the threat of predators or whatever is
experienced as threatening by the infant.

What happens when the needed person never comes back?
Anxiety eventually ceases, and is replaced by pain, grief, and
mourning, and perhaps despair. We may never get over the pain

of the loss. Worse, sometimes a loss leads to an apparently lasting inability to make any new relationship in which another person could become an important attachment figure. Others do find themselves able to make such new relationships. This has led to the concept of 'successful', 'healthy' mourning, and Bowlby quotes with approval (and some adaptations) Anna Freud's (1960) definition that it is

> 'the successful effort of individuals to accept both that a change has occurred in their external world and that they are required to make corresponding changes in their internal world, and to reorganise and perhaps re-orient their attachment behaviour accordingly.'

> (III, 1)

In the course of this effort, there may be reactions which seem neurotic and which certainly would not lead to well-being if persisted in:

- persistent disbelief that the loss is permanent,
- a repeated urge to call for, search for, and recover the lost person,
- prolonged yearning for the lost person,
- a sense of reproach against the lost person, combined with unremitting self-reproach,
- compulsive caring for other people.

Any of these reactions may be conscious or unconscious. If unconscious, the consequent behaviour, feelings, and mood-swings may seem very puzzling both to the mourners and to their friends, thus adding to the pain. The irrationality of some reactions may be obvious, and yet the feelings are sincerely felt; for 'healthy mourning', they need to be expressed and recognized, understood and accepted by those around, as part of the process of accepting the loss. It is because of this that Bowlby and many others warn against the dangers of preventing people from expressing the anguish they feel. Particularly, in the present context, children should not be prevented from doing so: they should not be told that they should not cry, or need not cry, or are silly to cry, or that they will be 'given something to cry about if they don't stop', or that they should not cry in order to spare other people's feelings. Adults all too easily engage in these conspiracies of silence, the more so if they have been made to deny their own fears and griefs.

Denial and detachment are characteristics of a badly mourned loss. Bowlby likened these reactions to a scar-tissue which prevents and distorts the development of later healthy growth (III, 2). The detachment consequent upon badly mourned losses does seem very like what some autistic children do when they turn away from people. It is as though the autistic child is experiencing a loss – Tustin actually called it a hole – where it should (constitutionally) experience an attachment figure. The anxiety which Bowlby traced back to the unattached infant's fear of predators has real echoes in Tustin's descriptions of the skinless infant's fear of contact.

The unsuccessfully mourning person is left with a deep sense of helplessness and vulnerability. Small wonder. In most forms of depressive disorder, including that of chronic mourning, the main issue about which a person feels so terrible is the impossibility (as it seems) of ever again finding someone to love who will love them and make them feel safe, when the most important one has slipped from their grasp without their having been able to prevent it (III, 14).

· 7 ·

Holding on to safety
versus
steering clear of danger

John Bowlby seems English to the core. By contrast, Balint, the author we next draw on, is, like Hayek and many others, indeed like Sigmund and Anna Freud, among the many immigrants who made important contributions to their adopted country. Balint was, like Bowlby, a psycho-analyst with wider concerns. He worked with doctors in general practice who wished to further their understanding of people (1957); he was a philosopher with a special interest in linguistics; and he seems also to have enjoyed life outside the study or the consulting room – in *Thrills and Regressions* (1959) the attractions of the fairground play an instructive role.

From this chapter onwards, we rely increasingly on ideas first evolved by psycho-analysts, and explore them further. Where do ideas come from? To a considerable extent they come from other ideas picked up during our learning years, from teachers and from books. They also come from our experience of life. In addition, writers on psycho-analytically based theories draw on their experiences with their patients. Typically they use a kind of backward reasoning which asks, 'If people can talk to me, a psychotherapist (or psycho-analyst), in this way, what does this tell us about their mental processes?' 'What kind of experiences of life must this person have had, particularly at the time when the personality was being formed, for him or her to be relating to

111

me in this way now?' They feel justified in this kind of theory-building because of particular assumptions:

1   That people relate to others on the basis both of their past experiences (Hayek's map) and of present perceptions of their situation (Hayek's working model);

2   That people at times experience the psychotherapist or psycho-analyst in terms of the past (map) more than in terms of the present (model). In psycho-analytic language, a *transference* can be observed;

3   That people can at times experience the therapist or analyst in terms of quite early maps. In psycho-analytic language, *regression* can be observed.

What happens in regression and transference provides the material from which theories of personality-development can be constructed.

Three psycho-analytic ways of experiencing self and others

Balint (1968) distinguished three levels of experience, each with its particular ways of relating, its own ways of thinking, and its own appropriate therapeutic procedures. They are easiest to understand if we back into them, starting at level 3.

Psycho-analysis began at level 3 – the level at which a person is capable of a three-sided experience – nearly a century ago, characteristically elucidating and interpreting triangular relationships, primarily the Oedipal problems between self, mother, and father. Classical psycho-analysis concerns itself with experiences which, though perhaps repressed, come from a time of life when words are already available, and when people are recognized as whole persons and are not just fragments of experience which come and go. The very complex processes of ambivalence belong to this period of life – quite a late and sophisticated stage of development, relative to the very early processes we have been considering.

The level Balint characterizes by the number 2 is the level at which a person is barely capable of experiencing self and other as differentiated. Balint saw this as the area of 'narcissistic' experiences. The other is not exactly a person at this stage, but more like an environment, a not-self. This level of experience is pre-verbal and patients can at first convey it to their therapist only by action, analogy, and implication; the phenomena belonging to this level have to be interpreted in the context of what the patient is actually doing in the relationship with the therapist – 'in the transference'.

The level characterized by the number 1, Balint called the 'area of creation', in which there are as yet no distinctions between self and other. Coming from a very different starting-point, some resemblances to Tustin and Bowlby are striking:

> 'According to my theory, the individual is born in a state of intense relatedness to his environment, both biologically and libidinally. Prior to birth, self and environment are har-moniously "mixed up", in fact they interpenetrate each other. In this world there are as yet no objects, only limitless sub-stances and expanses.'
>
> (1968: 67)

Here are no persons, no words, and no boundaries: to talk to a person in this state is to remove them from that state. If that is thought undesirable (and Balint has clear ideas about the value of regressing to this state of mind, to which I shall turn in my final chapter), the person must not be addressed until he or she is out of it and ready to talk. Being allowed to be in that regressed limitless state of mind is sometimes exactly what people need in order to get better. The important thing will have been that they got to feel like that and were allowed to be like that, not that it was discussed with the therapist and interpreted.

The infant's first experiences are at this deepest level, where what Balint calls Primary Love is to be found, a term he prefers on humane and theoretical grounds to the more generally used 'narcissism' – Primary Love, the first rudimentary experience of relationship with others (Balint 1952).

The harmonious interpenetrating mix-up

'The harmonious interpenetrating mix-up' is Balint's version of an idea we shall come across in various contexts, called by such terms as merging, symbiosis, primary narcissism, facilitating environment, self-object states, oceanic feelings, the pure sense of being, and so on. These words attempt to describe a state of mind in which self and other merge and drift apart like seaweeds in the sea, as it may be at the very start of the e-merging of self from (m)other. Balint considers how this might be experienced by the foetus in the womb. He thinks of it as an existence with hardly any structure, in particular with no sharp boundaries.

'Environment and individual penetrate into each other, they exist together in a "harmonious mix-up". An important example of this harmonious interpenetrating mix-up is the fish in the sea (one of the most archaic and most widely occurring symbols). It is an idle question to ask whether the water in the gills or in the mouth is part of the sea or of the fish. Exactly the same holds true of the foetus. Foetus, amniotic fluid, and placenta are such a complicated interpenetrating mix-up of foetus and environment-mother, that its histology and physiology are among the most dreaded questions in medical examinations. . . .

It is worth remembering that our relationship to the air surrounding us has exactly the same pattern. We use the air, in fact we cannot live without it. We inhale it in order to take parts out of it and we use them as we want. Then, after putting substances into it that we want to get rid of, we exhale it – without paying the slightest attention to it. In fact, the air must be there for us, and as long as it is there in sufficient supply and quality, we do not take any notice of it. This kind of environment must simply be there, and as long as it is there – we take its existence for granted, we do not consider it as an object, that is, separate from us; we just use it.'

(1968: 66–7)

Balint goes on to say that the situation changes abruptly if the environment is altered – if the supply of air is interfered with for instance; then the apparently negligible environment assumes immense importance.

All this is relevant to our interest in the question: Where is the boundary between self and other? How does the infant come to experience some things as 'me' and others as 'not me'?

Subjects, objects, and obstacles

Balint comes at these questions armed with linguistics, in a brilliant chapter called 'Object and Subject' in *Thrills and Regressions* (1959). He notes first that 'object' has two different meanings, more or less according to whether the word is being used as noun or verb. It can mean 'objective' as in 'target' (and the Hungarian Balint notes that the Hungarian word for object is *targy*). This is the meaning which Freud had in mind when he chose the word for his instinct-based theory, where the object is the body-area to which the instinctive drive is directed. The other meaning has to do with 'objecting to' something, experiencing something as having to be pushed away.

> 'The other meaning of "object" seems to be "obstacle in the way of action", in fact a resistant obstacle that has to be negotiated ... our very first perceptions about objects may be those of resistance, ie something firm against which we may pitch our strength. ... This conception is certainly in harmony, with the cluster of associations surrounding the word "object".'
>
> (1959: 60)

Balint then refers to the world of objects which scientific thought had created for our imagination during the nineteenth century. 'For quite a time, nature – or life – was conceived as a collection of solid, separate, clearly defined and sharply contoured entities called "objects".'

> 'Parts of the external world which are felt to be firm, resistant, and sharply contoured are called by a special somewhat aggressive name – "*object*" – which suggests both resistance against our wishes and aim or target for our strivings. Other parts of the same world, which are not solid, do not resist much, and have no real contours, are called by non-aggressive names, such as substance, substrate, both showing similarity to "subject", denoting ourselves. A third very generally used word – *matter* – describing these not so sharply contoured, less resistant parts of the world, derives from a root denoting mother. The inescapable inference is that at one time there must have been a harmonious mix-up in our minds between

ourselves and the world around us, and that our "mother"
was involved in it. Though this mix-up strikes us as childish
and primitive, we must admit that it preceded our "modern",
"adult" or "scientific" picture of the world which, so to
speak, grew out of it.'

(1959: 62)

Balint is here touching on the possibility that we may experience
some stimuli as intrusive and lumpy – impinging, as Winnicott
would say. He has surely in mind something very like the
frightened reaction of some children to lumps in their food – it
may be remembered that Tustin thought that autistic children
might be experiencing these as scary not-self intrusions into the
smooth evenness of life which they wanted so much.

'In psycho-analytic theory we are wont to classify mother's
milk among the earliest objects, but it is arguable whether
milk, a liquid, is ever considered to be an object by an
unprejudiced common-sense man. One cannot reject out of
hand the suspicion that the idea of milk as an object emerged
in the mind of sophisticated analysts and not necessarily in the
minds of infants. If I am right, milk would be another instance
of the friendly expanses with no objects in it, a matter, a
substance. If we accept this then the widespread inexplicable
fads in many people about the skin in milk might be understood. The skin is a hazardous object appearing in the substance "milk", painfully disturbing the primitive harmony.'

(1959: 67)

Homebodies and spacebats: ocnophils and philobats

For Balint, the experience of the harmonious interpenetrating
mix-up was 'a paradise in the womb'. This paradise is destroyed
by the discovery that firm independent objects exist. 'From then
on, the existence of objects with their resistant, aggressive and
ambivalent qualities must be accepted' (1959: 68). The moment
of this discovery does not coincide with the birth of the body:
it marks a rather later moment: the beginning of the individual
personality, of the self (which Balint because of his theoretical
orientation called the ego). The encounter with something so
definitely other that it cannot be controlled is, in Balint's view,

what starts the individual on the process of individuation.

Two reactions may come from this discovery. Unfortunately Balint chose to call them ocnophilic and philobatic. I shall call them home-loving (homebodies) and space-loving (spacebats), which keeps much of the meaning and also most of the letters from the words Balint used, so as to minimize confusion.

A homebody's reaction to the discovery of the 'other' is to create a world based on the phantasy that other people and things are useful, reliable, and kind; that they will always be there when needed; and that they will never mind being used as needed. By contrast, a spacebat reaction is to create a phantasy world which goes back to the time when there were no others, no obstacles/things/people, only limitless power.

A spacebat lives as far as possible in a phantasy of a still existing 'unity and harmony of limitless contourless expanses'. When other people or things cannot be ignored, they are experienced either as dangerous unpredictable obstacles and hazards (of which the autistic child's reaction is an extreme example) or as emotionally uninteresting equipment to be used as convenient. On the other hand, homebodies' reaction to the discovery that there are others, people and things, which resist them and which they cannot control, is to turn strongly to these others, to whom they then attribute the power to look after them in this dangerous world. This development leads them to the cultivation of strong relationships with others and to mistrust of their own independent individual endeavours. In these relationships

'the object is felt as a vitally important support. Any threat of being separated from it creates intense anxiety, and the most frequently used defence against this is clinging. On the other hand, the object . . . becomes so important that no concern or consideration can be given to it. It must have no separate interests from the individual's, it must simply be there and, in fact, it is taken for granted. The consequences of this type of relationship are (a) an over-valuation of the object and (b) a comparative inhibition against developing personal skills which might make the individual independent from his objects.'

(1969: 69—70)

A homebody's world consists of people and things 'separated by horrid empty spaces'. Homebodies live from person to person, cutting short their time in the empty spaces as far as possible. They are frightened when separated from their attachment figures; their fear is allayed when they rejoin them. Homebodies hold on to people (parents, friends, anyone) or things (toys, clothes, rooms, home-towns) or ideas (in art, philosophy, science, or politics). In the world of ideas they need certainty. Uncertainty and ambiguity are experienced as uncomfortable and somehow wrong. They imagine that as long as they are in touch with a safe attachment-figure they themselves are safe.

Spacebats, on the other hand, have the illusion that all they need is the proper equipment. They do not need people, certainly not one particular person. In fact, people are avoided as principal sources of danger. 'Provided the elements are not too inclement, the pilot is safe in the skies, the sailor on the high seas, the skier on the slopes, the driver on the open road, the parachutist in the air.' The spacebat fears danger only from other things and people, which have to be 'negotiated': the pilot has to land, the skier has to skim round trees and rocks, a boss has to be impressed, a lover pleased. The spacebat's world is one of friendly expanses dotted with dangerous and unpredictable things and people.

Spacebats cultivate their skills and ego-functions so that they can look after themselves. Thereafter they can put their trust in the assurance that they can cope, keeping also always a fascination for (but wary mistrust of) the environment (including the people) they were not able to control until they had cultivated the skills to do so. These skills they will continue to test and confirm throughout life, often through deeds of risk and derring-do. Such people's world is coloured by an unjustified optimism, which actually has its roots in the earlier world of Primary Love when all was well – this memory enables them to hold on to the belief that their skills and equipment will be sufficient to cope with anything as long as they can avoid the hazardous obstacles.

Fairground pleasures differ accordingly. The homebodies go for the simple human aggression of the rifle range or the greedy indulgence of hamburgers and candyfloss. Spacebats go for the non-attached thrills of the Big Wheel, the roundabouts, and the dodgems, which over and over assure them of their ability to survive. They look for danger which can be overcome with skill. For them, thrill goes with skill. It struck Balint that these thrills are to do with leaving a safe place for somewhere where there is nothing to hold on to, with perhaps the danger of collision, and then a safe return home. His hypothesis was that this is where the fear of separateness (the loss of an attachment figure) could be mastered in play. It is a regression – to the moment when the infant experienced itself as on its own, unattached and unsupported.

The very language of caring and relating is permeated by these two contrasting stances: 'we are contrasting the world of skin-contact with the world of the more distal sense of vision'. Home-loving relationships are more *tactile*: homebodies use *tact*, they like to be *in touch*, ideas are *grasped* and *comprehended*, stories *grip* them. Spacebat relationships are *eye-to-eye*, spacebats *look after* people and things, they have *regard* for them, *consideration*, *concern*.

> 'The three synonymous words "concern", "consideration" and "regard" came from Norman French into English ... in their original meaning they all describe a state of intense looking at an object from a distance.'
>
> (1959: 36)

To sum up:

Homebodies	*Spacebats*
need to feel in tune with their chosen person (attachment figure),	need to feel in tune with the whole world,
presume that they can win the favour of their chosen person,	presume that they can conquer the world without relying on anyone's favour,
need to be in contact (close, attached); they keep in touch with people.	need to be on the watch (distant, eyes and ears alert); they relate to people by making them safe through the use of interpersonal skills.

In the course of his discussion Balint makes some interesting observations. He notes that even the most intrepid spacebats hold on to something: skiers to sticks, tightrope-walkers to poles, lion-tamers to whips, and all have to be taught not to tense and 'hold on' with their muscles in the supreme moment of tension (1959: Chapter 2). I think this must be the same process as that which Tustin had in mind when she noticed how autistic children hold on to what she called an auto-sensuous object; she thought it likely that by holding hard on to this, the defenceless and frightened child gave itself a sense that the whole body had something hard to protect it.

There is a similar paradox about homebodies.

> 'By clinging one gets farther and farther away from the satisfaction of the original need, which was *to be held* safely. The profoundly tragic situation is that the more efficiently one clings, the less one is held by the object. (This ever-repeated experience during analytic treatment had a large share in building up our theories of ambivalence and frustration).'
>
> (1959: 86)

Both home-loving and space-loving are reactions to the e-mergence of self from (m)other. Both reactions involve the disappearance of something from which separation had been inconceivable. The home-loving reaction would be to cling so closely to the attachment figure that vision, which normally gives a sense of distance, is blurred and obscured and the gap between self and other acutely. The space-loving reaction makes the other dwindle out of sight so that one ceases to be reminded of the separation.

Both reactions provide a ready foundation for ambivalence. The home-loving side, so dependent for well-being on the closeness of the other, may make us suspicious, mistrustful, disappointed in the failings of the people we cling to; the space-loving side may make us feel superior and condescending to the very people we need to cooperate with.

> 'Both of them are in constant danger of marring or even destroying their relationships to their love-objects by exactly the same methods by which they gained their favour: the ocnophil by too much clinging, the philobat by the use of too

much superior skill. From this angle it would be equally correct to describe these two attitudes by words denoting hatred.'

(1959: 88)

Less frantically and more constructively, our home-loving side may enable us to cultivate a talent for psychological closeness and intimacy and tolerance, while the space-loving side may go exploring the great featureless expanses – a happy preparation for a safe return home.

PART · 3 ·

THE RELATION OF SELF TO OTHERS

THE BASIC UNITS OF EXPERIENCE

THE EMERGING OF PAINFUL RELATIONSHIPS

THE LANGUAGE OF SPLITTING

To sum up so far, especially for readers who like the landscape metaphor: there is a pool where we begin to live, a harmonious interpenetrating mix-up, a womb, an ocean. There is a deluge, an unorganized sensory flow which can be terrifying and chaotic, or smoothly flowing. Then new features begin to appear: volcanoes and lava flows of anger, pits of despair, rocks of detachment. The oceans are bounded and contained by shores. If the shores are calm and sweet we find ourselves as homebodies. If the shores have breakers and rocks, we turn away oceanwards and become spacebats. Near the shores may be breakers and rollers – but also harbours, reefs and tiny islands, and sandbanks.

In the next chapter we consider how land is made. Islands form in the limitless expanses of the sea, and in the lee of the shore. The islands will form clusters of islands, and eventually landmasses. Each island starts as a cluster of tinier islands. Each landmass starts as a collection of clusters.

From all this, something like a personality emerges, and we can begin to consider its structure.

· 8 ·
The basic units
of experience

Some technical terms

Kernberg is the first, of the authors to be met in this book, who writes purely from the point of view of a psycho-analyst addressing other psycho-analysts. He makes no concessions to the lay person, who therefore has to bear up under some pretty difficult language. For instance, like most psycho-analysts, he avoids the term 'learning' when considering the way in which people are shaped by their experiences. Just as Hebb wrote of sensory input organized into cell-assemblies and phase-sequences and phase-cycles in the association cortex, and Hayek wrote of stimuli which set off impulses which get organized into connections, maps, and models, so Kernberg writes of internalization, introjection, and memory-traces. It is difficult to match each of these words from one language to a precise equivalent in another, but we don't need to do this. (Schafer in a number of publications presents valuable discussions on this.)

Like most of his profession, Kernberg uses 'internalization' for processes I would call learning, and I reluctantly follow him in this chapter to avoid too much confusion. For Kernberg, internalization brings about 'psychic precipitates or structures'. Introjections are the simplest of these, and they leave 'memory-traces' (1976: 25ff). In his discussion of all this, he clearly has in mind the kind of classifying conceptualizing processes discussed in our first chapters.

Memory-traces, introjections, and internalizations are *processes* which happen as a result of external stimuli, and they are *also structures*, that is to say they endure after the stimuli have ceased. An introjection is '*both a process* of the psychic apparatus, *and*, as a result of that process, a *structure*' (1976: 25).

This way of thinking is very much in line with the structure-building connection-strengthening ideas advocated in the present book. There are no static structures, only dynamic processes moving at different speeds so that they seem relatively enduring or relatively fleeting. It is a way of thinking which allows us to regard all experiences as processes which in turn start off other processes which make it possible to retain memories of what is happening now so that these experiences can be recalled or built on at a late date. It allows also for the possibility that the memories of our experiences are not static and unalterable but continually subject to further changes with further experiences. Thus we can think of early introjections as contributing to the first outlines of a 'map' in Hayek's sense, and of internalization in general as contributing to map and working model in the continuous monitoring self-steering way which Hayek postulates.

The unitary nature of experience

One of Kernberg's most useful contributions to developmental theory is his acceptance of the unitary nature of experience. Almost without exception, Western psychological theories have tended to cut experience into different and separate and often contrasting basics: thinking *or* feeling *or* acting; conation *or* cognition *or* affect; will *or* emotion *or* thought *or* perception. Since Old Testament times, since Plato and Aristotle, we have tended to believe that thought somehow happens in one part of a person, feeling in another, will and action in another. For Kernberg, experience comes in wholes: any encounter provides an experience which has unity and leaves an integrated memory behind, though of course some parts of the experience may remain unconscious or preconscious or get repressed or remain unnoticed because the culture does not provide a word – a concept-label – for it.

Although experience comes in wholes, an observer, or a very self-aware person, might abstract from the experience afterwards. 'Abstract' would be precisely the right word for that, for it would be like considering the colour of a flower abstracted from its other qualities, such as shape or scent, each of which could also be abstracted. What is so interesting about Kernberg is that, while granting that the mature person can split experience in these abstract ways, he maintains that the newly born infant cannot, and will not do so for a while. The fact that we adults can do it, can analyse and abstract and split our experiences, makes it difficult for some of us to imagine a kind 'basic unit of experience' (Kernberg's term) in which this split does not exist. In trying to imagine what it might be like to be a baby having 'basic units of experience', we are handicapped additionally by the fact that the baby has not yet clearly differentiated 'self' from what is 'not self' so that we cannot use the word 'I' to describe the experience. We are of course also handicapped by the fact that we have to use words to describe the experience while the baby has no language as yet and is not having an experience with words in it! However, the idea of a basic unit of experience is so essential to what we are trying to think about in this book, that it is worth trying for an imaginative reconstruction even though it is bound to fail.

Imagine a tiny baby being lifted up:

There is a great whoosh which is frightening or thrilling or both.

There is a sense of very powerful things going on.

There is either a sense of sharing in that power (being it) or a sense of being at the mercy of it.

That experience, just described, has made a difference to that baby, in that there are now memory-traces. There is not yet an 'I' with a memory of that experience, but the memory-trace is there and will affect the next experience because there is now already something established with which the next experience will be met, and which forms part of its context. And the *whoosh* is there for ever, still going on now, in the reverberating memory-traces. And meaning depends on context. So these memory-traces — primitive introjections in Kernberg's language — can function as an organizing principle for what happens next: the next experience, which is affected by what has gone before, assimilated into it, and so confirmed.

Taking our imaginative reconstruction a bit further, suppose that the baby's feeling is of fright and not of thrill (and perhaps anger and distress at the nasty sensation), and that the next thing to happen is a bowel movement. Something unaccountable is felt to be happening and is felt to be part of the general discomfort of things. If nothing happens to allay this feeling, then the original feeling of fright, and perhaps distress and anger, is likely to be confirmed by the bowel movement.

In contrast, suppose that the feeling is of thrill and not of fright; then there is now, not a feeling of powerlessness, but rather a sense of glory. And suppose that there is a bowel movement next, then this might be experienced as part of a general splendidness, thrill, powerfulness.

If the baby could speak, it might say:

Either   'Oh! that was nasty, I didn't like that and now some-
         thing else I don't like is happening to me.'
Or   'Oh! I like that, it's thrilling, I feel grand and do
         wonderful things.'

Something like this is what I take Kernberg to mean when he writes that 'introjection is the earliest, most primitive and basic level in the organization processes. It is the reproduction and fixation of an interaction with the environment by means of an organized cluster of memory-traces' (1976: 29).

We do not start life as individuals

Another important and, in my view, useful way in which Kernberg differs from many other writers on the infant's early experiences is that he does not postulate an original ego, psyche, self, core, or anything of that sort at all. Kernberg, from his experience of how this happens with regressed patients, aims to give an imaginative insight into how the sense of self, of being a person, of identity, comes about. A person, in his view, is not born with these. I propose to follow Kernberg in this, rather than Freud (Sigmund or Anna), Klein (Melanie), Fairbairn, Winnicott, or Guntrip. Here again, Kernberg's approach is consonant with that in our previous chapters: there is a gradual emergence of a sense of self out of a set of experiences. *This set of experiences does not spring from an individual core-self but involves other people from the start.* Kernberg is entirely against the assumption that a person starts as a solitary individual who learns to relate to others for reasons of individual survival. On the contrary, the potential person-in-relationship-with-others is there from the start.

Kernberg starts with an experience of an event, typically an encounter with someone or something, often called an 'object'. Part of Kernberg's importance comes from the seriousness with which he takes this 'basic unit of experience' which he calls an 'internalized object-relation'. 'Internalized' reminds us that it is learnt and also that it is all happening inside the head of one person: the experience is not what an observer might see while watching a man talking to his dog, for instance, but what it is for the man.

The simplest internalized object-relation consists of

1 Some memory-traces which will eventually become organized into structures (processes) which will contribute mainly to a sense of *self*;

2 Some memory-traces getting organized into what will eventually contribute mainly to structures (processes) which build up our images and representations of 'objects' (that is of *other* people and things);

3 Some memory-traces of the feelings or relationships or transactions implicit in the experience – these can be said to *connect with both* the above.

This sense that experience comes in what Balint would call a harmonious interpenetrating mix-up of self and other is not easily arrived at by introspection. In our culture, just as we abstract from our experiences in terms of feelings *versus* thoughts, so we also abstract in terms of self *versus* others. Culture goes deep, which is what makes it hard for us to accept that our way of thinking about our experiences is not the only way, not necessarily even a good way.

The emergence of 'self' and 'other': the unintegrated or pre-integrated personality

Kernberg postulates that for a while after birth, the infant has experiences and memory-traces of experiences, but that these are isolated and not connected with each other. The infant's mind is then like the first map of an unexplored country, mostly blank spaces. Or, since that is too static a picture, the infant's mind is like the ships of a fleet afloat on the five oceans, before wireless communication. Each ship floats about full of life, but without contact with other centres of life.

So Kernberg's picture of the infant mind would have a number of what he calls units of experience floating around in it, more or less connected with each other but as yet in no ordered or meaningful fashion. Slowly they become organized in gradually more enduring ways. As experiences continue to happen, and repeatedly have common elements, connections begin to be made. (Actually, Kernberg does not use the term connection with the same enthusiasm as some of our other authors. Each author has his preferred metaphor. Hebb makes one think of threads – nerve fibres; Hayek makes one think of the straight lines of logical implication. In either case the word connection is appropriate. Kernberg makes one think of blobs of experience which merge. The processes referred to are similar but the pictures are different because the authors' imaginations are different.)

As further experiences become introjected, units of experience can begin to merge, to integrate. This integration is a complex business. There is both fusion and fission, both merging and separation as things begin to sort themselves out. Some units of experience will merge with others into more general organizations, but others will separate out (or more accurately will have 'followings' in Hayek's sense) before merging elsewhere. How this will happen will depend on what 'followings' the experiences have in common (see pp. 35–6 and 50–2).

Experiences, at this very early stage in life, integrate and develop toward conceptual status, but we can safely say that these experiences are very different from their adult equivalent. Infants cannot organize their world in adult fashion because not enough has happened yet to get more than some very blurry-edged units of experience, each rather separate from the others in some ways, and each incorporating what the observer might call inappropriate (that is misclassified) components.

We may think of a sea with floating bits of seaweed, shipwreck wood, fishes, and birds. Slowly, under the impact of further experiences, the flotsam and jetsam of events begin to fit together and to merge into more complex islands, floating in the sea. This merging is accompanied by all kinds of differentiation: all fishes are organized under the heading 'fish', all seaweed – wherever it is and of whatever kind – with seaweed, all gulls with gulls and separate from albatross, and so on.

In at least one way, the metaphor of 'islands' is a dangerous one, for the early clusters of memory-traces do not disappear upon reorganization, the way islands would disappear if they were magically shunted elsewhere to join up with others. We should rather say that, as Hayek would put it, new followings are created so that the original shape of the experience is embedded in new connections. The new followings both give new significance to the experience and also submerge it in the new contexts, just as a figure may be harder to find once it has been put into a new context, as in *Figure 28*. Meanings depend on context. But the original meanings are not destroyed in the process of further organization – in regression something like the original experiences can be re-experienced.

To return from these imaginative flights back to more sedate metaphors: from the beginning of life, experiences leave their mark. That is from the beginning of life, an experience becomes an internalized object-relation with potentially three elements: a sense of self, a sense of other people and things, and a sense of what goes on between these two. And almost from the beginning, some aspects of some experiences have something in common with what has already been experienced. The common factor may lie mainly in the regions of self-imagery, or in the regions representing other people and things, or in the regions registering relating and feeling, or in all of them, of course. Because of this, our experiences of ourselves are affected by the structures we already have, although of course the later experience may modify them. Similarly our experiences of other people and things are affected by already established structures reflecting our sense of other people and things, although these are, in turn, modified.

From the earliest days on, then, differentiating and integrating processes are expanding, solidifying, attenuating, structuring, organizing. The boundaries between self and other (Kernberg calls them 'ego-boundaries') become ever more clearly delin-

LITTLE RED RIDING HOOD IS ON HER WAY TO VISIT HER
GRANDMOTHER. HIDDEN IN THE PICTURE ARE HER
FATHER, HER GRANDMOTHER, AND THE WOLF.
CAN YOU FIND THEM?

Figure 28

eated, and what Kernberg usually calls the ego (and I usually call
the self) exerts increasingly more central control over perception
and action.

Integrating, metabolizing, and splitting

As life unfolds, experiences are integrated into more and more
complex structures. More object-relations are continually
acquired, internalized, differentiated, integrated, made part of
the person. This complex reorganizing and integrating does not
proceed evenly: there will be some highly organized structures,
and others less highly organized: some experiences will be more
tightly integrated (that is with many connections to other
structures) and some will be connected very loosely indeed.

The more easily new experiences are absorbed into structures which already exist (that is the more easily they are connected with them, and organized and integrated with them), the less we notice them. What the triangles in *Figure 29* have to tell us is

Figure 29

hardly ever seen for what it is at first glance – our existing structures are so tightly organized that we do not allow the actual information to reach us consciously (from Abercrombie 1960).

The images of Red Riding Hood's grandmother and father in *Figure 28* are strongly connected with other structures and therefore difficult to abstract out again. Red Riding Hood's shoes, and her face, are more tightly organized as structured patterns (that is they are less integrated with the surrounding structures and less embedded in them), and so they are more easily noticed.

Of course, readers who have made a hobby of these kinds of puzzles and deceptions will already have strongly established structures with programmes to look for the catch, and they will see exactly what is in the picture and in the triangles – but that is just the point I am making. Stronger and more tightly organized structures will act as context for new experiences, giving meanings which depend on the established context. A slap in the face can be experienced:

- purely as pain (non-integrated),
- or as mother attacking me,
- or as mother angry because I spilled honey all over the tablecloth,
- or as mother inadvertently hitting me as she whirled round while playing rounders with us.

The 'slap' can be integrated in different ways. In the final example the 'slap' may not have 'hurt' at all.

Meaning depends more on context in more integrated structures. It will become important later (see pp. 372–78, 410ff.) that we can use consciousness, words, and language to reassess the context and hence the meaning of an experience. By these means we can abstract even well-absorbed experiences from the context in which they have become embedded.

Kernberg calls the process by which an experience is integrated into an existing psychic structure 'metabolizing'. By this he means the transformation of an experience so that it becomes part of a person, in the same way that we metabolize a biscuit by eating it and it becomes part of our bodies. I used to amuse a small nephew by saying that my cat was someone who turned fish into puss. This metaphor of 'metabolizing' is useful, providing that we do not lose sight of the fact that the process may also be described by other metaphors, such as 'organizing' and 'integrating'.

Kernberg believes that 'pockets' of unmetabolized early object-relations may persist in a person's psychic system while, all around, other object-relations merge and are being integrated. Some early experiences are not integrated: they have no 'followings': they remain 'split off'.

Pleasure and pain as organizing principles

For Kernberg as for Freud, there are two basic feelings, pleasure and pain, attached to two basic drives: libidinal/pleasure-seeking and aggressive/destructive/pain-associated respectively. According to this view, all pleasurable experiences are associated with libidinal drives, all painful experiences with aggressive/destructive drives. Kernberg assumes that the emergence of self and other out of the earliest units of experience is attributable to these two drives and their associated feelings.

Like many others, Kernberg considers that the painful experiences which the infant encounters are the first to be organized, and that they are experienced as somehow inflicted on the infant by an 'other'. This primitive organization of experience constitutes the first differentiation of self from other. It is as though the baby knew that the self is good and the other bad. According to this theory, organization starts when something is experienced as bad — it does not start from an experience of well-being. The sense of 'other' is thought to come from times of distress which the infant experiences in terms of 'this is terrible but it is not me'. This is in contrast to what is thought to happen at times of well-being. These are so pleasant that it is thought to be of no advantage to the infant to organize the experience into 'this is very nice but it is not me'. On the contrary. This is how the sense of omnipotent well-being develops which Freud (1915) calls the 'purified pleasure-ego': 'all that is good is me and all that is me is good'.

The purified pleasure-ego and the pleasant experiences which lead to its construction are, in Kernberg's view, the core or germ of the self. In some graphic metaphors, he writes of the pleasant parts of the basic units of experience as 'precipitants' round which parts of the self 'consolidate'. They consolidate by virtue of the common element of pleasure in a number of experiences. 'What is important is the intense, overwhelming nature of early feeling and its irradiating effect on all other perceptual elements of the introjection'.

In this view, not only does distress not get organized at this stage with what will become part of the self, but also distressing experiences are not recognized as having a common factor — they are not given meaning except as 'other'. Unpleasant experiences are kept apart from each other, and from the sense of well-being — defensively.

From this viewpoint, pleasure and pain are the organizing principles for all experiences, taking precedence over any other means of conceptualizing experience. It is not difficult to imagine circumstances in which this could be so, for instance when the infant is so frequently uncomfortable that this makes an overwhelming impact on its development: distress and the absence of distress could come to matter more than anything else. And we may imagine how this can happen if we picture a system in which those neural pathways come to be the most dominant, down which pleasure-messages and pain-messages flow; this would be a system in which those pathways have more enduring and more extensive reverberations. We could also account for the relatively later conceptualization of distressing experiences, by imagining that, in early states of development, distress somehow disrupts normal message-sending. This disruptive process would be the same as that referred to when it is said of a human baby that 'the ego is overwhelmed by anxiety, and disintegrates'. In the adult, we call it panic. When distress disrupts the immature organism's organization, this prevents it doing anything other than calling for help from more mature animals. There may be survival-value in this. If the young organism is too immature to react to danger with fight or flight in a successful way, it is perhaps safest that it should be unable to try, and be reduced to only crying for help. Bowlby might support this line of thought.

However that may be, Kernberg, in a very classical tradition, attributes the differentiation of self from other to a defensive manoeuvre: the beginnings of ego-functioning are thought to be defensive in this tradition, the purpose being to maintain a sense of well-being and to ward off the infant's discovery that the distress is also its own. Kernberg writes as though this is the general case, as Freud did, and many others.

I do not think it so likely that the sense of well-being and the sense of distress can be the original organizing principles of self and other *in every case*, though perhaps it was the general case among those who sought psychotherapeutic help at a particular time during this century. To my mind, people need to be fairly well and integrated, before they are able to organize their experiences of the world in terms of 'I like' versus 'I don't like', 'libidinally' versus 'aggressively'. I think it is at least as possible for people's minds to be organized according to what happened in their early relations with others, *whether pleasurable or painful*. Greenberg and Mitchell (1983) write with great clarity about the logical puzzles created by various compromises between libido-based theories and relationship-based theories.

My own views are best understood as based on the early chapters of the present book, where sensations and emotions are thought of as organized into the landscape of what occurs as experience follows experience. I hold to the view suggested by Hebb and Hayek, among others, that psychic structures form because repeated experiences create them from the most commonly experienced connections, which after a certain point gain some independence from the structures in which they were originally embedded.

To my mind, the neurophysiological/classificatory/concept-attaining/structure-building approach favoured by Hebb and Hayek, and elaborated by them and others, provides the basic ideas in terms of which we should understand the emergence of self and other from the original state which William James (1890) called a 'big buzzing blooming confusion', and Balint a 'harmonious interpenetrating mix-up'. Pleasure and pain may profoundly affect this differentiation, but they are not solely responsible. The processes I have called concept-formation start off the differentiation of self from other, as they start every other differentiation and integration.

Abstracting, generalizing, and differentiating

Returning for a moment to the metaphor of 'islands', it has to be acknowledged that the islands undergo some weird developments in the course of time. As the infant encounters further experiences, we may think of the islands both as disintegrating and as merging in new ways. However, as this happens not on a geographical but on a multidimensional scale, it is not easily visualized on a flat map. It is as though all the trees on all the islands merged to contribute to a more general concept of 'tree', while each still remained also on its island of origin. It is as though all the green on all the islands (green of leaves, of sea, of stones) merged to contribute to the more abstract concept of 'green' without, however, bleaching the green objects on the islands. It is as though the flying of the birds and of the leaves in the wind were integrated to make the concept of flying. In short, each experience remains itself although generalized abstracted aspects may grow in relative importance as further experiences contribute to them. Differentiating, generalizing, and abstracting go together.

Abstraction, differentiation, and generalization are names for different aspects of the same process which was described in Chapter 3 in connection with learning to recognize triangles, oranges, and musical notation: the formation of concepts. The concepts now under consideration are at a higher level, that is all. In order to conceptualize the colour puce, I have to perceive and recognize as puce a particular shade in a variety of contexts – generalizing. I have to disentangle it from other features of the situation in which it is embedded – abstracting. And I have to distinguish it from other shades which are not puce – differentiating.

The three main sets of abstractions, generalizations, and differentiations with which we are concerned just now are to do with the achievement of some sense of self, some sense of other people and things, and, thirdly, some ways in which self is experienced as related to other people and things. These will be considered one by one.

However, perhaps yet another caution is needed before we do so. It is only for the sake of clarity we look at these three sets one by one and 'abstract' them. Except in very rare circumstances, my experience of myself is not of me in some pure abstract sense. I am aware at this moment, not of 'me', but of me-getting-an-idea-across-to-you-the-reader   and   of   you-the-reader-under-standing-me, you-liking-this-point, you-put-off-by-my-style. In short, and to say it yet again, our experiences come in units of relationship.

Identity: the sense of self

Gradually, if all goes well, a self, and a sense of self, is established, made up from all the bits of experience in which the person has been involved. The memory-traces of all these bits remain, but the structures which they form are profoundly affected by the context which the evolving structures provide for each new experience as it happened. Some experiences will have integrated with much that has gone before; some will have been left more or less isolated (1976: 33). 'Under the influence of a well integrated ego-identity', more central controls gain increasingly more dominance over new information coming in, and the map is no longer so easily modified by further ex-perience. New information, although registered, then has relatively little effect on behaviour or indeed on consciousness. Kernberg is here also referring to the process of selective perception, by which certain meanings come to predominate over others.

Through these processes the sense of self differentiates from not self. Strong psychological structures are created in which the self is involved – self-structures. Self-structures are often strong enough to be functioning as 'maps' to the working model of what is going on in and around the organism at a particular time. When this is so, they are strong enough to steer behaviour in a particular direction. When this has happened, we recognize a stable identity.

The 'other' and the 'depersonalizing' of feelings

As experience piles up, self-structures gradually establish themselves and, in doing so, separate out more and more from other structures which have less to do with one's identity. In the course of this process, as the self becomes more distinct, other people and things also gain coherence and individuality. There is a growing sense of 'Ah yes, this is me, and that is that, and you are you, and this is what goes on between us'.

Gradually, with further experiences, if all goes well, the personality develops a relatively stable sense of itself in its environment and a stable sense of what is not self but other people and things. Our life-experiences are increasingly re-organized and integrated, with more linkages to the more central regions of the self, and/or with more clearly delineated object-imagery. Our experiences can become more closely connected with (or, on the other hand, more distant from) the feelings or excitements which originally accompanied the experiences. This is a process through which our experiences can also become relatively less integrated with the person with whom we first experienced them, and relatively less integrated with the feelings or excitements with which we first experienced them. Thus feelings and excitements can be isolated from the structures in terms of which they were first experienced, isolated from structures of self and/or isolated from object-imagery.

To give an imaginary illustration of a very complicated process, the experience may be of a child being hugged by the mother and enjoying it. In words:

'I like being hugged by mother'

This may be broken up into such substructures as 'hugging is lovely' (whoever hugs whom: the 'depersonalized' relationship), as well as 'I like being hugged', 'I love mother', 'I like hugging', 'mother loves me', 'mother loves hugging me', 'mother likes hugging', and so on.

This example is also useful in letting us realize just how many structures can emerge out of one experience; it is a mistake to think of an experience being broken up into one self-concept, one object-concept, one relationship, one emotion.

Kernberg uses the word 'depersonalizing' for this process, acknowledging his debt to Jacobson (1953) who coined the term. In later chapters, where depersonalizing becomes a useful way of coping with distressing feelings, I shall often call it 'distancing' or 'disowning'.

In depersonalizing, emotions and objects differentiate. My first experience of a dog may have been frightening, but 'frightening' and 'dog' will eventually probably differentiate from each other, so that in due course I can distinguish between the dog which scared me, and dogs in general which have no personal significance for me either frightening or lovable, and so on. At that level of abstraction, dogs remain dogs, whatever my experiences of them: object-constancy has been achieved – see Natasha's struggle with object-constancy on p. 142.

In depersonalizing, emotions and self differentiate. 'I' and 'frightened' differentiate. More generally, I learn that I am not wholly (always) good or wholly (always) bad, or wholly (always) happy or wholly (always) unhappy. Later I have to discover that my feeling that someone or something is good or bad does not mean that it is so. And I have to discover that my feeling that someone or something is good or bad does not mean that other people think so. Subjectivity is thus turned into objectivity.

This process of depersonalizing may be patchy or superficial. Underneath what we have learned about dogs which helps us say we know that not all dogs are frightening although we once knew a frightening puppy, there may be unconscious connections very tightly integrated with a feeling of good or bad about dogs. Part of psychotherapy is to bring these unconscious connections into consciousness.

When thinking about feelings, it is useful sometimes not to think in a 'distancing' or depersonalized way of 'love', or 'distress', or 'fear'. It can be instructive to think for a while in terms of 'love-of', and 'distress-from', and 'fear-of', and 'hate-of', and 'greed-for', and 'bliss-with'. We risk being cut from our roots if we think of feelings apart from who-feels-what-towards-whom. Kernberg (from a rather different theoretical starting-point) insisted that feelings are experienced as relational – once stated, it seems obvious, at least for a healthily functioning organism. Feelings are relational from the start except when something has gone wrong with our biochemistry. When feelings are detached from the experiences in which they were aroused, that is normally due to a later and defensive manoeuvre.

This third component in the object-relation does not therefore separate out in an organized way, as self-structures or object-imagery do in the healthy infant. On the contrary, it looks as though health may consist in keeping feelings attached to the experiences with which they are bound up. Healthy people may have a clear sense of self and of the people and things around them, but they are not much visited by isolated waves of 'fear-of' or 'bliss-with'. Such feelings would normally be anchored in an experience.

Depersonalized feelings are very weird. One of the many contributions made by Melanie Klein and her associates comes from their intuitive understanding that 'I am angry (with a person or thing)' is very close to 'Someone or something is very angry with me'. The feeling 'angry-with' may be depersonalized, detached from particular experiences, and associated at random with self or with other. Similarly 'I feel torn apart (by something in the course of hunger)' may become 'I have torn apart (the breast associated with hunger)'.

For some people there is no differentiation between self-and-feeling; for others there is none between others-and-feeling. It seems that people vary in this respect. The former are likely to experience 'I am fine, sad, content, frightened, furious', etc. The latter are likely to experience 'He is nice, she is frightening, that is nasty, this is sweet, the other wicked'. Only people who are very out of touch would be assailed by feelings of fear or well-being or anger or love without any clear connections with anything. Illustrating the extreme, a person mainly organized in terms of self-structures, and distant from the world of people and things, might say,

'I was so worried when I did not hear. . . . I wondered what I had done wrong. I felt so guilty and worried, and then I remembered that I am always forgetting people's birthdays. Aren't I awful.'

Another kind of person, mainly organized in terms of other people and things, and distant from his or her own feelings, might say,

'They sent this letter which said they were closing down. With a cheque. The cheque was an insult. They have no right to send a notice like that through the post. I went to the Citizens' Advice Bureau round the corner from where I used to live – not last year but the year before. Almost everyone there was new, much younger and two were Asian.'

Yet another kind of person hardly experiences either self or other people, but picks up feelings without firmly attaching them to anyone:

'It was really eerie, a dangerous atmosphere. There were a lot of booming noises and a lot of talk which I don't remember. It felt very heavy and threatening. It didn't matter, though.'

People differ in how they are aware, more in some ways, less in others. One wonders at which point these types begin to become fixed. It is an interesting area to speculate in. Whole cultures or subcultures may be found which prefer one or other type, so that polite conventional speech requires more awareness of one aspect than another. Thus in some circles it is discourteous to talk about oneself, and in others it is bad manners to talk about others, and in yet other circles one should not talk about impersonal matters.

Natasha's struggle with object-constancy

'*Thursday 20 May, 1976*

Dinner.

Pussycat jumps on the table and sniffs at the cheese.
Daddy: Pussycat!
Mummy: Yes pussycat! Take him off. He may have something.
Natasha: What?

Mummy: Some germs that are bad for us.
Natasha: You've just made me unhungry.
Daddy: How?
Natasha: The soup's changed its taste.
Daddy: The soup's the same though it tastes different to you.
Natasha: No it isn't, the soup's changed.
Daddy: Mummy's soup hasn't changed.
Natasha: Yes it has.
Daddy: Mine's the same.
Natasha: Well mine's different. I don't want it now.
Daddy: The soup's the same. Mummy's remark about the cat made a difference to you but not to the soup.
Natasha: Well how does that make the soup taste different?'

(Laing 1978)

Introjections, identifications, and ego-identity hierarchically organized

At the very beginning of experience, the infant can take in (internalize, learn) only the simplest things and in the simplest way. As the person develops, more and more complex experiences can be taken in, recognized, given meaning, and acted upon. These more complex experiences are, it will be clear, composed of simpler ones, modified by them and modifying them in turn.

Kernberg marks out three levels of complexity in organization, three milestones in the development of the organized personality. The simplest of these – *introjection* – has now been sufficiently discussed. The next level is that of *identifications, or role-relationships.* If the differentiations and integrations of introjected experiences proceed well and normally, Kernberg holds that the growing infant will be able to register certain regularities in the relationships in which it is engaged, and these regularities can be called 'roles'. A conscious sense of role-relationships develops out of the unconscious primitive sense of object-relationships (on which, of course, role-relationships are built). There is then a time

'when the cognitive and perceptive abilities of the child have increased to the point that it can recognise the role-aspects of interpersonal interaction. Role implies a socially recognised function that is being carried out by the self, the other, or both. For example, when the mother does something with the child (such as helping it to get dressed), she is not only interacting with the child, but also actualising in a certain way the socially accepted role of mother (giving clothes, protecting, teaching).

(1976: 30–1)

At the same time, the child is learning what it is to be a good child and what it is to be a good mother. Here is an important channel through which the general culture enters the child.

Kernberg uses the concept of 'role' to build bridges from individual psychology to social psychology and eventually to anthropology and other social sciences. What a good child is, what a good mother does, differs from place to place. How a good mother does it, differs. Different cultures may differ in, for instance, the extent to which they allow mothers to comfort their children when distressed. And cultures which encourage mothers to comfort their children may still differ in the kind of comforting (oral, tactile, verbal) they favour. Here it is not basic object-relations which are being learnt, but complex role-relations.

In marking this milestone as one of *identifications*, Kernberg brings into focus the extent to which the child at this stage develops by grasping what is the right behaviour for it *in the role relationship* it is learning to understand. There is at this stage a much more developed clarity as to what is self and what is other; and what connects these more sophisticated concepts of self and of other is also much more elaborate; it is the sense of appropriate role-behaviour, and of the appropriate feelings which go with it. Because of this development, it is obviously also easier for feelings to be under better control.

Kernberg sums up the processes at this level in the following way: The cluster of memory-traces implicit in identification comprises:

1   an image of an object adopting a role in an interaction with the self,

2   an image of the self more clearly differentiated from the

object than in the case of introjection (and possibly playing a complementary role), and

3   an affective colouring of the interaction, of a more different-iated, less intense quality than in the case of introjection (1976: 31).

At the highest level, the *level of 'ego-identity'*, the personality is organized by 'an overall organization of introjections and identifications under the guiding principle of the systematic function of the ego'. Here we have Kernberg's idea of how people direct and control their actions. We first met it in Chapter 4. What he calls the ego is a controlling and evaluating system of the kind Bowlby had in mind — it will be remembered that he quoted Bowlby with approval (p. 61). This controlling and evaluating system is integrated with other psychic structures to a greater or a lesser extent. It is by this that people steer themselves; it constitutes their sense of themselves in relation to the world of other people and things as they have learnt to experience them (1976: 32).

In developing his views on 'ego-identity', Kernberg acknow-ledges his indebtedness to Erikson (1959), both in recognizing the importance of cultural influences on personality develop-ment, and in recognizing that the formation of an ego-identity is a lifelong process. He also takes seriously Erikson's (1950) sequence of eight developmental tasks faced by all human beings. In these respects he is less biologically deterministic than many other psycho-analytic writers, and leaves more room for culturally determined variations in human behaviour.

The argument in this book has now been brought to a point where something like a self or a personality can be imagined, in a continuous development which began with clusters and net-works of neural connections. We have also been able still to hold on to our landscape metaphor. Islands begin to cohere . . . from smaller clusters . . . integrating and differentiating into larger landmasses . . . developing specific flora and fauna. . . .

Now that we can think, however tentatively, about the self and its structure, we can begin, equally cautiously, to consider the effect which other people may have on these structures.

·9·

The emerging of painful relationships

W. R. D. Fairbairn, the main stimulus to the thoughts in this chapter, published just one book, a collection of articles and papers written in the twenty-five years between 1927 and 1952. It has, however, two titles, one in Britain and another in the United States. The page-references I use come from the British edition.

Fairbairn is only now beginning to be given the respect to which in my view he is entitled, having long been a prophet without much honour in his own country. Ernest Jones's preface to the book gives a flavour of this, of the man, of his colleagues, and of his times:

'Dr Fairbairn's position in the field of psycho-analysis is a special one and one of great interest. Living hundreds of miles from his nearest colleagues [i.e. in Edinburgh], whom he seldom meets, has great advantages and also some disadvantages. The main advantage is that, being subject to no distraction or interference, he has been able to concentrate entirely on his own ideas as they develop from his daily working experience. This is a situation that conduces to originality, and Dr Fairbairn's originality is indisputable. On the other hand, it requires very special powers of self-criticism to dispense with the value of discussion with co-workers, who in the nature of things must be able to point out considerations

146

overlooked by a lonely worker or to modify the risk of any one-sided train of thought.'

Dr Jones omitted to mention the risk of the deadening effect of group-pressure on thinkers of deviant thoughts!

'If it were possible to condense Dr Fairbairn's new ideas into one sentence, it might run somewhat as follows. Instead of starting, as Freud did, from stimulation of the nervous system proceeding from excitation of various erotogenous zones and internal tension arising from gonadic activity, Dr Fairbairn starts at the centre of the personality, the ego, and depicts its strivings and difficulties in its endeavours to reach an object where it may find support.'

Fairbairn and Kernberg have a great deal in common. Both are interested in the very very early stages of self-development and in the emergence of differentiation between the self and what is not self. Both also keep the reader constantly aware that there are three foci for the theorist to concentrate on: self, other, and the relationship between.

Kernberg was writing thirty important years after Fairbairn, and the intellectual climate had changed very considerably in that time. Fairbairn, for instance, like almost all his contemporaries wrote of the 'ego' when more writers now (though not, as it happens, Kernberg) would write of the 'self'. In the current chapter I write of 'ego' when I must, and of 'self' when I can do so without confusion.

Unlike Kernberg, Fairbairn does not look into the origins of the self. Like many in his time and since, he took for granted that people were born with one. The climate of his time was still subtly influenced by religious concepts. It was easy to think in terms of each person born already endowed with a soul which was highly individual from the start. Wordsworth's *Ode on Intimations of Immortality* expresses this belief in an unforgettable way.

'Our birth is but a sleep and a forgetting:
The Soul that rises with us, our life's Star,
    Hath had elsewhere its setting,
        And cometh from afar:
    Not in entire forgetfulness,

And not in utter nakedness;
But trailing clouds of glory do we come
    From God, who is our home:'

We do not have to be committed to Wordsworth's theology to recognize the feelings he is describing here, if we have been fortunate in our early years. Views not dissimilar to these are still maintained by many, an extreme example being the anti-abortion lobby who endow the earliest foetus with the soul it is to have ever after. Such an assumption has implications for psychodynamic theory, since it is difficult to think of a person both as having an individual soul well before birth, and yet as not having an individual self until well after birth.

I should perhaps add that I do not think I am here putting forward a general anti-religious or anti-soul argument. There is nothing in most theologies (including Christian ones) which forbids theories about the gradual evolution of a soul; indeed there is quite a bit about soul-making in some of them. Just as at one time, in Western cultures, the world was thought to have been created within a week, an idea which was later abandoned by many, so a soul may be thought of as coming about more slowly than has sometimes been assumed.

Fairbairn and those who read him were (to some extent still are) concerned with the matching of his ideas to the classical views of Freud, and it may be of interest to refer to some points of difference.

Like Kernberg, Fairbairn felt committed to a theory in which the focus was on people in their relationships with each other, rather than on the impulses of isolated individuals.

'How an individual is going to dispose of impulse-tension is clearly a problem of object-relationships, but equally a problem of the personality, since an object-relation necessarily involves a subject [i.e. a self] as well as an object. The theory of object-relationships thus inevitably leads us to the position that if impulses cannot be considered apart from objects, it is equally impossible to consider them apart from ego-structures. Indeed, it is even more impossible to consider impulses apart from ego-structures, since it is only ego-structures that can seek relationships with objects.'

(p. 88)

In the context of his time, Fairbairn's innovations are: his understanding that the infant is born into a relationship and develops in the context of that relationship, so that its developmental problems have to do with the differentiation of itself from others and with the relationship of self to others; his understanding that impulses are normally not isolated processes to which a person is somehow subject, but an expression of one's personality; his understanding of *dynamic structures*, which are best thought of as structures of experiences like Kernberg's 'identity-systems': organizations of the memory-traces of the experiences in which a person has been involved: physiological, neurological, and psychological actions and reactions and sensations and feelings, maps and models and TOTEs and all.

Fairbairn himself summarized the central points of his differences with Freud as twofold:

> '1   Although Freud's whole system of thought was concerned with object-relationships, he adhered theoretically to the principle that libido is primarily concerned with pleasure-seeking, i.e. with the relief of its own tension. This means that for him libido is theoretically directionless, although some of his statements undoubtedly imply the contrary. By contrast, I adhere to the principle that libido is primarily object-seeking, and that the tension which demands relief is the tension of object-seeking tendencies. This means that for me libido has direction.
>
> 2   Freud approached psychological problems from the *a priori* standpoint that psychical energy is essentially distinct from psychical structure. On the other hand, I have come to adopt the principle of dynamic structure, in terms of which both structure divorced from energy and energy divorced from structure are meaningless concepts.
>
> Of those two central points of difference, the latter is the more fundamental, since the former would appear to depend on the latter. Thus Freud's view that libido is primarily pleasure-seeking follows directly from his divorce of energy from structure; for, once energy is divorced from structure, the only psychical change which can be regarded as other than disturbing is one which makes for the establishment of an equilibrium of forces, i.e. a directionless change. If,

however, we conceive energy as inseparable from structure the only changes which are intelligible are changes in structural relationships and in relationships between structures; and such changes are inherently directional.'

(pp. 149–150)

The concept of dynamic structures

The concept of dynamic structures frees the theory of object-relations from having to depend on explanations in terms of impulse-frustration and impulse-gratification. It makes it possible to think in terms of psychological structures which can develop through processes other than instinctual drives.

The concept of dynamic structures was one of Fairbairn's major innovations, the starting-point of other original ideas. But it is interesting to notice, and difficult for the contemporary reader, that the climate of the times was so pervasive that he continued to write in inconvenient terms he could easily have discarded. Thus he continued to use the notion of 'libido' (at that time considered a form of general and/or sexual psychic energy which activates people) although libido is not directly observable and is a concept we can do without if we use the concept of dynamic structures. However, Fairbairn continued to use it, as for instance in the splendid statement that 'libido is not pleasure-seeking but object-seeking'. Fairbairn also continued, it seems to me in spite of himself, to think in terms of two different streams of psychic energy – libidinal and aggressive; again, we could do without these if we use the concept of dynamic structures.

Put in simple terms, Freud maintained that people were motivated by their (libidinal) drives to seek gratification, and that this gratification was pleasurable. Fairbairn, on the contrary, maintained that 'pleasure is the signpost to the *object*': people seek *people* and take pleasure in *them*: Fairbairn believed that only those people whose capacity to relate has somehow been impaired, have to make do with impulse-satisfaction as a second best. 'The strength of a child's physical needs for the parents' genitals varies in inverse proportion to the satisfaction of its emotional needs' (p. 122) – the happier the child is in its relationships with other people, the less it is likely to be physically attracted or driven to part-objects like genitals. Kohut was to say much the same thing a quarter of a century later.

Fairbairn was among the first to say it and, to my mind, we should accept his point. But we should use it to add to our general understanding of people rather than to make a controversy. Surely the classical theorists were right: there are many people who live for the satisfaction of their drives; even when analysed in depth that is how they function. We should understand Fairbairn to be saying that there are also people whose main concern is with others – even when analysed in depth they seek others. And naturally, there are people who in some circumstances show more of one kind of interest, and in other circumstances show more of the other. Fairbairn, like most of us, could not refrain from showing which kind of people he found more attractive and more likely to be happy in a way he favours – he preferred those who need to relate to others. (Balint, making a somewhat similar differentiation, tried more earnestly to be fair to both types.)

Fairbairn was aware (as Balint was) that his views carried important implications for the behaviour of a psycho-analyst or therapist:

'It is an accepted article of the psycho-analytical technique that the analyst should be unusually self-effacing. There are very good reasons for the adoption of such an attitude; but it inevitably has the effect of rendering the relationship between patient and analyst somewhat one-sided from the patient's point of view and thus contributing to the resistance.

When the self-effacing attitude of the analyst is combined with a mode of interpretation based upon a psychology of impulse, a considerable strain is imposed upon the patient's capacity for establishing satisfactory relationships – a capacity which must be regarded as already compromised by virtue of the fact that the patient is a patient at all.'

(p. 87)

Fairbairn went on to say that you do not help people by enabling them to identify and name the impulses to which they are subject. They must be helped to reorganize the personality-structures into which such impulses are integrated.

'*Impulses are but the dynamic aspects of psychic structures* and cannot be said to exist in the absence of such structures, however immature these may turn out to be.'

(p. 88, my italics)

Digression: speaking of people as 'objects'

Fairbairn had so many humane things to say that it must strike the non-specialist reader as odd that he continued to use the term 'object' when he meant people. In his defence I have to say that at least since the Judges in Old Testament days, when Jephthah used the word *shibboleth* to distinguish enemies from allies, it has been typical for in-groups to develop in-language, which facilitates recognition among people of like mind. However, 'objects' just does not seem a humane word to use for 'people', and I shall avoid it where I can.

'Objects', in psycho-analysis, is an umbrella-word for experiences which refer not to the self, but to someone or something that has significance for the self. Generally I have usually substituted 'other people and things' where it would be customary to write 'objects'. Wherever possible I have used more definite words like 'mother', 'cat', 'chair', and so on.

In the terms in which I am building up my main argument, objects are structures of memory-traces: images, concepts, whatever. What word is best to use? If I write consistently of 'structures' I may be more consistent, but I am also more boring and more distant from the experiences I want to describe, for which we already have acceptable words in common speech. If, on the other hand, I use words like 'concept' or 'image' where they feel appropriate and where they help us draw on our already existing understanding of life, I run the risk of misleading the more precise-minded reader: 'concept' gives a more cerebral and less motivational impression than I intend; 'image' gives a more visual and less motivational impression than I intend; and 'object' antagonizes less psycho-analytically minded people because it sounds so impersonal. I wish each of these words could have some flavour of all the others. They all refer to dynamic structures: by 'concepts' I mean structures of ideas which also involve feelings and action, by 'imagery' I mean structures which are also conceptual and involve action, and so on. In this book, unless otherwise stated, objects mean concepts which mean images which mean representations which mean dynamic structures, and so on. Often, too, I shall write of 'phantasies' in the tradition followed by Melanie Klein. 'Phantasy' seems to highlight the hopeful or fearful aspects of some concepts, the expectations that are hidden in them.

Clearly we are here considering objects which are not people or things, but which are a person's experiences of people or things. This focus can be strengthened by writing of 'inner objects', and some writers are always careful to do this.

'Splitting an object' refers to what happens when a person experiences more than one object where other people may be sure that there is only one. For instance, I might have split my experiences in such a way that I sometimes relate to a perfectly good mother, and sometimes to a perfectly bad one, when we all know that each person has only one mother, who is probably sometimes good and sometimes bad.

Where the point of a sentence is that a person's experience of something or someone is not being shared by other people, I have written of 'phantasy objects' or 'inner objects'. I have also referred to them as ideas, concepts, partial maps, dynamic structures, and so on. 'Phantasy', in psychodynamics, emphasizes that aspect of something which Hebb and his kind would call an 'expectancy'. We may think of the infant as passively undergoing experiences over which it has little control. But from the experience of some regularly recurring routines, it will come to expect that the first stages of such a routine lead to the rest of a sequence. This is one way in which an organization of memory-traces becomes a dynamic structure. The experience of many infants is that the emergence of a need – say, hunger – will lead to an expectation or an imaginative anticipation or a phantasy of something or someone coming to gratify that need: a complex concept of a gratifying person or a gratifying thing. This phantasy, once it is constructed, remains. Kernberg would say that the memory-traces persist. Even when the satisfaction does not come, the concept – the phantasy – is not wiped out. So one can keep thinking about it, making up stories about it, and so on. This does not depend directly on how often the good thing actually happens. If it does not happen so very regularly, the infant can build up two phantasies of the mother – of one who is good and satisfying, and of one who is uncontrollable and is sometimes satisfying and sometimes not. The fact that the latter is sometimes satisfying, helps to maintain the phantasy of a satisfying 'good object', and the fact that the object sometimes does not bring satisfaction helps to maintain the phantasy of a 'bad object'. It, too, persists. Once a nasty or frightening concept has been established, it can keep alive and dynamic, independent of whatever good experiences may also be taking place.

Objects are bad by virtue of having been experienced as painful, or as not-there when they should have been there, or as there when they were not wanted, or generally causing too much tension. Fairbairn, like Melanie Klein and Kernberg and many others, believed that bad objects were conceptualized much earlier than good objects. They thought that if the infant was not frustrated, it would not register what was going on. If the transition from feeling a need to having it met was smooth and without pain, they thought the baby would not register it, at least in the very early stages of psychic development. (See, for instance, his footnote on p. 93.)

Looking at infants I have met, it seems clear to me that they do register pleasant sequences of excitement and gratification as well as unpleasant ones of excitement and frustration. I believe these pleasant sequences to be important in the development of a strong, realistically trusting and optimistic personality. However, for Fairbairn and many others, bad objects are the first to be internalized.

Some inner objects − or concepts or images or representations or phantasies or structures − start to develop very early. Those which have to do with the mother are likely to be very early indeed, and Fairbairn and some of his contemporaries formed hypotheses about this development. In my view it is a fair criticism of most of these theories, that they are too focused on the *mother* and how *she* is experienced by the child. Tustin (who of course was working much later) provides a useful counterbalance, reminding us that before person-experiences there are tactile, auditory, and visual sensations which may or may not be organized into person-experiences. For all children there are, from the start, stimuli which have nothing to do with the mother; these may become organized as part of 'mother', but it will not do to insist that it must be so. It is not valid to assume, as is often done, that all early object-experiences are 'mother'-experiences or that all early object-imagery is 'mother'-imagery.

Freud is not one of those who fall into this error. This is partly because even a hundred years ago enough was known about the neurology and physiology of perception and learning to recognize this as an error, and we know from his *Projekt* (1895) that he knew enough. But it is also partly because Freud's interest was not in objects of this kind, inner or outer; the theories of perception and thinking which were current in his time had no connection with theories of motivation. Images were not thought of in ways which gave them dynamic power. It was to instincts that motivating power was attributed − instincts had built-in drives toward objectives; these objectives (also often translated as objects) were not thought of by him as persons, but as the natural target of instinctive drives − a drive towards food, or somebody's genitals, the attainment of which is accompanied by pleasure. It is to this idea that Fairbairn (and others) opposed the later idea of dynamic structures in which people were necessarily involved.

However, one inner object was of interest to Freud. For him, the super-ego was a parental image created by a mixture of the child's experience of its own anxieties and its experience of its parents' prohibitions and threats. Freud saw the super-ego as having motivating power in so far as the child took over the parental threats and prohibitions as part of its imagery ('internalization'). This made the super-ego an inner object with motivating force because the child's instinctual drive was thought to be directed to what the parent had; the energy of this drive, should it not reach its target, was thought somehow to be diverted and deflected back to the child. Thereafter the energy was available to the child and reinforced the child's acceptance of parental prohibitions and threats. Freud called the super-ego the 'limbo of abandoned object-cathexes', that is a collection of instinctive energies which had not been expended in gratification, because they had not reached the object(ive) to which they had been directed.

Melanie Klein − who was contributing very new and challenging ideas in the 1930s when Fairbairn was formulating his ideas − thought in terms of a much greater number of inner objects.

When she started to publish, she wrote of objects as the objectives of instinctive drives. She was then mainly interested, as Freud was, in what could be said about the development of the instincts. However, in time the focus of her thoughts extended over the 'objects' themselves, as they appeared in the phantasies of the children she was analysing. These phantasied 'objects' became more and more a part of an inner world stocked with such images as 'breasts', 'nipples', 'penises', and 'insides' – part-objects (Segal 1964).

The term 'part-object' is used when a person relates to just one aspect of what would normally be experienced as a whole object. Melanie Klein's part-objects are unintegrated bits of experience to which we perforce have to give names (verbal labels), if we are to talk about them. It is important not to take the labels too literally, however, as the experiences belong to a pre-verbal and highly unintegrated level of being. This level may be so primitive that there may not yet have been much differentiation, either of self from other, or between various other things. So Melanie Klein is writing of an infant's pre-verbal experiences of the breast, the nipple, digestive processes, and so on, without any accompanying sense that the breast is not its own but its mother's, or that the digestive processes are its own insides and not the mother's. The unintegrated bits are not yet organized with a unifying sense of itself or of the world of other people and things.

When some integration and differentiation has taken place, the phantasied inner world, as Melanie Klein conceived it, has various images of the self. These are in relationships with other objects in the inner world – relationships of terror such as are implied in the phrase 'persecutory anxiety', or greed or envy or hate, and later of guilt and concern for others. 'Object-relations' were for Melanie Klein, and later for Kernberg and others, the drives and accompanying feelings which linked the self to the object. Because of their belief that unsatisfying objects are the first to be differentiated from the original general confusion, these early feelings all seem pretty horrifying, and the objects are 'bad objects'.

Melanie Klein's inner objects, being very early structures, were very partial maps of reality indeed. Fairbairn's inner object-relations sound as though he was thinking of a slightly later stage of development, say, the toddler's, and so the events he described rely on rather realistic maps. This discrepancy may be because it is difficult to get one's language and one's concepts to reach imaginatively into these earlier more primitive regions, though we shall see in due course that Guntrip, Fairbairn's disciple and analysand, did this very convincingly.

Were objects whole to start with?

Melanie Klein was the first to base therapy on the idea that a person's inner world was stocked with part-objects. She, and many inspired by her, seem often to assume that there was originally a whole object which was later split into separately experienced part-objects. Fairbairn certainly writes of the splitting of the object as though the object had once been whole and was then split into parts; I am not clear whether he actually thought this or not – Guntrip, his great exponent, certainly did, and Fairbairn, who took it for granted that the infant is born with a self from which bits split off later, wrote of an internalized mother from which bits are later split off (1952: 134). I think it must be clear that I do not think this a correct description of what happens. The infant does not begin with a single image of 'mother'. The infant has a lot of experiences with mother, and these are gradually differentiated into 'my experiences with mother who soothes me', 'my experiences with mother who hurts me', and so on. Different experiences of the object remain as separate structures – 'islands' – unless and until they become connected through experience. Even then, how strongly connected they are will depend on the stage of development reached before the connection was made – that is how mature the personality was when object-constancy was achieved. It follows, incidentally, that while a person's conscious experience may be whole-object experience, a split may be maintained at less conscious and more primitive levels.

All this is easier to think about if we think in terms of images, which are more easily thought of as separate and as merging, as they do in the process of focusing for instance, stereoscopically. If we think too concretely in terms of objects, as the theorists in the mid-twentieth century have done in my view, we may find ourselves confused by our own metaphors.

Were selves whole to start with?

It must be clear by now that I believe that there is a gradual differentiating out from a general confusion in which the sense of self and the sense of other were originally submerged. And I believe that complete differentiation is difficult to achieve, so that there may be all sorts of ways in which an adult person's sense of self may still be confused (merged) with what is not self but other. Fairbairn realized this, but his understanding is not always firm. He wrote that the whole of development is from an infantile merging kind of dependence to a mature separated-out interdependence, but he could not always use this idea simply. However, once this idea has been grasped – and the whole of the present book is meant to strengthen this grasp – many difficulties disappear with which Fairbairn and his contemporaries struggled: they become difficulties which beset only particular kinds of people.

The concept of the psychological unity of mother and baby does not seem to have been easily available to Fairbairn and his contemporaries, partly, I guess, because of the general climate of the time, which too easily took it for granted that each person was distinctively individual and born with a self. And so, faced in the consulting-room by people who talked as though they confused their mothers with themselves (or as though they confused their therapists or others with themselves), psychotherapists at that time believed that their patients' *original individuality had been lost* through a process they called 'identification', a process which does indeed exist. What they did not allow for was the possibility that there were people whose *individuality and selfhood had never been established*.

Believing in the original individuality of the infant, Fairbairn and others necessarily confused those who had lost their sense of self with those whose identity had never really established itself. For much the same reason they also confused those who in phantasy were still at one with their mothers though their 'False Selves' presented an appearance of individuality, with those who had an individual self but on occasion regressed back to a state of mind in which they were still merged.

These writers saw all these types of relationships as the infant 'identifying' with the mother after an original state of separateness, and they saw identification mostly as swallowing. Fairbairn, for instance, wrote that 'infantile dependence is characterised not only by identification but also by an oral attitude of incorporation'. In that discussion he incidentally also demonstrated something further considered in Chapter 13: that the metaphors of 'inner' and 'outer' create at least as many problems as they appear to solve.

> 'In virtue of this fact, the object with which the individual is identified becomes equivalent to an incorporated object, or, to put the matter in a more arresting fashion, the object in which the individual is incorporated is incorporated in the individual. This strange psychological anomaly may well prove the key to many metaphysical puzzles.'
>
> (1952: 42–3)

I think it is a puzzle created purely by the metaphors which were popular at that time.

The 'oral attitude of incorporation' has been assumed to be typical of all infants by many writers from Abraham onwards. In fact, the earliest relationship of the infant was thought to be an oral – swallowing – one. It seems to me true that there are people who experience their closeness with others in terms of swallowing and being swallowed; some of these appear to me to be deeply disturbed, others not. (And some deeply disturbed people do not have swallowing phantasies, so this is not a well-understood dimension.)

For people for whom being at one with = identification = swallowing, being separate may be about spitting out and evacuating or being spat out and evacuated, with a good deal of smearing and soiling. To anyone who has had dealings with behaviour categorized as 'deteriorated schizophrenic', this description of how some people experience life is instantly convincing: the swallowing of unsuitable and repulsive things, the spitting out, the smearing on to others. There is evidence that such processes are part of the phantasy life of many of us – what is questionable is whether they typically represent the experiences of at-oneness, individuation, and differentiation for us all.

We are considering a stage in the life of the infant where

imagery is not so sophisticated that all aspects of an experience are easily or accurately registered as 'me' or 'mother' or 'other'. At this stage there will be many mistaken attributions so that aspects of the environment are organized with self-structures, and aspects of the infant's own visceral or other sensory responses are organized as 'not-me' objects. In short, there is a gradual process during which experiences (and hence imagery, phantasies, and other conceptual structures) are sorted into 'experiences of myself in the situation', 'experiences of others', 'experiences of relationships between myself and others in certain situations', and so on. Maybe this sorting process rarely goes as far as we like to think it does, and maybe we act on these more blurry concepts more frequently than we like to think we do. I certainly believe so.

The emergence of painful relationships: frustration and rejection

Freud really only had one 'inner object'; Melanie Klein had a multiplicity of them. Fairbairn concentrates on three: three primitive ways of encountering the environment, around which later experiences are organized: exciting (libidinal), anti-libidinal, and feelingless. The development of these three object-relations keeps pace with the development of three dynamic organizations of self-imagery, which Fairbairn sometimes calls ego-structures: the 'Libidinal Ego', the 'Anti-Libidinal Ego', and the 'Central Ego'. He seems mainly to have had patients to whom these three phantasies meant a lot – there is no guarantee that they are dominant in everyone's psychic life, but it is worth looking out for them.

Let us start by considering a simple sequence of arousal and satisfaction or frustration, a basic building-block in the construction of a theory of personality-structure: hunger is soothed by food, bowel-tension by evacuation, muscle-tension by rocking, soreness by cream and powder, and so on. Now the time has come for the baby to have one of its needs met. Secretions begin, muscular responses, and so on. Anticipatory phantasies arise. There is nothing painful or disturbing about these for a while. But hope deferred makes the heart weary and, if gratification is painfully delayed, the anticipation starts off a set of painful associations. We might say with Fairbairn (and others) that the infant feels excited by something and dissatisfied with it. An infant may be excited while a lovely experience comes to it – the 'good object' of happy experiences – or it may be excited by a phantasy of something *lovely but not there*. This latter experience is for Fairbairn an experience of the *Exciting Object*: it is a particular area on the map which charts imagery of the mother: the mother experienced in her frustrating aspect. The Exciting Object *excites but does not satisfy* – to remind us of this I shall write of it as the Frustrating Exciting Object.

While the infant is evolving the Frustrating Exciting Object, it is at the same time registering a dynamic structure or image of itself as excited and excitable. This experience of the self is the *Libidinal Ego*.

When Fairbairn writes of the 'Libidinal Ego' he is thinking of an 'ego-structure', a part of the self, a dynamic self-structure. Just as people in his time thought in terms of originally whole objects which subsequently split into parts, so Fairbairn thought of people as having an original wholeness which split into parts – this he called ego-splitting, a major innovation at the time, which has proved of use to many later theorists. However, the contemporary interest in the splitting of the self (the ego) put in the shade what seems to me an equally profound and, to begin with, more difficult notion, to which we now turn.

For Fairbairn, the Frustrating Exciting Object and the Libidinal Ego mutually define each other. They are two characteristics of a relationship, like two sides of the same coin – they must not be thought of as independent of one another: one cannot exist without the other. Between them they refer to one thing – a relationship – defined by Frustrating Exciting Object and Libidinal Ego, just as a coin is defined by heads and tails. For Fairbairn makes it clear, as in a different way Kernberg does, that our experiences are relational from the start. 'I have a wonderful mother who has wonderful things she sometimes gives me' emerges as an experience not after but at the same time as my experience of mother as 'mother with wonderful things' and of myself as 'me liking wonderful things'.

On parallel lines, Fairbairn identified a more punishing, vindictive, and rejecting relationship between a phantasy mother who was a *Rejecting Object*, experienced as not giving what the child is asking for, and a self experienced as an *Anti-Libidinal Ego* hating itself for having asked and/or needed something from the mother which she did not give. (Sometimes Fairbairn called this anti-libidinal attitude the Internal Saboteur: it is the bossy, harsh, sneering, belittling voice which some earlier writers called the sadistic super-ego.)

Just as Libidinal Ego and Frustrating Exciting Object are paired aspects of one experience, so Rejecting Object and Anti-Libidinal Ego are also paired. Libidinal excitement forms the link between the former; rage and hostility between the latter. An example would be

'It was idiotic of me (anti-libidinal experience) to expect that old wretch who does not like me (rejecting-object experience) to promote me (exciting-object experience) when I want it so much (libidinal-ego experience).'

If the various emotions running through this remark are clearly understood and kept separate by the reader, this is because I have taken trouble to lead up to that remark. The speaker of the sentence does not experience anything as tidy as that. The excitement, the frustration, the hostility, the lack of hope are there, so is the bad self-imagery and the bad object-imagery. The speaker may well feel self-reproach on one day, blame the world on another occasion, and just feel mopey or angry at yet another times. Many many people live a life in which self, other, and relationship have not been tidily separated. To distinguish between them is hard work. The reason is that originally the experiences came in *basic units*, as Kernberg would say, basic units in which self and other had not yet differentiated. We, the observers, see something of the excited child and the exciting but frustrating world around it, but the child's experience is (this theory assumes) one of alternating excitement and disappointment, in which there is as yet little or no consciousness, let alone self-consciousness and perception of the other person in a mutual relationship. We are not nearly as good at keeping self, other, and situation conceptually and verbally distinct as we like to think.

Before the end of this subsection, some footnotes:
• Fairbairn's descriptions of excitement and frustration some-

times have an air of being tremendously sexual or sexualized, especially when one comes to them after reading someone like Kernberg. This mother who rejects, who excites and does not come, who frustrates, what can she be refusing? This is a very Oedipal way of relating. Fairbairn is not focusing on Oedipal (triangular) experiences here, but pre-Oedipal theories were not yet part of the intellectual climate, so we get descriptions which are particularly accurate for people who have sexualized their experiences: either they have experienced life in a rather sexualized way from the start for some reason, or this was the only way they could be helped to verbalize their feelings at all, by psycho-analysts who were thinking in Oedipal terms because they had not yet formulated pre-Oedipal ones. Whichever, we must remember that the kind of 'sexual' here involved is not exactly what Freud had in mind – it is a more interpersonal sexuality even at this early stage.

• At a more primitive level, we may entertain the possibility that such frustrating, exciting relationships come about when separation-anxiety has gone past some critical point of tolerance ('Where *was* you, mummy?'), when the attachment figure was needed and not available. I think Fairbairn's theories encompass such experiences and apply to people hurt in this way, but these ideas did not come into general circulation until after Fairbairn had completed his thoughts, and so he does not refer to them. But we should, for they fit here. On the other hand, compared with the children who had autistic experiences, we are here considering a stage where quite a lot of structure of self and of other has already developed. The other *is* there (at least in phantasy) as exciting and potentially satisfying; we are not in the realm where the other is experienced as a black hole, an agonizing place where an attachment should have been.

• At a more primitive level still, we need to pay tribute to Fairbairn's clinical perspicacity in that, well before his contemporaries, he could guess at a state of mind in which the infant is making no distinction about where the distress is coming from. He is thinking of a state of mind which is not yet sufficiently structured to be capable of the question 'Is this me or is it another?' 'Am I wrong to expect help or is she wrong to withhold?' 'From whom does this excitement come, me or her?' The feeling is in the basic unit, in self and other and relationship.

That self and other should be so easily confused, and so hard to tell apart, may seem amazing at first glance. And yet it is an experience which almost all of us must have come across in close relationships, in making love, for instance, and in quarrels, where it is almost always hard to feel sure at first whether it is 'their' fault or 'mine'. 'Am I too intolerant or should I have protested long ago about this behaviour?' is a typical question people ask themselves when a relationship goes wrong, 'Am I imposing on them or are they imposing on me?' We do not always know which!

Reactions to distress: anger, unconsciousness, and phantasy

The child, dependent on the mother, may find itself at the disposal of an exciting but often frustrating or rejecting person. What are the consequences for a child locked into relationships with Frustrating Exciting or Rejecting Objects? The child feels that its mother does not care about it, not even about its love for her, and it has somehow to come to terms with this situation.

It may be angry. But how can a child dare to let its life depend on someone with whom it is angry, someone who appears to be already in a mood to be annoyed, frustrating and rejecting – someone who already sees the child as in the wrong and deserving of punishment? (Most parents feel like this toward their offspring at times, so there is likely to be some ground for the child's worries to grow in – enough for them to be maintained once they have sprung up.) The child who feels that its parents find its needs insufferable, will expect its anger to be even more intolerable to them. This will be a very worried and fearful child. The process is an escalating one, for when fear becomes associated with the steps that lead to anger, signal anxiety sets in. The child will now be worried and frightened when it wants what it knows it won't get, because this will make it feel disappointed and rejected, and that often makes it angry, and that will make the parents more rejecting.

Fairbairn is deeply concerned with the extent to which life can be frustrating, painful, and frightening for the infant personality. He was, after all, working at the same time as Melanie Klein, who first formulated and put into words the hell of terror and rage which can be the infant's daily experience. A world of frequent arousal and disappointment is a painful world to live in; painful too is the accompanying experience of the self. It is a devastating experience to be in a relationship where you are mostly expressing your feelings to someone who does not care what they are, or is angry about them. Fairbairn distinguishes gradations in this misery. For a start, there is the humiliation of having your feelings so depreciated. At a deeper level the shame, at having feelings which are not valued but rejected, can reduce a child to a constant sense of worthlessness and destitution. It feels wicked, inferior, inadequate, and altogether wrong to be expecting so unjustifiably much, to be so demanding a nuisance. It may come to regard its own loving feelings as somehow shameful and bad, and may keep them to itself so as not to lose altogether the sense of being loving (even if not lovable). At a deeper level still, writes Fairbairn, the child feels quite emptied – an experience of disintegration and imminent death (p. 113).

How can the child find some protection against such feelings? By various splits in the imagery of itself and others.

To disown your feelings is a kind of protection. An older child, with more firmly established self-structures, might perhaps be able to do this by distancing itself from the memory that it had been excited and frustrated. But in the very early stages of development, a worried infant may keep even the imagery of itself-capable-of-excitement split off and separate from other self-imagery – this knowledge of itself as excitable is never integrated; those partial maps are not available.

To protect itself a child may disown the knowledge of its own excitement, and of its own excitability, its own capacity to get excited and have hopes, needs, and wishes. The child may disown the memory of having ever wanted what it could not get. It may cease to acknowledge any image of itself as capable of wanting what it cannot get. That part of the map may be unavailable to the everyday world of the working models.

Or, having kept away from the imagery which goes with itself wanting nice things, the child may conclude that there is something wrong with what appears nice and satisfying. Either that he or she is wrong, or that everyone is wrong to want nice satisfying things. It may even conclude that satisfaction is bad.

The child may take another course to protect itself from the idea that its world is a bad place. It may disown not just aspects of its own feelings, but aspects of the world of other people and things. It may make splits in the world of others. Where frustrating, exciting, and rejecting relationships predominate, the child develops the idea that the way people relate to each other is arousing and exciting but not satisfying, or that people are at heart angry with themselves and each other, and that what happens to wishes and hopes is that they get disappointed and denied. These discoveries may be too painful to hold on to, and so the child may keep them apart from other aspects of its experience of the world. Also kept apart may be the information (potentially there, because it registered when it happened) that there are satisfying things and people; acknowledging this would bring with it the knowledge that good things are being withheld, that good people have gone away.

Anger augments these processes. For when a child experiences its grown-ups as unloving and rejecting, it may feel anger. This it will fear to express lest its anger make them more rejecting than ever and thus increase their 'badness' (by making them more real in the child's eyes as 'bad objects'). Or the child may fear that its anger will make them less loving and thus less capable of being 'good objects'. The child, perhaps already angry in its hurt frustration, may fear that its very recognition of its parents' lack of love and care is the hostile act which will destroy their goodness. (This incidentally provides a good example of the fear of anger acting as a signal anxiety, warning us to keep something out of mind which might pain us, or to avoid seeing something that is there in front of our eyes.) By controlling its imagery, the child tries to control its world.

Small wonder if such a child is tempted to transfer its lovingness to the world of 'inner objects'. This helps to preserve its sense of itself as a loving person. Having made the transfer, the child feels love, and phantasizes about it, and about the people it loves. Perhaps it even feels itself loved – or, rather, perhaps it maintains a phantasy of itself as loved by a phantasy mother. But none of this is given expression in a way another person can know about. There may be a vivid life of remembering, thinking, imagining, planning, even suffering – but in phantasy, not 'now', not 'here', involving only phantasy objects in a phantasy world. The child has withdrawn from the world which is mediated through the senses.

Both Fairbairn and Melanie Klein conceived of a state of mind in which life is so grim that the senses are dulled and messages from the world of other people and things do not penetrate: nothing sensory is processed into the state of organized clarity which lets the world of other people and things break through. Instead, the person experiences life in terms of a set of selectively organized phantasies: 'Exciting Objects', 'Rejecting Objects', 'Ideal Objects'.

One might suppose this phantasy world to be a haven of reciprocal love and care. To some extent this may be so, but when children or adults come to psychotherapy because of the straits in which they find themselves, it is usually discovered that this inner world is not a happy one. Phantasies are not necessarily agreeable. They can be very nasty and unsustaining. However, they have one use for the damaged child (in us all): they are familiar and they set us more manageable problems than we think real life will set us. Many of us have had experience of managing our phantasies, if we ever had a dream in which we went through some events, thought 'Oh I don't like that', and redreamt the events with differences which made the story more acceptable to us. For most of us, phantasy objects are probably more controllable than everyday people, and this feels good at times when we feel very powerless and vulnerable. Concepts and images are more amenable – or so it would seem from a disadvantaged position – than parents, teachers, bosses, spouses. The schizoid reaction is one in which the cowed personality withdraws as far as possible, from actual relationships with uncontrollable people and events to phantasied relationships with rather more abstract figures. 'The schizoid state', writes Guntrip (1969: 67) in discussing Fairbairn's ideas, 'is not an aspect of an inevitable developmental position, but a fear-dictated flight from object-relations.'

A person's inner world may be full of tension, dominated by daydreams about self-sacrifice, unrequited love, undeserved blame, and punishment. Small wonder, if these were the main relationships which the child could make: the child needs attachments, and will make painful relationships rather than none at all. Even when, later, a person learns that relationships can be happy, the art of making happier relationships has still to be achieved, the pain of having had bad relationships has still to be lived with: tolerated and integrated, not disowned or flinched from. And alas, happier experiences subsequent to the initial damage sometimes have relatively little effect on long-established structures – the very understanding of what they are, or should be, and of what relationships other people enjoy, can be highly distorted.

The phantasy world gives us an opportunity to disown to some extent both the world of other people and things, and our own unwelcome thoughts, memories, and feelings. Hence it is very hard to renounce phantasy-relationships with phantasy-objects, and to risk making relationships with real people again, who are unknown, who may be very rewarding but also may be very hurtful, whose possibilities have to be discovered, not invented.

The relationship between 'Central Ego' and 'Ideal Object'

In our phantasy world we are engaged with ideas which have the nature of dynamic structures, acting as 'authority figures', 'goodies' and 'baddies', 'persecutors', 'victims', 'rescuers', and so on. Fairbairn's great contribution – obvious when stated but easily ignored when using the metaphor of 'objects' – is that mostly we define these stagey figures in such a way that our way of dealing with them or relating with them is implied in the word itself. We love 'goodies' and we try to be like them and feel bad when we aren't. We hate 'baddies' and persecute or feel persecuted by them. We identify and sympathize with 'victims' (if we didn't, it would be because they're 'baddies' – *their* suffering serves them right!) and we welcome and cheer on the 'rescuers' (if we don't, it is because we see them as 'persecutors'). As Fairbairn formulates his theory, we have learnt to relate to the world in an excited but frustrated way, or in an angry need-rejecting way, or, thirdly, in a spuriously calm matter-of-fact way.

What is left after the libidinal and the anti-libidinal organizations of the self have been disowned? There remains a self shorn of both enjoyable and painful components, but still capable of engaging in the survival functions, mainly perceiving, remembering, comparing, planning, and so on – the ego-functions. Fairbairn calls this left-over bit the Central Ego; it is almost entirely a monitor of events. It is an organized region of the self which registers that there has been arousal of need, and gratification or frustration of needs, wishes, impulses to approach or retreat, but it does not register the accompanying feelings. Though of necessity in touch, however, minimally, with whatever dynamic structures enable the organism to survive, there is not much contact with the arousing, gratifying, or frustrating sensations themselves (which have formed 'libidinal' and 'anti-libidinal' organizations).

The Central Ego relates to what Fairbairn calls the Ideal Object. The phantasy is that if a child does not 'make a nuisance of itself', is not unjustifiably demanding, and avoids whatever makes its grown-ups reject it, *if* it does all this and maybe more ... *then* the child will be behaving in an ideal way and the grown-ups, who of course are ideal, will be able to respond in an ideal way. Fairbairn calls this the Moral Defence (against the intolerable anxiety of living in a hostile world). Alas that it should sound so plausible a term.

The world 'central' might suggest that the Central Ego is somehow at the core of a person, but this is not what Fairbairn meant. The Central Ego is the monitor at the boundary between the self and other people and things. In this it closely resembles what Freud meant by 'ego' – he also did not mean the self but only that monitoring process. It is also like Winnicott's False Self, the Caretaker Self which protects more vulnerable feelings which are conceived of as deeper, further away, or further back. In Chapter 17 I call it the Coping Self.

There are therefore circumstances when the Central Ego is divorced from much that is part of a person; there is only the sort of consciousness which is expressed in 'I must get along somehow', not feeling much or needing much or dreading much, since all that is almost entirely split off. Being out of touch with most of the springs of action, the mode of speech is passive. This is how a withdrawn person does feel. The more personal pronouns are also removed: 'That's life', 'That's how the cookie crumbles', 'No use complaining'. The Central Ego holds summarized abstracts of the environment: concepts not percepts.

In these circumstances, the environment, too, is shorn of anything that might make for strong feeling. An Ideal Object, it is stripped of its exciting or rejecting aspects, bland. Sometimes Fairbairn calls it the Accepted Object, since everything is experienced as acceptable: 'My family is just ordinary', 'We get on well', 'We don't have problems'. Harold Pinter excels in conveying the flavour. 'What's anything to do with anything?' asks a character in *The Dumb Waiter*.

A person who represents the extreme condition described by Fairbairn, or, more likely, a person in this mood, might say 'I have no wishes; I do not care about anything or anyone'. Such people have a simple system of guidance – pleasure-seeking/pain-avoiding, or survival, or a cause, or a set of values – by the light of which they manage their lives, rather as managers of industrial organizations may impersonally manage the organization on lines laid down by others. They manage; they do not enjoy. They may think of this matter-of-fact region as their real and most central self. It is a region of thoughts and calculation – an entrepreneurial self-region, or a managerial one, individualistic. The extent to which it is cut off and isolated from other self-regions varies of course – people differ. I would not be surprised if it varied from social class to social class in systematic ways which would be shown up by research. I certainly think that it varies between the sexes, by and large, the men's Central Ego being on average more pronounced and more isolated, and also more highly valued than the women's.

Personality-structures here, as so often (see Fromm 1946), reflect the institutional structures of our society. So, perhaps to an even greater degree, do the theories we construct, since they are constructed by those of us who have done well by our institutional arrangements. There are people whose Central Ego is the most conscious and valued aspect of their self-imagery. They seem to be conscious of themselves mainly as thinkers, believing themselves to be most uniquely themselves when thinking. It is interesting to note how often philosophers are like this. Descartes wrote, 'I think therefore I am – Cogito ergo sum'; Pascal called himself a mere fragile reed but, he added quickly, 'un roseau pensant': a thinking reed. Perhaps professional thinkers, academics, and theory-writers are particularly prone to this kind of personality structure, which they thus believe to be characteristic of the whole human race. Being thinkers, they are good at words, and get themselves into print. However, they may not be accurately describing how it is for all of us.

Depressed, schizoid, and schizophrenic reactions

One reaction to painful early experiences leads to an easily *depressed* personality. As Fairbairn says in his discussion of the moral defence, the child may find it more tolerable to organize its misery in terms of its own badness rather than in terms of the badness of the world around. The child then experiences the frustration of its needs as its own fault for having those needs. It organizes its experiences in terms of its own demandingness, unreasonableness, lack of merit, unlovability, and so on. This is a sad cast of mind for, besides the disappointment, the child now also feels guilt and constant self-belittling. Fairbairn would say that the Anti-Libidinal Ego – the Internal Saboteur – is constantly attacking the Libidinal Ego.

It may be that inner conflict and trouble will eventually arise when the child can no longer resist very strong evidence that not itself but the actual mother or the actual environment is at fault, uncaring, or hostile – a very depressing discovery full of further guilt. However, when the evidence can no longer be ignored (that is selectively perceived and disowned), a person may be forced to make a more realistic assessment of what is happening.

Such a *depressed* reaction leads to a more integrated personality-structure than does the *schizoid*. The schizoid reaction to painful early experiences is simply not to integrate. People who have left much experience unintegrated will experience both bad moments and good moments, but the connection between moments or experiences or events is only tenuous, and is not integrated with their total experience of themselves and of life. Their wanting something is not strongly connected either to getting it or to not getting it. No experience of wants, needs, or wishes is strongly associated with other experiences of the self; neither is the experience of being frustrated or angry or hurt strongly associated with any other self-structures. Nor is the experience of wants, needs, wishes strongly associated with experiences of mother or other people or things. There are dynamic organizations, but they are fragments: Libidinal, Anti-Libidinal,

Central. Having them separate and not much in communication with each other enables a person not to be constantly in touch with misery and frustration and rage.

Fairbairn is much struck by the sense of futility and emptiness which goes with the schizoid structure, and he rightly associates this with the environment's lack of appropriate response to the child's expression of itself: lack of appropriate response does give a sense of futility to one's doings.

He also makes the very interesting point that much of what used to be diagnosed as hysteric behaviour in the nineteenth and early twentieth century, the empty-feeling person, looking for a relationship to fill that emptiness, may in fact have been schizoid, the personality-structure being tragically such that no ordinary responsive and loving relationship could heal the split which maintained the empty feeling (see also Khan 1983).

The *schizophrenic* reaction would take these splits a stage further. There has been drastic depersonalizing. Fear of, love for, hate toward, bliss from, are experienced with no coherent connection to either self or other. 'My' enjoyment is not mine, I do not feel it is 'I' who is enjoying. 'My' relationships – of fear, love, hate, and so on – are not 'mine'; I do not feel that it is 'I' who is fearing, loving, or hating. Objects float around without any constant handles of 'enjoyable', 'hateful', 'terrifying'. Yet there is enjoyment, fear, hate. Is it yours? Or yours? Or theirs? Or mine? It is hard to know for sure.

A modified version of Fairbairn's diagram

The drawing reproduced in *Figure 30* was inspired by Fairbairn's diagram on p. 105 of his book. However, his theories at that time (1944) were modified later (1952: 179) and I have held to the later views throughout. The lines represent boundaries between regions, and I have allowed openings to indicate a certain amount of communication between major regions of the personality, as viewed by Fairbairn.

> It will be seen that this differentiation of ego-structure corresponds roughly to Freud's account of the mental apparatus – the central ego corresponding to Freud's 'ego', the libidinal ego to Freud's 'id', and the internal saboteur to

Freud's 'super-ego'. It is integral to my conception, however, that the three structures just described are all dynamic ego-structures assuming a dynamic pattern in relation to one another, whereas Freud's 'id' is conceived as a source of energy without structure, and his 'ego' and 'super-ego' as structures without energy (except such as they derive from the 'id').

(p. 171)

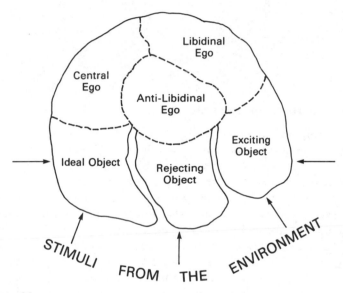

Figure 30
Source: Fairbairn, W. R. D. (1952) *Psycho-Analytic Studies of the Personality*. London: Tavistock.

The previous chapter ended with a view of the personality as something like a cluster of islands, a scattering of islands on the map. Fairbairn has presented us with a view of the personality best represented on a map by three landmasses. We now need a chapter to enable us to think with more precision about such differences in structures, and particularly about the ease with which regions can communicate with each other.

· 10 ·
The language of splitting

Recapitulation on dynamic structures

Just to remind ourselves, things begin to be recognized for what they are when they become 'classified', as Hayek put it, when the memory-traces of sensory stimuli combine, creating more central processes in the association cortex. There they become integrated (1) with messages which give information about body movement and posture, and also integrated (2) with messages which give information about chemical states, which contribute to what we eventually learn to recognize as emotions, and also integrated (3) with the memory-traces of previous messages which used part of the same neural structure.

Thus messages (from the inner and from the more distant environment) are registered in a network of concepts which between them produce something like a record of the previous associations which similar and related messages had in the past. This sort of record Hayek called the *mental order*: he meant by it the organization (structuring) of brain activity into a psychologically meaningful order. The mental order gradually approximates to an order which we assume to exist in the world we share with others, an order which arranges the memory-traces of our experiences in such a way that we get ordered and consistent patterns (structures) of meaning from them.

The order of the world we experience is mapped on to the order which exists in the brain's activity.

'In discussing the relationship between the network of neural
connexions and the structure of external events which it can
be said to reproduce, it will be useful sometimes to employ the
simile of the *map*, which reproduces some of the relations
which exist in certain parts of the physical world.'

(Hayek 1952: 5. 25)

At the beginning of life, there may be no map, or only a very
general unstructured one. Then comes the process of constructing one from incoming experiences. With more and more experience, its detailed structures become more and more clearly
defined, and each succeeding message has relatively less impact
on the increasingly strong structures which already exist. On
this map are regions, representing concepts, images, phantasies,
experiences, and so on. Regions are *dynamic* structures – they
induce action as appropriate. Such structures may be quite
specific or they may be very general and comprehensive indeed,
and they may be connected with each other in very loose or very
tightly organized ways. The task of this chapter is to clarify what
we mean by 'loose', 'tight', 'close', and so on, so that we can use
words like 'integrated' and 'split' with more precision.

First, we need to give a moment to consider what structures
are. Practically everything, from moths to months to medieval
cathedrals, has formal structure. Structure is the word for how
parts relate to each other. A picture like *Figure 31* can be a

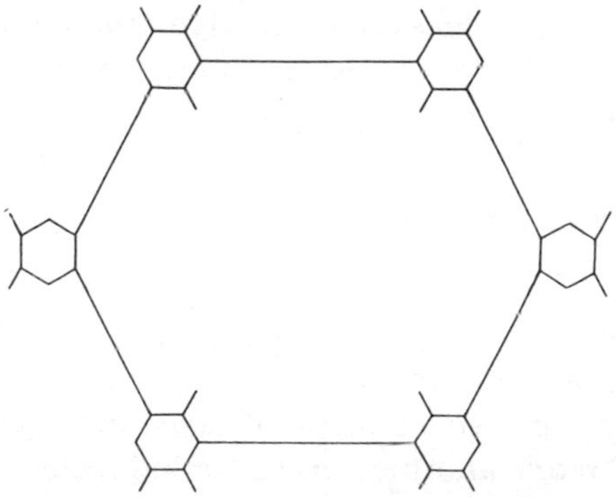

Figure 31

diagram of how atoms are arranged in a molecule, or how children are dancing ring-a-roses, or how houses are built round a close. In the present context, it can be a picture of how cells in the association-cortex relate, or of how cell-assemblies relate in higher-order concepts, or of how these higher-order concepts relate in even larger structures such as those I have called 'images', 'objects', 'regions'.

The slightly more complex structures pictured in *Figure 32* could be concepts consisting of interconnected nerve-cells, or they could be higher-order organizations of interconnected concepts. They would then be structures made up of smaller structures. An organization of interconnected higher-order concepts would be a structure of structures of structures. The complexity which can be built up in this way is obviously tremendous, ranging from neurons, through Kernberg's basic

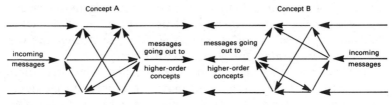

Figure 32

units of experience, to the major dynamic structures emerging out of people's experiences of themselves and of other people or things. Words, symbols, abstract ideas, and ideals are also higher-order structures.

The integration and differentiation of dynamic structures

Over time, concepts integrate and differentiate. What does this mean in terms of structure?

We can picture two conceptual structures which have no connection with one another, as shown in *Figure 32*. We can also picture these two concepts with a lot of interconnections, as *Figure 33* shows.

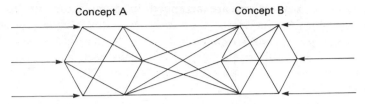

Figure 33

We can picture these two conceptual structures integrating (that is merging), if we picture the connections between them increasing in number until both are activated whenever messages come in to (what used to be) either concept.

This would happen when particular experiences have often been connected in space, in time, in words, or in symbols. People's structures become more complex as they live on and pile up experiences. In the course of this process, the meaning of the experiences can change. No memory-traces disappear: nothing neural ever vanishes. It may, however, be 'reorganized' or 'metabolized'. With further experiences, the neural or conceptual context may change, and because of this the significance of the original experience may change. Meaning, after all, depends on context. Take, for instance, an experience of pleasure and an experience of distress (see *Figure* 34).

An experience of pleasure   An experience of distress

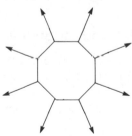 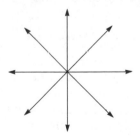

Figure 34

Interconnections come to be made between these two experiences because they have elements in common – they happen to 'me', for one thing. When this happens, the experience of pleasure is tempered by its associations with distress, and vice versa. As *Figure 35* shows, the context is changed.

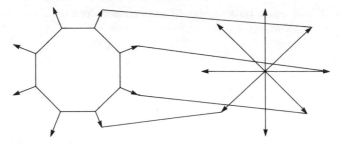

Figure 35

Isolated events become interconnected and begin to make a person's map. This map is the context for later experiences. In the course of this process, 'the memory I have now' becomes different from 'the experiences I had then'. 'Ah yes, I remember it well'.

The context can change in many ways. After more experiences, there may simply be more of one kind of thing than of another – for lucky people a lot of pleasure becomes the context for rather little distress. In other circumstances, a lot of distress is the context for very little pleasure. For rather dry people, a lot of ideas have become the context for relatively little feeling of either a pleasant or a distressing kind. In yet other circumstances, a lot of feeling *and* ideas get centred on only one person, or on many, and so on, and so on.

Dynamic self-structures: their context and integration

'Self' and 'other' are obviously higher-order concepts. It is tempting to think of them as clearly delineated from one another, as 'chalk' and 'cheese' are. But previous chapters have already shown us that this would be an error. Experience comes in wholes, in basic units in which our selves are intertwined in the situations in which we are. We may have to achieve a very high level of sophistication to get a sense of self which is not intertwined in and dependent on the situations in which we find ourselves, and to get a view of people and things which is unaffected by our memories, hopes, or fears. Even then, this achievement will mark only the more conscious tip of an iceberg: below, there will be all kinds of connections going back to the earliest and most basic units of experience. We do not usually experience our selves 'in essence', as the philosophers would say, but in relationships with other people and things. Most of us are not interested in our selves in the abstract but in 'me-liking-toffee' or 'me-hating-the-cold', and in role-relationships: 'Father-and-me', 'me-quarrelling-with-Jill'.

In the same way, I do not think that most of us are usually interested in the philosopher's *Ding an sich* – the essence of a thing itself. We are interested in things because of what they mean to us: 'the-safari-park-I-visited-with-John', 'the-TV-personality-everyone-is-talking-about'.

Chapter 8 examined the way in which the basic units of experience contribute to more generalized structures in the process of 'depersonalizing'. This could happen in different ways: besides people who characteristically experience life mainly in terms of others (as in 'They sent me a letter saying they had closed down'), there are people who experience life mainly in terms of themselves (as in 'I felt so worried when I did not hear'), and others again who experience life mainly in terms of feelings which come and go. The first kind are people for whom whatever happens in life comes to be rather intricately integrated with other people and things: anything that does not involve other people means rather little to them and is therefore only vaguely taken in and remembered, and rather infrequently a spur to action. The second kind are people for whom whatever happens in life comes to be rather intricately integrated with self-regions, and what cannot find much connection with themselves is experienced as rather irrelevant, only half taken in, rather vaguely remembered and rather infrequently a spur to action.

People differ, of course, and it is interesting to classify people according to the extent to which they are involved with (that is tightly or loosely integrated with) others. When I say 'Brown is horrible', I speak as though there is only one universe (one map – mine), and in it Brown exists and he is horrible: I seem to take myself for granted and seem unaware of my relation to Brown. At another extreme, I might say 'Brown? What he does never bothers me. I just take no notice'. I would then be speaking as though there were only one universe (mine) in which I exist and Brown only barely does so. When I say 'In my view Brown is

better on the production staff than as a sales manager', I
acknowledge that there are a number of alternative universes. I
allow Brown to exist, as it were, in his own right: on my map, on
his, and on other people's.

Self and other can be integrated in a person's map in a great
variety of ways. Different people feel, and express themselves,
differently.

> 'Brown annoys me.'
>
> 'I am angry with Brown.'
>
> 'I feel angry with Brown.'
>
> 'I have angry feelings toward Brown.'
>
> 'I have angry feelings about what Brown has done.'
>
> 'I don't think Brown should have done this or that.'
>
> 'Brown is very different from me and has his own ideas.'
>
> 'Brown has nothing to do with me, or I with Brown.'

It cannot be said too often – in matters psychological, few
boundaries are firm, or invariable, or sharp. I can be involved
with what an outside observer might call 'Mr Brown' to varying
degrees (that is the associations between my self-structures and
my Mr-Brown-structures may be few or many). Also, I can be
different when 'I' am in different situations and role-
relationships (that is different regions of my self-structures are
active at different times). Also, the extent to which my self-
structures are dynamically associated with other structures
varies from time to time. Sometimes even an experience only
loosely connected with 'me', (that is connected to 'me' by only a
few strands of previous memory – via associations with the
Argentine? ... acne? ... alcohol advertisements?) will form
part of my current awareness. At other times only experiences
which are closely connected with me will be included, as when I
have a bad toothache and cannot take an interest in anything
beyond it.

Conceptual structures need to be both inwardly integrated
and yet not too isolated from one another. If too isolated, as chalk
and cheese are for most of us, it is difficult to compare and
contrast them, or to arrange them in relation to each other. If, on
the other hand, they are not sufficiently isolated, we seem
featherbrained grasshoppers unable to focus and concentrate.

We can imagine a continuum. At one impossible extreme, we can try to imagine how we would feel if our personality were a totally integrated structure which responded in a totally unified way to each situation as it arose. This is hard to imagine. More desirable is something rather less impervious and less lumbering: we can imagine our selves to possess highly complex structures, broad-ranging and flexible, capable of registering a wide variety of stimuli and capable of responding flexibly and in highly specific ways to what is going on.

At the other extreme, as Kernberg pointed out, we may be inconvenienced by split-off infantile experiences which we never integrated into our map of our selves – 'unmetabolized' 'encapsulated' 'pockets'. In that case, though all our experiences would still be on the map somewhere, there would be some memory-traces isolated in this encapsulated way, and they would lack sufficient connections with words and symbols to be capable of our conscious attention. Such experiences would never have been conscious; we would not now (or ever) be able to 'give an account' of them; they could not be fitted into any working model of our situation. The meaning of whatever reaches such pockets is not determined by what is currently going on as our adult selves would understand it. Isolated in a pocket, it is not affected by later experiences and more adult perspectives. Context will not change it. So it remains in its primitive form. Yet behaviour characteristic of that archaic split-off object-relationship can be triggered into expression. When this happens, everyone is surprised. We may then 'account for' what we did by rationalization. Or we may disown it. 'A bolt from the blue', we say. 'It wasn't me.' 'I don't know what came over me.'

Regions of the self

How does a sense of self, of identity and continuity, emerge out of all these contexts? What, given a collection of interconnected self-structures (self-regions, self-images), creates that quality of 'self'?

The common factor in all the infant's experiences must be . . . its experience of itself! Whatever happens to it is registered in that infant's nervous system. There is a continuous mapping, more centrally, of sensations as they arrive, both from the external world through the appropriate senses, and from internal processes which record the infant's body-movements, posture, glandular state, and so on. That is happening all the time – all the time there are messages about what is happening inside the little baby and on its surfaces. And the baby has been born with at least two inborn patterns – the *homunculi* – which the various sensory and motor messages connect with as they come in.

At first, these connections are likely to be of a very fragmentary kind, as we see when we watch a baby repeatedly discovering its toes as though for the first time. The baby does not seem to have a unified self-image from the start, only isolated and transient experiences of an arm, a foot, a mouth – fragments of the self, one might say. But it is logical to suppose that these bits of self-imagery will get organized earlier than bits of what will turn out to be other people and things. For the self of the newborn baby, newly experiencing life, is always the common factor in the situation. The baby keeps experiencing itself, whatever else it is also experiencing. Whatever the baby encounters – sometimes a breast, sometimes a blanket, sometimes a light-source – may happen quite often and be registered quite often. But this cannot be happening as often as its experience of being the place where all this happens, which becomes, pretty soon, its experience of being the 'me' to whom it happens.

So the 'self', the 'me', comes to consist of a set of overlapping (interconnected) memory-traces. These are organized into overlapping (interconnected) self-structures, which include the original *motor homunculus* and the *somato-sensory homunculus* with which we are born, *plus* all the experiences in which we had something done to us (our selves as objects), *plus* all our experiences of ourselves doing something (our selves as agents). A map is formed on which the contours of all these self-structures are outlined. This map is my sense of self, 'myself', the place where all these experiences reside.

It is easy to imagine that all the regions will integrate into what eventually becomes *the* self-image, or *the* self. The fact that there is only one body per person would tend toward creating just one dominant self-structure to go with that body's experience. But it is not as simple as that, and in my view we tend to overestimate the probability of there being only one major self-region on the map. The self and the sense of self do not seem to be consistent and reliable and unchanging experiences for everyone. On the contrary, different self-structures may be evoked in different circumstances. It is wiser to regard the self as an organization of interconnected structures or self-regions. A relatively loosely-organized self would be one whose self-regions had relatively little intercommunication – many splits: communication between those regions would be relatively slow. A more integrated self would be one with more intercommunication – fewer splits; communications between those regions would be relatively faster (see *Figure 36*.) The contrast would be between a person who behaves very differently in different role-relations – kind as a parent, harsh as a teacher, unobtrusive among people who threaten – and a person whose personality comes through as the same in a variety of contexts. The fewer the interconnections, the slower the person is to see the connections between events, and the more isolating the splits: each region is activated only in particular circumstances, without much affecting other regions – it would take such people a while to catch up with themselves.

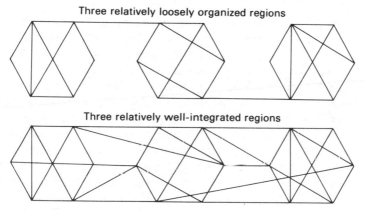

Three relatively loosely organized regions

Three relatively well-integrated regions

Figure 36

There are many kinds of self-regions, overlapping in different personality-types to a greater or a lesser extent, and dominant in them to varying degrees:

- myself as the place where things happen,
- I, the agent doing things,

- me, the person to whom things happen,
- 'I', 'me', 'myself', 'mine', etc.,
- that part of the self composed of needs and drives, wishes and wants,
- the conscious self – the 'I' that give an account of my self,
- parts of the self as experienced in a variety of other role-relationships,
- the self that is known in the context of domestic relationships: son, brother, husband, father,
- the self that is defined and described and related to by others – as edgy, kind, important, not worth bothering about, etc. – that is the 'self-image' that others give one,
- the self (or selves) that is/are edited or elaborated versions of the above – the self as I see my self – a person's own conscious self-imagery,
- my 'episodic self', and my 'semantic self'.

Bowlby (1980) introduces these two interesting variants, the 'episodic self' and the 'semantic self', from a distinction drawn by Tulving (1972) between two ways in which we know ourselves. We may think of ourselves in terms of our memories of ourselves in various 'episodes', as when we spilled the lemonade on auntie, or painted the dog with our new water-colours. We remember what happened, and what happened next, and what happened after that. This kind of knowing is memory of the actual sensory experiences and so it is bound up with our deepest sense of identity and continuity. By contrast, we may think of ourselves in a more general and abstract way, as in 'I am stubborn' or 'I don't mind baby-sitting'. In this way of knowing ourselves, we draw on some mixture of our own remembered experiences and what other people have told us. This is Tulving's 'semantic self'.

There may be relatively little connection between some of these various self-regions. If 'I' (the active self) and 'me' (the passive self), or if my 'semantic' self and my 'episodic' self, remain separate (relatively speaking, of course) and do not integrate, the whole of me is never *there* either for myself or for other people.

Consciousness

Consciousness plays an important role in differentiating and integrating regions of the self. Or, rather, our ability to use language is important. As Hayek sees it, a set of established neural connections may include the neural equivalent of words. To put this the other way round, words are connected to sets of established connections, which they can thereby 'stand for' or 'represent' or 'symbolize' or 'mean', in the same way that an angle can stand for a triangle and vice versa. Once this is possible, words can evoke sets of connections (that is conceptual structures) which resonate to those words. We talk to ourselves in words, we can give an account to ourselves of our world, of our place in it – we are conscious, we are conscious of ourselves.

Words will also come to be connected with one another, not just with the original connections. (Indeed, for many of us the connections between words may be quite as strong as the connection between words and the experiences for which they stand.) We can construct verbal versions of our experiences. And a verbal version may leave some things out which were actually experienced, or may include things which were not experienced. For instance, I can write 'A tiger is nibbling my pen as I write', although this is not my experience.

The verbal form of our experiences, being verbal, allows us to be self-aware. We can give some account of our selves. In these accounts there is always 'I myself' or 'me myself', at least as an observer. The reflexive 'I myself'/'me myself' experience is always in the region which carries my awareness. This region is at different times in touch with different other regions; whichever one it is in touch with, that is the one I am conscious of.

This way of thinking goes back to what was foreshadowed in Chapter 4. What we know is determined partly by our map and our working model, and partly by our consciousness – that part of the map and the working model which we can give an account of. Map and model include self-regions. All self-regions are on the map. The model carries the current representation of a person in his or her situation, *here and now*. This need not be conscious, but it is when I am able to 'give an account' of myself. Then we can say, 'This is how it is', 'This is how I see it', 'This is how I am', 'This is who I am', 'This is what I expect', and so on. Hearing ourselves say it, remembering saying it and thinking it, strengthens our ideas of the world and of who we are in the world.

We may think of ourselves as having a map on which all our self-regions are represented. When these regions are fairly well integrated with one another, I feel that I am a fairly integrated person: there is fairly instant communication between the regions of my self so that no region is long cut off from consciousness. This would be registered in my self-awareness as if I were walking in the gently hilly landscape of 'myself', conscious of other areas around wherever I might be standing. The whole area is composed of self-regions, all contributing to my 'sense of self'. When I give an account of myself, I am conscious of any and all of it – quite a large part of my map of reality.

When I 'give an account of myself', I am conscious mainly of where I am standing now. The less integrated my personality, the less communication there is between the regions, so that each may be rather isolated. This would be registered in my self-awareness as if I were walking in one narrow valley out of sight of other nearby narrow valleys. In this case, different contexts or relationships or situations involve somewhat different separate self-regions, each of which I may experience as my self. Which self-region will be the source of action at any time will depend on the general situation at that time – the 'model' in Hayek's terms.

In the most extreme case, each region is an organization of self-structures with the memories, hopes, objectives, plans, schemes, and other ego-functions, *including consciousness*, which belong solely to that set of experiences. The 'split personality' of fiction.

So much for a summary of ideas already expounded. Now for a change of pace; we build some more on what has gone before.

Fissures between regions of the self

Three different kinds of fissures may usefully be distinguished in the landscapes of the mind. I shall call them 'gaps', 'lids', and 'splits' respectively.

A *gap* is where two or more experiences which could be

organized together happen not to be organized together, as for instance when a person has never made a connection between 'nameless' and 'salesmen' (its anagram). These two little structures have never been integrated in the reader's mind until now: there was never any connection between them.

Gaps occur because the processes of integration tend to confine themselves along certain boundaries. In the normal course of events, incoming messages from the senses construct an ever more accurate and coherent organization of dynamic structures, with plenty of intercommunication where appropriate, because ideas associate on the basis of past experiences. When all goes well, the structures which between them define 'me with cats', for instance, are different from those which define 'me with dogs', though in many contexts the mind would sooner or later drift from the one to the other. Whether sooner or later would depend on the number of interconnections between these two concepts.

Gaps account for a lack of connection between quite complicated types of organizations of experience. Tulving's distinction, between an 'episodic' understanding of one's experience and a 'semantic' one, is of this kind – I may be able to remember the sights, sounds, and feelings of my fifteenth birthday party, and I may think of myself as shy at parties, and yet for some reason these two memory-structures have never got connected.

The other two kinds of fissure are actively maintained by forces which are stronger than the natural processes of integration. There is what the French neuro-psychiatrist Janet, as long as 100 years ago, called 'dissociation' (Guntrip 1961: 399; 1969: 96). When there is dissociation, the personality somehow lacks the strength to hold itself together. Structures which had been integrated fall apart again. This is the kind of fissure to which the word 'split' applies most vividly – something is split that had been whole. It is interesting that Janet worked with what were then called 'hysterics', people who might now be recognized as 'schizoid', and 'falling apart' seems a very accurate description of how they feel at times. Interest in this kind of structural weakness was lost for some time while the focus came to be on Freud's concept of repression – 'putting the lid on things' – another way in which fissures can be actively maintained (Guntrip 1969: 252).

Both 'splits' and repression usually involve anxiety. The difference lies in the personality-structure already in existence when the anxiety is generated. If there has been too much anxiety before there is as yet much integration of the self, you get dissociated states: splits in the structure of the mind. Then connections may have to be made in a remedial setting, lest the split persist for ever. Repressive structures ('lids'), on the other hand, depend on the existence of more central organizations to do the repressing. These more central organizations are strong enough to 'put the lid on' an anxiety-creating structure. They are a later development, and alleviating their adverse effects requires a very different therapeutic relationship.

The role of anxiety in preventing integration: an example from Fairbairn

Unless something actively intervenes, experiences with a lot of factors in common are normally organized together, integrated in other words. The something that intervenes is likely to be an incongruity between already existing structures and new information now coming in which, if integrated, would cause an intolerable change in the existing structure. Such an incongruity sets off a feedback process: 'Is what is going on in accordance with the desirable situation I have in mind?' If it is not, the incongruity may be a very alarming one, with the reaction 'No! No! This cannot be!' (see pp. 66 and 351ff.). Then either the existing structures on the map, which define the desirable situation, have to be divorced from the conscious self-regions, or the incoming information has to be disregarded – kept apart from the current model of the self-in-the-situation.

Anxiety intervenes at the point where associative processes would normally lead to something that has to be avoided as painful. We are here in the realm of what Freud first called signal anxiety: anxiety aroused by the expectation that yet more anxiety or distress will be experienced unless further integration of the current experience is halted. A split then has to be maintained between what is being experienced and what might be experienced.

The diagram of Fairbairn's personality theory on p. 173 (*Figure 30*) depicted people with three rather isolated self-regions. It showed a 'Libidinal Ego' directing its wishes and hopes to the 'Frustrating Exciting Object', and affected by but out of touch with the 'Anti-Libidinal Ego' which directs its rage and fear to the 'Rejecting Object' – the connection between the Libidinal and the Anti-Libidinal Ego being such that the latter comes into action when the former is active. Thirdly, there was the 'Central Ego', which directs itself to surviving in an environment that offers little of either pleasure or distress, and is more or less out of touch with the other two regions.

People with this kind of personality-structure might almost be conscious of only one set of object-relations at a time, and barely in touch with other parts of the map. For them, the three regions would be almost alternative to one another: immersed in one set of object-relations they would be nearly unconscious (out of touch) with the possibility of other ways of relating. In a more fortunate personality, the three regions are less out of touch with one another, less contrasting, less sharply alternative, more like three moods which a person might have on different occasions.

Other forms of dissociation arise after some integration of central processes has taken place. Once central processes have become organized, they can have the effect of maintaining a fissure, thereby preventing further integrations. Normally these involve anxiety, but not always.

Selective attention: the role of central processes in preventing integration

Selective attention is a comparatively simple way of maintaining a fissure, at least for a while. To recapitulate, attention is an instruction from more central processes (pp. 42ff., 57ff.). Attention requires organizations of concepts, ideas, and feelings, which are sufficiently enduring to be capable of reverberating (pp. 34–5 and 58). These reverberations can bring parts of a person's map into prominence, and this makes the feedback processes possible, through which selective attention operators: 'Is what is going on in accordance with what I have in mind? If yes, carry on. If not, cease that activity and try another.'

Bowlby (1980: Chapter 4) relates these processes to what he calls defensive exclusion. He argues, along lines by now familiar, that sensory input goes through several stages – reception, evaluation, interpretation, and so on. Each of these stages involves successively more strongly organized conceptual structures, and each is successively more central to the whole organization than the previous more ephemeral stage was. New information is thus able to make an impact. But equally, it goes through filters – what is already established and 'known' affects more recently required information, and indeed may keep it from consciousness altogether. Bowlby cites an amusing experiment which illustrates this, showing how newly arriving information was kept isolated, and yet was able to influence what happened next.

> 'In this type of experiment, two different messages are transmitted to a person, one message being received in one ear and the other in the other. The person is then told to attend to one of these messages only, say the one being received by the right ear. To ensure he gives it continuous attention, he is required to "shadow" that message by repeating it word for word as he is hearing it. Keeping the two messages distinct is found to be fairly easy, especially when they are spoken by different voices. At the end of the session the subject is usually totally unaware of the content of the unattended message. . . .
>
> In one such experiment, subjects were required to attend to and shadow ambiguous messages, of which the following is an example:
>
> "They threw stones towards the bank yesterday."
>
> Simultaneously with this message, either the word "river" was presented in the unattended ear, or else the word "money". Later, subjects were presented with a recognition test for the meaning of the sentence, in which they were asked to choose between the following:
>
> (a)   "They threw stones towards the side of the river yesterday";
> (b)   "They threw stones towards the savings-and-loan association yesterday".
>
> Subjects who had had the word "river" presented to the unattended ear tended to select (a) as the meaning, whereas

subjects who had had "money" in the unattended ear tended to select (b). None of the subjects remembered what word had been presented to the unattended ear and they were unaware that their subsequent judgement of meaning had been influenced. Clearly, in order for the word presented to the unattended ear to have had the effect it did in this experiment, it must have undergone sufficient processing for its meaning to have been recognized.

A similar conclusion emerges from another experiment that also used the technique of dichotic listening. Before the experiment proper, the subjects went through a few training sessions during which they were exposed to an electric shock when any one of a set of selected words was spoken to them. As a result, subjects became conditioned to the word-shock combination so that whenever one of the selected words was heard, it was responded to by a change in the Galvanic Skin Response (a measure of sweating, thought to indicate anxiety). In the experiment proper, the subjects were required to attend to and shadow a message in one ear while a list of words was presented to the other, unattended, ear. Words in that list were of three kinds: neutral words, some of the words that had been conditioned to shock, and both synonyms and homonyms of those words. Despite the facts that no shocks were given during the experiment itself, there was an appreciable rise in the Galvanic Skin Response whenever a conditioned word was presented in the unattended ear. Of even greater interest is that there was also a substantial – though lesser – rise in perspiration when the homonyms and synonyms were presented. Here again, the findings indicate that every word presented in the unattended ear must have undergone considerable processing and its meaning established.'

Bowlby concludes:

'From these findings it is but a short step to infer that, just as people's judgement and their autonomic responses can be influenced by cognitive processing outside awareness, so also can their mood.'

(Bowlby 1980: Chapter 4 quoting Norman 1976: 31–2)

We exclude certain things from consciousness in order to be

able to attend to the things we need to attend to without being distracted. We do this all the time. But we also do it in a defensive way, to isolate information which might worry us – create anxiety. Some of this excluded information remains unorganized at the sensory and perceptual levels – it never gets organized conceptually, though it is in principle capable of such organization. In other circumstances, information does reach conceptual and verbal levels of organization, but is excluded from consciousness and use at this level. 'Analytic psychotherapies can be understood as procedures aimed at enabling people to accept information that hitherto they had been excluding', writes Bowlby (1980: 46).

Central processes, ego-functions, and the self

Selective attention is one of the simplest cognitive processes by means of which the direction-giving function of the organized personality operates. There are more complex central processes which guide our behaviour and our self-awareness. But however complex they may eventually become, the basic mechanism is still the feedback: 'is what is happening congruous with the desirable situation I have in mind, or not?.'

Feedback processes operate at all levels of complexity. 'Has my fork speared this potato?' 'Is my action pleasing to God?' There is quite a range here: the second question includes a good many more regions than the first. It feels more central: more comprehensive, more inclusive of more regions with which the self is concerned. More self is involved, and more control is involved: the more central self-regions are acting as attention-directing, direction-giving, orientating, and steering processes for the less central regions.

When certain messages arrive centrally, the feedback can produce anxiety, with the result that potentially relevant information is not incorporated in the working model of the-self-in-the-situation. The mechanism is the same as that which keeps any two regions from integrating, the difference being simply that we are now looking at dominant central regions in relation to the rest of the personality structure. We are looking at monarchies rather than federations of equal states. Central organization makes exclusion and repression easier (Reich 1935, 1975).

Feedbacks involve expectations or, amounting to the same thing, values, wishes, hopes, prejudices, and all kinds of non-rational non-cognitive features. They also involve the accumulation and organization of incoming information, that is they involve ego-functions; at a simple level these would be such processes as perceiving, conceptualizing, categorizing, remembering, comparing, and planning. The dominant central regions are the ones where the ego-functions are located. Ego-functions develop as the personality develops, guiding people to find their way in situations, much as Lorenz's little shrew did. Thus Kernberg (1976: 35) quotes, from an unpublished list compiled by Murphy (1963), some higher-order ego-functions clearly performing a central steering role:

'regulating the general level of psycho-motor activity,

regulating control over delay,

planning activities and giving them an orientation,

shifting attention in flexible ways,

differentiating between stimuli,

integrating experience and actions (skills).'

Bowlby (1980: 54) similarly gives a list of functions performed by what he called Principal Control Systems, processes through which incoming information is organized and selected or discarded, at successively higher levels of organization (more centrally). These processes are clearly cognitive functions of a very high order – ego-functions:

'ordering, categorizing, and encoding information,

retrieving information from memory,

juxtaposing information so as to make reflective thought possible (comparing, patterning),

framing alternative plans for "high-level decisions",

inspecting certain overlearned and automated action-systems, together with the representation-models linked to them, that may be proving maladapted. As a result of such inspection,

systems and models long out of awareness become available
for reappraisal in the light of new information, and if
necessary, attempts can be made to reorganize or perhaps
replace them.'

The last of these is clearly a feedback process.

The use of the term 'ego-functions' raises a small but confus-
ing problem of terminology. Most classical writers have tended
to use the word 'ego' where I would use the word 'self'. Balint,
Kernberg, and Fairbairn do, for instance. There is then a danger
that 'self' and 'ego' will be equated, whereas all agree that there
is more to the personality than ego-functioning – see the whole
of Guntrip (1971) for a discussion of this. I would like to restrict
the word 'ego' to be the collective noun for all cognitive
functions. This would enable us to use the word 'self' as the
collective noun for all self-regions.

The tendency to equate ego-functions with 'the self' easily
creates philosophical problems about what motivates us. When
we think of the self, we can make it into a thing, an object on an
inner stage. The metaphor of 'inner object', which puts the self
on an inner stage together with other figures representing other
people and things, is a useful metaphor. It seems to come
naturally to us, and it gives recognition to the mobility and
active purpose which these figures display in our heads. It is a
useful way of thinking but it is a misleading one. The self is a set
of self-regions, a more or less tightly organized congeries of
processes or functions. If we think of it as more unified than it is,
and give it more substance than in fact it has, then we may start
asking 'what motivates this thing? What makes this figure act?'
Not to fall into this trap, we have constantly to remember that
self-regions are dynamic structures of processes – *they move and
act by virtue of what they are.*

Obviously some regions are more 'self' than others, standing
more accurately or more easily for the whole self; these are
normally likely to be more central regions, but not always.

Types of dominant central process

How may self-structures be organized into more or less integrated selves?

First, we may distinguish structures with a strong central organization, from those without. Structure (1) in *Figure 37* shows a centrally integrated structure. It has a number of fairly distinct but highly interconnected regions, with one 'central' region more in touch with all the others, so that the whole can be given direction from this centre. The centre will be a dominant image, or a dominant object-relation, or a dominant set of instructions about how to behave. This is the typical hierarchical structure, familiar in many different contexts. The central organization affects the working model of the situation, the model on which a person acts: people will get anxious when there is incongruity between expectations arising from the central region and information coming in about the actual situation.

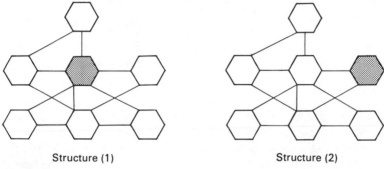

Structure (1)   Structure (2)

Figure 37

The lines between regions indicate which regions communicate and integrate. This is simplified here, because there are many degrees of communication whereas lines show only whether regions do or don't. In (1) and (2) the central region integrates easily with any of the others and this is how the organism is steered. In (1) consciousness (indicated by hatching) resides mainly in the central region. In (2) consciousness resides in the region on the right, although the organism is steered (by definition) by the central region.

In *Figure 38* Structure (3) has no centre. Some people of this kind find that their consciousness resides mainly in one particular region, rather as in (1) or (2); other people's consciousness

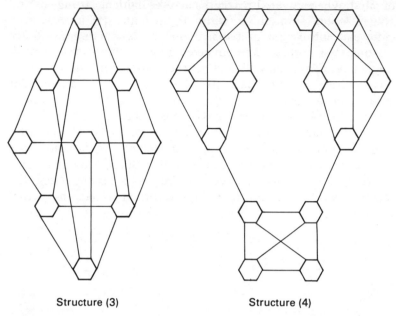

Structure (3)   Structure (4)

Figure 38

wanders freely among the regions. Structure (4) shows a personality-structure with three vertical splits.

When there is no strong central organization, as in Structure (3), we may still have an integrated structure, with a number of fairly distinct but highly interconnected structures. But in this case, no region is more in touch with all the others, so no region gives more direction than any other. We may think of this as a federation of equal states without a dominant president or senate – perhaps the European Community provides a good analogy. This personality-structure may be just what is needed for at least some kinds of artistic and other intuitive endeavour. With advancing years, people with strongly influential central processes necessarily become more and more firm in their expectations as to how things should be, and increasingly conventional in thought. But those whose organization is less tight, and less centralized, may have access to the more primitive earlier states of mind, where covered-up truths may be hidden, and where the apparatus for new ways of seeing things may be found.

Second, we can distinguish according to where consciousness normally resides. There are people who usually know what they are doing and where they are going and why, people who can give an account of themselves – centrally organized and conscious people whose consciousness is centred too (Structure 1). Then there are people whose consciousness does not reside predominantly in the central region, although they are centrally organized and therefore directed from the centre (Structure 2). In this case, the region which actually dominates is not known to the person concerned, whose image of himself or herself is therefore rather partial, depending on what region is the conscious one – this would be the regions in terms of which such people would give an account of themselves. Such people may well surprise and puzzle the onlooker.

As for the people who are hardly centrally organized at all (Structure 3), some of these may be flexibly and widely conscious and able to give an account of themselves whatever circumstances they are in. Such people can be said to have several distinct centres of consciousness, each containing some capacity for consciousness, some self-regions, some object-relations, and so on. These would be people who adapt very responsively to different situations, without feeling that their integrity or their identity is threatened by having to behave very differently in different circumstances. It would seem natural and obvious to them to do so. The fact that they are stern here, and jolly there, only means that they are sometimes stern and sometimes jolly, as seems appropriate. It would be wrong to say that they are 'really' one or the other – they are really the lot.

On the other hand, with little centralized control, if there is also little consciousness, people may be rather scatter-brained. They might find it difficult to concentrate or to be consistent, and they might find it hard to understand themselves and other people, and to explain what they want, even to themselves. Because so much is left out of any model they happen to be using, they may also have a sense of not being real or genuine or honest in what they say.

Vertical and horizontal splits – dissociation and repression

We may think of each self-region as a set of interconnected object-relations. There is in each region some self-imagery and some object-imagery and some relationships and some feelings. Each region has in this sense something rather like what we think of as a self. It is because of this that Kohut writes of 'vertical splits' in the personality, to be contrasted with the horizontal splits created by repression. Vertical splits in the personality isolate self-regions, each of which is capable of being an 'independent centre of consciousness'. Each is capable of producing a working model of the-self-in-the-situation which takes account of some important aspects of the self and leaves others out. It is mainly with vertically splitting personalities that the present book is concerned. However, we need a brief consideration of 'horizontal splits' (that is *lids*) for comparison and perspective.

'Horizontal splits', like vertical ones, isolate some self-regions, but they do so as a result of a dominant central self-region 'putting the lid on' sub-regions which are not capable of being organized as 'independent centres of consciousness'. 'Horizontal splits' ('lids') create repressed *bits* of self-imagery, or object-representations, or self-object relations (Kohut 1971: 176ff.; 1977: 211ff.).

A central organization has to exist if repression is to be the preferred defence against anxiety. Repression occurs when a dominant central region does not integrate, but rather rejects, information which would reveal an incongruity between it and something that is about to happen. This dominant central organization may be a *self-image*: I have either to give a penny to the beggar or, conscious of incongruity, cease to regard myself as a kind person. What will I do? I may go through the process of modifying my behaviour and give some money, so that I don't have to modify my image of myself, or I obscure the issue with further considerations and contexts so that the incongruity ceases to cause anxiety. Or my anxiety may be so great that I do not do the necessary work but keep the new information (that I did not give a penny) isolated from integration with the rest of my self-imagery – I repress it.

A more complex version of a repressive central process involves an *idealized image of the self*. This region is not mapped according to the contours of what I was or am, but according to what I wish to be.

Sometimes idealized imagery is derived from another person's wish, which is then used as guidance. A feedback system becomes established between one person and another, often between a child and a parent, sometimes between husband and wife. In some circumstances we may be so desperate for something that feels good in a miasma of bad feelings, that we *idealize another person*, or try for *idealized relationship* in which we can please the other. Such idealizations may become central to the personality. Particularly in childhood, we are under pressure, both within and without, to idealize our parents. And we are always under pressure to idealize the loving relationship between parents and children. Evidence that parents are not inevitably the best people to look after children arouses deep anxiety and is strenuously resisted. At least until the early 1980s, it was fair to say that this was the dominant ethos of the caring professions who, like others, found it hard to accept that the two may be best apart. The pressures to idealize the marriage-bond used to be as strong, but common sense has begun to prevail in this area.

Anxiety when the ideal and the actual are not congruous creates the conditions for repression, once there is a central organization which strongly holds to the ideal. We then get horizontal splits. This is how Bowlby writes of the process:

'Both the nature of the representational models a person builds of his attachment figures, and also the form in which his attachment behaviour becomes organised, are regarded in this work as being the results of early learning experiences that start during the first year of life and are repeated almost daily throughout childhood and adolescence. On the analogy of a physical skill that has been acquired in the same kind of way, both the cognitive and the action components of attachment are thought to become so engrained that they come to operate automatically and outside awareness. Similarly, the rules for appraising action, thought and feeling, and the precedence given to each, associated with the concept of the super-ego, are thought also to become engrained ... and applied automatically and outside awareness.

Plainly this arrangement has both advantages and disadvantages. On the one hand, it economises effort and, in particular, makes no demands on the limited capacity channels which mediate advanced processing. On the other hand there is the disadvantage that, once cognition and action have been automated, they are not readily accessible to conscious processing and so are difficult to change. The psychological state may then be likened to that of a computer that, once programmed, produces its results automatically whenever activated. Provided the programme is the one required, all is well. Should an error have crept in, however, its correction not only demands skilled attention but may prove troublesome and slow to achieve. ...

Hence some of the difficulties encountered in psychotherapy. For the task of changing an engrained programme of action and/or of appraisal is enormously exacerbated when rules long implemented by the evaluative system forbid its being reviewed. An example of this is when people find themselves unable to review the representational models they have built of their attachment figures because to do so would infringe a long-learned rule that it is against one or both parents' wishes that they should study them and their behaviour objectively. A psychological state of this kind, in which a ban on reviewing models and action systems is effected outside awareness, is one encountered frequently during psychotherapy.'

(Bowlby 1980; 55–6)

The function of idealized figures in putting the lid on certain structures of the personality is explored at the end of the next chapter.

SOURCES OF STRENGTH

the great advantage of being alive
(instead of undying)is not so much
that mind no more can disprove than prove
what heart may feel and soul may touch
– the great(my darling)happens to be
that love are in we,that love are in we

and here is a secret they never will share
for whom create is less than have
or one times one than when times where
that we are in love,that we are in love:
with us they've nothing times nothing to do
(for love are in we am in i are in you)

this world(as timorous itsters all
to call their cowardice quite agree)
shall never discover our touch and feel
– for love are in we are in love are in we

(e.e. cummings, *selected poems 1923–1958*)

·11·
Feeling 'grand'

The self and the selfobject

Kohut thought of the self as emerging slowly out of the process by which self and other differentiate.

> 'In trying, in analysis after analysis, to determine the roots of the selves of my analysands, I obtained the impression that during early psychic development a process takes place in which some mental contents that had been experienced as belonging to the self become obliterated or are assigned to the area of the non-self, while others are retained within the self or are added to it. As a result of this process, a core self – the nuclear self – is established.
>
> This structure is the basis for our sense of being an independent centre of initiative and perception, integrated with our most central ambitions and ideals, and with our experience that our body and mind form a unit of space and a continuum in time.'
>
> (Kohut 1977: 177)

Kohut believed that many of his patients had suffered disturbances in the process of self-formation, and that therapy could help them in specific ways to repair that early damage.

> 'I have become convinced that, to some extent at least, a properly conducted analysis of patients suffering from a

203

disturbance in the formation of the self creates a psychological matrix that encourages the re-activation of the original developmental tendency. The nuclear self of the patient is consolidated, the talents and skills of the analysand that are correlated to the nuclear self are revitalised, while other aspects of the self are discarded or recede.'

(p. 178)

Kohut invented the word 'selfobject' for the state of mind – with which adults are still at times in touch, both in everyday life and in psychotherapy – when differentiation between self and other has begun but has not yet proceeded very far. This state of mind may be a development which becomes possible soon after the development of the 'auto-sensuous mother' which Tustin writes about. In the selfobject there is already some 'me', some sense of identity, although this sense of 'me' is associated with some powers or abilities which do not actually belong there. For instance, the milk-giving breast may be included in the infant's self-structures and therefore experienced as 'me', and so may other aspects of the mother, like the arm which carries 'me' around five feet above the floor – these have not yet differentiated out as 'not me'. The experience of 'me' conveniently equipped with a milk-giving breast or a mother or an extra arm, is an experience of that state of mind which Kohut calls the selfobject. The resulting sense of well-being and self-esteem must be pretty gratifying to the infant.

Narcissism and self-esteem

The sense of self-esteem, self-liking, or self-respect is one of Kohut's basic interests. He reaches his own valuable perspective on it from the starting-point of the classical concept of 'narcissism'. I should warn the unwary reader that this does not mean in classical psycho-analysis what it has come to mean in other circles. For a classical definition we may turn to Fenichel (1945), the great authority on the psycho-analytic concepts of that time. Quoting him now also shows the present-day reader how difficult it was to think about these processes in the days when all human behaviour was considered to be rather directly concerned with instincts and their vicissitudes. Those were the days, too, before evidence had begun to accumulate about the important place held by mothers in their babies' lives from the moment of their birth onwards.

The whole of Fenichel's chapter on early mental development is still astonishingly appropriate, considering it was drafted in the 1930s or early 1940s. Like Freud, Fenichel starts from the idea that there is a state of 'primary narcissism', in which there is as yet no differentiation of self and object. Without this differentiation there can be no object-representation, and this makes it possible for the wonderful feelings of goodness, rightness, safety and omnipotence which belong to that stage for the lucky ones. He quotes Ferenczi (1916) who spoke of a first limitless sense of omnipotence which persists as long as no conception of objects exists – obviously the prototype of a space-loving feeling; Balint was deeply indebted to this fellow-Hungarian. Traces of this original object-less condition, which Freud (1927) called 'oceanic feeling', persist into adult life, or at least the longing for it persists. Narcissistic feelings of well-being are also sometimes felt as a union with some omnipotent force – obviously the prototype of home-loving feelings.

To my mind, narcissistic feelings come from the memory-traces of what it was like in the days of oceanic feelings and harmonious interpenetrating mix-up when the self and a beneficent and powerful (m)other were still merged in the infant's experience. This must have felt good. Fenichel has a rather more instinct-based formulation but in the present context that does not matter: the baby's self-esteem is determined by the gratification of its (instinctual) needs. 'The first supply of satisfaction from the external world is simultaneously the first regulator of self-esteem.' When being gratified, the baby feels wonderful, indeed omnipotent. When the baby has a need which is not being satisfied, it feels irritated, frustrated, deprived, and it longs for what will remove the 'disturbing displeasure'. (We have here an example of the theory Bowlby did not care for, which assumes that motivation comes from the wish to restore equilibrium.)

'The longing for the return of omnipotence and the longing for the removal of instinctual tension are not yet differentiated from each other. If one succeeds in getting rid of an unpleasant stimulus, one's self-esteem is again restored.'

(Fenichel 1945: 40)

and

'The individual's experiences connected with omnipotence lead to a most significant need of the human mind. The longing for the oceanic feeling of primary narcissism can be called the "narcissistic need". "Self-esteem" is the awareness of how close the individual is to the original omnipotence.'

(ibid.)

Its (instinctual) needs make the child dependent on the parent. Interestingly Fenichel's theory requires that the child renounces its own instinctual satisfactions. 'The tendency to participate in the parent's omnipotence, after renunciation of one's own, differentiates itself from the desire for instinctual satisfaction. Thereafter every token of love from the powerful adult has the same effect as the satisfaction of instinctual needs.' The nature of the child's dependence is thus changed.

'The small child loses self-esteem when he loses love and attains it when he regains love. This is what makes children so educable. They need supplies of affection so badly that they are ready to renounce other satisfactions if rewards of affection are promised or if withdrawal of affection is threatened. The promise of necessary narcissistic supplies of affection under the condition of obedience and the threat of withdrawal of these supplies if the conditions are not fulfilled are the weapons of any authority.

(p. 41)

By the time Kohut is writing, a less instinct-based theory of personality-structure has become possible, but Fenichel's clinical insights have lost none of their power. The sense of omnipotence reappears in what Kohut (and many others, see especially Horney 1950) called grandiosity.

Narcissism, mirroring, and the grandiose self

Working in depth, Kohut came across a primitive region in some of his patients, which he called the grandiose self. He found that, in the course of psycho-analysis, some people would start to behave as though any flaw, any difference of opinion, any lack in total harmony between them and their analyst, was quite intolerable. At those times they would feel great distress and outrage, that their perhaps not yet even spoken thoughts and feelings had not been responded to by their analyst, whom they required to mirror their every move. To Kohut's mind, the patient was back in a developmental phase where he or she needed a totally accurate and absolutely competent selfobject. He called this way of relating the 'mirror-transference' and saw in it a revival of the condition Freud (1915) had called the 'purified pleasure-ego',

> 'in which the child attempts to save the original all-embracing narcissism by concentrating perfection and power upon the self – here called the grandiose self – and by turning disdainfully away from an outside to which all imperfections have been assigned.'
>
> (Kohut 1971: 106)

There is an evocative resemblance here to Tustin's little patients turning away from what they experienced as harmful. In ordinary life, when children or older people behave as though they are entitled to everyone's deference and subservience, we call them cheeky or demanding or pompous, and we usually respond by setting limits, through noncompliance, ridicule, scolding, or whatever. To my mind it is not the least of Kohut's contributions that he makes this irritating behaviour so understandable.

The selfobject and mirroring/confirming

The selfobject state of mind exists exactly to the extent that the mother is prompt to bring to the baby what it needs precisely at the moment the baby needs it. This confirms the illusion, so necessary at that stage, of harmony, security, and invulnerable power. For the selfobject is the baby's experience of its *own* competence, of its *own* power to have whatever it needs. We can get a glimpse of what this experience may feel like, in a sentence such as 'To get what you want makes you feel grand, wonderful'. This sentence can mean both 'makes you feel grand, wonderfully satisfied' and 'makes you feel you're a grand, wonderful person'. This distinction between 'I feel grand' and 'I feel that I am grand' is more sophisticated than infants (and many adults) are capable of making.

So the mother who is prompt to cater to her baby keeps the baby feeling grand and confirms the baby's sense of goodness *and* well-being. Kohut (like others) gives to this promptness and accuracy of response the name of 'mirroring': there is a symmetry between the baby's phantasy-image of what it needs and the mother's intelligent and caring supply of that need. I will often call it confirming, because it also confirms the baby's sense of its own rightness: its right to exist, to have these needs, to have these gratifications.

The confirming/mirroring process has important implications for the development of the infant's sense of self:

'the human environment reacts to even the smallest baby as if it had formed a self. . . . When, within the matrix of mutual empathy between the infant and its selfobject, the baby's innate potentialities and the selfobject's expectations converge, is it permissible to consider this juncture the point of origin of the infant's primal rudimentary self?'

(1977: 99)

Dibs in search of self

Virginia Axline (1964) gives a moving and convincing account of successive stages in this process at a mature level, in the story of her therapy with a troubled 4-year-old boy, Dibs. (See also p. 270.) At their first meeting, they walked together into the playroom.

'I sat down on a little chair just inside the door. Dibs stood in the middle of the room, his back toward me, twisting his hands together. I waited. We had an hour to spend in this room. There was no urgency to get anything done. To play or not to play. To talk or to be silent. . . .

Dibs just stood in the middle of the room. He sighed. Then he slowly turned and walked haltingly across the room, then around the walls. He went from one toy to another, tentatively touching them. He did not look directly at me. . . .

He walked over to the doll house, ran his hand along the roof, knelt down beside it, and peered inside at the furniture. Slowly, one by one, he picked up each piece of furniture. As he did, he muttered the name of the objects with a questioning, halting inflection. His voice was flat and low.

"Bed? Chair? Table?" he said. "Crib? Dresser? Radio? Bathtub? Toilet?" Every item in the doll house he picked up, named, carefully replaced. He turned to the pile of dolls, and sorted slowly through them. He selected a man, a woman, a boy, a girl, a baby. It was as though he tentatively identified them as he said, "Mamma? Papa? Sister? Baby?" Then he sorted out the little animals. "Dog? Cat? Rabbit?" He sighed deeply and repeatedly. It seemed to be a very difficult and painful task he had set himself.

Each time he named an object I made an attempt to communicate my recognition of his spoken word. I would say, "Yes. That is a bed," or, "I think it is a dresser," or "It does look like a rabbit". I tried to keep my responses brief, in line with what he said, and with enough variation to avoid monotony. . . . And that is the way our conversation went with every item that he picked up and named. I thought that this was his way to begin verbal communication. Naming the objects seemed a safe enough beginning.'

(Axline 1964; 1971 paperback edition: 22–3)

Somewhat later in the therapy:

'"I'm going to start work, now," he said. "I am going to build a high hill. A high, high hill. And the soldiers all fight to get to the top of that hill." He quickly built his hill, selected some toy soldiers and placed them in various positions, seemingly climbing up the hill.

"They really do seem to want to get up to the top of that hill, don't they?" I said.

"Oh, yes", Dibs replied. "They really do" . . .

"I'll take more and more soldiers," he said. "I'll let them try to get up that hill – up to the very top of that hill. Because they know what is up there on the very top of the hill if they could only make it to the top. And they do so want to get to the top".

He looked at me. His eyes were shining. "Know what is at the top of that hill?" he asked.

"No. What is?" I asked.

Dibs laughed, knowingly, but kept his own counsel. He inched each soldier up slowly toward the top. But after he had moved all the soldiers a fraction of an inch toward the goal, he sifted more sand on the top of his hill and made it a little higher. He then turned each soldier and slowly, one by one, brought them back down. One by one, he marched them into the little metal house, standing in the sandbox.

"They were not able to get to the top today," he said. "They all go back into their house. They turn and wave. Sadly, they wave. They had wanted to get to the top of that hill. But no one of them could do it today".

"And they felt sad, did they, because they couldn't do what they so wanted to do?" I commented.

"Yes," Dibs sighed. "They wanted to. And they tried. But they couldn't quite do it. But they did find their mountain. And they did climb it. Up. Up. Up. Quite a way! And for a while they *thought* they would get up to the top. And while they *thought* they could, they were happy."

"Just trying to get to the top made them happy?" I asked.

"Yes," said Dibs. "It's like that with hills . . ."

"Those things seem important to you, do they?" I asked.

"Yes," he answered. "Very important".

He picked up the shovel and quietly and intently dug a deep hole in the sand.'

(pp. 90–1)

Mirroring and the two stages of 'transmuting'

Kohut saw mirroring as part of a two-stage process. Accurate empathy is the first step – knowing what the baby feels. Doing something about whatever is troubling the baby is the second step – but only the second. Except in extreme situations, the first is the more important. The first requirement is not that something be 'done for' the child; the first requirement is to understand and absorb what the child is experiencing and to communicate back some recognition and acceptance of its experience. In short, don't just shovel the spoon in, confirm the child's right to hunger and satisfaction. When that happens in the right way, the child's sense of its self is strengthened. The child then experiences hunger (or whatever), but not to such an extent that it becomes oppressed, humiliatingly dependent, or hurt – certainly not to the explosive extreme extent which would disrupt the emerging organization of self-structures.

In fortunate circumstances, the mother's anticipation of the child's needs, and of the anxiety it would feel if satisfaction is too long delayed, will have brought about what Kohut called 'empathic resonances in the maternal selfobject' (1977: 86). The mother picks up the distressed baby and responds to it while carrying it or holding it, in ways which create conditions likely to make the child feel better. These are, in Kohut's words, 'conditions which are phase-appropriately experienced by the child as a merger with the omnipotent self' (ibid.). The child's rudimentary sense of itself merges with its experience of the caring mother ('the maternal selfobject'), and her 'highly developed psychic organization is transmitted to the child via touch and tone of voice and perhaps by other means' as though this organization were the child's own.

Kohut draws continual parallels between parenting and therapy. There are times when the therapist is the patient's selfobject. Then

'the same principle underlies the analyst's attitude towards his analysands. Every interpretation, in other words, and every reconstruction, consists of two phases: first, the analysand must realise that he has been understood; only as a second step will the analyst demonstrate to the analysand the specific factors that explain the psychological content he had first grasped empathically.'

(1977: 88)

Only then will the 'transmuting internalization' take place – the learning which changes the patient.

Is it two-stage?

Is this a two-stage process? Yes and no. I think it worth just spelling out what I think happens, as it were in slow motion, because it becomes increasingly important in the course of this book. The simple sequence might look like this:

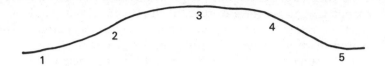

1   A sense of well-being (which is the foundation for a sense of a grand self) is interrupted by

2   some discomfort, and mounting anxiety, which could lead to disruption of the sense of well-being (that is of the foundation for sense of a grand self), and eventually to disintegration and the spread of panic, but which is fortunately followed by

3   empathic merging with the selfobject's mature psychic organization, followed by

4   need-satisfying actions performed by selfobject, followed by

5   calm well-being (which is the foundation for a sense of a grand self).

Or, after some internalization:

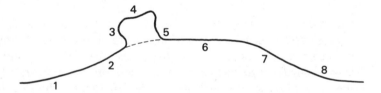

1   A sense of well-being (which is the foundation for a sense of a grand self) is interrupted by

2   some discomfort, and mounting anxiety which could lead to disruption of the sense of well-being (that is of the foundation for a sense of a grand self) and eventually to disintegration but

3   this discomfort acts as a signal anxiety which leads to

4   a phantasy of merging with the selfobject's mature organization, followed by

5 stabilized manageable anxiety (showing that the panic has not spread), which ought to be followed by

6 actual empathic merging with the selfobject's mature psychic organization, followed by

7 need-satisfying actions performed by selfobject, followed by

8 calm well-being (which is the foundation for a sense of a grand self).

In the second instance, there is enough internalization of the good mother ('the selfobject's mature psychic organization') to allow the infant to tolerate a longer interval before something is actually done about its distress, before panic anxiety sets in. This interval provides an opportunity for ego-functioning to develop in a confident, unhurried way.

The development of autonomy and skills

How and why can the infant move, from the blissful sense that it is grand and entitled to everything, to a less arrogant position in which it can and does take some responsibility for its own well-being? Kohut sees this in terms of a gradual process by which it comes slowly to accept that there are limits to its power to keep the universe harmonious with its wishes. (Most other writers seem to concern themselves mainly with the circumstances around less harmonious acceptance, or around the development of guilt at bad feelings towards other people and things.)

We owe to Kohut the concept of the *transmuting internalization* (nine alien syllables). It is the process we have in mind when we say *we have really learnt something* (seven plainer English syllables). What is learnt concerns our place in the world: the infant moves from a state in which something good that felt like a part of 'self' (in a selfobject way) turns out to be 'not self'. If we do not learn this, we can never feel confident that we can work to make good things happen in fact and not just in phantasy. It is only when we recognize a good thing as not (yet) ours, that we can set about making it ours.

Imagine a process in which, for instance, milk and biscuits arrive so soon after the child begins to form an expectation of milk and biscuits, that to the child it appears that they arrived because it thought of them, the mother's prompt reaction having accustomed the child to this. The child is in a selfobject state of mind. Later, on some occasions, the biscuits do not arrive soon enough for the child to believe it has omnipotently created them. It then begins to learn that the arrival of milk and biscuits is not completely under the control of its thoughts. However, it may have come to associate milk and biscuits with hearing someone say 'bikky' and this lays the foundation for shouting 'bikky', whenever it has a wish for milk and biscuits, and *thereby* getting them (*Fig. 39*). The milk and biscuits now arrive not by being

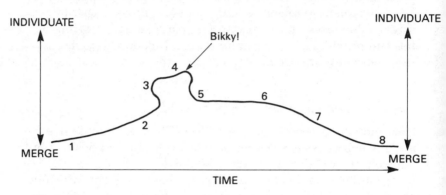

Figure 39

merely thought of. The child has to do something to make them arrive: shout, and they come. The child is learning a skill. Later still, it may learn that they now no longer arrive unfailingly when it shouts, but that it can make its way to the kitchen and find them, or it can ask, 'Please may I have a biscuit'. More skills, more autonomy. We have come a long way. And so the child, and the patient, come to be able to do something for themselves which previously had to be left to parent or therapist. It is like an extended weaning process.

'The mother's responsiveness to the child's needs prevents traumatic delays before the narcissistic equilibrium is established after it has been disturbed, and if the shortcomings of the mother are of tolerable proportions, the infant will gradually modify the original boundlessness and blind confidence of his expectations of absolute perfection. With each of the mother's minor empathic failures, misunderstandings and delays, the infant withdraws narcissistic libido from the archaic imago of unconditional perfection (primary narcissism) and acquires in its stead a particle of inner psychological structure which takes over the mother's functions in the service of the maintenance of narcissistic equilibrium.'

(Kohut 1971: 64)

If all goes well, the acquisition of more autonomy and skill is matched and supported by the natural development of the child's (or the patient's) growing interest in the world of other people and things, in exploration as Bowlby would say, in play as Winnicott would see it. This is a very different process from the enforced instinctual renunciation which Fenichel and the older psycho-analytic theorists put forward as the major cause of self-regulation and the internalization of parental advice. Although most children are probably still subject to a very great deal of instinctual renunciation, it is pleasant to know that there are cheerier developmental possibilities. Interestingly, these possibilities are created by the failure of the mother to mirror the child's needs in every particular. Putting it all in a nutshell, however jargon-ridden:

'It is the experience of this sequence of psychological events via the merger with the empathic omnipotent selfobject that sets up the base-line from which optimum (non-traumatic, phase-appropriate) failures of the selfobject lead, under normal circumstances, to structure-building via transmuting internalisations.'

(Kohut 1977: 87)

These 'optimal failures' come about because of a longer than hitherto normal but still manageable delay before gratification, or because of a misunderstanding of what the infant wanted, so that it did not get what it wanted on that occasion, but still felt generally loved and understood. A comforting thought for fallible parents and psychotherapists.

Of course, if the mother's support is withdrawn too abruptly, we may get the kinds of effects Tustin writes about, and Fairbairn and others. But Kohut stresses that deprivation, though harmful, is nowhere near as damaging as a constant lack of empathy would be.

> 'Even seriously realistic deprivations are not psychologically harmful if the psychological environment responds to the child with a full range of undistorted empathic responses. Man does not live by bread alone.'
>
> (1977: 87)

In due course, the merged state comes to an end, as the mother makes time for her own needs. In this she serves her child better than an obsessively devoted one might do, who might fail to give the child a chance to grow up. There have to be appropriate preconditions for development, in child-growth as in therapy.

> 'What the child needs is neither continuous perfect empathic responses from the selfobject nor unrealistic admiration. What creates the matrix for the development of a healthy self in the child, is the selfobject's capacity to respond with proper mirroring at least some of the time. What is pathogenic is not the occasional failure of the selfobject but his or her chronic incapacity to respond appropriately.
>
> (1977: 187–88)

The discovery of limitations

An empathic selfobject gives the infant tremendous self-esteem. Although new experiences will inevitably change the context, part of the selfobject organization will remain. There will always be a region on the map to signify 'I am grand; I can do anything; I can have what I want' (1971: 107–09).

In the most fortunate circumstances, development consists of a gradual mapping of other experiences of the self and the world, in such a way that there is no damage to the established structure of self-esteem when the child discovers limitations to what it can do and what it can have. It is bound to discover limitations. We are not in fact omnipotent, and mother cannot continue to hide this from us. But the discovery of skills can compensate to a greater or lesser extent:

> 'I am grand, I can do anything, I can spoon porridge into my mouth.'

'I am grand, I can tie my shoe-laces, I can read my John-and-Janet book.'

If all goes well with optimal failures, the sense of self-esteem is rather painlessly embedded in the child's gradual discovery of its limitations. 'I am grand, I can do anything' (the original selfobject omnipotent feeling) becomes intricately connected with other experiences:

'I am grand, I can do this and this, but not that and that.'
'I cannot stop the rain when I want it to stop, but I am grand in other ways.'
'I am grand — and so are Andrew, Brian, and Cathy (that is, other people).'
'I am grand for everyone loves me. Not just Mummy but also Daddy, Annie, Betty, and Charles (that is, other people).'
'Everyone loves me. They also love the new baby, but still, I am grand.'

Eventually we can even bear the thought that not everyone loves us, or that some people may love other people more than they love us!

These later additions and finer structurings of our maps of our selves can be closely organized and integrated with the original 'I am grand' contours. It is these connections which create 'grand' rather than 'grandiose' phantasies. In happy circumstances, 'being grand' (the original sense of omnipotence generated in the selfobject state) becomes inextricably and not very painfully organized with an appreciation of what others can do and be. What others can do and be does not diminish what I can do and be, except if I develop my original omnipotent feelings into the grandiose idea that 'only I am grand, there is no one else'. Similarly my discovery, that there are things I cannot do, need not detract from my positive self-regard except in so far as I am unable to let go of my sense that 'I can do everything'.

However, we all probably get anxious sometimes when the original 'I feel grand' organization gets threatened by too many reservations, qualifications, or invidious comparisons. For meaning depends on context, and when the context changes, my sense that I am grand is modified. I may begin to fear that my feelings will get hurt — 'narcissistic injury'.

The development of autonomy and skills is in the first instance encouraged by feeling grand enough – the natural outcome of good mirroring. If the child feels safe, it will turn to the world round about. If the child does not feel safe, however, it cannot feel free to exercise its curiosity in exploration and play. It will remain more inert and passive. It may then switch from one adult to another, and change its approach, in the hope of finding a better source of self-esteem, rather on the lines of 'I can't make *her* do what I want, but I can try to get closer to *him* and share in the grandeur which surrounds *him*'. Kohut believes that if good mirroring does not engender the sense of being grand, we have a second chance: we can identify with admired figures and feel grand by reason of our association with them. The wholesome development of the latter depends on whether the idealized parental figures were happy to let themselves be idealized without disturbing the child by mockery, competition, or shaming.

Two sources of strength: 'I am grand', 'You are grand'

'I am grand' is one early organization of experience. According to Kohut, there is a second organization, which becomes especially important when the environment has failed to provide sufficient grounds for the phantasy that I am grand. The child may find (or even in large measure create) a grand figure to identify with, which takes notice of the child and allows it to come close and belong to the grandeur which this grand person possesses.

> 'The central mechanisms ("I am perfect", "You are perfect but I am part of you") are the two basic narcissistic configurations employed to preserve a part of the original experience of narcissistic perfection.'
>
> (Kohut 1971: 27)

In this way, Kohut does justice to the idea of the essentially dynamic nature of self-structures. With growing individuation, the child reaches out to others for recognition and confirmation. And it also reaches out to a world which is grand and of which it is a part. The child reaches out to explore and experiment and imitate. 'I've just discovered that the world is full of a million

wonderful things and THIS PERSON can make them happen and
embodies them! Can I come close to that? Can I be like that?' The
phantasy is of being as wonderful and grand as the admired
person. This phantasy can be given much strength and much
hope if the admired person will let the small child share in his or
her wonderful activities. Then, if all goes well, the child will get
something from the activities and from the very self – the
identity – of the admired person. Especially in the matter of
skills. 'You are wonderful and I can be like you. I can hammer
nails like you. I can bake cakes like you. I can tell stories like
you. Someday I will get it just right. The nails will knock in
straight. The cakes will rise. The stories will make people
spellbound. I'm not quite as good as you (yet), but I'm learning
fast. (I've nearly done it now, you finish it off).'

We all need this experience, and not just to remedy any
shortcomings in the mirroring we had. Besides 'I'm grand
because you love me', we need the sense that 'I'm grand because
you love me and this leads to all sorts of interesting things. I can
grow up and do grand things. Because I love you because you
love me and let me grow up and be like you'.

There is so much hope here. But there are also dangers.

'The two chances relate, in gross approximation, to the
establishment of the child's cohesive grandiose-exhibitionistic
self (via his relation to the empathically responding merging/
mirroring/approving object) on the one hand, and to the
establishment of the child's cohesive parent-image (via his
relationship to the empathically responding self-object parent
who permits and indeed enjoys the child's idealisation of him
and merger with him) on the other hand.'

(1977: 185)

Note how naturally Kohut uses the pronoun 'he' when turning
his attention to this idealized parent-figure! It feels as natural to
us as the air we breathe. Mostly the woman is expected to be
around in an unobtrusive way, experienced more as a selfobject
state of mind than as a person, to see to everyone's needs without
making anyone uncomfortably aware that these services are
being performed. She does the mirroring. The man is still
thought of as characteristically the one who lends significance
and splendour to the endeavours of women and children, by his

appreciation, enjoyment, and praise. But it does not have to be the father, though this is so easily taken for granted. It can be the mother. It can be a grandparent. Sometimes it is a teacher.

In connection with this it is interesting to note that in upper-class Britain, according to many autobiographies, either parent or both together could be cast for this idealized role, because the nanny and other servants did what mirroring/confirming was done. 'Vivre? Nos serviteurs le peuvent pour nous.' These autobiographies tell of the wonder of being washed, brushed, and brought to the drawing-room at tea-time, to meet those marvellous grown-ups with whom it was a privilege to spend time, and they recall the magic of being kissed good-night by the fairy-tale apparition of mother in a ball-gown, and of being put on their first pony by father, or given their first gun. I wonder if we may connect this with a propensity for hero-worship and hierarchical leadership-structures?

The two chances compared and related: the 'bipolar self'

'The child has two chances as it moves towards the consolidation of the self, disturbances in the self occurring only to a pathological degree if there is gross failure in both these developmental conditions.'

(1977: 185)

So there are two quite different experiences, both of which will help the child to enjoy the discovery that there are other people in the world.

It can be a great help, to a child whose initial capacity for self-esteem has been damaged, to find a grown-up who will satisfy the longing for there to be a wonderful person somewhere in the world. How many women have accepted this value-by-proxy accommodation as their life-goal? 'If it can't be me that's grand, at least it's you, and I belong to you.' Kernberg would say that the basic role-relationship has been internalized: it matters less whether I or the other is grand, what matters is that there is a relationship in which someone belongs to a grand person and that I am part of that relationship.

Self-esteem injured by imperfections in the first stage can be soothed by the experience of being allowed to be part of something or someone wonderful. Of course, the ability to use this second chance must itself depend on how much well-being and self-esteem the child has already been able to establish. One could not expect an autistic child to be able to use it; it is at an extreme of unready encounter with the world of other people and things. To a lesser extent, rage and envy and the feelings of persecution which go with this, springing from a less extreme but still very distressing encounter with 'the other', must also impair the ability to use the second chance: feeling persecuted by others is not very compatible with finding them wonderful and taking easy uncomplicated pleasure in their company.

However, in more favourable circumstances, the grandiosity and exhibitionism of the archaic grandiose self are tamed by gradually finding their context within more reality-based experiences, while yet 'supplying the fuel' as Kohut put it, 'for our ambitions and purposes, for the enjoyment of activities, and for important aspects of our self-esteem. And under similar favourable circumstances, the idealised parent-image, too, becomes integrated into the adult personality' (1971: 27, 28).

Kohut estimates that the roots of these processes come from very early on. Developments go on into the fourth, fifth, or sixth year, the confirming/mirroring relationship being the earlier to blossom (1977: 179). The more satisfying this early phase, the more outgoing and spontaneous the person, the more confidently impelled by his or her wishes, and the less attracted towards abstract ideals and goals set in the future. But if things have been less satisfactory in the early stages, people may be less in touch with their wishes, and go in for some quite tense grandiosity and exhibitionism: 'look what I can do'. This may nevertheless find a useful place in a personality attracted towards strong ideals and long-term goals.

We can get by on reduced amounts of either of these self-structures; if one of them is missing to some degree, we can get by on the other. People who have been insufficiently mirrored, admired, and confirmed may go in for rather idealized hierarchical leadership-structures and hero-worship. Conversely, people who had lots of confirmation but lacked the opportunity to create and copy admired figures are more liable to sit around like garden gnomes being agreeable and democratic and lovable and cosy − even while Rome burns.

Splitting off one's self-esteem

The original experience of narcissistic perfection is of being merged in what Tustin called the auto-sensuous mother, and Kohut the selfobject state. If something goes wrong at that stage, natural gaps remain where they should not, and we get 'splits'. Tustin's 'encapsulation' and Kernberg's 'unmetabolized (that is unintegrated) pockets' are of this kind. It is in this connection that Kohut developed his concept of a 'vertical split'. A vertical split preserves the sense that 'I am grand' *in isolation* from other experiences, so that we only become conscious of it in particular circumstances. More dangerously, by the same token people are able to keep the sense of their own limitations isolated from other experiences, so that they will behave 'grandly' when they should not, ignoring aspects of the situation which are obvious to the bystander. At other times, in other circumstances, such people will behave in a depressed and lifeless manner, feeling totally worthless, not at all in communication with the sense of 'I am grand', again puzzling the bystander who can see all sorts of pleasant things to enjoy in the situation.

Vertical splits are between self-structures. The sense of self is split. This makes it possible to say that there are two distinct and separate self-structures (among others) − 'I am grand' and 'I am wretched' − with very little communication between them. The development of such a split seems to depend on how empathic and ready the mother was who helped create the self-object, and on the abruptness with which 'self' differentiated out of 'self-object'. If things go badly, there may be what Balint calls a Basic Fault, a drastic break (see Chapter 17). The sense of being 'grand' is then split off from later understanding, and may be evoked unexpectedly and quite unrealistically in some circumstances, while at other times it is equally unrealistically absent.

the grandiose self	*the wretched self*
'I am grand and can do anything'; 'I am the greatest, the only one'.	'I am wretched and no good, I can't do anything well'; 'These others are good, I am not'.

These two organizations may be related in such a way that when one operates, the other is in abeyance. There is the split. It is interesting to wonder how the switch is made from one to the other.

This kind of split is more likely to come about if the infant did not get much self-esteem from its selfobject, so that it has not had sufficient encouragement to feel grand. This can happen in accidental ways, and it can also happen when parents have been too restrictive, punitive, inhibited, tired, or powerless to act as sensitive implementers of their child's needs. In any case, the child may build up a self-image of not being worth bothering about, or worse. From this angle, the grandiose self and the wretched self correspond rather closely to Fairbairn's Libidinal Ego and Anti-Libidinal Ego.

A split of this kind is also more likely when the child discovers too abruptly and unexpectedly the limitations to which it is subject. For instance, if the mother has let herself be used as a selfobject beyond the appropriate time. This is in turn more likely, according to Kohut (and also Khan 1979), if the mother saw the child as an extension of her own self-esteem and her own grandiose phantasies, so that there was a merging beyond the time when this was necessitated by the infant's weakness. Such mothers, and anxious phobic mothers also, obstruct the child's normal development, which would otherwise have taken it beyond a desire to be merged in a selfobject state. Fixation in the selfobject state interferes with the development of identification with an admired figure who *does things*. We then get the kind of person who, smugly or desperately, conveys the impression 'I am wonderful because I am so lovable'. Such children may have a hard time when they must finally be left to their own resources, as on going to school, for instance. They will not have had the opportunity for gradually developing the skills needed for a more independent exercise of their functions. So, as in the case of the autistic child, but of course rather later in development, the child will discover its lack of power. It will discover the extent to which it is defenceless and subject to intrusion, and that will be a terrible blow. Just going off to infant-school for the morning can be a terrible experience for children who are not yet psychologically individuated.

'Vertical splits' and 'horizontal lids'

Kohut differentiated between vertical and horizontal splits (1977: 185ff.). It may be both helpful and amusing to call them 'splits' and 'lids' respectively for a few pages.

Splits are due to inadequate recognition and confirmation: inadequate mirroring. They are due to things going wrong in the development of appropriate integrations and individuations: the infant has not been appreciated in the right way for what it is and what it can become. Its grand and its wretched self are isolated from one another.

Repression is different. It 'puts the lid on' certain experiences and feelings. Repression creates a 'horizontal split'. This is a later development, when a more realistic self is beginning to be formed. Neither wretched nor grandiose self are very realistic: elements of both will be integrated in more realistic self-structures when development goes as it should. With a more realistic self, the child becomes able to take pride and pleasure in what it is and what it can do. Kohut calls this 'the child's natural self-assertion', in contrast to the unrealistic grandiosity attributable to unresolved selfobject merging. When the lid is put on the child's sense of being grand, when its natural excitement and self-assertion are met with disapproval, the child feels bad, and in some circumstances it may become anxious whenever it thinks of doing anything unbidden that might be fun or feel good (1977: 120ff.). This is a repressed, guilty child.

In some strata of British life, and probably elsewhere, people are shamed as a matter of routine at the very moments when they feel they have done something good or done something well – jokingly, of course, so that the ill-will can be disowned. There appears to be a determination that no one shall feel 'bigheaded' or forget for a moment that 'if there is laughter in the morning, there will be tears before bedtime'. Even the very possibility of someone achieving something has to be counteracted by 'taking them down a peg or two'. No wonder that children brought up in this atmosphere avoid being noticed as far as they can, and are quietly angry: 'sullen'.

Whereas splitting has to do with defects in mirroring, repression has more to do with identification with admired figures, and especially with the idealization of rather ungiving and unforgiving figures – the dour, the jealous, the exhausted. Such people can confirm the fears and phantasies of weakness and inadequacy which the child has necessarily accumulated already. Watch Daddy put the lid on:

'Can I bash this nail, Daddy?'
'No, son, not until your arm is strong enough and your sense of aim is developed and you have some understanding of mechanical principles. And moreover you must learn not just to copy me but to develop a sense of individual handiness and leadership. And you must be able to identify what is needed in the situation, such as going over there out of my sight and scrubbing the floor.'
'Oh. I am going to have to be pretty clever before I can bash nails. I was very presumptuous to think I could be as grand as that. I am going to have to become very good indeed, not like I am now. I shall never be able to do all that. I am not as good as Daddy.'

The ideal has been made too big, too general, and too future-centred. Good ideal figures are giving and forgiving. Then (1) you get to bash the nails and (2) you get a little bit of confirmation too. You bash your thumb, but they don't do what mum does, which is to bandage it. They look round slowly and grin, and pause, and then in tones of strictest confidence they say, 'Did that myself last week. Hurts, doesn't it.'

Skills, ego-functioning, and self-esteem

Kohut is at home with the idea that a person may have a number of selves rather than one Self. He at times identifies three self-structures which he thinks of as 'major constituents of the nuclear self', the two contrasting ones – the grandiose self and the ideal-parent self – and a third which I think epitomizes an active non-repressive giving and forgiving ideal (m)other who does things. This third self-structure comprises the ego-functions and all the talents and skills which give self-esteem. Thus Kohut writes in his discussion of Mr X:

'The damage done to his nuclear self was widespread. It affected all three of the major constituents of this structure, namely, the two polar areas – the grandiose-exhibitionistic self and the idealised-parent image – and the intermediate area – the executive functions (talents, skills) needed for the realisation of the patterns of the basic ambitions and basic ideals that were laid down in the polar areas.'

(1977: 49)

Seeing ego-functions as special self-regions makes sense. In terms of the map-metaphor, ego-functions certainly have a place in our imagery of our selves in the world, and they certainly contribute to the sense of self. They can in principle be isolated from other sub-regions, much as Fairbairn's 'Central Ego' is isolated. Kohut is particularly interesting about this in connection with work-problems. He believes that a strong sense of self-esteem brings not only a sense of well-being, but also generally improved functioning. As, through the right therapeutic approach, patients feel better about themselves, their capacity for work improves. Conversely, many of the most severe work-disturbances are, in Kohut's experience, due to a decline in self-esteem and subsequent fear of fragmentation. People will often attempt to counteract painful feelings of unreality or fragment-ation by forcing themselves into activities, ranging from the physical (in sport or sex) to overwork. Their work (or their sex or their sport) is made the isolated activity of an isolated self-structure, a pocket lacking pleasant associated connections. Such people engage in their activities in an 'automatic' way, passively, without pleasure or initiative, simply responding to cues or demands. Kohut reports that if things go well in therapy, patients will one day report that their work has changed, that they are now enjoying it, that they now have the choice of whether to work or not, that they now undertake it on their own initiative rather than by passive obedience. Last but not least, they find that their approach has now some originality rather than being humdrum and routine. Kohut quotes Hartmann (1939, 1947): 'a living self in depth has become the organising centre of the ego's activities' (1971: 120).

Compensatory and defensive developments

Kohut's approach to psychotherapy has a relatively hopeful air. Though the damage done in early days cannot be undone or erased as if it had never been, Kohut envisages other good things which can happen instead. He allows for later chances. If a child starts with little self-respect because of too unempathic an early environment, a later sense of worth can be achieved through attachment to an admired and powerful figure with executive skills, who can be copied. Whether there is this second chance or not, the child can still develop what Kohut calls compensatory structures. Tasks which we set ourselves, and to which we feel committed, can play an important role in giving meaning and validity to what might otherwise be a rather more fragile personality-structure (see the last pages of Chapter 19). A skill is a good example of a compensatory structure. I may not be lovable or interesting to people, but I know that I can run faster than anyone in my town, or come first in exams, or make up fine stories, or impress others with my sexuality.

Kohut draws a contrast between compensatory developments which add to self-respect by achievements which are generally respected, and other more defensive manoeuvres which can do no more than serve to hide the pain suffered through lack of self-respect: unrealistic values, hostile phantasies, perversions. Clearly this is a tricky area in which to make pronouncements, since it depends so much on what is admired in the culture. To make yourself the most outstanding competitor would normally be seen as compensatory in our culture, but it might be seen as a defensive perverted individualism in a more collectively minded culture. Kohut is careful to say that he is not presenting a contrast but a broad spectrum, with rather more compensatory developments at one end, and rather more defensive developments at the other, and a good deal of overlap in the middle (1977: 4). In the pages which follow, we shall see that developments which other writers have called 'False Self' bear a marked resemblance to Kohut's compensatory and defensive structures.

·12·
The joy of being

Winnicott had for years been paediatrician at St Mary's Hospital in Paddington, and had met hundreds of mothers and babies there before he even trained as an analyst. His thoughts on the psychological development of the tiny infant thus arise from two sources: from the infant brought him by the mother, and from the infant in us all brought him by his patients.

> 'My experiences have led me to recognise that dependent or deeply regressed patients can teach the analyst more about early infancy than can be learned from direct observation of infants, and more than can be learned from contact with mothers who are involved with infants. At the same time, the clinical contact with the normal and abnormal experiences of the infant–mother relationship influences the analyst's theory, since what happens in the transference (in certain regressed phases) is a form of infant–mother relationship.'
>
> (1960: 141)

In my view, Winnicott's understanding of the child (in us all) is unparalleled in its depth and variety. But partly as a side-effect of these qualities, he presents us with some new problems. For one thing, he makes it so clear what is good for the baby's future well-being. The burden he thereby places on us feels at times almost unbearable. He himself partly gets round it by writing of the 'good enough' (that is the not necessarily perfect) mother,

228

and by writing as though practically all of us were good enough. This is reassuring. Yet he has opened our eyes to some dreadful things that can happen to children in their earliest months. We now know so much more about what is good and bad for them, and about how hard it is for parents to be good enough. We know we fail at times to be good enough. Also, our knowedge is a burden in another way: how may we be of use to other ignorant and distraught parents in their distress? The facts seem too overwhelming to tackle. (See for instance, Bowlby 1973: Chapter 20, 'Omission, suppression and falsification of family context'; also Chapters 15 and 16.)

Another worry springs from changes in the climate of opinion since Winnicott's day. In the writing of that period, the baby was always 'he', and he was always looked after by his mother who was supported by her husband, his father. In various ways I have tried to represent Winnicott fairly and yet write in such a way as to minimize the pressure these assumptions exert on single parents, on parents who wish to share the work of parenting, and on households in which people bring up children for whom they were not biologically responsible.

Thirdly, to the annoyance of, for instance, Greenberg and Mitchell (1984), and probably others, Winnicott does not write precisely but impressionistically. When it suits his purpose, he uses the same word to mean different things in different contexts, or different words to mean the same thing. For our purposes, it is especially trying that in the tradition of English pragmatism, he uses such words as *self* and *ego* as though they were self-explanatory. On many pages, he has both ego-functions and self-structures in mind. His great follower, Guntrip, coming from a very different academic tradition, has attempted to clarify some of the difficulties this presents (in *Psychoanalytic Theory, Therapy and the Self*, 1971).

Lastly, I should confess that I have sometimes paraphrased some of the more difficult passages quoted, in order to make them clearer to myself and perhaps to other readers.

Being and the sense of self

Winnicott seems to me to have had a special gift for understanding the baby's point of view, even at a time when, from the baby's point of view (and often, according to Winnicott, from the mother's point of view as well), there is one entity only, formed by mother and baby, not yet separated out. 'There is no such thing as a baby', he is often quoted as saying, meaning that 'if you set out to describe a baby, you will find that you are describing a *baby and someone*. A baby cannot exist alone, but is essentially part of a relationship' (1964: 88). That is where his account of development begins.

> 'However complex the psychology of the sense of self and of the establishment of an identity eventually becomes as the baby grows, no sense of self emerges except on the basis of this relating in the sense of BEING. This sense of being is something that antedates the idea of being-at-one with, because there has not yet been anything except identity. Two separate people can *feel* at one, but here at the place that I am examining, the baby and the object *are* one.'
>
> (1974[1971]: 94)

Winnicott was writing here about something very like Kohut's selfobject. But it is a less busy phase of that state of mind. The selfobject is active in understanding and doing, in procuring safety and sustenance; Winnicott's 'being' is 'resting-in-being'. Poets, lovers, and mystics know that state of perfect harmony, complete oneness, total surrender of individuality, in which there is no call to do anything. Freud wrote of it as an 'oceanic feeling'. Balint knew it as a 'harmonious interpenetrating mixup'.

When two people feel at one with each other, this sense of bliss may have its roots in memories of an early state when, as babies, we *were* at rest and at one with the mother. The longer, the deeper, the better this early experience, the more favourable the conditions for the establishment of a secure and resilient sense of self later. In terms of the language of our early chapters, in fortunate circumstances the very earliest homunculus-based self-structures are associated with memory-traces of perfect satisfaction and bliss. How many good associations there are will depend on how well the baby's needs were recognized and attended to. Good associations create the sense of being, of being-at-one, and of well-being – all connected and preserved together with having one's needs taken care of. (It will be remembered that Kohut also insisted that being understood and recognized is as important as being taken care of – see pp. 210–11.)

Being and doing

The blissful state of being is a state of perfect well-being in which we are not called upon to make an effort. Many of us cannot help feeling that having to be 'doing' is a second best state, for instance when the alarm clock rings on a cold, gloomy morning. Winnicott argues that doing is what the infant feels forced to engage in when something has disrupted its blissful state of being. Doing means work, a task, autonomy, responsibility, the exertion of effort and skill. For Winnicott, the sense of being is primary, the sense of doing an outgrowth of it. The satisfactions of doing something and the satisfactions which come from achievement are for him, perhaps only by a small margin, second best – substitute-satisfactions for not being perfectly at rest and at one any more. (There is a resonance here with Kohut's and Balint's interest in the development of skills to provide safety for the vulnerable self.)

Winnicott links the two experiences, of doing and of being, with male and female elements in the human psyche. He does not always write of this in a way everyone is quite happy with. However, he might not have quarrelled with a formulation which I prefer: that for a variety of reasons people tend to associate doing and activity with masculinity, while passivity and restful being tends to be expected of women. The social sciences are now beginning to explore the extent to which these associations have been used to enforce conformity on men and women. There is a circular argument by which such associations are used as social pressures to guide boys and girls into behaviour which is insisted on as natural to their sex. Winnicott does not fall into this trap, but he does associate the sense of being with 'a female element in the personality both of men and of women', and the need to be doing with 'a male element' (1974[1971]: 95).

The experience of being is about union, continuity, and caring between people; the experience of doing is about individuality, drives, excitement, assertion. Boldly, Winnicott uses the example of the baby at the breast to mark the contrast between the active process of instinctual drive-satisfaction and the quiet state of being at rest, at one. The satisfactions of sucking and being fed, Winnicott allots to the male element in us all. But something else is also going on.

> 'Object-relating backed by instinct drive belongs to the male element. . . . I have arrived at a position in which I say that object-relating in terms of this pure female element has nothing to do with drive or instinct. The mother either gives the infant the opportunity to feel that the breast is the infant, or else not. The breast here is a symbol not of doing but of being. . . .
>
> At the risk of being repetitious I wish to restate: when the girl-element in the boy or girl baby or patient finds the breast, it is the self that has been found. If the question be asked, what does the baby do with the breast? – the answer must be that this girl element *is* the breast and shares qualities of breast and mother and is desirable.
>
> In the course of time, desirable means edible and this means that the infant is in danger because of being desirable, or, in more sophisticated language, exciting. Exciting implies: liable to make someone's male element *do* something.'
>
> (1974[1971]: 95)

As I pursue Winnicott's ideas on being and doing, I am struck by the number of times I find a sidelight on other writers. A sidelight on Kohut's two chances:

> 'Clinically one needs to deal with the case of the baby who has to make do with an identity with a breast that is active, which is a male-element breast, but which is not satisfactory for the initial identity, which needs a breast that *is*, not a breast that *does*. Instead of "being like" this baby has to "do like".'
>
> (p. 96)

A sidelight on Melanie Klein's theory of envy:

> 'The mother who is able to do this very subtle thing . . . does not produce a child whose "pure female" self is envious of the breast, since for this child the breast is the self and the self is the breast. Envy is a term that might become applicable in the experience of a tantalising failure of the breast as something that *is*.'
>
> (p. 96)

On Fairbairn's contrast between drive-satisfaction and personal relating:

'The object-relating of the male element to the object presupposes separateness. As soon as there is the ego-organisation available, the baby allows the object the quality of being not-me or separate. . . . Drive satisfaction enhances the separation of the object from the baby, and leads to objectification of the object. Henceforth, on the male-element side, identification needs to be based on complex mental mechanisms, mental mechanisms that must be given time to appear, to develop, and to become established as part of the new baby's equipment. . . .

Psychoanalysts have perhaps given special attention to this male element or drive-aspect of object-relating, and yet have neglected the subject-object identity to which I am drawing attention here, which is at the basis of the capacity to be. The male element *does*, while the female element (in males and females) *is*.'

(pp. 94–5)

On Guntrip's description of schizoid lack of vitality:

'It seems that frustration belongs to satisfaction-seeking. To the experience of being belongs something else, not frustration, but maiming.'

(p. 95)

How (m)others help infants develop a True Self

For Winnicott, the child's sense of self evolves slowly from a period in which there is no such thing. He thought of the mother as performing functions for the child which the child would later perform for itself. This is one sense in which, from the child's point of view, there is no differentiation between itself and the mother. Like Kohut, Winnicott imagined the mother providing for and protecting the child, so that no harsh experiences can reach it from anywhere. The mother is a 'facilitating environment'; she sees to it that there is no impingement. In keeping with this view, Winnicott also imagined that the child does not necessarily recognize its own needs as its own. 'In the area that I am examining, the instincts are not yet clearly internal to the infant. The instincts can be as much external as can a clap of thunder' (1965[1960]: 141). There is a time when the sense of self and its ego-functions are as yet only in process of building up strength; they may not yet have reached the stage in which bodily needs and reactions are felt to be part of the self, and so they may be felt as alien and intrusive. What a difference this would make to an experience of colic – or teething!

In Winnicott's view, it is essential for the best kind of well-being and mental health, that there be a period in the infant's earliest life when it feels 'grand' – magnificently omnipotent and in control. Winnicott here clearly had the same feelings in mind as Kohut when the latter wrote about grandiosity. But whereas Kohut often took his examples from the toddler's 'showing off' stage, Winnicott took his from the earlier pre-differentiated selfobject stage of resting in the mother. No doubt the roots of the toddler's grandiosity come from this earlier experience.

A facilitating environment is the pre-condition for the safe development of what Winnicott called a 'True Self'.

> 'The True Self appears as soon as there is any mental organisation of the individual at all, and it means little more than the summary of sensori-motor aliveness.'
>
> (1965[1960]: 149)

> At this stage, the infant is most of the time unintegrated and never fully integrated; cohesion of the various sensori-motor elements belongs to the fact that the mother holds the infant, sometimes physically, and all the time figuratively.'
>
> (p. 145)

The True Self is firmly associated with all things bodily, including the *homunculus* core of the self, where all perceptions, all movements, all reactions are mapped.

The fortunate infant develops self-structures whose core is homunculus-based. The me-to-whom-things-happen and the I-who-do-things are homunculus-based. Winnicott calls this fortunate state 'indwelling': I dwell in my body and my body is very much 'me' – I have the sense that my body and mind are integrated, and not isolated each from the other (Winnicott 1965[1962]: 68; also Davis and Wallbridge 1981).

If there has been no more than 'optimal frustration' (enough for the infant to begin to feel an individual but not enough to cause the misery of loneliness), then the infant's experiences of want-leading-to-satisfaction will establish associations of goodness as part of the general integration of a me-to-whom-good-things-happen and an I-who-makes-good-things-happen. The self-structures have a lot of self-satisfied associations for this baby. The more good associations, the happier the sense of indwelling. Strong links with very good early associations leave people with an inextinguishable fund of optimism and well-being.

Even when the infant's early experiences are not very happy, the structural characteristic which Winnicott calls indwelling is in itself a blessing. For it is from these earliest body-based experiences that what Winnicott calls the True Self grows. This natural development is very different from the intentional fabrication of a False Self, which has no strong links with the homunculi, leaving the person with a much weaker foundation for the development of a genuine sense of self. A False Self is weaker, in the sense that we cannot gain strength from it when life is difficult, because it is not linked to any blissful memories of well-being when we were at rest, nor can it bring us spontaneous joy and inspiration when life is easy.

The self quickly develops complexity as structures become established, and in due course becomes a complex set of coherent interconnecting structures, appropriately mapped. If there has not been a traumatically disruptive event – what Winnicott calls an impingement – each stimulus from the environment finds its place in the inner world of the infant without having had to be somehow encapsulated in an autistic way, or otherwise defended against. The success of such developments would depend on the constitution of the infant and on the capacity of the parental figures to react so appropriately to the infant's signals as to avoid breaks in continuity.

In so far as the (m)other is able to interpret correctly the little signs of the infant's impending needs (for food, warmth, stimulus, or whatever) and brings about the satisfaction of each need before frustration has had time to build up too far, the infant has the sense that anything it wants to happen does happen. There is then a clear unbroken chain of events from the first arising of a need to its satisfaction. The True Self is then composed of all that ever happened to the baby from the beginning, with no hindrance to appropriate integration, and with no splits except where they should be. The early sense of security and omnipotence is then retained as central to the infant's personality – the quality which Erikson (1950) called 'trust'.

The (m)other's prompt satisfaction of the infant's needs caters to its sense of well-being in two other ways as well. To have a hunger which is satisfied after I have experienced it, but before I find it painful, validates the rightness of my hunger, making it a good experience to have and not a bad one. This constrasts both with the experience of having been painfully hungry for too long, and with the experience of eating at intervals which have nothing to do with whether I am hungry.

Secondly, if a baby gets what it needs when it needs it, it feels grand: it feels itself to be a grand baby. (The factual difference between I-feel-grand and I-am-grand requires a more sophisticated distinction than the baby has as yet made.) (M)others who are prompt to bring the baby what it needs confirm the baby's sense of well-being and goodness. Kohut and Winnicott (among others) give this promptness and accuracy the name of 'mirroring', to emphasize the symmetry between the baby's phantasy image of what it needs and the (m)other's caring supply of what it needs, but I will often call it confirming (the baby's sense of rightness). When the baby coos, (m)others welcome it; when it cries to express a need, they satisfy it in a confirming kind of way – the baby develops a sense that anything it does is welcome and wonderful. This is what we do when we stand around a new baby and say: 'Look, isn't it lovely, it's got little toes, and oh look, its eyes are open.' The baby feels grand although it has not done anything except have toes!

Mirroring the infant's self-image, and confirming its self-esteem

Kohut and Winnicott bring slightly different perspectives to the process of mirroring. For Kohut, empathic mirroring confirms the infant's self-esteem in terms of its skill, power, and competence to survive. For Winnicott, it confirms the infant's self-esteem whatever it happens to be doing, whatever its needs and responses. Doing versus being, again.

'What do babies see when they look at the mother's face? I am suggesting that, ordinarily, what they see is themselves. In other words, the mother is looking at the baby and *what she looks like is related to what she sees there*. All this is too easily taken for granted. I am asking that this which is naturally done well by mothers who are caring for their babies shall not be taken for granted. I can make my point by going straight over to the case of the baby whose mother reflects her own mood or worse still, the rigidity of her own defences. In such a case what does the baby see?'

(1974[1971]: 130)

In happy circumstances, the baby sees its own charm, worth, and lovability when it looks into the (m)other's face. The first definitions of the self are influenced on the one hand by the internal climate and, on the other, by what you discover about yourself from the mirror of the other. All this is very relevant to the process of psychotherapy, in which people discover parts of themselves which had hitherto been hidden. This uncovering makes people feel unsure and vulnerable. They are not as they thought they were. How will other people react now? Can they accept their new discoveries? The recognition and acceptance found in other people's eyes (in some circumstances the psychotherapist's) may make all the difference between renewed defensiveness and a change for the better.

For Winnicott, when (m)others are sensitive and loving, the infant is able to experience a smooth sequence from feeling-a-need to having-that-need-met. This smooth sequence makes for integration in at least three ways. It welds the arousal of the infant's needs strongly to the satisfaction of those needs; it also welds satisfaction to a self-image in which needs are valid and good; and it also welds satisfaction to an idea of the world as a-place-where-needs-are-met. So the satisfaction of experienced needs contributes to the infant's expanding imagery of itself and of the world. This is a very different focus from Fairbairn's and Kernberg's: they believed the infant's earliest imagery to be of 'bad objects', that is of unsatisfied needs, of a world which does not satisfy needs, and perhaps, of their own unsatisfactoriness in having needs which are not met.

For both Winnicott and Kohut, good mothering makes the

move from a merged selfobject existence to an individuated existence a gradual and gratifying process. The (m)other does the things that need doing if the infant is to have a sense of well-being. While the infant has not yet individuated, it experiences itself as doing all these things which need doing. Gradually it does in fact take over from the (m)other and begins to look after itself in certain respects. The child who has been fortunate in its parents is supported by the confidence (1) that it can do the things which it-and-the-mother did while they were at one, and (2) that the environment is benevolent and not frustrating or hostile. Such a child's self-imagery is replete with confident self-congratulatory feelings, such as some socially successful parents' children have who – although they themselves have not yet achieved anything – nevertheless feel that they are somehow more meritorious than the children of parents who are less well off.

At a later stage, good parenting brings about not only the infant's experience that it can cope, but also the experience that it can cope with occasional times when it either is not getting the gratification it is looking for, or is not getting it straight away or not so well. If things have gone well, the child can absorb a certain amount of strain of this kind and can put up with the discovery that the world is sometimes less than entirely beneficent. The 'right' amount of anxiety has been generated for the child to develop its own powers. Not too little, not too much, but just right: 'optimal' frustration.

The development of a 'False Self'

In general, Winnicott had great faith that parents are good enough to meet the infant's needs in the way most likely to promote the development of a secure and spontaneous personality. However, in the chapter on ego-distortion (1965[1960]) he allowed himself some thoughts on the effects of having parents whose reactions are not adequate for this purpose. With an insufficiently facilitating environment there may be fatal breaks in the sequence of connecting processes which link the infant's earliest and most physical experiences of needs and their satisfaction – at the very core of the self – to its later experiences of the world of other people and things.

Where, for whatever reasons, the environment is less facilitating, there is not so smooth a sequence of connections and so these integrating links are less strong, or absent. The infant may even come to associate its needs with distress and inadequacy, and not with satisfaction and well-being. In such circumstances – which we already encountered in our discussion of Fairbairn's contribution – the infant may feel compelled to shift away from an interest in its own needs to an interest in the (m)other, before it is developmentally ready to do so.

Fairbairn, among others, focused mainly on what happens when pain and distress have regularly been associated with aroused but frustrated needs. Winnicott, among others, focused mainly on what happens when the infant's needs are satisfied but not satisfied in relation to the time when they were being aroused. The child then misses out on the idea that *when* it experiences a need, *then* is the time to satisfy it. The link is missing. The infant has gratifications but does not connect them with the needs it has experienced. Similarly, the infant at times has deprivations, and these are not connected with their source either.

When the link is missing, even if there are no other ill effects, there is no 'cathexis' to the arousal of needs: a person will not experience the arousal of a need as a pleasurable or desirable experience, since satisfaction has never become directly associated with excitement or arousal. At worst, the deprivation may be so intense that the whole biologically-based personality is dissociated, the whole conscious personality may break away from the experience of arousal and interest. This kind of breakaway split is what interested Fairbairn and Guntrip, among others, and must be what Balint called a Basic Fault (or, at least, one kind of Basic Fault). The infant's needs, biologically associated with the earliest mapping and the original homunculus, become a matter of emotional indifference or even, in severe cases, the cause of panic fear because they are experienced as dangerous intrusions.

Meanwhile, emotional attachments do develop. Through these, arousal and interest come to be connected, not with the needs the infant experiences, but with the perceived or imagined needs of those who bring the infant its gratifications – at times which are connected not to the infant's biological clock but to the (m)other's ideas. The (m)other must therefore be watched and taken notice of. Attachments made on this basis will be strong but anxious: insecurity is built in.

An anxious infant has to stop 'being', in order to deal with distress and in order to deal with the needs of the (m)other from whom help is needed. Unlike the more relaxed infant, who will eventually start an interest in the (m)other because it begins to explore the interesting environment at the biologically appropriate developmental stage, the more needy and distressed infant will begin to be interested in the environment for what it can get out of it. This infant needs to start *doing* things. The premature shift from being to doing may mark another point of development at which Balint would locate a Basic Fault. For the infant is at the developmental stage at which it needs to feel in tune with the world. It needs to feel confirmed as a secure, interesting, and interested self, in a secure relationship with the interested and interesting world of others. But the need to survive may make it fearful about the world, and interested mainly in seeing where distress and the alleviation of distress may come from. The question ceases to be 'Who am I?' 'Who are we?' 'Who are you?', and becomes 'What are you good for?', 'How do I have to behave to get what I need from you?' The environment becomes something to be exploited. The self and the other stand over against each other, and the primary relationship is not unified but exploitative.

What does such a child see when it looks into the face of the mother?

'Of course nothing can be said about the single occasions on which a mother could not respond. Many babies, however, have to have a long experience of not getting back what they are giving. They look and they do not see themselves. There are consequences. First, their own creative capacity begins to atrophy, and in some way or other they look around for other ways of getting something of themselves back from the environment. . . . Second, the baby gets settled in to the idea that when he or she looks, what is seen is the mother's face. The mother's face is not then a mirror. So perception takes the place of what might have been the beginning of a significant exchange, a two-way process in which self-enrichment alternates with the discovery of meaning in the world of seen things.

Naturally, there are half-way stages in this scheme of things. Some babies do not quite give up hope and they study the object and do all that is possible to see in the object some meaning that ought to be there if only it could be felt. Some babies, tantalized by this type of relative maternal failure, study the variable maternal visage in an attempt to predict mother's mood, just exactly as we all study the weather.'

(1974[1971]: 130–31)

The types of skills which an anxious child develops are characteristic of its situation. Children with a sense of security and competence, and an interest in the world of challenging unyielding things, are likely to look for new things and enjoy the challenge. Children with a more insecurely-based self will feel more dependent on others, unsure whether they will be given good things and unsure whether they are allowed to get good things for themselves; they will therefore have less practice in developing the skills which lead to control over the environment in any direct way. The skills they develop are more likely to be in the area of getting others to comfort or approve or achieve for them. They may be a good deal more perceptive than their more secure friends, their sensitivity to others developing from the time when voice and body-language might yield clues on what others were good for and how they could be got to be kind, pleased, not offended. Other people's expectations can become of overriding importance, overlaying or contradicting the original sense of self, the one connected to the very roots of one's being, the *homunculi* and the very earliest memory-traces. This second development, a kind of compensatory structure, is what Winnicott calls the False Self.

Warning: It may be that, in the interests of clear presentation, Winnicott sometimes distinguished too starkly between True-Self and False-Self structures. Or the occasionally jarring starkness may be due to his overestimation of the integrity of the normal self. In fact, all of us have a collection of overlapping selves or 'roles', some of us more so, some of us less. Some of these selves are 'falser' than others: more strongly linked with being acceptable, less strongly linked with our deeper feelings.

One of my friends has 'George', a robot bit of her very nice personality, whom she switches on at formal do's and occasions when genuineness and spontaneity are very much not called for! It makes it pleasant for the rest of us to have her around, false self or no.

In any case, the False Self is not a structure that should be unthinkingly denigrated. All of us need protective defences and devices against hurt. Winnicott had the rights of it when he described some developments of the self as primarily defensive, deriving from the need to carry on even when life no longer feels like a continuous stream of satisfying (or at least manageable) experiences. And he gave due respect to False-Self structures when he wrote of them as performing a caring and care-taking role, even capable of bringing a person to psychotherapy!

> 'In the analysis of a False Personality the fact must be recognised that the analyst can only talk to the False Self of the patient about the patient's True Self. It is as if a nurse brings a child, and at first the analyst discusses the child's problem, and the child is not directly contacted. Analysis does not start until the nurse has left the child with the analyst, and the child has become able to remain with the analyst and has started to play.'
>
> (1965[1960]: 151)

Premature ego-functioning

Premature development of the ego-functions (conceptualizing, and all the cognitive skills one needs to size up others and guide one's actions for survival in an indifferent world) seems very close to what Winnicott thinks of as a False Self. 'Being' needs no skill – all you need is someone to look after you; it is 'doing' that requires skills. If the ego-functions develop without strong links to the original sense of oneness and trust, they are part of a False-Self structure, very like Fairbairn's Central Ego – managerial but unfeeling.

The development of self-imagery, of object-imagery, remembering, connecting, comparing, planning, evaluating, and so on, proceeds at its own pace if there is no premature worry about survival (Guntrip 1971: Chapter 5). It is only in the context of

THE JOY OF BEING 243

safety — Bowlby would call it a context of secure attachment — that normal curiosity and play and exploration can proceed. It will be remembered that Bowlby maintained that, in the course of normal development, purposive behaviour and the search for gratifying experiences naturally supersede the infant's insistence on being close to the mother, except when insecurity has led to clinging over-dependence (Bowlby 1973: Part 3). Normal healthy development, in Bowlby's view, starts with a strong biologically determined attachment to a mothering figure, while exploration of the environment comes naturally at a later stage, exactly because the growing young thing feels secure and safe, not terrified, starving, or desperate (Bowlby 1969: *passim*).

I prefer this point of view to the more orthodox psycho-analytic one held by Winnicott and others, that the ego-functions develop *only* as a result of insecurity and anxiety.

Lack of secure attachment forces the immature organism into action, but the action is accompanied by terror and stereotyping. Real understanding is lacking when the infant has had no opportunity for a leisurely and secure playful exploratory phase, during which it has a chance to familiarize itself gradually with the fascinating world of other people and things. Mental representations of the self-in-the-world will have had to form *prematurely* for the sake of avoiding distress; because of this, a lot of enriching connections which might otherwise have been linked to these representations, will be missing. If the baby has been too worried to linger and enjoy, the adult will think, 'Never mind the sunset, let's get home before something goes wrong.'

> 'We find either that individuals live creatively and feel that life is worth living, or else that they cannot live creatively and are doubtful about the value of living. This variable in human beings is directly related to the quality and quantity of environmental provision at the beginning of each baby's living experience.'
>
> (1974[1971]: 83)

Some unfortunate people have almost no complex ego-functioning, they just react. As soon as a need appears or an alarm is signalled, the instant any meaning or pattern begins to emerge, they respond with scarcely a moment of reflection. Premature development of the ego-functions means doing too much, being too little. Premature ego-development is experienced as a continual pressure to respond and react, what Guntrip calls 'a sense of straining'.

Playing

Playing is the opposite of premature ego-development. It enables an integrated self to emerge, equipped with skills and confidence, a self that is happy just being, but also capable of happily doing work in a non-compulsive way.

Non-purposive activity – playing – is a way of being yourself and knowing yourself: it can be a way of discovering who you are by discovering what you are doing. Playing can be letting impulses work themselves out – 'having id-experiences', Winnicott calls it – without organizing them into patterns as purpose or anxiety would make us do. The child discovers what its impulses are by becoming aware of its phantasies or its actions, not by being told that it has them. There is a warning for psychotherapists here, against being too assertive in psychotherapeutic interpretations. Being told what your impulses are, when you have not discovered them for yourself, can lead to compliance and to role-playing the personality you have been told you have; it can lead to a false idea of yourself, to a False Self.

> 'I am concerned with the search for the self and the restatement of the fact that certain conditions are necessary if success is to be achieved in this search. These conditions are associated with what is usually called creativity. It is in playing, and only in playing, that the individual child or adult is able to be creative and to use the whole personality, and it is only in being creative that the individual discovers the self.'
>
> (1974[1971]: 63)

It is clear that by the 'self' Winnicott here means the whole personality, conscious and unconscious, integrated and non-integrated, the whole map as well as the current working model. As far as Winnicott is concerned, 'to use the whole personality' does not call for any 'misapplied rationality': the self is something that can be experienced and apprehended: it cannot be accurately described in words. But then, in Winnicott's philosophy, the self is not for describing but for being; almost, the self is for playing.

A child that is playing happily is exploring what happens in various manageable circumstances — what people and things feel like when it handles them, what it feels like when handling them, what they can do, and what they can be made to do. In play we have freedom to overcome timidity by trial and error, uninhibited by the fear of mistakes. Interest can build up gradually, at our own pace, and we can stop when we want to. There is no impingement, however helpfully it is meant, from the world of others. Others are not wanted just then, however loved they may be at other times.

In the chapter entitled 'The Baby as a Person' (1964), it is a baby's spontaneous play that Winnicott uses to convince his listeners that babies are persons. He describes a little boy ten months old, sitting on his mother's knee in his consulting room, seeing a shiny spoon.

'You may be sure that if he is just an ordinary baby he will notice the attractive object and he will reach for it. As a matter of fact, probably as soon as he has reached for it, he will suddenly be overcome with reserve. It is as if he thought, "I had better think this thing out; I wonder what feelings mother will have on this subject. I had better hold back until I know." So he will turn away from the spoon as if nothing were further from his thoughts. In a few moments, however, he will return to his interest in it, and he will very tentatively put a finger on the spoon. He may perhaps grasp it, and look at mother to see what he can get from her eyes. At this point I will probably have to tell mother what to do, because otherwise she will help too much, or hinder, as the case may be; so I ask her to take as little part in what happens as possible.

He gradually finds from his mother's eyes that this new thing he is doing is not disapproved of and so he catches hold of the spoon more firmly and begins to make it his own. He is still very tense, however, because he is not certain what will happen if he does with this thing what he wants to do so badly. He does not even know for sure what it is that he wants to do.

We guess that in the course of a little while he will discover

246 OUR NEED FOR OTHERS

what he wants to do with it because his mouth begins to get
excited. He is still very quiet and thoughtful but saliva begins
to flow from his mouth. His tongue looks sloppy. His mouth
begins to want the spoon. His gums begin to want to enjoy
biting on it. It is not very long before he has put it in his
mouth. . . .

We can now say that the baby has taken this thing and
made it his own. He has lost all the stillness that belongs to
concentration and wondering, and doubt. Instead he is
confident and very much enriched by the new acquisition.'

(1964: 75)

Playing and ego-relatedness

The True Self starts with a sense of being-at-one both with an
interesting, helpful, friendly world and with whatever impulses,
needs, and wishes may arise.

What are the conditions in which the True Self can survive
and maintain itself? Being securely held by a facilitating
environment is apparently essential. It is noteworthy that
Winnicott did not write of the mother as an 'object' in this
connection: he wrote of a 'matrix' or a 'framework of ego-
relatedness'. Balint may have been thinking of something similar
when he wrote of substances existing before there are objects.
Both had in mind conditions which provide the security and the
freedom to explore, to find, to create, to play.

When parents provide such sure and unobtrusive protection
that the child feels totally secure, the child does not need its
watchful and defensive ego-functions, and they do not develop
prematurely: this gives a longer time for the True Self to
establish itself and ramify.

> 'Behold the Child among his new-born blisses,
> A six years' darling of a pigmy size!
> See, where 'mid work of his own hand he lies,
> Fretted by sallies of his mother's kisses,
> With light upon him from his father's eyes!
> See, at his feet, some little plan or chart,
> Some fragment from his dream of human life,
> Shaped by himself with newly-learned art;

        A wedding or a festival,
        A mourning or a funeral;
            And this hath now his heart
        And unto this he frames his song:
            Then will he fit his tongue
    To dialogues of business, love, or strife;
            But it will not be long
            Ere this be thrown aside
            And with new joy and pride
    The little actor cons another part;
    Filling from time his "humorous stage"
    With all the persons, down to palsied Age,
    That Life brings with her in her equipage;
            As if his whole vocation
            Were endless imitation.'
    (William Wordsworth, from *Intimations of Immortality from*
                    Recollections of Early Childhood)

To relax into non-purposive activity, to be undefended and not
on the watch, that is a very rare state for most of us. It is
sometimes achieved in psychotherapy, and by some children in
infancy and childhood. When a silence falls between people who
feel secure with each other, we have something like it. Winnicott
calls it 'the stuff out of which friendship is made' and goes on to
say in italics that it 'may turn out to be the matrix of
transference'. If we have had no experience of this state, it is
hard to imagine it – or to allow it to happen. Winnicott calls it
ego relatedness, for the e merging self is not conscious of relating
to anyone, but does not feel alone either, and is in fact not un-
related (not without an attachment figure), since someone is
there, though without impinging on the child's awareness. Balint
uses the German word *arglos* to describe this state, another
example of a word for a feeling for which there happens to be no
convincing English equivalent; 'guileless', 'undefended', or
'vulnerable' will have to do. In this state, there is another person
looking after you, but you do not experience this other, except
through knowing that it is safe for you to forget about yourself
and about any dangers which might threaten. Because of
this other, however, nothing can go wrong. Being safely held

makes ego-relatedness possible. Ego-relatedness makes play possible.

Ego-relatedness and being oneself and being alone

A moment's reflection will show that a person's capacity to be alone is very convincing evidence that that person is capable of being separate, individuated, an individual. Winnicott set a yet more stringent test: not whether you can be on your own, but whether you can be in other people's company, and yet be yourself, and feel comfortable and unthreatened. Winnicott considered that the capacity to be alone is based on the experience of being 'alone' in the presence of someone else. This is the experience he called ego-relatedness. In that state 'the ego-immaturity of the infant is naturally balanced by ego-support from the mother' (1965[1958b]: 32). Without sufficient experience of ego-relatedness, the capacity to be alone cannot develop.

Winnicott examines the phrase 'I am alone'. He points out that the concept 'I' implies that there has already been considerable emotional development: it implies the differentiation of 'I' from 'other', 'an internal world and an external one'. The phrase 'I am' shows that the individual has not only shape but also life. In the beginnings of 'I am', the individual is raw, undefended, vulnerable. The individual can achieve the 'I am' stage only because a protective environment exists, created by the mother and other caring adults, though the baby is probably not aware of this. Next comes the phrase 'I am alone',

> 'a development from "I am" which depends on the infant's awareness of the continued existence of a reliable mother whose reliablility makes it possible for the infant to be alone and to enjoy being alone, for a limited period.'
>
> (p. 33)

Ego-relatedness as a state of mind comes, I imagine, after selfobject states of mind have started to develop: ego-relatedness seems to require a little more consciousness that there is something or someone beside yourself. The next development, in which transitional objects are created, probably cannot begin

until after the state of mind in which selfobjects predominate
has declined.

After ego-relatedness, transitional processes

While the infant is still totally dependent on the (m)other,
various phantasies float through its mind. Some have been
conceptualized by Freud as omnipotence phantasies, some by
Kohut as selfobject states, some by Winnicott as ego-relatedness.
They have in common that the infant is not differentiating an
internal world from an external one; in none is the existence of
the (m)other quite recognized. One of Winnicott's greatest
contributions to our understanding is that he noticed and
elucidated another state of mind, just a bit closer to allowing
other people and things a separate and independent existence
than those already mentioned. In this state of mind the infant has
in one sense complete control over the other, but it uses some of
that control to give a phantasied independence to that other.
Winnicott first understood this phenomenon in terms of children
playing with dolls and teddy bears. The naughty disobedient
bear was of special interest. From the point of view of an
observer, the child makes the bear be whatever the child decided
the bear shall be, and what the child makes the bear be is . . .
disobedient. From the child's point of view, that proves that the
bear has an existence independent of the child's wishes: the bear
is not under the child's control but does disobedient things
which the child then reproves. (Of course, bears are also loved,
cuddled, and generally treated companionably.) Winnicott saw
this kind of play as part of the process by which the child, in a
series of easy stages, comes to terms with the 'other' – the part of
the environment which is in fact not under its control.

In his later writings, and generally in more recent literature,
the comfort blanket and the 'sucky' seem to have taken over as
most frequently mentioned things used in this way, bears having
led the way to a better understanding of their function. The
comfort blanket and the 'sucky' appear earlier in the child's life.
They are more noticed now because we have now learnt to
notice these things, all of which give the child some reassurance
that its environment is a benevolent one and can provide what it
needs.

The fortunate child is able to imagine the blanket or the bear as sufficiently 'not self' to allow this 'other' occasionally to take over the ego-relating functions which the mother's arms, presence, voice, and actions had been providing. And yet the other is not so 'other' that it is not always immediately available to the child. The child can thus ensure that it never feels alone, powerless, or abandoned.

The bear experienced as having a will of its own, the blanket experienced as able to give reassurance, and other such, were called 'transitional objects' by Winnicott.

> 'The object represents the child's transition from a state of being merged with the mother to a state of being in relation to the mother as something separate.'

(1974[1971]: 17)

We are now able to recognize a whole range of transitional processes. They can be arranged on a dimension which has, at one end, experiences in which there is a great deal of merging with the (m)other, for instance where the thumb which is being sucked is experienced in terms of the mother's nipple. When the child has to some extent e-merged, it has experiences with bears and other toys on whom it can exercise its curiosity about what can happen when small persons have a will of their own. Such transitional experiences help the child develop. They allow it to experiment and come to terms, by easy stages, with some unpleasant facts when it is developmentally ready to accept them: that it is not in total control of the world but does have some control; that a relationship has two ends to it – self and other; that both ends of the relationship can be practised in play so as to get a better grasp of their nature; and that self-assertion is not too dangerous – the bear can be naughty.

I have often wondered about the place of pet animals in people's lives. It seems to me that pet animals are for many people another step in the progressive differentiation of self from other.

There is a range:

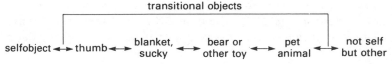

Idealized grown-ups also belong on this dimension or are just off it – they are not self but other, and so involve transitional processes to a markedly lesser extent. To begin with, a thumb or a blanket or a teddy bear was enough to satisfy the child with phantasies of comfort. It only wanted lulling. But when the self begins to be strong enough to tolerate moments of frustration, the child may create a grown-up based on the nearest human being who will stand still for it. And then: 'Oh, brave new world, that has such people in it.' Transitional processes are active and reach out and create the needed world, given half a chance.

To this creative process we turn in Chapter 14, but we need an intervening chapter to make the most of it.

·13·
The language of relationships

This chapter serves as an interlude to remind us that the boundaries of the self are quite different from the boundaries round ordinary physical objects. Even my body-self has boundaries which are different from the boundaries to cups and saucers and postage-stamps. When I drive in my customary car and am getting through a gap, I think 'I' am this wide. In someone else's car it takes a while for me to learn that 'I' am a different width. When playing tennis, 'I' reach the ball with no more movement than is required. When I use a mallet and chisel, 'I' cut the wood. This is how I think of the things I use every day. Any tool is difficult to use while I behave as though 'it' did the work. I have to feel that it is I. When strangers look in the garden from the street, I feel intruded on. I have a personal space round me, and I feel invaded if a stranger comes too close to me. If a burglar comes into my house and shits on the floor, I feel broken in on and dirtied.

We must not think of ourselves as having boundaries as definite as a shell round an egg. It is like believing that objects are separated from each other by black pencil lines, the way they are in drawings. Physically we are all separate. My eye is mine, not yours. Your digestion is yours, not mine. His measles are his, not ours. Psychologically this simply is not so. 'My' mother is more mine than 'my' teacher is; 'my' apple is even more under my control but it is less reciprocal. I am my mother's daughter,

252

my teacher's pupil, but hardly my apple's eater. Then again, my mother is also my sister's mother; and interestingly, 'my mother' may be more mine than 'our mother' is – or less, it depends on the facts of the situation. But what is not in dispute is that, when I say 'my mother and I', the boundaries between and around us are different from when I say 'our mother and I'.

Again, I can think of 'I' in a very narrow sense as in 'I am thinking of going to Australia' – the boundaries round my person and my plans sound clear. But what if I say, 'We are thinking of going to Australia'? Does this represent picture of me thinking, and of my two friends, each also thinking? Or does it represent the result of our discussion in which each of us has contributed? How are we to think of 'us' and 'we'? We go wrong, I think, when we cling too tenaciously to metaphors which make our psychological boundaries correspond to our bodily ones. Our digestive processes happen in a place – the stomach – which has a distinct skin round it, *but we do not have skins round our minds. Our boundaries are where we are in touch with other people and things.*

To keep fresh, we need from time to time to re-examine the language in terms of which we try to understand our relationships to others. This chapter represents an attempt to get away from too strong a reliance on the distinction between inner and outer worlds. This has in my view created some unnecessary problems, not least because of the emphasis it places on the separateness of you from me.

Inner and outer worlds

To some extent, the distinction between inner and outer worlds derives from our experience of our bodily self. As Balint (1959) pointed out, the senses develop in a sequence which, if all goes well, brings the infant only very gradually into encounters with other people and things.

'The two most important senses that provide the perceptions which form the basis for the discovery of "objects" are sight and touch. Both of them are undeveloped in the first post-natal months, as they need a considerable degree of muscular co-ordination to work properly; as is well known, binocular vision does not exist in the first weeks of life. Moreover both sight and touch, together with hearing, are projective senses; they feel, place or construct the object outside the body, either at a distance (sight and hearing) or at its surface (touch).

The situation is utterly different with the two lower senses, which are well, perhaps even fully, operative at birth. In their function there is hardly any projection; we feel smell and taste inside our body – *in* our mouth or *in* our nose; moreover, the sensations themselves, more often than not, have nothing to do with objects, only with substances. Here we get some idea of how and why the mixup between ourselves and the world around us has come about. Looking at it as an external detached observer, we recognise that it is based on an interaction between the individual and the external world; one may say that the world has intruded or penetrated into the individual's mouth or nose, and equally correctly that the individual has taken in parts of the external world – penetrated into it.

The same kind of mixup occurs with the sense of temperature, though to a lesser degree. In fact, it forms a transition between the lower and the higher senses, i.e., those based on mixup and those using projection. Cold and warmth are felt partly as coming from outside, partly as a state of our own body or even of ourselves: *we* feel warm or *it* is warm.

(Balint 1959: 62–3)

Pribram, last quoted in Chapter 4, also considers the organization of our senses to be the cause of the way we think about 'in here' and 'out there' (1971: Chapter 9). He argues that by virtue of having *two* eyes and *two* ears we can locate stimuli whose source is 'out there', as it were stereoscopically.

> 'From the energy configurations that excite some of our receptors, we are able to construct a "World-Out-There". The excitations of sight and hearing we especially tend to interpret as distant from the receptors excited. ... We sense we are touching, tasting, or smelling something apart from our own receptor reactions.'
>
> (Pribram 1971: 167)

When our perceptions are patterned in conditions of 'bilateral symmetry', 'the sum of such perceptions constitutes our World-Out-There. When these conditions are not present, we do not perceive objects and occurrences; instead we construct a world-within on the basis of our subjective feelings.'

(p. 183)

'In contrast to perceptions, subjective feelings are those phenomena, those ghosts which we immediately attribute to what is within the boundary, that bag we call the skin, which demarcates "Us" from the "Other".'

(p. 167)

Similarly, Winnicott wrote of a 'limiting membrane' separating the inner world from the outer:

'Of every individual who has reached the stage of being a unit (with a limiting membrane and an outside and an inside), it can be said that there is an inner reality to that individual, an inner world which can be rich or poor and can be at peace or in a stage of war.'

(1958[1951]: 230)

This way of thinking is very common – in the West at least – and it usually works well enough as a metaphor, providing we do not go construing the world in this way and then believing that that is the way the world is. It led Winnicott almost immediately into difficulties about 'a third area, neither inner nor outer' – 'a potential space', 'a cultural space', concepts we consider in Chapter 14.

Christian theologians and probably mystics of many persuasions have had conceptual problems of exactly the same nature: while the devout are said to live in Christ, Christ is also said to live in them. Fairbairn (1952: 42–3) put the paradox in terms of the complex psychodynamic concepts of his time:

'The process of differentiation of the object derives particular significance from the fact that infantile dependence is characterised not only by identification, but also by an oral attitude of incorporation. In virtue of this fact, the object with which the individual is identified becomes equivalent to an incorporated object, or, to put the matter in a more arresting fashion, *the object in which the individual is incorporated is incorporated in the individual.* This strange psychological anomaly may well prove the key to many metaphysical puzzles. Be that as it may, however, it is common to find in dreams a remarkable equivalence between being inside an object and having the object inside.' (my italics)

Matte Blanco (1975) who used set-theory to elucidate some of our unconscious processes and structures would recognize this kind of symmetry.

Thinking about ourselves in terms of an inside and an outside can lead us into some tenacious traps. This kind of allocation creates a spatial phantasy of our psychic world: an inner world with an outer world around it, like the pre-Galilean system of the earth with the sun, stars, and the planets circling round it. This spatial way of thinking has proved so powerful that people have drawn conclusions from it which might perhaps be warranted if there really were such spaces, but which can also cause confusion.

Admittedly, in the history of thought it has proved a useful discipline to regard some facts as subjective and others as objective: facts which several people agree on have normally been regarded as more objective than those which are held only by a single person. Facts held by only one person are usually not called facts, but views, opinions, or less politely, delusions or hallucinations, and they are regarded as subjective, not objective. The more people agree on a fact or on the scientific propriety with which something has been established as a fact, the more objective that fact is considered to be. It is, therefore, not surprising that objective facts have come to be thought of as belonging to a realm called 'the outer world': the world of shared reality. Similarly, the subjective experiences of individuals have been allocated to a realm called 'the inner world'. But is this the best way to think of my experience of you?

Getting in a muddle about the skin as a boundary between people

The metaphors of inner and outer space, of what comes from 'inside' and what comes from 'outside', seem to have an immediate appeal to most people. It is easy to understand why.

Food comes from 'out there'; we swallow it and it is 'in here'; we evacuate the waste and it goes 'out there'. Most of us feel that no metaphor is involved in these descriptions of bodily processes. Nor do most of us feel that a metaphor is involved when we think of a noise or a sight or a smell or a slap coming from 'out there', which we 'in here' perceive and think about. The noise, sight, smell, touch, originate outside our skins, out there, while we are perceiving and thinking from a point inside our skins, 'in here'.

We tend to experience our selves, our identity, our soul, our ego, as located somewhere within the 'bag of skin', the 'limiting membrane' which covers our bodies all over. Some of us feel we live behind our eyes; others feel they live behind their rib-cage, in the solar plexus, in the genitals, or just 'all over'. Still each individual 'I' is normally experienced 'inside' while the rest of the world is felt to be 'outside'. And the other way round also: what is inside my skin is *me*, what is outside is *not me*.

The skin surface does help to establish a sense of where self ends and not-self begins, but it can lead to a dangerous metaphor, tempting us to use language which cannot accurately describe our experiences. As Balint writes in his high-spirited way in his chapter on 'Object and Subject' (1959: 66):

> 'By the way, the air is not an object but a substance. Further, it must be pointed out that there is no need to define exact boundaries at which the external air stops and we ourselves start. In fact, it would be a kind of hairsplitting to do so, as it would amount only to a play with words to ask, for instance, whether the air contained in our lungs is part of ourselves or part of the external world. Obviously it is both, it is a mixup. Almost the same is true, by the way, of the contents of our bowels. In some way they are our "inside" in the strictest sense of the word; in another way they belong to the external world though undeniably they are inside us.
>
> May I add that this neither-here-nor-there psychological state is reciprocated by the embryology and histology of the same organs? Both the intestines and the lungs are lined with a special kind of epithelium which is contiguous with the skin that covers our body; moreover, though it is morphologically different, embryologically it is a derivative of it. So here, too,

we have a kind of mixup between outside and inside; at any rate, the boundaries are so uncertain and vague that it is hardly possible to say where inside ends and outside begins.'

Our boundaries are where we touch other people and things

The idea that our boundaries are experienced mainly when we encounter others has been in the background of the developing narrative of this book from the beginning. It solves some theoretical problems, and, though it creates others, the new problems seem to me more manageable, more interesting, and more productive of further insights.

Perhaps the most immediately obvious difficulty created by the new hypothesis is that we experience boundaries in so many different ways: with love, with frustration, with fear, with shock – as obstacles, as opportunities, as absences, as stone walls, as bridges. What an interesting difficulty to work with! It seems to suggest, for instance, that boundaries are kinds of relationships: that people are defined, enriched, frustrated, and delimited by their boundaries with others.

The boundary between me and a person I love and trust is very different from the boundary between me and someone I experience as indifferent or intrusive. People who love and trust each other feel 'identified', so that the other person's well-being feels almost like their own. People in such a relationship will think of themselves as 'we'. Then, though you and I are individuals, the boundary between us is very different from the boundary between us and them. The boundary between me and you-who-are-one-of-us is very different from the boundary between me and those-people-over-there: their well-being is not identified with mine. They are different and the boundary is different because the relationship between them and us is different.

For various reasons, our thinking has been forced into a misleading either/or form:

| experientially | I | versus | Not I |
| psychologically | Self | versus | Other |

spatially	Inner	versus	Outer
philosophically	Subject(ive)	versus	Object(ive)
socially	Us	versus	Them

The boxes on the left represent something nearer to our very own private experiences, while those on the right represent something nearer to our experiences of whatever we feel to be 'not me'. The contrast is

Something is happening which (or someone is there who) can be affected by my hopes, fears, and my feelings.	versus	Something is happening which (or someone is there who) cannot be affected by my hopes, fears, and my feelings.

This new formulation achieves an important change, for now we no longer have to think of experiences as *either* altogether 'me' *or* as altogether 'other'. The dichotomy has gone; instead, there is a continuum – a range of experiences, from those in which we feel very much in charge, to those which feel very much inflicted on us:

Something happens! Someone is there! I can affect what happens: I can keep things as they are or make them go away. I am in charge.	Something happens! Someone is there! I can affect what happens next to some extent.	Something happens! Someone is there! I cannot affect what happens. I cannot keep things as they are or make them go away. I am powerless.

This way of thinking makes available a whole subtle range of relationships/boundaries. At one extreme, I feel in total control of a person or a thing – at this end I am boundless and omnipotent. At the other extreme, I am definitely not in control: this is where I touch other people and things, and feel limited by them.

A new language for talking about self-regions: mine, ours, yours, theirs

We need a new language, with metaphors as concrete as 'inside' and 'outside' but less divisive and more relational. Such a language in fact exists. It is already so established, and so proven in practice, that it is astonishing that it has not yet been taken over by psychologists. I mean, of course, the language of personal pronouns, the language in which ordinary people speak to each other.

Why should I not use 'I' to refer to my own self-regions, and 'me', 'mine', 'myself', 'the self', and so on, as appropriate? Similarly we could use 'we' (and also 'us', 'ours', and so on) to refer to those regions which map the experiences in which both 'I' and 'you' participate. In effect, we can regard each pronoun as a region where certain processes are grouped.

Before we consider 'you', some warnings and other considerations.

1   My experience of 'us' will be different from your experience of 'us' – the boundaries of the region will be different, and the relationships will be different.

2   Before there is experience of self and others, there is the selfobject state, which leaves blissful oceanic memory-traces. It is tempting to think of the selfobject state as an 'us' region, but this can be misleading. The selfobject state is best thought of as a necessary but not a sufficient forerunner for the experience of 'us'. 'Us' should refer to the experience of you-and-me, a structure whose development comes later than the selfobject state, since it depends on individuation and on the separating out of me from all that is not me. On the other hand, 'us' is a mere bit of grammar or bit of arithmetic except for those whose selfobject memories are awakened by the use of the word.

3   What Winnicott called the 'male element' in the personality is very much the 'I', since it is the active doing self-region of the personality which he has in mind. What he called the 'female element' is very much the 'we' or 'us' self-region – it is the region of at-one-ness which originates in the selfobject state but already has some differentiation. 'We' and 'us' are regions of relating and interacting and giving; they are not competitive but sharing.

4   It will be remembered that Balint derived two distinct personality-types from the infant's first reaction to the discovery of other people and things. Some people prefer

others to be cosy and close to others, reproducing to some extent the bliss of the selfobject state and the harmonious interpenetrating mixup. But other people see others more as a hindrance and prefer 'them' out of the way. The former would feel incomplete if circumstances prevented the formation of a strong sense of 'us'; the latter would feel uncomfortable unless there were sufficient opportunity for experiencing a strong sense of 'I' unimpeded by 'them'. Their respective experiences of 'you' will be correspondingly different.

I propose the words 'you' ('yours', 'yourself', 'yourselves') as normally appropriate for a person's experiences of another person. It is relevant to remember, however, that these words mean very different things to different people, depending on how much 'us' they are capable of. There are people for whom 'I', 'you', and 'us' are mere ways of speaking. Some use these words in a grammatically correct way, and yet have little of the sense of identity which should be expressed by the word 'I'. Others may have little of the sense of the other person's identity implicit in the word 'you', or little of the sense of fellowship which should lie behind the word 'we'. Also, there are variations in how much 'us' is involved. Probably most of us would feel more 'us' when with Abel than when with Cain, yet both can be addressed as 'you'. The more I think of it, the more I think it odd that we do not have different pronouns for the relationship 'you-as-part-of-us' in contrast to 'you-as-a-part-of-them'. It would be really convenient. Perhaps the languages which distinguish 'tu' from 'vous' and 'Du' from 'Sie' have an advantage here. Perhaps we could put the archaic 'thou' to a new and profitable use. Or was that its original use?

This way of using pronouns experientially has its roots deep in our common life. In many parts of Britain, it is considered offensive to refer in terms of the third-person-singular to someone who is present in the room or to someone who is valued by those in the room. The common retort is 'Who is "she"? Someone the cat's brought in?' For similar reasons, I think the third-person-plural is often used to express alienation, as in 'They don't care', 'They're out for what they can get'. In some languages the alienating effect of the third-person-plural is customarily used to acknowledge social distance, as in the Italian 'Lei', the German 'Ihr'. ('Yr', by the way, refers in Hannah Green's *I Never Promised You a Rosegarden* to the powerful dangerous forces which had control of Deborah's world.)

'He', 'she', 'it', 'they', 'them' are words used for others when no 'us' is felt. They are truly other, not 'I', not 'us'. As Hudson's diagrams at the end of this chapter illustrate, there is no relating, no give-and-take, no sense of 'me-as-part-of-us' and 'you-as-part-of-us', no sense of 'us'. The sense of 'me', 'you', 'us' accompanies our growing awareness of the reality and reliability of the people in our world. Where this is missing, there can be no free sharing and giving, only power and control, manipulation, calculation, and exploitation.

Now that we have left the inconvenient artificial world of dichotomy, and entered the world of I and Thou, we and you and they, we can play a little.

Consider also

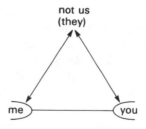

Blobs may convey a more accurate impression, as well as allowing us to use the principles of sets and subsets (Matte Blanco 1975)

Consider also

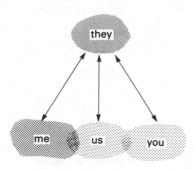

Also

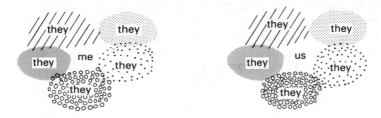

Liam Hudson (1975: Chapter 4) offers a scheme somewhere in
between tidy lines and blurry blobs.

'The octagon is the figure we walk upon in most Victorian
hallways: the eight-sided tile. Set side by side, octagons yield a
mosaic that in some ways resembles the beautiful six-sided
pattern of a honeycomb. Conceptually speaking, octagons
start to acquire interesting properties when overlapped. If we
draw nine octagons, overlapping as in the diagram, we find, in
the middle of the pattern, a structure I shall call the "cell".
Like a fortified town, this has an external boundary, internal
subdivisions, and also an internal boundary.

The cell is "fortified", both inside and out. On the outside
against the alien world of other people: and on the inside
against those aspects of our own mental functioning over
which we can exert no conscious control. . . .

Look again at the diagrams; and especially at the relation of
any one cell to its neighbours. These relations are of three
sorts. There are neighbours at a distance, with whom no

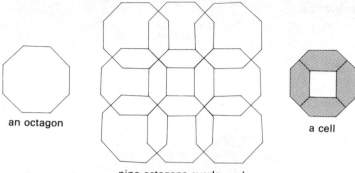

an octagon

a cell

nine octagons overlapped

boundary is shared. There are the four much closer cells, with whom an external boundary wall is shared. And, closer still, there are the four that overlap. In this last instance, the external wall of one cell forms part of the internal wall of the other. And vice versa. Our octagons offer, in other words, three degrees of relationship: acquaintance, friendship, and intimacy – 'he', 'you', and 'thou'.

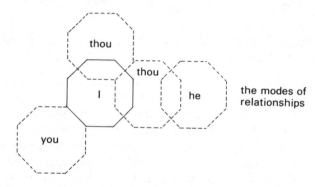

the modes of relationships

The diagram also suggests a distinction between friendship and intimacy that we may not have foreseen. It implies that, in friendship, we use our perception of the other's public "face" in constructing our own external defences. In an intimate relation, the two concerned are each using the other's public presence in controlling their own irrational desires and fears. To lose a friend is to lose part of one's public presence: to lose an intimate is to lose part of the bulwark that protects us from our own helplessness.

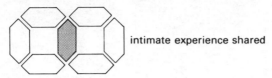

intimate experience shared

Nor is this all. Each cell has four segments; and each segment can be constructed as a body of experience we share with someone. Each cell consists, then, of a unique combination of intimate relations. We *are* what we share with those close to us – our parents, our spouses, our children.'

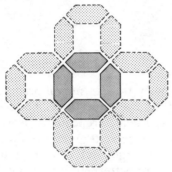

the set as a unique combination
of shared experiences

·14·

Discovering, inventing, creating, and using symbols

Experiences leave memory-traces – neural processes organized in structures which reflect the experience. Concepts form when similar patterns of experiences repeatedly leave similar structures of memory-traces. *Figure 40* gives an impression of how a concept, the letter B, emerges out of a mess of what at first appears to be just an unpatterned lot of dots. But it is not unpatterned – it is just that the pattern has not yet become distinct: we have not yet learned to see it for what it is. Each time the patterned stimuli reappear, the concept will be stronger and clearer.

Repeated similar experiences develop simple concepts. Eventually further experiences develop these concepts into more complex organizations. These are to some extent records of the past: more 'central' or 'higher order' processes, and eventually 'maps'. A time comes when these records of the past, built up from experiences, themselves affect new experiences, creating expectations, directing attention, and so on. 'Phantasies' is the word used for such concepts in psycho-analytic circles.

Discovering the object

We are now able to take up our reflections on Winnicott's ideas where we left off in Chapter 12. He had some remarkable ideas on the interplay between more central processes and the sensory

266

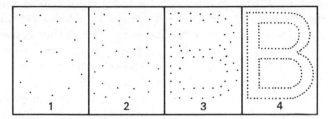

Figure 40

life: the very development of a True Self depends on whether the baby's needs were met when it experienced them or at more arbitrary times. Winnicott wrote one of his most moving and poetic passages on the role of the mother's empathy in detecting what her baby is unconsciously hoping for.

'When I see in what a delicate way a mother who is not anxious manages the situation, I am always astounded. You see her there, making the baby comfortable, and arranging a *setting* in which the feeding may happen, if all goes well. The setting is a part of a human relationship. If the mother is feeding by the breast, we see how she lets the baby, even a tiny one, have the hands free so that as she exposes her breast the skin can be felt, and its warmth – moreover the distance of her breast from the baby can be measured, for the baby has only a little bit of the world in which to place objects, the bit that can be reached by mouth, hands and eyes. The mother allows the baby's face to touch the breast. At the beginning babies do not know about breasts being part of mother. If the face touches the breast they do not know whether the nice feeling comes in the breast or in the face. In fact babies play with their cheeks, and scratch them, just as if they were breasts, and there is plenty of reason why mothers allow for all the contact that a baby wants. No doubt a baby's sensations in these respects are very acute, and if they are acute we can be sure they are important.

The baby first of all needs all these rather *quiet* experiences which I am describing and needs to feel held lovingly, that is, in an alive way, yet without fuss and anxiety and tenseness.

This is the setting. Sooner or later there will be some kind of contact between the mother's nipple and the baby's mouth. It does not matter exactly what happens. The mother is there in the situation and part of it, and she particularly likes the intimacy of the relationship. She comes without preconceived notions as to how the baby ought to behave.

This contact of the nipple with the baby's mouth gives the baby ideas! "Perhaps there is something there outside the mouth worth going for." Saliva begins to flow; in fact, so much saliva may flow that the baby may enjoy swallowing it, and for a time hardly needs milk. Gradually the mother enables the baby to build up in imagination the very thing she has to offer, and the baby begins to mouth the nipple and to get to the root of it with the gums, and bite it, and perhaps to suck.'

(1964: 'Close-up of Mother Feeding Baby')

Winnicott here imagines how a baby's sensory experiences, when repeated in the right emotional atmosphere, eventually build up expectations: phantasies. He then goes on to imagine how the fortunate baby's phantasies lead to desired sensory experiences – in plain language, how the baby's wish for a particular experience seems to bring it about: the baby wants something, discovers the nipple, and discovers that the nipple is what it wants.

'Gradually the mother enables the baby to build up in imagination the very thing she has to offer, and the baby begins to mouth the nipple and to get to the root of it with the gums, and bite it, and perhaps to suck.

And then there is a pause. The gums let go of the nipple, and the baby turns away from the scene of action. The idea of the breast fades.

Do you see how important this last bit is? The baby had an idea, and the breast with the nipple came, and a contact was made. Then the baby finished with the idea and turned away, and the nipple disappeared. This is one of the most important ways in which the experience of the baby we are now describing differs from one placed in a busy institution.

How does the mother deal with the baby's turning away?

This baby does not have a thing pushed back into the mouth in order that sucking movements shall be started up again. The mother understands what the baby is feeling, because she is alive and has an imagination. She waits. In the course of a few minutes, or less, the baby turns once more towards where she is all the time willing to place the nipple, and so a new contact is made, just at the right moment.'

Winnicott's final comment in this passage marks the difference between the early experiences of people whose lives are governed by their instinctual drives and the early experiences of those whose lives are governed by their relationships with others. When the conditions Winnicott here describes are repeated again and again,

'the baby drinks not from a thing that contains milk, but from a personal possession lent for a moment to a person who knows what to do with it.'

At first, as far as the baby's experience is concerned, the baby and the mother are merged into one another: the mother is a sensory experience of the baby's. However, someone not merged with the baby has to make actual what the baby is ready to find. There then follows a time of to-and-fro while the (m)other is repudiated, reaccepted, and finally perceived as less under the baby's control than the baby had assumed.

This process is highly dependent on there being someone prepared to participate in the baby's phantasies. It may seem paradoxical at first glance that, for the best development of a child's autonomy and self-respect, there has to be this period of utter dependence. But if adults will play the required part for a time, then the baby will have had some actual experience of magical control, of omnipotence, of almightiness and creation. For what the baby thinks of, there it is, and it is good. I think it is this which the psychotherapist Virginia Axline practised so perceptively, that when, years later, Dibs, a previously unhappy and disturbed little boy, was asked what had helped him, he replied: 'Everything I did, you did; everything I said, you said' – the essence of support and confirmation. The whole passage is worth recalling. Dibs and Virginia Axline are pictured as having met by chance on a street.

'"Hello, you," he said.

"Hello, Dibs."

"I know who you are," he said.

"You do?"

"Oh yes! You are the lady of the wonderful playroom," he said. "You are Miss A."

We sat down on the front steps of an apartment house along the way to talk.

"Yes." I said. "And you are Dibs."

"I'm grown up now," he said. "But I do remember when I was very, very small and first came to see you. I remember the toys, the doll house and the sand and the men and women and children in the world I built. . . . I remember our office and our books and our recording machine. I remember all the people. And I remember how you played with me."

"What did we play, Dibs?"

Dibs leaned toward me. His eyes were shining. "Everything I did, you did," he whispered. "Everything I said, you said."

"So that's the way it was." I said.

"Yes, 'This is your room Dibs' you said to me. 'This is all for you. Have fun, Dibs. Have fun. Nobody is going to hurt you. Have fun.'" Dibs sighed. "And I did have fun. I had the most wonderful time in my life. I built my world with you in the playroom. Remember?"

"Yes, Dibs, I remember."''

(Axline 1971: 190)

A pictorial metaphor for 'discovery'

We need to look at these processes in further detail, and explore further implications. Suppose we use patterns of tiny circles to represent messages which do not come directly from the environment but are effects of central processes – messages from the 'map'. We can then decide to let a baby's phantasy of something, say a phantasy experience of the breast, be represented by a pattern of tiny circles in the shape of a B, for Breast, as in *Figure 41*.

Suppose we use patterns of black dots to represent messages which derive more directly and recently from sensory stimuli.

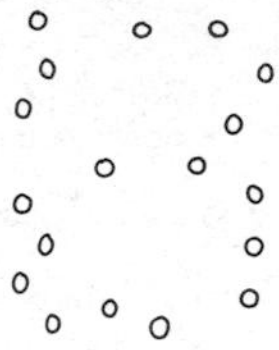

Figure 41 This is a phantasy, unconformed by new sensory experience.

These are potentially object-representations; they come from the working model of the situation. We can then imagine the baby registering a sensory experience of the breast when it is in touch with it (*Figure 42*). This is a purely sensory experience: in itself it has no meaning.

Figure 42 This is a set of sensations — it does not mean a thing.

Whether these sensations are noticed at all, or noticed as pleasant or as disturbing, depends on other factors (for instance, on whether the baby just then had a pleasant phantasy of a breast and what that stands for, or of a bath or a sleep).

When the tiny infant has a mother of the kind Winnicott described on pp. 267ff., who puts the breast where the baby's phantasy, too, has put it, the infant has an experience which Winnicott called 'object-finding-and-creating' or 'discovering the object'. The phantasy experience created by the baby is then very closely connected with the sensory experience made possible by the mother presenting whatever the baby had a phantasy of just then. Combining the two sets of neural input, we can then represent the neural pattern as in *Figure 43*.

In this representation, there is no gap between the expectation/ phantasy/hope/need/wish and the experience wished for. The two coincide. The gap, between what the baby needs and what

Figure 43 Neural representation of a discovered object. Here is a meaningful and recognizable concept, and a meaningful and recognizable object.

it is given, is bridged when the object is found at the right moment – when phantasy (central processes) and the sensory input coincide. So the phantasy is confirmed by the world.

In adult life we know this experience, of phantasy confirmed by sensory input, mainly in disconcerting contexts, as in the tiny confusions which result when you blow your nose at the precise moment that a train whistles or when a roll of thunder breaks just as you turn your head: 'Did I do that?' This omnipotent element is characteristic of the age at which we originally experienced such coincidences as part of normal well-being; we were feeling 'grand'.

Discovery as a source of strength

Before differentiation, mother and child are one, from the baby's point of view. As Winnicott said, there is no such thing as a baby. Tustin goes entirely along with this, quoting Winnicott (1958a: 239) on this difficult-to-describe situation: 'Psychologically, the infant takes from a breast that is part of the infant, and the mother gives milk to an infant that is part of herself.' For Tustin this seems inherent in our human biological equipment: 'In earliest infancy, the coincidence of inbuilt patterns with correspondences in the outside world seems to me the first "holding situation".' And, quoting from Winnicott again: 'The mother places the actual breast just where the infant is ready to create, and at the right moment. Mother, baby, teat and tongue work together to procure the illusion of continuity and to confirm it'. She comments: 'Both Winnicott and Milner (1955:

100) have stressed the importance of ample opportunities for such illusion in early infancy and the dangers of a premature impingement of separateness' (Tustin 1972: 33).

When the tiny infant engages in Winnicott's object-finding-and-creating, then the object of its phantasy will be mapped in very close connection with the infant's self-regions, for the object of its phantasy appears as soon as it is thought of or wished for. For a moment we need this complicated way of saying that the infant feels it has 'created the object'. On the other hand, if things come to the infant at times when it has not 'created' them, if the not-self thing is brought near the self unexpectedly, then it is experienced as threatening, as an impingement − as tremendously not-self. Even though needed, food or relief then feel 'other'.

Between these two poles lies a range. Messages from the (inner and outer) environment are received, evaluated, and so on, and attached strongly (or less strongly) to self-regions and thus they become less (or more) a part of the world of other people and things. And, of course, babies differ in what they create and what they experience as impingement. One infant may create food and find company imposed on it, another will create company and find food imposed on it. Different vulnerabilities or faults will be consequent on such differences as to what feels 'other'.

Suppose I have a phantasy of whatever will make me feel good, and then what makes me feel good comes about and I feel good. Then this experience is almost wholly one of 'me' and hardly at all of 'not me'. I get a sense of strength and well-being. Suppose, however, that I have a phantasy of whatever makes me feel good, but the event does not come about just then and there. After a brief and quite painless delay, whatever makes me feel good does happen, and I feel good. I don't have the experience that I made it happen (created it). But I do have an experience of a nice not-self that appears at more or less the right time and makes me feel good. This, I imagine, happens after a relatively short delay.

The effects of a relatively longer delay are even less likely to make me feel that I am powerful and that everything is under my control; the delay may make me feel that the world is quite a difficult place to handle.

In all these instances, however, my phantasy of something good *is* confirmed. Good things are there for me: they are mine or somebody's who is willing to share them. And my phantasy of what makes me feel good does materialize and make me feel good. However, if the delay is too long, my phantasy of what makes me feel good is not confirmed, the good thing does not come, though some other thing (not necessarily bad) does – this disturbs me and makes me feel impinged upon. (See also the discussion on pp. 326–29 and 364–65.)

We have a clue here about how different experiences may variously contribute to people's self-imagery or their imagery of the world. Beginning with our experience of much or little impingement, we organize other people and things not just as good or bad objects, but as self, or other, according to the amount of impingement and otherness that has been experienced in their connection.

When, as Winnicott puts it, 'object-relating matches with object-presenting', the fortunate baby feels in charge. It is not subjected to the kind of impingement which can result from being fed when not hungry, played with when sleepy, left alone 'to sleep' when it is not ready to sleep. A fortunate baby gets its pleasures the very moment it begins to think of them and begins to look for them. The looking is a kind of anticipatory experience based on memories of having its needs met soon after it has begun to want.

This is important. If the phase of dependence on others goes badly, the child is left with memories of helpless and frustrating dependence on others, for the good things are experienced as not coming at its behest but at the whim of an uncontrollable other. If the phase of dependence goes well, the child retains memories of a state pretty close to omnipotence – 'I get what I want, all I have to do is want it.' What a source of self-esteem!

Repeated experiences of finding whatever it wished for, at the very moment when that thing was first thought of as desirable, help the child build up a sense that the world is a good place, that it is able to take care of itself, is safe, strong, competent, and skilled – a sense that starts as omnipotence and becomes ego-strength. Erikson (1950: Chapter 7) calls it Basic Trust, 'an inner population of remembered and anticipated sensations which are firmly correlated with the outer population of familiar and predictable things and people'.

We can put this in the language of Being and Doing. Because all this has taken place at a time when self and other were still merged, the really fortunate baby's experience is that of being 'grand'; and this self-region of 'being-grand' becomes established before there has been any association of this self-region with others in which it was doing something. That is a good start: the baby feels it is grand before it has to prove itself by doing grand things.

This baby's good fortune stands out the more clearly when we contrast it with a baby who has had prematurely to develop ego-functions, the doing side of its personality. However good and competent such a baby may feel, its 'I-do-things-well' structures are not so fed and sustained by connection with 'I-am-grand' regions.

When the baby's phantasies are confirmed by the world, 'I-in-the-world' is associated with a sense of being competent, able, skilled (see *Figure 44*).

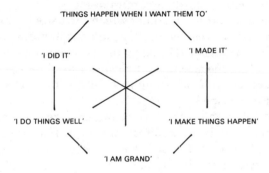

'THINGS HAPPEN WHEN I WANT THEM TO'

'I DID IT'

'I MADE IT'

'I DO THINGS WELL'

'I MAKE THINGS HAPPEN'

'I AM GRAND'

Figure 44

When events coincide felicitously with the child's phantasies, it can think of itself as active and strong, an important effect for a baby so much of whose experience is likely to be at the receiving end of other people's purposes. The sense of 'I' goes with the sense that 'the world is mine', 'I made it'. When phantasies and events do not coincide so well, the child is more likely to have an image of itself as acted upon, 'me', rather than 'I'. 'They do it to me'. So what looks like the same thing – a dress for Dolly, a song written in praise of apples, a holiday – can be experienced with a strong 'this-is-I' component by one person, and can be a proud expression of that person's personality, while someone else might experience a strong sense that 'they made me do this' – which makes the same thing not a source of self-esteem but of shame.

Playing as discovery

The baby has a problem of adjusting what actually is happening (mediated through its senses) with what was happening in its phantasy (at the level of its more central processes). Suppose baby has a hunger pain in its stomach, and suppose that its phantasy of what will ease it does not include a teat of a particular shape. It will have a shock if relentlessly presented with a teat which did not match its phantasy. It may not be able to use it. It may stay hungry. It needs time to sort out what the essential pattern is – the baby needs to play with the teat to establish the conceptual pattern which its phantasy and its current experience can then confirm.

Playing is the activity through which the baby is able to make the adjustment between what it already has in mind and what is presented for it to find. The baby needs time and space to play, to explore, to experiment, and during this time the imagined phantasy 'other' can be brought in line with who or what is waiting to be grasped.

The world of the 'other' thus becomes real for the infant through play – it learns what it can do in that world. In this process, the world of the other has no chance to remain entirely nice (or entirely nasty) in any idealized way – its actual properties will gradually be discovered. Play-time gives the baby an opportunity to identify the other as an object that either will or won't do what is required, the baby's central processes (phantasies) changing under the impact of the incoming sensory information. In view of this important function, it may seem paradoxical that playing is an activity which has no aim or purpose – it is just . . . playing. 'What are you doing?' 'Nothing – just playing.' It is in this sense an opposite to doing, just as being is an opposite of doing.

From a merged or selfobject state, through playing, the infant can begin to learn its separateness from the other.

'Two babies are feeding at the breast. One is feeding on the self, since the breast and the baby have not yet become (for the baby) separate phenomena. The other is feeding from an other-than-me source, or an object that can be given cavalier treatment without effect on the baby unless it retaliates.'

(1974[1971]: 104)

Until there is a 'you' and a 'me', there can be no 'us'. Playing helps distinguish 'me' from 'you', preparatory to building a strong 'us'.

Playing leads to the discovery of the other as the other 'really' is. I mean here the discovery of the other we cannot control, the other who exists regardless of our needs, hopes, fears, and wishes. Playing corrects our phantasies of what we imagine the other to be, using the evidence which we allow the other to present to our senses. Of course, we do not play with those we fear too much, and so we cannot discover who or what they 'really' are in this sense. But we do watch the late-night horror film; we play with what we fear a little, hoping to reduce our fear through finding less danger than we feared, or more skill in coping.

The discovery of others who are the source of good things leads to gratitude and confidence. But there must surely be many times when the baby responds with anger to the discovery that it is not omnipotent but must put up with a delay before it will get what it wants. This anger has a special role: it can test and at times establish the reality of the other person's separateness (see also pp. 400–01).

Using or testing as discovery

Winnicott (1971/1974: Chapter 6) was interested in a kind of behaviour which he called 'using the object' and I shall call 'testing'. This is a process which allows us to distinguish between the people and things we can imagine or phantasize about, and the people and things whose actions are not under our control. By testing I can discover what is under my control and so 'mine', and what is in the world which Winnicott called 'shared reality' (1974[1971]: 107) and which is not under my control. I think that quite a lot of such discoveries happen in a painless way in the process of playing and exploring. However, the case of particular interest just now is what happens when the test results in disappointment and disillusionment. (In later chapters we explore what happens when the disappointment is so great that the person cannot face it and retreats back into phantasy, denying the painful events which occurred in shared reality.)

Imagine a baby playing: diddle diddle; wave rattle wave wave; trala trala; wave wave; fine fine. The rattle falls overboard: Where is it? I'm not feeling nice. No rattle. No wave no wave. I'm still not feeling nice. Absent rattle hurts. Something hurts. Why don't I feel better? I should feel better. No one makes it better. I'm angry. No one makes it better and I've done my yell and it doesn't get better and I yelled very loud and it doesn't get better and It Hurts And I'm Angry And If It Doesn't Get Better I'M GONNA FIX THEM AND I'LL DESTROY THEM AND I'LL SHOW THEM . . .

When things (or persons) are no longer 'subject to omnipotence' – no longer imagined to be under the baby's control but discovered to be part of 'shared reality' – they cease to be part of the baby and become separated out. The loss of omnipotence may frustrate and anger the baby, but it has a focus for its anger – the (m)other. The distress of deprivation becomes the anger of frustration, anger which may be so great that the baby fears it will destroy the (m)other in its rage. But it is now in 'shared reality' and so it is bound to learn that destroying people in phantasy does not destroy them in shared reality, thank goodness. And so, when the rage subsides, the baby discovers that the (m)other is still there and so is the baby itself. Thus, in Winnicott's view, the baby discovers a class of objects not destroyed by rage, to which it can then begin to attend in a new way. The world is a safer place when you can stop thinking of yourself as omnipotent, powerful, and destructive in a world which has other powerful and destructive people in it. The (m)other has been tested and has survived.

> 'The subject says to the object "I destroyed you", and the object is there to receive the communication. From now on the subject says "Hullo object! I destroyed you. I love you. You have value for me because of your survival of my destruction of you."'

> (1974[1971]: 105)

So, gradually, either through playing or more perilously through testing, other people become more real as *other* people. They have been discovered as able to survive both love and hate. This makes realistic ambivalence possible. In phantasy, the good and the bad can be kept separate. We can have a phantasy good mother, who comes when wanted, separate from a phantasy bad mother, who never comes when wanted. In shared reality, we have to put up with the fact that mothers (and others) are both good and bad together. To some extent they will be just as we imagined them; and to some extent they remain obstinately their own selves.

That is why Winnicott stressed that transitional objects – bears, dolls, imaginary playmates – are normally not tested to destruction, however savagely the child treats them. The child *could* destroy them – they are sufficiently under the child's control to be capable of destruction – but this is not what the child normally wants to do to its transitional objects. It is partly because the child does not normally test its transitional objects to destruction that it eventually turns more to other people and things: transitional objects cannot be 'discovered', the way other people and things can be discovered, to be either the sort of person or thing we hoped for, or not. There is a particular gratification or disappointment which comes from relating to real people and things in 'shared reality'. Transitional objects, by contrast, are useful because they help the child come to terms with the discovery of its own limitations: they put the child in touch with the possibility (disillusioning? comforting?) that it is not omnipotent.

So we have here been considering a developmental period when the child feels strong enough to discover real people to relate to in an honest way, taking the rough with the smooth, as regards itself, and as regards others.

Illusion and disillusion, and the gap between

We have been tracing a baby's progress from illusion through disillusion to acceptance of its limitations. Winnicott described the process as it happens at its best: starting when the infant is still tiny and when the mother is good enough, and has arranged things just as the infant imagined them:

'As a consequence the infant begins to believe in external reality, which appears and behaves as by magic, and which acts in a way that does not clash with the infant's omnipotence. On this basis the infant can gradually abrogate its sense of omnipotence. The True Self has a spontaneity and this has been joined up with the world's events. The infant can now begin to enjoy the illusion of omnipotent creating and controlling, and can then gradually come to recognise the illusory element, the fact of playing and imagining.'

(1965[1960]: 146)

At first,

'Psychologically, the infant takes from a breast that is part of the infant and the mother gives milk to an infant that is part of herself. In psychology, the idea of interchange is based on illusion.'

(1958[1951]: 239; see also 1974[1971]: 13)

Disillusionment is the process of discovering that you are not omnipotent after all, that phantasy does not by itself create what you want, that there had been someone all along who was not under your control, who had been letting you believe that you were in control and who is now no longer letting you believe that. 'The infant can . . . enjoy the illusion of omnipotent creating and controlling, and can then gradually come to recognise the illusory element.'

The illusory element is, in my view, the merged selfobject state which is the precursor of the experience of 'us'. The emergence of the distinct concepts of 'you' and 'I' creates a gap which does not exist in the selfobject state. The experience of 'us' is the bridge across that gap. How I need that bridge, that sense of union, after losing the phantasy of well-being and omnipotence which characterized a good selfobject state! Illusory it may have been, but it felt safe. This safety is now being rebuilt in the relationship called 'us', or to put it in a different way, this safety is being re-established as part of the concept of 'us'. *After ego-relatedness – 'us'-relatedness.* In that safety, the fortunate baby can discover the world of other people and things not under its control, but in shared reality.

I believe that, in thinking this out, Winnicott got trapped by too strong an adherence to the particular spatial metaphors which we considered in the previous chapter. He writes of

> 'the third part of the life of a human being, a part that we cannot ignore, an intermediate area of *experiencing*, to which both inner reality and external life contribute. ... It is a resting place for the individual engaged in the perpetual task of keeping inner and outer reality separate yet interrelated.'
>
> (1974[1971]: 3; also in 1958[1951]: 230)

Part of what he meant we have just looked at:

> 'The intermediate area to which I am referring is the area that is allowed to the infant between primary creativity and objective perception based on reality-testing.'
>
> (ibid.)

This intermediate area is for Winnicott 'between': 'In between the mother and the infant is some thing, or some activity, or sensation' (1965[1960]: 146). This is the 'third part' – the part that Winnicott thought of as a transitional or a 'potential' space. How else may we think of it, this 'between' thing or activity or sensation? To my mind it is best thought of in two ways, one to do with people (discussed in this and the next subsection) and one to do with creativity (discussed in the subsection thereafter).

The 'intermediate area between people' seems to me an experience of 'us', and is not a space but a process. This process, the experience of 'us', developing as it does in favourable circumstances from selfobject states, requires the differentiation of 'you' from 'me': we are then *separate yet interrelated*, as Winnicott specified in the quotation. To maintain that way of relating is indeed 'a perpetual task'; to be in such a relationship is indeed to be in a resting place.

Figure 45 gives a simplified visual representation of the mutually stimulating concepts reverberating in the baby's head; the concept 'you' is used instead of '(m)other' for the sake of neatness, though it is of course a slightly later development.

Filling the gap between 'you' and 'me' with a symbol

The selfobject state is succeeded, in a facilitating environment, by the baby's phantasy that the satisfying object is there when wanted. This phantasy helps the baby not to be overwhelmed by

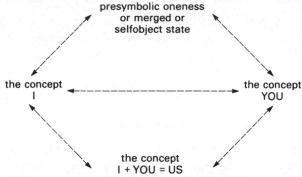

Figure 45

distress when it begins to feel ever more individual and separate from the (m)other. For, as this happens, it may more often have to wait for, or to work for, or even forgo, the gratification of its wishes. But though it must now change from 'good things are there when needed' to 'you bring me good things when I need them', it need not lose its feeling that it is a grand baby. That confident trust may remain, that memory of the reliable availability of goodness. In fortunate circumstances the baby may after differentiation feel that it is a grand baby in a grand environment. Here is the beginning of the useful process by which we can turn our phantasies into symbols.

Just to remind ourselves: a memory, however simple or however complex, is a concept, an image or part of an image, part of a dynamic structure. The more complex of these structures we can call phantasies. A phantasy can be a symbol: it can stand for, stand in for, represent something. Thus the memory that good things come when they are needed 'represents' the good thing and 'stands for' a guarantee that it will come. I think that this is what Winnicott meant when he wrote:

> 'In between the infant and the object is some thing, or some activity or sensation. Insofar as this joins the infant to the object, so far is this the basis for symbol formation.'
>
> (1965[1960]: 146)

This process is a complex version of the one discussed in Chapter 3, pp. 30–1: an angle may come to activate a phantasy of a whole triangle.

On this very simplified foundation, I propose to construct, bit by bit in succeeding chapters, everything that has to do with the inner life: concepts, symbols, and internal relationships. For the way the concept "triangle" is arrived at, illuminates not only how people come to see a particular triangle as a triangle, but also how people begin to recognise triangles wherever they occur, whatever their angles, and, even, how people begin the process which will eventually lead them to think of triangles when they see an angle, so that an angle can "stand for" or "mean" a triangle and a triangle can "stand for" or "mean" an angle.

stand for = mean = symbolize

When one aspect of something stands for the whole, the whole may be activated although the person registers only the one aspect.'

A memory can stand for – be symbolic of – a future event. It can be maintained as an active phantasy for a while, even in the absence of sensory confirmation. The process is like that of 'reverberation', whereby a concept continues to be maintained for a while even without sensory reinforcement. It can operate to prevent a rise in anxiety, such as a baby might feel in the absence of the mother. So the baby is able to hold the mother in mind, and the comfort and security which are associated with the mother, while she is not there – even when there is no sensory reinforcement of that complex concept of comfort and security which 'mother' connects with.

The presence of a transitional object which can be held on to, helps to keep the reverberations going. Blanket edges, teddy bears, and such stand in for the phantasied (m)other. They stand on the margins of shared reality, representing the more uncontrollable mother and others who are known to come eventually, if not now.

Creativity

There is a close connection between frequent and solid experiences of 'us' and the development of symbols for more elaborate creative purposes. This is derived from the close connection between you being here with me now when I am not

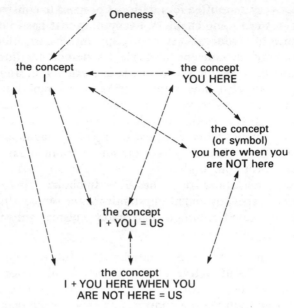

Figure 46

needing you (I am not thinking of you) and me thinking of you (having you as part of my current experience) when you are not here.

The fortunate baby will have had many many times when it was with the mother but not aware of her except for the security of knowing that she was there when needed. The baby was fortunate because its environment was fulfilling one of the essentials needed if it is to have a highly developed creativity. Because the baby somehow had the mother there when she was not an obvious part of its experiences, the baby can 'discover' her after she has been absent (from its experience) for a while. The baby will have had the experience of tolerating her absence without having felt the terror that she might be lost for ever. The baby's experience will have flickered between 'you here when you are not here' and 'you not here when you are here'. It has thereby discovered that it can hold on to a concept – a symbol – which stands for the available mother. The concept of the available mother – the symbol of the available mother – has become pleasantly and interestingly established. It can play

'peekaboo' with it. It can make the symbol happen while waiting
for the mother to come along. The symbol can fill the interval of
waiting, a small space of time.

The symbol stands for 'mother' − it stands for 'you who
normally come soon after I realize that I need you. Something
arose in my mind, an anticipation, a phantasy of something good.
Then there was a small gap, an absence, an interval of time. Then
you came.'

Symbols can stand for what will come. But, equally, they can
stand for what may come, what may not come, or what will not
come again. All kinds of conceptual processes can fill the interval
between the moment when we have a phantasy of something and
the moment of finding something. Transitional objects and other
symbols appear where there had been either nothing, or an
experience of something not there.

The art critic Peter Fuller has written a striking account of this
process in visual terms. He is looking at a painting by Robert
Natkin.

'About a third of the way down the picture, a little off centre,
there is a roughly rectangular area wedged between two
passages of whitish cross-hatching. As you continue to look at
this constellation it sharpens into a focal point. The rectangle
appears to be "in perspective": it seems further away from
you at the top than at the bottom. And so it lifts itself
upwards and outwards and the fragile curtain of paint, the
sensitive surface or skin, is apparently ruptured or torn. As
you ask yourself where the rectangular shape is within the
picture space, you become aware of what has been imaginatively called "the hum of light" which reverberates across the
whole surface, setting it in motion, disrupting it, and trans-
forming the way it reveals itself to you, the viewer. Although
you will in fact probably be looking at the painting in a
constant light, it is *as if* it were illuminated through a
succession of continuously changing filters.

All this commotion on the surface draws you in through the
skin of paint. In front of the picture itself you may even find
yourself expressing this involuntarily by moving a step or two
closer to it physically. In any event, you discover that the first
phase of your involvement was no more than a prelude or an

overture before the curtain vanished. You come to see that Natkin began by enticing you with an illusion – the illusion of a light-filled, elastic membrane of paint like the tinted underbelly of a gecko glimpsed against a sun-drenched window – and to accept that what you are in fact confronted with is nothing more or less than the successive layers of the thinnest of honey-comb marks laid down gently in whispers of paint upon the canvas surface. In this work the pigment is as tightly packed, as literally fleshly, as in any of this series.

But no sooner have you recognised the facticity of the materials than you become aware of yet another way of reading the painting. For now it is as if the curtain has risen and yet the painting continues to suck your eyes into itself, to engulf and entertain them. The uniform skin of light evaporates in part because its tenuous existence came about only through the mixing of colours and the organisation of forms into a shimmering, illusory film on the retina. But as this film disintegrates it gives way to billowing and boundless hazes of colour, to seemingly limitless vistas of illusionary space.'

(Fuller 1980: 178–79, Abstraction and 'The Potential Space')

Later in his chapter Fuller relates this process to other ways in which voids and blanks may be filled with creations of intense significance, aesthetic, spiritual, or practical. Here we find the roots of much imaginative endeavour. For some people, a space feels like an invitation to bridge it. Spacebats may engage in it for the thrill of having dared to risk themselves. Confident people, who can draw on a sense of competence ('I am grand – I can do it') may find a void pleasurable and attractive: it can be filled with all kinds of efforts. The gap, the emptiness, the interval, the space, seem inviting to creative people. We see faces in the clouds. On a larger scale, the Brontës on their lonely moors, with their isolated lives, their dead mother and empty father, filled their world with vivid people and events. Painters need their empty canvasses. Dr Barnardo, Albert Schweitzer, and others who are creative about people, see what is missing and what is needed, and set about putting it there.

Two people who encounter one another may create a relationship where there had been nothing. This is the more fascinating because, if the creation is to endure, there has to be an element of truth, which makes the encounter one of exploration and discovery. Who can tell how much invention-creation there is in such a relationship and how much discovery-creation? It must vary from person to person. Indeed, who can insist on the difference between invention and discovery in our love and hate of each other? We are so varied in our potential qualities, and so prone to have them called into being by other people's love and hope, or hate and coldness. Do not the old stories of cruelty and redemption tell us so?

Scientific invention is also a matter of filling a blank. This kind of creativity seems to come in two forms: interpolation and extrapolation (Bartlett 1932). Interpolation is closest to the process of 'discovering the object': the scientist has a set of starting-points, which seem connected with a phantasied end-point or outcome which he or she wishes to reach. At first this gap can conceivably be filled with a shifting multitude of possibly useful concepts. Some of these are eliminated when we cannot get evidence, cannot get the facts to coincide with our phantasies. Eventually, if we work hard enough and are lucky enough, the pieces fall into place and bridge the gap from phantasy to outcome in a way which can be tested further.

The process of extrapolation is of a more space-loving kind – discovery rather than invention. 'Surely if we sail west we will come to the Indies', said Columbus – and landed in America! Starting from the known, the discoverer takes the next step (perhaps the next logical step) and then the next and then the next . . .

All kinds of good things can happen when conceptual activity does not eventuate in the anticipated outcome. Creative processes happen, imaginative play, artistic endeavour, invention, discovery. They all start with the kind of mental processes called phantasy (that is, untested unconfirmed concepts). In this state of mind there are (at least during the 'period of hesitation') no clear concepts, no clear contours. Bits of 'self' and of 'not self' are available for potential concept-formation.

Symbols, words, and the holding function

Creativity requires, it seems to me, two conditions. One is access to the blurry shapeless pre-symbolic states of mind where concepts and symbols are *potentially* to be found. The other is the capacity to shape, hold, contain − conceptually organize − some of what is to be found there. We need to conceptualize and integrate the unprocessed material into shape. To create something, we need chaos, but we also need order. Otherwise we encounter the turbulence met by some of the autistic children described in Chapter 5. If there is nothing to hold us, we shall have a black hole instead of a psychic core. In order to develop, we need symbols with which we can hold and organize what would otherwise be confusion.

It looks as though symbols can have a holding function only after the child has experienced other kinds of being held and holding. The child must therefore have had experiences of the separateness of self from not-self; otherwise 'holding' makes no sense: there must be two things for one to hold the other; there is no holding when there is merging.

Margaret Little (1981: Chapter 5) notes this connection between the development of symbol-use and the development of self−other differentiation, working with people for whom the merged state, which she called 'undifferentiatedness', persisted, as a delusion, into adult life. In those areas of their lives where they held on to this delusion, they could not use 'the sophisticated processes of deductive thinking, drawing correct inferences, symbolisation or metaphor'. They said, 'What's yours is mine, what's mine is my own' and 'What's yours is half mine, and half the other half's mine, so it's all mine'.

> 'This comes from the undifferentiatedness itself, as here the symbol and the thing symbolised are absolutely one; as are the deduction, its source, and its consequences. For this same reason, these patients are not able to test reality in many areas; they have first to *find* it. They are engaged upon processes of differentiation and integration, and not upon such things as projection and introjection, identification and repression, all of which pre-suppose a separateness of subject and object.'

Similarly Tustin (1980):

> 'Symbol formation is based on the capacity to use *substitutes* for actual things and situations. It is also based on the capacity to feel separate from the outside world and thus to use

abstractions. The use of material objects which are felt to be part of its body and permanently replace the real thing, has prevented the psychotic child from doing this.'

Tustin (1984) contrasts an autistic boy's play with that of another child, whose mind was disturbed in a different way. The latter would use the toys he was playing with to *represent* (Tustin's italics) his feelings about himself and his world. But the autistic boy felt the toys to be actual bits of the village and of Mrs Tustin.

'An important part of modifying such children's pathological use of their autistic objects seems to be the realisation on the part of people caring for the child that these objects are not experienced by him as *substitutes* for longed-for people. For him, they *are* that person, because they give him the sensations he desires, the sensation of an object being of pre-eminent importance to him.'

(1984)

Mrs Tustin recounts an important session in which she felt that she understood something that this boy was doing, and that he understood her and felt understood by her.

'I said I had turned over his "shapes" in the stomach of my mind, and he had turned over my "shapes" in his, and something new had come out, to which he had replied "I suppose that's thinking".'

(1984)

Mrs Tustin was using words to communicate with the boy. Words are communicable symbols and can be part of shared reality. Shapes are private experiences and they are pre-symbolic. Words can interplay with other people's words. We can hold ourselves and each other with words. Words are for many people the supreme holders, binders, and organizers of meaning. Words are symbols: they stand for experiences. Words can be inner objects; they can be transitional processes; and they can be shared between people. They tidy up the pre-verbal and only blurrily conceptual wash and sway of our primary processes – they give us access to them and they preserve us from being taken over by them. Bad things happen when, for whatever reasons, this holding function fails.

The autistic children described by Tustin illustrate some of
this. They used little speech and they used it badly. Their
thinking was described as 'restricted and meagre'. They were
thought to be 'a-symbolic', not using symbols. Certainly they did
not play like other children of their age, or day-dream, or
imagine, or form expectations. These are all processes which
depend on the use of concepts, images, and phantasies to stand
for other things.

Symbols 'hold' us. Here, at the beginning of the processes of
conceptualization and symbolization, we also find the beginnings of the emotional and social virtues connected with tolerance
of frustration. Symbols enable us to bear with long delays
between needs and their fulfilment: they fill that gap of time. At
the simplest level, we fill the gap with phantasies of the
satisfying object or with the idea that it will come soon. At a
more complex level, the gap is filled with images of the world or
of our selves. This keeps us from being overwhelmed by
frustrated needs – the images provide a soothing context for our
frustration. We restrict our diet and put up with craving because
we want to look nice on the beach. We go on working after we
are tired because it will be good to see the finished product. We
do without for a little longer, so as not to have to put up with
second best. The ability to put our frustration in perspective
enables us to persevere for long periods in frustrating situations,

Once you discover Perrier, nothing else will do.

Figure 47

which will eventually yield major rewards (J. Klein 1965: 500–26).

We hold ourselves and each other with words. Not surprisingly, therefore, psychotherapists have tried, from their different perspectives, to understand the use of words and symbols in the context of what might be called shared ego-functioning. Tustin acknowledges her debt to those who influenced her:

> 'It will be obvious that in this work with Peter I was influenced by Bion's (1962b) formulations concerning "maternal reverie" and its importance in the transformation of what Bion calls "raw beta elements" by what he calls the mother's Alpha function. I was also influenced by Segal's (1957) paper on Symbolic Equations. "Autistic shapes" and "autistic objects" are part of the early pre-symbolic mental phenomena dealt with by these writers. Both Milner and Winnicott were aware of the importance of providing a containing medium for the expression of these entirely personalised "shapes" so that violent passions could be held and expressed through the shared experience of fun and play which had a very serious purpose. Milner (1969) by her "doodles", and Winnicott (1975) by his use of the "Squiggle Game", enabled the child to share his personal shapes so that mental and emotional assimilations could take place.'

All these writers show the profoundest awareness that concept-formation and 'thinking' come not from individual but from interpersonal activities. If things have gone wrong in the course of a child's development, so that its concepts are distorted, a social relationship, an 'us', has to be established before the organization of concepts can take place in a more orderly fashion.

The idea of developmental or remedial ego-functioning on another's behalf, first alluded to in Chapter 11, has recurred in each successive chapter. We next look at a detailed account of how one analyst helped a disturbed young woman to form concepts and symbols, and how much empathy and feeling it required.

PART · 5 ·
SPLITS

RENÉE

INADEQUATE ENVIRONMENT AND FRAGILE SELF

BASIC FAULTS AS THE CAUSE OF SPLITS

BEING SCHIZOID

The piers are pummeled by the waves;
In a lonely field the rain
Lashes an abandoned train;
Outlaws fill the mountain caves.

Fantastic grow the evening gowns;
Agents of the Fisc pursue
Absconding tax-defaulters through
The sewers of provincial towns.

Caesar's double-bed is warm
As an unimportant clerk
Writes I DO NOT LIKE MY WORK
On a pink official form.

Unendowed with wealth or pity,
Little birds with scarlet legs,
Sitting on their speckled eggs,
Eye each flu-infected city.

Altogether elsewhere, vast
Herds of reindeer move across
Miles and miles of golden moss,
Silently and very fast.

(W. H. Auden, *The Fall of Rome*)

293

·15·
Renée

The case of Renée, presented by Madame Sechehaye (pronounced, approximately and delightfully, Sashay) is remarkable because it describes how an adult went through many of the experiences normally experienced by an infant, in the process of acquiring concepts which become increasingly accurate representations of shared realities. It is also remarkable in that the work was done in the 1930s, when very little theory was available to guide her.

Mme Sechehaye was a psycho-analyst working in France and Switzerland. Her patient, Renée, was eighteen when they started to work together, and twenty-six when the account ends. Sechehaye was no better served by her translators than many other writers on psychological topics, so no pleasure can be got from the language of the text. There are two translations, with different titles. The quotations in this chapter come from the translation published in 1951.

Sechehaye called her method 'symbolic realization'. She meant by this the use of symbols to make something real to someone else, to make something real that was not real to them before: she gave Renée symbols to help her to conceptualize her experiences. Twenty-five years later, Hannah Segal (1957) wrote of a related process which she called 'symbolic equation'. It refers to what happens when a person experiences a symbol as though it were the thing it stands for. By using Renée's capacity for symbolic

295

equation, Sechehaye was able to make things 'real' to her. She also helped her to base the symbols on concepts which were in turn based on good sensory experiences – this is partly what makes symbols 'real'.

Sechehaye did two things: she worked in an astounding way with Renée, and she wrote it up so well and in such detail that we do not need to take her theoretical ideas where we do not want to.

Renée had grown up with an almost unworkable set of concepts. She had had a very deprived life. Although well-to-do, neither of her parents seems to have been able to devote time or feeling to her, and she seems to have been the victim of some strange sadistic and exploitative phantasies. Some of these account in part for her failure to thrive as an infant. Her mother, 'without realizing', put too much water in the baby's bottle, and the doctor somehow came to the conclusion that the child's constant crying was due to the richness of her mother's milk, and advised further dilution! When the grandmother came to stay, the three-month-old baby was visibly and grossly undernourished. It was the grandmother who decided that the milk was already over-thin and changed the mixture. Grandmother looked after Renée from then on until the eleventh month, when she abruptly left. Clearly Renée was surrounded by many destructive influences from the start.

In early puberty Renée became noticeably disturbed, and by her mid-teens she was behaving in the way schizophrenics did behave in the early 1930s, grossly deluded, dirty, dirty-minded, sly, and violent, perhaps because her doctors also behaved as they did in the 1930s, with forceful attempts at hypnosis, with terrifying physical restraints and baths, with occasional starvation-diets and sudden 'rest-cures' in the country. The damage to Renée's self-esteem must, from the beginning, have been frightful.

Mme Sechehaye seems to have been naturally kind, not repelled and not frightened. She seems to have had an intuitive understanding of Renée. Especially she seems to have understood that there was something to understand, unusual for people working with this kind of disturbance at that time. Like so many pioneers, she began with the classical methods she had been taught – psycho-analysis as this was practised over there at the time, with lots of explanations about complexes and where they came from. She modified her approach as she began to understand Renée better.

One breakthrough came when she went to visit Renée, who was at that time on a farm in the country. Renée would not eat. (From the distance of fifty years on, we can see that this was what we would now call 'anorexia', and we would connect it with Renée's need to keep some aspect of her life under her own control.) On this occasion, Mme Sechehaye had brought her an apple, and Renée accepted and ate it. So little was understood about these phenomena at that time, that, at the end of her visit, Sechehaye arranged for a great dish of apples to be always available to Renée. Of course, Renée did not touch them: on a later visit she explained that 'those apples are shop apples, apples for grown-ups, but I want apples from Mummy, like those', pointing to Mme Sechehaye's breasts. 'Those apples there, Mummy gives them to me but only when I'm hungry'. Mme Sechehaye wrote:

> 'I understand at last what must be done. Since the apples represent mother's milk, I must give them to her like a mother feeding her baby. I must give her the symbol myself, directly and without intermediary, and at a fixed time. To verify my hypothesis I carry it out at once. Taking an apple and cutting it in two, I offer Renée a piece, saying: "It is time to drink the good milk from Mummy's apples, Mummy is going to give you some". Renée then leans contentedly against my shoulder, presses the apple upon my breast and, very solemnly, with intense happiness, eats it.'
>
> (p. 51)

Winnicott commented:

> 'When we attempt to assess what Sechehaye did when she gave her patient an apple at the right moment (symbolic realisation), it is of but little moment whether the patient ate the apple, or just looked at it, or took it and kept it. The important thing is that the patient was able to create an object, and Sechehaye did no more than enable the object to take apple shape, so that the girl had created a part of the actual world, an apple.'
>
> (1965[1962]: 60)

Giving Renée an apple was, as Sechehaye saw, a symbolic communication: 'Mother wants you to eat and wants you to live.'

> 'The symbolism of the apples was the revival of all the shocks that Renée had had in infancy in regard to food, which represents maternal love. First of all, the mother had put so much water in the milk that it had hardly any consistency at all and could not satisfy the child. Then the mother had pretended to nurse the father and let him eat her up, in order to tease the baby. Furthermore, the mother had nursed the siblings one after the other, in front of Renée, which revived the memory of past privations in her unconscious.
>
> Renée had remained in the stage of moral realism: that which the mother grants is good, to desire it is permitted; that which she refuses is bad and if one allows oneself to desire it, punishment is merited. Renée's mother, by her behaviour, seemed to condemn her desire for nourishment; it was bad to want to eat, and consequently the desire to live was blameworthy.'
>
> (p. 51)

Sechehaye wrote of this feeling as guilt, but we now are more likely to see it as persecutory anxiety – the primitive fear of annihilation. In regularly handing Renée bits of apple,

> 'the "bountiful mother" has in this way taken the place of the "depriving" mother which permits Renée to live and love herself. . . . The new mother has proved that she wants her child to live and the child's confidence is able to assert itself since it has now received the right to live.'
>
> (p. 53)

Renée received the reassurance, and a way of conceptualizing the reassurance – the apple.

> 'Anxiety had attached itself to oral need. It was therefore necessary to correct in an appropriate manner the wrong done to the baby Renée.'

It is important to notice, Sechehaye points out, that it was a *symbol* of food that Renée needed – a symbol that would not arouse so much anxiety that she could not accept the corrective experience.

'When Renée had returned to the oral phase, she would have been angry to receive real milk, and that would have made her more ill. It was necessary for her to receive a symbol and not a reality ... because guilt feelings made it necessary to camouflage the repressed desire. Once guilt feelings have been calmed, one can accept reality.'

(p. 52)

Sechehaye intuitively recognized that the good mother is the facilitating environment, so she was willing to let Renée relax and regress to a very infantile way of being, and looked after her. Whenever Sechehaye forgot her role as facilitating environment, Renée immediately felt convinced that she should not be alive. From this Sechehaye concluded that she had to do a little bit more than be accommodating: she had also to take positive action and provide events from which Renée could continue to get the reassurance that she had permission to live, to enjoy life. Renée could not take this for granted. It had to be confirmed on many occasions, presumably because there was so little of it when she was a baby.

'Once, when I was present at her meal, I said with a certain impatience (trying in vain to get her to eat): "Well, if you don't feel like eating, don't". This was the end! I had revived her conflict in relation to food: I, the "mother"! I had encouraged her not to eat.
    The following night, Renée had a terrible fit, during which she knocked her head against the wall to destroy herself. It seems that my remark had provoked a new schizophrenic episode. Renée had to be sent to the clinic again where she was very agitated, biting her arm, pulling out her hair, ripping her clothing and constantly attempting suicide. ... She felt disintegration: "The roof crumbles, the monkey has something in his head that does not work any more". She wrote to me ... "I am going to sink, come to my rescue. Will you understand for once SOS – SOS – SOS".'

(pp. 64–5)

When she came out of this crisis she was completely inert, incontinent, refusing all food, being fed by tube; she spent days lying down without reacting to anything. After several disasters of this kind, Sechehaye became aware how careful she had to be never to suggest that Renée was in any way not wanted.

> 'Renée still hears voices. These voices say to her "Eat by yourself" [as a trap to provoke what Sechehaye calls guilt but we would call persecutory anxiety]. The analyst mother must say in turn: "I do not want you to eat alone, it is much too soon. I still want to give you your food".'
>
> (p. 54)

> 'Furthermore, when Renée was able to wish for something (to desire something is to want to live), I immediately gave it to her. For example, I said to the nurse "Please go quickly and get an apple-tart for Miss Renée, go quickly". Renée always seemed extremely astonished that anyone would put himself out for her. . . .
>
> One day Renée ventured to ask to feed herself. But this time I was on my guard and said to her, "Yes but only a little bit of bread because Mummy loves to feed Renée herself". She then said with a sigh of relief, that if mother continued to feed her she would be able more often to try to eat alone.'
>
> (p. 78)

At this time, 'mummy's feeding' was still the major concept through which the right to live was confirmed. 'Renée has a right to live' was becoming established as a concept but it was very closely connected with Sechehaye, who was experienced as giving her that right when she gave her things to eat. Eventually, we discover in a lovely quotation, Renée began to attach this concept to her own experiences and processes, to her 'self' we might say. Sechehaye overhears her talking to herself, on a number of occasions:

> 'At first she spoke to herself as a very loving mother speaks to her child, and I heard her say "Drink your milk [symbolized by the tea], my darling, it is mother who has prepared it, and then get quickly into bed. Mother is coming, curl up into a ball, my darling, mother loves you so". Some time later the tone changed, it was more lively, firmer, more adult: "Quickly to bed, your tea, your book!" And when the introjection was complete "Some tea? Oh I don't need any, it would cut my appetite for dinner. I am going to rest a little and then I shall

read''. She has now become aware of herself, the symbols were becoming unnecessary since reality had asserted itself.'

(p. 81)

The childish language would come back every time there was something new to learn, and would disappear again as soon as she had learnt it (p. 81).

Renée needed many repeated experiences to get some sense of continued existence – Sechehaye's, her own. In her fifth year:

'One day I left her outside in the street for a moment while I entered a shop to leave an order. When I returned I found her in a terrible state of anguish, completely lost and confused, believing herself abandoned.'

(p. 80)

In the course of her time with Renée, it became impressed upon Sechehaye that new concepts and connections could be established only by careful continuity and in slow degrees. Thus after a major relapse, Renée would eat only green vegetables. Not being nourishing, thought Sechehaye, they did not arouse anxiety about the right to live. Neither did the green unripe apples Renée picked off the trees. Sechehaye brings some ripe red apples; Renée refuses: she will eat only bits personally handed to her by Sechehaye.

'After the raw apple, she accepts an apple cooked in water, then a baked apple which represents foreign milk – that is to say, cow's milk – then porridge with milk [stepping into reality, Sechehaye says a bit mysteriously]. But each innovation has to be accompanied by a piece of raw apple given by the analyst-mother, just as in the beginning of the weaning period the breast is still offered occasionally. The child is shown in this way that she will not be weaned completely before she no longer needs the maternal milk. Two whole apples are always left on the mantelpiece, so that Renée can run to them in case her confidence is shaken. Little by little it is possible to add biscuits, bread, rusks such as are given to a weaned child, then sandwiches, oatmeal soups and so on.'

(pp. 53–4)

The first concept which Renée needed to establish was the right to survive. The apples, and all they came to imply, stood for this. Later stages of progress were each marked by an appropriate symbolic realization. After the right to survive, the right to be herself and to be cared for. A little plush monkey stood for this, which Sechehaye had given to Renée and which she treated with great concern and solicitude. Just as Renée could not always accept food directly, she could not at first accept solicitude without being panicked, for she was not sure yet that she deserved to have people care for her. But she could accept concern on behalf of her monkey, which conceptualized a part of herself, 'the Queen of Thibet', which had long been established. Renée could also begin to take care of herself via the monkey; she could, in Sechehaye's words, exteriorize her compassion for her own condition. 'Poor little monkey. He has a headache', said Renée (p. 55).

So now we have a symbol for the self as well as a symbol for an environment that wants Renée to live and to be an object of concern and solicitude. Next, Sechehaye found a symbolic way to communicate to Renée that she had a right to pleasures. Warm baths were the first symbolic representations of such pleasures (p. 57). Next came a toy tiger. 'Immediately he took over the role of good mother-analyst, frightening for the wicked but good to Renée (p. 67). Sechehaye thought that this tiger also enabled Renée to focus her assertive aggressive and hostile feelings, so that these did not suffuse too many inappropriate parts of herself or her world. 'Renée became less hostile and could be approached more easily: better contact was obtained. Anxiety diminished' (p. 67). The tiger was also useful in attacking the inner voices which persecuted Renée at times, denying her right to life and happiness.

Having established the right to live, and a channel through which love and care could reach her, Renée began to take an interest in the wide and varied world of other people and things. Having established the rudiments of self, we find Renée interested in what is 'not self':

'Imperceptibly, interest in reality broke through. One time, Renée was impressed with the contrast between the plains and the mountains. Another time, she was amazed at the meaning of certain words. She asked questions on general history. She asked for a watch, to keep track of time. She drew a branch of a grape-vine which hung in front of a window.'

(p. 77)

Sechehaye appreciated the importance of skill, and helped her classify and order the object world.

'I taught her to recognise certain species of butterflies and flowers, and to classify the pictures we had of them. She understood that to classify was to take possession of things and act upon them.'

(p. 77)

Classifying also pins the world down, removes some of its unboundaried, unconceptualized confusion.

'I gave her little tasks, intended to take her away from the indefinite, and thereby greatly relieved her.'

(p. 77)

And, throughout, to help her grow:

'Each time she did something, I complimented her, in order to strengthen her ego.'

(p. 78)

Mme Sechehaye began to work with Renée in 1930, when Renée was eighteen. In 1940 Sechehaye was able to write that 'the mental illness is over and in spite of her frail health Renée is fully engaged in intellectual activity, accomplishing good work with success and ease' (p. 127). Seven years later,

'Renée has not only remained cured, without any recurrences of pathology, but her personality has continued to develop and has gained in strength. . . . After she brilliantly finished her studies, Renée settled down in a city near Geneva. She lives with a girlfriend who is also a biologist, and with enthusiasm they collaborate on the same work. Renée has remained deeply attached to me and comes to see me as often as circumstances permit.'

(p. 131)

·16·

Inadequate environment and fragile self

Guntrip was one of the earlier British psycho-analytic theorists to want to shift the focus of psychotherapeutic theory towards 'schizoid' problems – the problems some people encounter in trying to maintain a vital sense of self in a realistic relationship to other people, while feeling continually undermined by anxieties about falling apart. In his introduction to *Schizoid Phenomena, Object Relations and the Self* he wrote:

> 'It is necessary to bring out very clearly the fact that psychodynamic theory has moved on beyond the original classic theory of superego control, guilt and depression.'
>
> (1969: 12)

And he quoted disapprovingly from a recently published book whose principal chapters bore such titles as 'Psychological Forces; Control of Desires, Derivative Desires . . . Deprivation of Desires; Aggression; The Super-Ego', commenting:

> 'Here is the old "moral psychology", all of it important but with no hint at all that the basic anxiety-producing conflicts in human beings are not over the "gratification of desires" but over the frightening struggle to maintain themselves in existence at all as genuine individual persons. . . .
>
> Of course guilt is a real experience and must be accepted, and there is no therapeutic result unless feelings of guilt are cleared up, but I hope that this book will disprove conclusively

that guilt is the core of psychological distress. *Pathological guilt* is, as we shall see, a struggle to maintain object-relations, a defence against disintegration, and is a state of mind that is preferred to being undermined by irresistible fears. The core of psychological distress is simply elementary fear, however much it gets transformed into guilt: fear carrying with it the feeling of weakness and inability to cope with life, fear possessing the psyche to such an extent that "ego-experience" cannot get started.'

(ibid.)

Guntrip was a considerable scholar of the old school. Deeply respecting the thoughts of others, he characteristically wrote as if he were only clarifying what others had said: he is only gradually coming to be recognized as a thinker with a unique perspective of his own. Though often taking other people's theories as his starting-point, he based his ideas also on his experiences with the people he took into therapy, and on his experiences in his personal analyses: he was first analysed by Fairbairn, whose views influenced his own thoughts greatly, and later went to Winnicott through whose help he came to accept another part of his personality hitherto blocked off from consciousness. The story is told in a moving article (1975). The dating of his writing is relevant as being either post-Fairbairn or as after both Fairbairn and Winnicott, but I confine myself mainly to his later ideas.

Guntrip's theory is in the main about the adult experiences of people for whom things had gone badly wrong at the stages when 'I' and 'you' and 'us' are forming. These structures cannot develop properly when the baby is not adequately protected against distresses which might overwhelm and obliterate them. And if the baby has not been adequately protected, if 'I', 'you', and 'us' structures are not properly developed, it cannot develop adequate defences against later distresses. Moreover, 'us' can be a great consolation in distress, and it is much harder to bear pain when recourse to 'us' is not possible. It is exactly this us-relatedness which is lacking in the people Guntrip describes as schizoid. Without at least a modicum of us-relatedness, 'I' cannot be properly established as a strong structure and will remain unintegrated: fragmented.

We are now considering early relationships, between the infant and the environment or the mother, which allowed things to happen which the child just could not bear. The child feels 'I wait for her and she never comes', 'I need her and she is not there', or worse 'They do not care what happens to me', even 'They do not care if I die', even 'They are killing me'. (I have put these feelings into the present tense here, because the young self has not yet a strong sense of the flow of time, and so whatever is happening then may persist in later object-relations as though it were forever happening – an experience on which such notions as hell might be based. I have also used third-person pronouns. There is no sense of 'us' – no sense of being held by another in a relationship. It is 'I' versus 'they'.) Such experiences leave lasting traces of pain and vulnerability.

The need for contact and support

The sources for this subsection and the next come mainly from Chapter 6 of *Schizoid Phenomena, Object Relations and the Self* (1969), and from Chapter 5 of *Psychoanalytic Theory, Therapy and the Self* (1971).

Guntrip used Winnicott's concepts of maturational processes and of the facilitating environment to underpin his own ideas on how the biology of the infant relates to the environment which will enable it to survive. Maturational processes govern the infant's biologically given potentialities, causing them to unfold in a biologically determined way. But these innate potentialities do not mature inevitably 'in sublime indifference to the outer world'. The infant is dependent on the opportunities which the environment offers; its potentialities flourish best in an environment that understands, supports, and encourages individual growth. If the environment is unsatisfactory, development may be distorted or arrested. The True Self is as yet only potential; it will not be realized in unfavourable circumstances.

Guntrip then looked at Winnicott's concept of ego-relatedness (a pre-condition for us-relatedness, see pp. 280 and 262f.). He considered ego-relatedness to be similar to, though perhaps more characteristically human than, the concepts of attachment-behaviour and separation-anxiety with which Bowlby was working at much the same time in a different corner of the field:

'Vulnerability to separation-anxiety exists when the human being is not ego-related' (1969: 223).

Ego-relatedness allows the young child to be protected by the presence of others without being impinged on by them. Given this, the vulnerable child is able to develop in its individual way, without fear either of devastating loneliness or of devastating damage.

> 'Birth is mere separation, and will speedily result in isolation, in the snuffing out of the sense of self, unless good mothering at once restores "connexion" of such a kind that it can lead to the evolution or realisation of the potential self of the infant.'
> (1969: 222)

In Guntrip's view, ego-relatedness is Winnicott's way of describing the process by which an infant who started life in total emotional identification with its mother can begin to experience its separateness from her, without losing its sense of security. 'The infant's ego-immaturity is naturally balanced by ego-support from the mother.' The sense of belonging, of being securely in touch, that grows in the baby by virtue of the mother's living reliability, becomes an established property of its own psyche. We have seen that there is a subtle transitional stage between feeling securely related when the mother is holding it, and feeling securely related when the mother is absent (see pp. 281–83). This can happen because of those moments when the baby who is actually with the mother can forget about her being there, because it feels totally secure – invulnerable. The baby gains proof that its trust is justified by finding, when it remembers the mother again, that she is still there (Guntrip 1971: 118ff.). This is the context for the development of us-relatedness which will replace the biologically-based sense of oneness. Clearly all this can only come about if the mother or other attachment figure is capable of experiencing us-relatedness. Not all (m)others are in this fortunate position.

People who have not had enough of this good experience are, in Guntrip's view, excessively vulnerable to even the slightest loss of support. Their chronic overdependence is a genuine compulsion which they cannot evade by effort, will-power, or intellectual understanding. Their only hope is to find someone who can understand them and help them grow out of it. That is what psychotherapy is.

The help Guntrip had in mind is only partly intellectual or dependent on insight given by a shrewd interpretation; rather it is mainly emotional – the need is for a relationship in which people can experience being securely held while they venture to be in touch with thoughts, feelings, or parts of the self from which fear has long kept them estranged. To this process, the final two chapters of the present book are devoted.

The inadequate environment: love made angry and love made hungry

Guntrip distinguished two types of reactions to the moment when the infant feels unprotected and uncared for. Which reaction occurs, depends on how much strength and confidence (or shame and fear) the budding 'I' has already accumulated. The stronger and safer-feeling personality reacts with anger and with the kind of depression that comes with anger. The less fortunate personality reacts with hopelessness and the kind of depression that comes with hopelessness. Here are two different kinds of depression arising from different sources. Guntrip (1969: 24) referred to these two types of reaction as 'love made angry' and 'love made hungry'. In his view, Freud's interest and focus lay more in understanding the former, which has to do with guilt, while Fairbairn (and other later writers) brought new understanding to the latter, which involves more schizoid reactions.

'Love made angry' is what happens when you want love from a person who is not giving it – you become angry with them in an attempt to force them to give you what you want. This is Bowlby's 'coercive anger'. Obviously, at some point this anger must lead to worry that your anger will drive away the very person you need, and for some this will lead on to guilt at having hurt the feelings of someone they care about. Not getting what you want, worrying about losing a loved person, having to live without love and mutual concern, makes you depressed as well as angry. On the bright side, however, you may in your anger turn to another person in the hope that they will love you better, and so you have another chance.

'Love made hungry' describes Guntrip's view of the 'schizoid position'. When you cannot get what you want from the person you love and need, it may be that instead of getting angry you simply feel more and more needy, with an ever stronger craving to get total possession of the loved person, to ensure that you will never be left wanting. But then you may be visited by the terrible fear that your love has become so overwhelming and devouring that it will destroy your loved one, and that then there will be nothing left of them. And indeed, this can happen. The depression which comes with this craving brings aloofness with it: you withdraw from loving because loving destroys those you love. In this case, there is no second chance, because if this is what you believe to be the nature of love and this is what you do, you dare not love anyone for fear that it will lead to the destruction either of them or of you.

In Fairbairn's terms, the love-made-angry depressed person looks on his or her loved one as a hateful denier (a Rejecting Object), while the love-made-hungry schizoid person sees his or her beloved as a desirable deserter (an Exciting Frustrating Object) never to be fully possessed.

Fairbairn's Exciting/Frustrating and Rejecting Objects played an important part in the evolution of Guntrip's thinking. Fairbairn himself used the metaphor of the infant reaching out and 'finding nothing there': the infant's excitement about life meets with no response in the world of other people and things, so that it must turn back on itself and be satisfied with phantasies of what it wants, ceasing to look for satisfaction in a world devoid of interest. (In psycho-analytic language, cathexis is withdrawn from the object-world.)

This sense of emptiness and void may be experienced where there would normally be connection with people and things, so that the child feels it has nothing to hang on to and lacks any sense of secure attachment. In this case, the (m)other is experienced as void and emptiness. At other times, void and emptiness may be experienced as coming from the self, as a frequent experience of hunger, for instance – the child experiencing itself as hungry-empty-needy-urgent-demanding-greedy-tearing-emptying in relation to the (m)other.

It is Guntrip's special contribution to emphasize always the two-endedness of relationships. This is not less the case when

310 OUR NEED FOR OTHERS

one end of a relationship is experienced as not there: the experience that 'the world is empty and does not hold anything for me' may be equivalent to 'I am empty and cannot hold anything or anyone securely'. Similarly 'I am empty and will destroy, swallow, overwhelm the world' may be experienced as indistinguishable from 'The world is empty and will overwhelm, destroy, swallow me'. People may experience all these possibilities, either simultaneously or in mood-swings up and down consecutively, however mutually contradictory they may seem to common sense (or rather to the 'Central Ego').

Needing people and fearing to need them: the in/out programme

Guntrip described in moving terms the plight of those who dread entering personal relationships which demand deep and genuine feeling on both sides. Such people may have felt compelled to withdraw their consciousness into a relatively small area because, although their need for love is as great as anyone's, it operates at the emotional level of absolute infantile dependence filled with need and greed and the terror of abandonment. At that level, dimly aware of their enormous need, they feel faced with the risk of total loss and destruction, both of themselves and of those they love. It is the form their own love has taken and they have little knowledge of any other. Loving, therefore, seems to present them with a terrifying choice, in which both alternatives lead to loss and destruction for someone. If they let themselves be loved, that means they must let themselves be swallowed up and taken over: they must be totally compliant and cease to be an individual. If they let themselves love other people, this means that they themselves will inevitably take them over, insisting on their total compliance and swallowing them whole. Then the loved ones will disappear as real people.

In this plight, some people try a compromise which Guntrip has called the in/out programme. Driven by their need to love and be with others, they go into a relationship but at once feel driven out again by their fear of exhausting the person they love with the demands they want to make on them, or by their fear of losing themselves through overdependence and compliance.

Others escape this painful oscillation by withdrawing from

feelings and relationships altogether. They then feel a dreadful meaningless emptiness. In Fairbairn's terms, their consciousness is confirmed to the unfeeling Central Ego, which relates only to idealized perfectly good and perfectly bad 'inner objects'. Such uncomplicated phantasy-figures are all that they (selectively) perceive of all that the varied world of people and things has to offer. Libidinal relationships are quite disowned, though anti-libidinal ones may be used to keep libidinal strivings down. We can imagine such an effect transmitted down the generations if we imagine parents who feel like this being emotionless and unresponsive when their children try to relate to them. We can imagine the children's greed for love and their fear of needing it. We can imagine the children summoning up all their strength, in turn, to avoid evidence of feeling, and growing up, and becoming parents, and so on down the generations.

When dependence is painful

The problem about being dependent on others is that infants need (m)others whether these are adequate or not. For many reasons, realistic and unrealistic, the infant (in us all) may construct a concept of being trapped in a relationship with a bad absent disobliging (m)other, the witch of many fairy tales.

Guntrip writes that in the first discussion he ever had with Fairbairn, the latter said that the basic neurotic conflict was between dependence and independence; when the person one turns to is the person one must get away from (1971: 116). How are we to rely on others without feeling trapped, and how are we to feel free from others without feeling cut off? Again we are reminded of Balint's philobats and ocnophils, who represent the fear of being committed versus the fear of belonging nowhere and having no attachment-figure. For both Fairbairn and Guntrip, the origins of schizoid traits lay in some failure of the early environment to provide combinations of support and freedom in an acceptable form, a form which would foster both relationship and individuality, and which would make it possible to feel comfortable both with 'I + You = Us' and with 'You and I disagree'.

When we are weak, we are vulnerable and need protection, and so we are necessarily dependent on whoever will protect us and look after our needs. Suppose now that the people on whom we are dependent resent our dependence. Then we will feel we are rejected *because* of our dependence, about which we are helpless to do anything. Our very situation makes us contemptible.

Some people are constantly afraid for this reason. Their experience of vulnerability and dependence has made them so: afraid of being dependent on people who dislike their dependence on them, afraid of appearing weak, afraid of looking a fool in other people's eyes. People committed to this internalized object-relation are in the more dire a plight because they regard themselves with the same hostile gaze which they experience from others. They feel shamed and disgraced by their own dependence and weakness and terror, believing that other people despise them for it. Guntrip had a patient who

> 'whenever she made any slight mistake, would begin shouting at herself at the top of her voice: "You stupid thing! Why don't you think! You ought to have known better!" and so on, which were in fact the very words her mother used against her in daily nagging. We see in an unmistakeable way the anti-libidinal ego as an identification with the angry parent in a vicious attack on the libidinal ego which is denied comfort, understanding and support, treated as a bad selfish child, and even more deeply feared and hated as a weak child.'
>
> (1969: 191)

In this frame of mind, people feel that the whole world is against them and waiting to humiliate them, yet they feel too weak to do without these hostile people. They are trapped. 'I need them but they don't want me; even my being here with them annoys them.' They may then make an effort not to feel those needs which make them dependent on the people who resent their dependence. In these circumstances, a person's sense of inadequacy does not come from doing this or that imperfectly; it is an 'unremitting state' of feeling in the wrong and in the way (Guntrip 1969: 175ff.).

To keep anxiety at bay, some people then develop a marked interest in competence and self-sufficiency, rather as the space-bats do. They may try to run their life so that their need for others is minimized. This is how the premature ego-functions of 'doing' rather than 'being' develop, with emphasis on adequacy and skills. But in the depths there is still terror, and the memory of being unable to cope, of being unable to keep 'them' friendly and concerned, and of the passionate overwhelming need for the forbidden dependence.

'I' split from 'me' lest they find and hurt me

The experience that 'I depend on a mother who does not care' or that 'I depend on another who does not care' will, in relatively mild circumstances, lead the child (in us) to the sense that 'I cannot direct my hopes towards this (m)other'. In more severe circumstances, there is likely to be a sense that 'the (m)other in whose power I am, is against me'. I believe that in truly severe cases, not only does the child feel 'You and I are not us', but the sense of 'us' does not develop at all. Hence neither does the sense of you-as-part-of-us, nor the sense of me-as-part-of-us. The child then has to live by relationships between 'I' and 'them', 'him', 'her'. There is no real 'you'. The (m)other can then be experienced only as impinging and exploiting, never as protecting or sharing.

When there is no 'us' in which 'I' and 'they' are embedded, it must seem natural that others should resent any reminder that I have feelings and needs of my own in competition with theirs. The other disappears except as a menace: 'I must not leave myself open to attack – I must not be found. I must keep myself safe from the (m)other.' (We need perhaps to be reminded again at this point that we are not considering the (m)other as known by other people – we are here considering how a child may experience the world. But perhaps we need also to remind ourselves that there are many more desperate and occasionally out of control (m)others than we dare publicly acknowledge.)

'I' keep 'myself' safe from 'them'. This sentence, which is grammatically correct, is full of splits and sharp boundaries. It might indeed describe a peson's mind correctly, but a person on whose map such splits and boundaries are very marked could not be a happy and rich and psychologically integrated personality. The 'I' regions are cut off from 'myself', and both are cut from 'them'. 'We' and 'you-as-part-of-us', both integrating structures, are not established.

Such splits would cut off a person's conscious 'I' from much that is going on with 'me' at the level of the body – the level of feelings and emotions, needs and impulses. In order to survive, I may have to make a habit of disregarding or disowning my feelings and my needs – I may have to alienate some regions of my self from other regions which have to do with feelings and needs. (In the theory propounded in this book, it is assumed that needs and feelings and impulses and hopes were originally part of my 'self' regions as these got established, so that a major effort has to be made to separate them out, a deliberate disintegrative effort of the kind discussed in the next chapter.)

One of Guntrip's patients, very like the one quoted on p. 312, shows the depths at which 'a cruel despising of weakness' can maintain a dramatic split between an active 'I' and a suffering 'me'.

'She would rave against girl children and in fantasy would describe how she would crush a girl if she had one, and would then fall to punching herself (which perpetuated the beatings her mother gave her). One day I said to her, "You must feel terrified being hit like that". She stopped and stared and said, "I'm not being hit. I'm the one that's doing the hitting".'

(Guntrip 1969: 191)

This woman achieved an almost complete split of 'I' from 'me' and withdrew consciousness from those regions of herself which were 'me'.

Differentiation between self-regions is obviously a necessary ego-function. We all have to establish a split between 'I' and 'me'. When I say 'I can see what is happening to me', I reveal a split between 'I' and 'me', but it is a necessary one, not a dangerous one. It is clear that I am not unconscious of 'me', rather that my consciousness can cover both 'I' and 'me'. But sometimes there is too great an erosion of the natural connections between regions, as when someone says, 'I don't know what is happening to me'.

Withdrawing from the unmanageable world of others

When most of life is frightening, and I usually feel inadequate, I may decide that being an onlooker is safer than being a doer: it is less obtrusive and hence less likely to attract hostile notice in my direction. When the watching 'I' is out of touch with emotions, feelings, and impulses, I develop something like Fairbairn's Central Ego, one of whose functions is to keep me out of situations so painful that I cannot cope.

Being wounded and terrified, people may withdraw into themselves in order to avoid further hurt. The danger is that they will withdraw so far that they will be left totally bereft, and get so far out of touch with their needs and feelings that they get no signals from them: it appears to such people that they have no needs – they don't feel anything. Paradoxically that may be a terrible feeling! The memory of having had feelings once, the capacity for which seems now lost, can fill a person with distress and longing. And in the present, I may want to keep in touch with the signals which come to me, yet be afraid of being overwhelmed by them if I do attend to them. I may oscillate in and out of my feelings because I do not have the energy or strength to contain them at a practical level.

We find in Guntrip further examples of the kind of people Fairbairn also described, people to whom messages from the world of others come only in very shadowy form, people not much in touch with what happens in the world of living-rooms, streets, or media. At first sight, this may not be obvious. However, slowly we realize that we are listening to someone who is not talking about people as we know them, in the round, but about 'them'. We are listening to someone who can perceive only a few highly selected aspects of the world of people and things. 'They', the others, are not realistically perceived, but are experienced only in terms of their imagined capacity to aid, threaten, or frustrate. Sometimes, 'they' are selectively perceived in such a way that the speaker can be both in touch with feelings, and yet able to keep them remote. 'Don't be silly' or 'Don't be so depressing' are examples of people speaking repressively to another person, while perhaps at the same time also disowning their own unacceptable notions. Similarly 'He's out for what he can get' or 'She sets her sights too high' may be said principally to enable the speaker to keep his or her own ideas isolated and disowned. Such people sometimes give us the impression that we and others are not experienced as independent people who existed before they walked into the room and who will continue to exist after they are out of sight; we are known only as experiences which must be controlled and kept away from contact with the self-image.

Small wonder that such people complain, in Guntrip's words, of feeling unreal, cut off, out of touch, out of focus, futile, the point having gone out of life, things seeming shadowy and meaningless. Guntrip (1969: 18) writes that, though they certainly complain of depression, this depression 'lacks the heavy, black, inner sense of brooding, of anger, and of guilt, present in classic (object-related) depression'. Schizoid depression is a state in which objects have been renounced:

> '*Patient:* I'm very depressed. I'd just been sitting and couldn't get out of the chair. There seems no purpose anywhere: the future is blank. I'm very bored and want to change but I feel stuck. . . .
>
> *Therapist:* Your solution is to damp everything down, don't feel anything, give up all real relationships to people at an emotional level and just "do things" in a meaningless way, like a robot.
>
> *Patient:* Yes, I felt I didn't care, didn't register anything. Then I felt alarmed, this was dangerous. If I hadn't made myself do something, I'd just have sat, not bothered, not interested.
>
> *Therapist:* That's your reaction in analysis to me. Don't be influenced, don't be moved, don't be lured into reacting to me.
>
> *Patient:* If I were moved at all, I'd feel very annoyed with you. I hate and detest you for making me feel like this. The more I'm inclined to be drawn to you, the more I feel a fool, undermined.'
>
> (Guntrip 1969: 19)

Cut off from the external world and living in my own phantasy, I cannot feel for others, for they are not real to me. My therapist and the other people around me are no more than stick figures which enable me to act according to the phantasies in my head which do seem real to me. I can imagine some of them to be so powerful that I must keep an eye on them and manipulate them to keep things smooth for myself. Or I may act compliant and behave nicely to them because I imagine that is what they want, and I imagine that I must do what they say because they are always right. Or I may imagine them as needing my consideration and concern. What I fear to do is to know them as they are, to 'discover' them. So I am left with the choice of either feeling well but rather unreal, or feeling real but terrible. I may veer between these two in an attempt to get some relief from each in turn.

Bad relationships may be better than none

It is hard to do without other people altogether. I may cling compulsively (and to other eyes tiresomely) to a loved person or valued idea, in order to keep unconscious my feelings about some of their more hateful aspects. Worse, I may cling to a relationship with an unloving or hating or unloved person, in order to keep at bay the sense of hopelessness, meaninglessness, and futility which would result from giving them up and being without anyone at all.

Some people may be able to keep anxieties at bay by relating mainly to causes and ideas, and interacting with other people mainly through these.

> 'If I stop believing in what holds me together and gives meaning to my life, only constant and unremitting self-monitoring will keep me from falling apart.
> 'I shall believe in psycho-analysis or monetarism or Adam and the Ants – they make life worth living.'

Somewhat better off are those people who can relate to others more directly, provided everyone's duties and roles are carefully and minutely defined. They relate to others mainly in the meticulous execution of tasks, not risking more unpredictable and spontaneous contacts.

Then there are people who prefer some kind of in/out compromise. However weakened they may be by the continual advance and retreat, it is better than nothing.

Yet others may be able to make relationships, albeit tainted by fear and suspicion because they cannot help feeling that people are dangerous and easily cruel or mean.

It is hard to do without people and relationships. When I fear and avoid them, something happens to myself, the self which needs to be attached to and in touch with others. Void and emptiness threaten me. My very identity feels as though it is disintegrating – it lacks boundaries where I should be in touch with others. I mobilize a host of defences. I look depressed, I feel depressed. Guntrip, however, argues that this depression may be what I hold on to as a defence against feeling overwhelmingly anxious. And indeed, the anxieties which a person is willing to know about may be a cover to conceal anxieties about falling apart or ceasing to be a person at all (Guntrip 1969: Chapter 8).

The defences against falling apart may be strong enough to be called False Selves; they may be the only parts of the personality that a terrified person dare show. One of the attractive things about Guntrip is his insistence on a person's need for defences. He does not speak of the False Self in condemnatory terms; he sees it as a necessary defensive organization, a survival kit, a caretaker self, the means by which a threatened person has managed to survive. It is worth reminding oneself, when exasperated by someone who acts flighty, irresponsible, dishonest, evasive, or snooty, that these are all defensive ploys.

A frightened person may make a show of anger as a way of hiding weak, scared feelings. It is easy for others to see such a person as an angry person (and to attempt a therapy on the basis of the hidden anger and the guilt which goes with it – after all, hidden anger and guilt form part of the psychoneurotic personality which was the first to be analysed and restored to relative well-being by Freud nearly a hundred years ago). But anger and hidden guilt are not at the root of all distress, and it is possible to use the appearance of hidden anger as a defence against even more unacceptable feelings. Guntrip writes eloquently about our culture's preference for these 'strong' feelings.

'In a word, the core of psychological distress is not *guilt* but *fear*. Guilt is itself a form of fear, but it arises at the stage when the child is becoming socialised and capable of realising the effect of actions on other people, and the nature of their reactions of anger and condemnation. The child feels ashamed, sad and frightened to find that he has hurt those he loves and needs. There are much more primitive fears than that, fears not of the effect of our *strong* and dangerous needs and impulses, but of our infantile *weakness*, littleness, and help-lessness in the face of an environment which either fails to give the support we needed as infants or else was positively threatening. Human beings all prefer to be bad and strong rather than weak. The diagnosis of guilt allows us to feel that the source of our troubles with ourselves and others is our possession of mighty and powerful instinctive forces in our make-up, which take a great deal of controlling and civilising. The philosophies of Nietzsche and Machiavelli, and the "power politics" of the present age, all make it plain that human beings feel at least a secret and often an openly admitted admiration for the ruthless strong man, however bad his ideas and actions may be. In our competitive Western culture (including communism which is every bit as competi-tive as capitalism) contempt is felt for weakness. We have always known that sympathetic care for the weak and suffering, fostered by Christianity, had to fight its way forwards, and survive on the basis of much compromise; as in the often cited cases of Victorian capitalists who made fortunes by the most ruthless business methods on the one hand, and endowed churches, charities and hospitals on the other. The main stream of the world's active life has been carried on in the tradition of the struggle for power in which the weakest go to the wall. The superman is the criminal who has the courage to fight and does not mind hurting other people. The Christian with his slave-morality of self-sacrifice to save others is weak and gets crucified. A diagnosis which traces psychological troubles to our innate strength supports our self-respect and is what is today called an ego-booster. A diagnosis which traces our troubles to deep-seated fears and feelings of weakness in the face of life has always been unacceptable.'

(1969: 31)

·17·
Basic faults as the cause of splits

In this chapter we are interested in ways in which the integrity of the personality can be disrupted by splits which come about after a period of what had seemed to be normal integration. Psychic structures which were at one time organized together may lose their interconnections and fall apart. This return to simpler structures is variously called 'dissociation', 'de-differentiation', 'disintegration', 'regression' to a simpler state of mind. It is how we feel – to a mild extent – when we feel not very well, as in a bad bout of flu. Everything is simplified, we do not have the energy to maintain a highly differentiated set of responses. We feel surprisingly fretful and in need of in-dulgence. We revert to childish comforts which we thought we had outgrown – sweet, mouth-filling, warm, relaxing things. Ego-functioning is slack; we are more child-like, more easily distracted, more vulnerable to slights and hurts we can usually take in our stride. The controls are weaker.

> 'Turning and turning in the widening gyre
> The falcon cannot hear the falconer;
> Things fall apart; the centre cannot hold;
> Mere anarchy is loosed upon the world.'

The values at the centre do not feel connected with the impulses demanding expression.

320

'The best lack all conviction, while the worst
Are full of passionate intensity.'

And yet, as the final lines suggest, new and very constructive
things may come from such anarchic states.

'And what rough beast, its hour come round at last,
Slouches toward Bethlehem to be born?'

Yeats's poem 'The Second Coming' describes deep and mysterious processes of dissolution and renewal relevant to many kinds
of creative work. Nina Coltart (1985) used it to illustrate the
work of psycho-analysts. Ehrenzweig (1967) based his whole
theory of art on similar premises. We cannot create anything
new if we cannot tolerate incoherence, disorganization, splitting.
For a more general discussion of breakdown, we therefore return
to the metaphor of personality-structure as landscape. In particular, Balint's concept of the Basic Fault (1968) helps us to
understand the kind of splits which may fragment structures
that had seemed integrated until a moment of stress caused
disruption. Balint likened the personality to a landscape with a
geological history. In this landscape are features caused by long-
ago events: mountains and oceans, scarps, crags, and valleys left
behind after major upheavals; millennia of weather and the slow
grind of glaciers have had their effects. Now plants cover the
earth; not immediately apparent in the landscape are faults in the
geological structure – faults not in the sense of errors or sins, but
weaknesses in the terrain, where the ground may crumble and
crack in times of strain.

A number of writers have contributed to our understanding of
the causes and development of such faults. I shall try to list what
each has to say without arguing. Each of them may have seen, or
been impressed by, a different kind of weakness. In the present
state of knowledge it is certainly pointless to try to argue them
into consistency.

Bodily damage

One kind of fault or permanent weakness is the result of bodily
damage. Regardless of a parent's loving wishes, it may happen
that a child is left for long periods in extreme conditions of

hunger, heat, cold, sensory deprivation, or whatever. Or it can happen that a child is born with a physical handicap. Or permanent damage may be done by disease, or when a child is accidentally badly hurt in wars or famines or earthquakes – or modern traffic. The effect of disaster at a bodily level may be to inflict so great a wound on the self-image – 'a narcissistic wound' – that the memories of it are kept isolated for ever, and the rest of the personality develops out of touch with those memory-traces. That is where the weakness will be, the fault. Hannah Green's *I Never Promised You a Rosegarden* (1964) gives an example of a traumatic bodily event leading to a later breakdown. In this story, the trauma happened when the child was four. She was not helped to recognize, put into words, express, or accept the pain and outrage she had experienced at the time of a surgical operation. On the contrary, all around her denied that anything bad had been happening. The experience remained so isolated that the girl had no *idea* of it, but she did feel the feelings associated with it. She tried to be good, living in a family which was certainly 'good enough' in spite of some shortcomings, but she battled ineffectually with the sullen resentment, hatred, and contempt which kept rising up in her, which no one could understand.

To me, it seems urgent to have more research into the consequences of injury to the body before body-imagery is stabilized. Body-imagery is the precursor of self-imagery, with which the sense of identity is closely connected. It is surely important to know more about the psychological effects of the incubators used to protect very premature or very ill infants, who necessarily must put up with an abnormal amount of sensory deprivation. And how are those infants affected, whose eyes are treated with a tincture at birth, as a medically approved preventative measure – a procedure which blinds them for the first few days of life?

There must be many ways in which the normal gradual development of imagery about what it means to be a bodily person – and of imagery about what the world has to offer – is so disrupted as to leave ill effects which we do not know how to eradicate. Moreover, we must do more research on damage caused, not by bodily distress or injury, but by other bodily circumstances. Who can tell the good and bad effects of leaving infants on their own in cots for long periods, instead of letting them be in touch with a human being much of the time? Who can tell the psychological advantages and disadvantages of the rocking cradle?

Separation anxiety and the loss of attachment – Bowlby

Bowlby has presented some convincing arguments from the animal world that attachment and separation-anxiety are biological phenomena, and he and his colleagues have provided both theoretical and factual (even visual) evidence of the sufferings of little children ill-prepared for separation from those to whom they are attached (Robertson 1952). According to this viewpoint, the infant animal has built-in as well as built-up expectations that its needs will be met by what Bowlby called an attachment-figure, normally the mother. If there is a delay in having these needs met, two kinds of distress result: first, distress caused by the unmet need – hunger, cold, pain, or whatever, and second, distress at the loss of the attachment-figure. According to Bowlby, the crying of the young of the species is biologically bound to create tension and anxiety in adults who hear it, and this does not abate until the distress-signals cease. The adult comforts the infant both by meeting its needs and by relieving the fright it got when it found itself unattached and subject to unmanageable distress. It is this distress which one of Tustin's little patients described as a black hole – a hole where there should be a button to attach the infant to what Kohut called the selfobject and Winnicott the facilitating environment; it is distress caused when the illusion of omnipotence has to be given up.

Premature loss of the selfobject state – Kohut

There is a time in infancy, when body-experiences and other processes have not yet integrated into a coherent and whole self; there is not yet a single dominant self-image, nor yet a set of interrelated ego-functions. For Kohut, the development of an identity is 'the growth of self-experience as a physical and mental unity which has cohesiveness in space and continuity in time'.

'The mother's exultant response to the total child (calling him by name as she enjoys his presence and activity) supports, at the appropriate phase, the development from auto-erotism to narcissism – from the stage of the fragmented self to the stage of the cohesive self.'

(Kohut 1971: 118)

The mother's (and other people's) love of the baby is the beginning of the baby's self-love. Empathic, competent, loving people generate a selfobject state of mind which enables the infant to experience itself as whole, lovable, in control and capable – 'grand'. It is love that causes integration – 'cathexis' – between the different experiences which happen to an infant, so that it feels itself to be 'grand'. 'A fragmented self is the consequence of a poorly cathected self' and falls more easily apart. The cause of such disintegration lies, in Kohut's view, in the unmanageable loss of the selfobject state: the infant abruptly loses the sense that it is whole, lovable, and competent – a sense which good care would normally provide – before it can cope with such a discovery by looking after itself. This is Kohut's formulation of a basic fault.

'While a relationship to an empathically approving parent is one of the preconditions for the original establishment of a firm cathexis of the self, and while in analysis disturbances in this realm are once more open to correction, the opposite sequence of events (from a cohesive self to its fragmentation) can often be observed both in analysis and in a child's interplay with its pathogenic parents. The fragmentation of the self, can, for example, be studied in patients who, with the aid of the analyst's presence and attention, have tentatively re-established a feeling of the cohesiveness and continuity of the self. Wherever the mirror-transference cannot be maintained, the patient feels threatened by the dissolution of the narcissistic unity of the self.'

(1971: 120)

An empathic and competent mothering figure (or therapist) will understand and provide for the baby's needs in such a way that the child (in us) can begin to build on a foundation of self-confidence and trust in the goodness of the world. But the abrupt failure or loss of the selfobject state damages the child's sense of itself as a whole person: to be cut off from one's selfobject, before one has grown out of this state in a natural way, must be like being cut off from one's arm or leg, certainly as traumatic. Thereafter the person is prey to a host of related anxieties, all to do with what it feels like when you fall apart:

- fear of loss of the reality-self, caused by longing for ecstatic merging with an idealized parent-figure;
- fear of loss of contact with reality and fear of permanent isolation because of experiences of unrealistic grandiosity;
- frightening experiences of shame and self-consciousness, caused by the intrusion of exhibitionism;
- hypochondriacal worries about physical or mental illness due to obsessional interest in disconnected aspects of the body or the mind.'

(Kohut 1971: 152–53)

These are commonly interpreted in psycho-analysis as castration fears. Kohut explicitly warns against this: *these* fears come from earlier breaks in integrity. In general, his views on instinctual drives take the whole of life as their context:

> 'Let me emphasize again that rage and destructiveness are not primary givens but arise in reaction to the faulty empathic response of the selfobject. . . . An isolated striving to search for an outlet for rage and destructiveness is not part of the primary psychological equipment of man, and the guilt with regard to unconscious rage that we encounter in the clinical situation should not be regarded as a patient's reaction to a primal infantile viciousness.'

(1977: 123–24)

> 'It will bear repeating at this point that the tenets I propose with regard to the experiences of aggression and rage also apply to the libidinal drives. The infantile sexual drive in isolation is not the primary psychological configuration – whether on the oral, anal, urethral or phallic level. The primary psychological configuration (of which the drive is only a constituent) is the experience of the relation between the self and the empathic selfobject.'

(1977: 121–22)

In Kohut's view, drives are normally integrated into the personality in the course of development. But when there is fragmentation, when the person falls apart, they become important in isolation from the self-organization, which no longer provides a context which transcends and contains them. Healthy drive-experiences, writes Kohut, always include both self and self-object. But if the self is seriously damaged or destroyed, then the drives become powerful in their own right. 'Such drive manifestations only establish themselves in isolation after traumatic and/or prolonged failure in empathy from the selfobject.'

$x + y + z$ amount of desolation – Winnicott

Bowlby's attachment figure and Kohut's selfobject are very like Winnicott's facilitating environment and 'good-enough mother'. None of these concepts is exactly like the others, but they have a common core of meaning. A facilitating environment allows a child to notice its needs and wishes, and to begin to imagine what would make it happy, and then to find its wish answered. For this to happen, the mother or other care-taking persons need not be there all the time, but they must not be away so long that the baby feels abandoned. They can safely be away for a little while and the baby will not mind, picking up the thread of its phantasy of their continued care at the point where it loses the sensory stimulus of their actual presence but still retains the remembered sense of their presence (= care). There may, however, be a brief delay between the first arousal of the need and the coming of the mother (or other care-taking person). When this happens, the baby may cry, and this will bring, let us say, the mother, to do what is needed.

Winnicott invented a mathematical metaphor for the amount of frustration or desolation an infant may be able to tolerate. The baby can recover without ill-effects from x amount of delay before someone comes to cope. Winnicott says the baby may even be able to stand an absence for $x + y$ amount of time, and still be able to pick up the threads of its good phantasy. But sometimes there may be a yet longer interval: $x + y + z$. This is too long, says Winnicott, and the infant becomes traumatized – wounded, damaged.

This is where Winnicott would locate the basic fault. The environment has now been irrevocably experienced not as facilitating but as indifferent at best, hostile at worst. The infant is now forced to develop ego-functions, so that it can look after itself – before it has reached the phase of development where a self arises naturally out of play experiences. A problem has had to be faced prematurely – how to get along in an unhelpful environment. A False Self (for Winnicott a set of cognitive functions disconnected from the life of feelings and emotions) begins to develop and to manage the environment so that further traumatic experiences may be avoided. When help finally comes, the whole experience is shut away. But the sense of indwelling may have been impaired by repeated bad experiences, and a rather lifeless self will develop, in which thinking and feeling and doing are dissociated from each other, with no strong sense of being or of being whole. Here is the place of the basic fault, where the break may come.

> 'Trauma implies that the baby has experienced a break in life's continuity, so that primitive defences now become organised to defend against a repetition of "unthinkable anxiety" or a return of the acute confusional state that belongs to the disintegration of the developing self-structures.'
>
> (Winnicott 1974[1971]: 114)

A break in being is different from a frustration, and here again we see a writer warning us that it is not castration-anxiety he is thinking of. Frustration belongs with 'male-element' drive-satisfaction-seeking. 'To the experience of being belongs something else, not frustration but maiming.' Something should be there which is not there – the indwelling self.

The pain of $x + y + z$ amount of desolation may have created a practically permanent break, with an accompanying practically permanent agony, of which a person may not be continuously aware, but which is nevertheless there all the time, sapping the capacity for work and happiness. In an important article, published posthumously, called 'The Fear of Breakdown' (1974), Winnicott made the point – important to those who live with this agony and to their therapists – that the fear of breakdown may in fact be a fear of reviving the memories of a previously experienced breakdown: there is a basic fault. In other words, there was a time when the process of integration was devastatingly interrupted and the infant had to remain in its distress; it could not return to the safety of a mother's enveloping and holding presence, but was left with the chaos of half-individuated processes not properly synchronized with one another. Winnicott called this state an agony. He thought the pain so great that 'anxiety' did not seem a strong enough word. He listed five 'primitive agonies' as examples, the first – the fear of returning to an unintegrated state – being the most basic, while the others in one way or another represent memories of later developmental disasters:

- failure of indwelling, when the body seems not to be the place where 'I' dwell,
- loss of the sense of reality,
- loss of the capacity to relate to other people and things,
- the sense of falling for ever with nothing to hold on to.

Winnicott sometimes writes in what seems to me a surprisingly optimistic vein.

> 'We must assume that the vast majority of babies never experience the $x + y + z$ quantity of deprivation. This means that the majority of children do not carry with them for life the knowledge from experience of having been mad. Madness here *means* simply a *break-up* of whatever may exist at the time, of a *personal continuity of existence*. After "recovery" from $x + y + z$ deprivation, a baby has to start again permanently deprived of the root which could provide *continuity with the personal beginning*.'
>
> (1974[1971]: 114–15, Winnicott's italics)

I am less optimistic than Winnicott about what happens to us in infancy, and believe that many of us have had this experience, quite often perhaps. But if we base ourselves on what we have learned from him and others, I also believe we can afford more hope. It is permissible to think that, while some parts of the developing structure fall into chaos and terror, other parts of the growing order remain intact and make a rebuilding of the destroyed connections possible. Only repeated deprivation in major areas of development would be likely to wipe out the possibility of reconnecting with the early roots of experience, the True Self. Winnicott himself actually goes on to say as much:

babies are 'constantly being cured' of the effects of $x + y + z$ degree of deprivation by the mother's comforting, her 'localised spoiling that mends the ego-structure'.

This is an important issue for psychotherapists: can this person be helped to find enough associations of goodness, and to bring them into operation often enough to have them contribute to greater ego-strength? If not, is there any point in helping him or her to become more aware? Or will such efforts leave the unfortunate person as disabled as ever?

Lack of fit and the unempathic environment – Balint

Balint was one of the earlier writers to consider seriously the point at which one becomes aware that there is a world of other people and things – the point of individuation. At this point, there may be either a more home-loving or a more space-loving orientation, but either way, if all goes well, a person will emerge with an integrated personality. However, all may not go well. Paraphrasing Balint, a person may be struck by a trauma, after which development will be fundamentally influenced by the method which that person invented to cope with the trauma. The Basic Fault is at the point at which people begin to have to 'cope'.

How Balint would have liked the use of the English 'coping' to refer to ego-functioning! It gives recognition to our ability to survive and to deal with people and things in order to survive, not necessarily with much regard to the moral dimension. 'Coping' has two independent and equally relevant roots, according to the *Shorter Oxford English Dictionary*: A. From the Old French *coper*, Modern French *couper*, to strike (a blow), to cut. From this root we get our meanings (1) to strike; to come to blows; encounter; engage; (2) to be or prove oneself a match for, contend successfully with; (3) to have to do with; (4) to meet, to come in contact (hostile and friendly) with; (5) to match a thing with another equivalent. B. From Middle English *kopen* – to buy (cf. cheap). From this root we get (1) to buy; (2) to exchange, barter; (3) to make an exchange, bargain. There is even a third root, from cope meaning cape: to cover with a cope, to hang over like a coping. All very appropriate.

To return to our theme after this linguistic digression, Balint does not think of trauma as necessarily a single event. Trauma is more likely to be caused by a long-standing situation in which there was some painful misunderstanding – a lack of fit – between the child and the adults around it. 'True, despite the general lack of fit, in some cases some adult may be on the child's side, but much more often, immature and weak individuals have to cope on their own with traumatic situations: either no help is available, or the only help is of a kind that is hardly more than a continuation of the misunderstanding, and thus useless.' For lack of the right support, the child is forced to find its own method of coping, 'a method hit upon in a time of despair or thrown at it by some un-understanding adult who may be a well-wisher, or just indifferent, or negligent, or even careless or hostile'. This method will be incorporated in the child's personality, and therafter 'anything beyond or contrary to this method will strike the person as a frightening and more or less impossible proposition'. 'The individual's further development will then be prescribed or at least limited by this method which, although helpful in some respects, is often costly, and above all, alien' (1968: 82n).

> 'Most patients cannot tell us what causes their resentment, lifelessness, dependence, what the fault or the defect in them is ... some can express it by phantasies about perfect partners, perfect harmony, untroubled contentment. ... Over and over they repeat that they feel let down, that nothing in the world can ever be worth while unless something they were deprived of is restored to them.'
>
> (Balint 1968: 88–9)

Balint notices the influence of the theories of his time. 'Sophisticated patients may express this something irretrievably lost or gone wrong as the penis or the breast, usually felt to have magical qualities, and speak of penis or breast envy, or castration fear.' However, says Balint, in nearly all cases this is coupled with an unquenchable and incontestable feeling that if the loss cannot be made good, the patient himself will remain no good.

Ontological insecurity – R. D. Laing

It is largely to R. D. Laing and his associates that we owe the popular growth in sympathetic understanding of what it is to feel 'schizophrenic' and of the concepts of the False Self. The publication in 1960 (paperback 1965) of Laing's *The Divided Self* made an enormous impact on the intelligent public of those days. He argued that our lack of understanding of many confused people is due to our own unconscious *unwillingness* to understand them (and ourselves), and that they are confused because we need to keep them (and us) confused. This was a revelation at the time. The crucial passage is a re-examination of what Kraepelin (1905) described as the typical behaviour of a patient 'in an excited condition', when being displayed to a lecture-hall full of students.

'The patient I will show you today has almost to be carried into the room, as he walks in a straddling fashion on the outside of his feet. On coming in, he throws off his slippers, sings a hymn loudly, and then cries twice (in English), "My father, my real father!" He is eighteen years old, tall, rather strongly built, but with a pale complexion on which there is often a transient flush. The patient sits with his eyes shut, and pays no attention to his surroundings. He does not look up even when he is spoken to, but he answers beginning in a low voice, and gradually screaming louder and louder. When asked where he is, he says, "You want to know that too? I tell you who is being measured and is measured and shall be measured. I know all that, and could tell you, but I do not want to." When asked his name, he screams, "What is your name? What does he shut? He shuts his eyes. What does he hear? He does not understand; he understands not. How! Who! Where! When! What does he mean! When I tell him to look, he does not look properly. You there, just look! What is it! What is the matter! Attend: he attends not. I say, what is it, then? Why do you give me no answer? Are you getting impudent again? How can you be so impudent! I'm coming! I'll show you! You don't whore for me. You mustn't be smart either: you're an impudent lousy fellow, such an impudent lousy fellow I've never met with. Is he beginning again? You understand nothing at all, nothing at all; nothing at all does he understand."

Kraepelin notes here among other things the patient's "inaccessibility": "Although he undoubtedly understood all the questions, *he has not given us a single piece of useful information*. His talk was ... *only a series of disconnected sentences having no relation whatever to the general situation"* [1905: 79–80, Laing's italics].

Now there is no question that this patient is showing signs of excitement. The construction we put on this behaviour will, however, depend on the relationship we establish with the patient, and we are indebted to Kraepelin's vivid description which enables the patient to come, it seems, alive to us across fifty years. What does this patient appear to be doing? Surely he is carrying on a dialogue between his own parodied version of Kraepelin, and his own defiant rebelling self.

"You want to know that too? I tell you who is being measured and is measured and shall be measured. I know all that, and I could tell you but I do not want to." This seems to be plain enough talk. Presumably he deeply resents this form of interrogation which is being carried out before a lecture-room of students. He probably does not see what it has to do with the things that must be deeply distressing him. But these things would not be "useful information" to Kraepelin except as further "signs" of a "disease".

Kraepelin asks him his name. The patient replies by an exasperated outburst in which he is now saying what he feels is the attitude implicit in Kraepelin's approach to him: What is your name? What does he shut? He shuts his eyes. ... Why do you give me no answer? Are you getting impudent again? You don't whore for me? (i.e. he feels that Kraepelin is objecting because he is not prepared to prostitute himself before the whole classroom of students), and so on ... such an impudent shameless, miserable, lousy fellow I've never met with ... etc.

Now it seems clear that this patient's behaviour can be seen in at least two ways, analogous to the ways of seeing vase or face [see also pp. 46–7]. One may see his behaviour as "signs" of a "disease"; one may see his behaviour as express-ive of his existence. ... What is the boy's experience of Kraepelin? He seems to be tormented and desperate. What is he "about" in speaking and acting in this way? He is objecting to being measured and tested. He wants to be heard?'

(1965[1960]: 29–31)

Laing and his associates differ from the other writers in this chapter, in not going back to events in childhood or infancy to demonstrate the existence of splits in the personality. For a variety of theoretical reasons, they do not need to. In particular they do not assume that the personality must once have been a whole which subsequently split. Rather, they see each person presenting different facets to each other person, according to the expectations which have evolved between them.

'Let us suppose that Jill has a father and mother and brother, who all live together. If one wishes to form a complete picture of her as a family person, let alone as a person outside the family, it will be necessary to see how she experiences and acts in all the following contexts:

Jill alone
Jill with mother
Jill with father
Jill with brother
Jill with mother and father
Jill with mother and brother
Jill with father and brother
Jill with mother, father and brother.

People have identities. But they may also change quite remarkably as they become different others to others. *It is arbitrary to regard any of these transformations or "alter" ations as basic" and the others as variations.*

Not only may people behave quite differently in their different alterations, but they may experience themselves in different ways. They are liable to remember different things, express different attitudes, even quite discordant ones, imagine and phantasize in different ways, and so on.'

(Laing and Esterson 1964: 6–7, my italics)

This is a theory of natural splits. It maintains that people will feel that they have integrity and identity, provided first that they are not under pressure to be wildly different in different role-relationships, and second that each role-relationship is fairly consistent from day to day. The examples given in *Sanity, Madness and the Family* (1964) are all of impossibly contradictory pressures. Here is 'Ruby', daughter of the Eden family:

'When Ruby, aged seventeen, was admitted to hospital she was in an inaccessible catatonic stupor. At first she refused to eat, but gradually she was coaxed to do so. After a few days she began to talk. She rambled in a vague and woolly way, often contradicting herself so that we could get no consistent story from her of her relationship with her family or with others. One moment she would say her mother loved her, and the next that she was trying to poison her. She would say that her family disliked her and wanted to get rid of her and abandon her in hospital, and then she would say that they were good and kind to her. . . .

She complained of bangings in her head, and of voices outside her head calling her "slut", "dirty", "prostitute". She thought that "people" disliked her and were talking disparagingly about her. She said she was the Virgin Mary and Cliff Richard's wife. She feared crowds and "people". When she was in a crowd she felt the ground would open up under her feet. At night "people" were lying on top of her having sexual intercourse with her: she had given birth to a rat after she was admitted to hospital: she believed she saw herself on television.

It was clear that the fabric of this girl's "sense of reality", of what is the case and what is not the case, was in shreds.

The question is: Has what is usually called her "sense of reality" been torn in shreds by others?'

(Laing and Esterson 1964: 118–19)

The authors then give an account of some of Ruby's background. (For the sake of clarity the names of her biological relatives have been printed normally, and the names by which she called them and/or by which they referred to themselves in quotation marks.)

'Ruby and her mother lived with her mother's married sister, this sister's husband ("daddy") and their son ("brother"). Her father ("uncle") who was married, with another family elsewhere, visited them occasionally. Her family violently disagreed about whether Ruby had grown up knowing who she was. Her mother ("mummy") and her aunt ("mother") strongly maintained that she had no inkling of the real state of affairs, but her cousin ("brother") insisted that she must have known for years. They (mother, aunt, cousin) argued also that no one in the district knew of this, but they admitted finally that, of course, everyone knew that she was an illegitimate child, but no one would hold it against her. The most intricate splits and denials in her perception of herself and others were simultaneously expected of this girl and practised by the others.

She fell pregnant six months before admission to hospital and had a miscarriage at four months. ... The family was haunted by the spectres of scandal and gossip, with what people were saying and thinking, and so on. Ruby's pregnancy intensified all this. Ruby thought people were talking about her, and her family knew that in fact they were, but when she told them about this they tried to reassure her by telling her not to be silly, not to imagine things, of course no one was talking about her.

This was just one of the many mystifications surrounding this girl. Here are a few of the others.

In her distracted state she said that she thought her mother, aunt, uncle, and cousin disliked her, picked on her, mocked her, and despised her. As she got "well" again, she felt very remorseful about having thought such terrible things, and said that her family had been "really good" to her, and that she had a "lovely family".

They in fact gave her every reason to feel guilty for seeing them in this way, expressing dismay and horror that she should think that they did not love her.

They told us, however, with vehemence and intensity, that she was a slut and no better than a prostitute. They tried to make her feel bad or mad for perceiving their real feelings.'

(Laing and Esterson 1964: 120–21)

In *The Divided Self*, written at much the same time, Laing helps us understand how Ruby comes to be feeling and acting as she does – she is protecting her inmost self from destruction.

'We have our secrets and our needs to confess. We may remember how, in childhood, adults at first were able to look right through us, and into us, and what an accomplishment it was when we, in fear and trembling, could tell our first lie,

and make, for ourselves, the discovery that we are irredeem-
ably alone in certain respects, and know that within the
territory of ourselves there can be only our footprints. There
are some people, however, who never fully real-ize themselves
in this position. This genuine privacy is the basis of genuine
relationship; but the person whom we call "schizoid" feels
both more exposed, more vulnerable than we do, and more
isolated. Thus schizophrenic patients may say that they are
made of glass, of such transparency and fragility that a look
directed at them splinters them to bits and penetrates straight
through them. We may suppose that precisely as such they
experience themselves.'

(Laing 1965[1960]: 37)

'We can now state more precisely the nature of our clinical
inquiry. People may have a sense of their presence in the
world as real, alive, whole, and in a temporal sense, continuous. As such, they can live out into the world and meet
others: a world and others experienced as equally real, alive,
whole and continuous.

Such basically *ontologically secure* people will encounter all
the hazards of life – social, ethical, spiritual, biological – from
a centrally firm sense of their own and other people's reality
and identity. It is often difficult for people with such a sense
of their own integral selfhood and personal identity, of the
permanency of things, of the reliability of natural processes, of
the substantiality of others, to transpose themselves into the
world of an individual whose experiences may be utterly
lacking in any unquestionable self-validating certainties.'

(p. 39)

Laing makes it clear that both secure and insecure people may be
tormented, sad, full of doubt and anguish and uncertainties. This
is not what distinguishes ontologically secure people from
others. Being secure does not mean being happy, only being
secure.

Laing classifies three kinds of danger which characteristically
beset the insecure.

1 *The danger of engulfment* – I may be taken over and swept
   away by someone or something.

2 *The danger of implosion* – I may be invaded and impinged upon and totally filled with whatever they put into me when I am empty. In reaction to these dangers, I may withdraw, which leads to

3 *The danger of depersonalization* – I may feel that nothing and no one is real any more: 'This is not happening to the "me" that matters.'

I may begin to think of my 'real' self as inviolable – no one can reach it. I may tell myself that whatever I am being forced to do, whatever roles they feel I must play, this is not happening to my real self. And indeed this is so – ontologically insecure people are not consenting to what they are saying or doing. Their true self is hidden away. Their behaviour and their bodies are being coerced, but somewhere is a 'me' that is not involving itself. Laing thinks of this as the 'unembodied self'. It is as though the person said, 'I must keep in mind that this is not happening to me, only to my body; it does not touch the real me.' As Laing puts it, 'Instead of being the core of his or her true self, the body is felt as the core of a false self which a detached, disembodied "inner", "true" self looks on at with tenderness, amusement or hatred as the case may be' (1965[1960]: 69).

However, this divorce of role from self destroys the integrity of the personality.

'We shall suggest that it was on the basis of his exquisite vulnerability that the unreal man became so adept at self-concealment. He learnt to cry when he was amused, and to smile when he was sad. He frowned his approval, and applauded his displeasure. "All that you can see is not me" he says to himself. But only in and through all that we do see can he be anyone (in reality). If these actions are not his real self, he is irreal: wholly symbolical and equivocal. He is a purely virtual, potential, imaginary person, a "mythical" man, nothing "really". If, then, he once stops pretending to be what he is not, and steps out as the person he has come to be, he emerges as Christ, or as a ghost, but not as a man: by existing with no body, he is no-body.'

(p. 37)

Here are people constantly reminding themselves 'This is not happening to the essential me', 'This does not touch the real me', 'What they say and do to me does not really matter', 'This is a dream'. What is happening to that part of the person which the person does experience as 'me'? What does 'touch me'? The answer is, nothing from the senses touches 'me'. That part of the person has retreated to the world of ideas. But the sense of self started with body-imagery, which, if all goes well, is refined and structured and in various ways continually confirmed by messages from the sensory world. If, now, there is a constant inhibition of messages from the senses which would confirm that the world exists, then the body-image, the self-image, and the very self are inevitably weakened. The experience of being connected with the body will be weakened and confused. But body-imagery has been connected with the sense of well-being from the early days on, when all well-being was physical, and so the sense of well-being is dissipated. Moreover, even when good things are happening (regular breathing, good digestion, regular heartbeat, the soft touch of clothes, the good taste of food), the effect does not enhance well-being as it would do in a less divided self.

The frustration and rejection of excitement – Fairbairn

Fairbairn was the first great exponent of splits in a person's self-regions. His ideas were given extensive consideration in Chapter 8, but some will need to be summarized here because Guntrip based his own formulation on them, and the next chapter takes Guntrip's ideas further. Fairbairn was interested in the developments which issued from the infant's experience of the mother as Frustratingly Exciting and/or Rejecting. He thought of the infant as having needs governed by the pleasure-principle – Freud called these the Id, collectively, and Fairbairn the Libidinal Ego. Children whose experiences were dominated by phantasy relations with a Frustrating Exciting and/or Rejecting Object will come to feel more and more that it is no use wanting good things. They will eventually cease to reach out for what they cannot get. Eventually the phantasy of something good simply raises anxiety or anger rather than a wish to get it: an Anti-Libidinal Ego has developed which protects the child from the pain of frustration, though it in turn may be painfully experienced. The Anti-Libidinal Ego is a set of reactions to the Libidinal Ego which ensure that the child's needs remain hidden; it remains unconscious of them. Thus the Anti-Libidinal Ego keeps the libidinal part of the personality out of touch with the world of potentially satisfying as well as frustrating people and things – there is a basic fault between Libidinal and Anti-Libidinal Ego.

A third personality-structure, which Fairbairn called the Central Ego, rather like Freud's Ego, comprises the set of calculating reactions through which currently incoming information is registered and evaluated and retained for future planning – a useful structure for survival purposes. There may not be much connection between this structure and the other two – another basic fault.

The regressed ego – Guntrip

Guntrip subscribed to Fairbairn's ideas about the structure of the personality. He added, however, an important concept of his own: the withdrawn 'regressed' ego (1971: 172). Guntrip considered that there were three stages in the process he called the withdrawal of the regressed ego.

1 At stage one, following Fairbairn, there is a deepening of the split between the (already existing) Central Ego (more in touch with the world of other people and things) and the (also already existing) Libidinal Ego (where a person's more bodily feelings originate). This is a true 'vertical' split.

2 At stage two, an Anti-Libidinal structure interposes between the Central Ego and the Libidinal Ego. This makes it additionally difficult for people to be in touch with their libidinal feelings, and for their libidinal needs to find expression in the world of other people and things. People then experience (rejecting) anger, because of the (frustrated) existence of these (excited) feelings, but they are not conscious of the source of their anger. The structure here under consideration is a repressive one, more a horizontal 'lid' than a vertical split.

3 At stage three, a further vertical split occurs, this time within

the Libidinal Ego, that is within the structures which involve libidinal feelings. This split ensures that, while some libidinal needs eventually find expression, however painfully they may be hampered by their connection with anti-libidinal anger and rejection, others are withdrawn from communication with any sources of pain. These latter are then out of touch with the realities mediated by the Central Ego, and out of touch with the moralities of the Anti-Libidinal Ego, and out of touch with other (libidinal) feelings, needs, hopes, wishes. They exist, but they are unknown to the person. The result is a (vertically) split-off personality of which the person is not usually conscious. This is Guntrip's 'passive regressed ego which seeks to return to the ante-natal state of absolute passive dependent security. Here, in quietude, repose, and immobility, it may find the opportunity to recuperate and grow to a rebirth, as Winnicott (1954) holds' (1969: 74).

The phenomenon Guntrip calls the regressed ego is a very important one. The next chapter considers it in detail, and depends heavily on Guntrip's insights. But before we get to it, we must take the opportunity to clear away some misconceptions about regression, about the meaning of Guntrip's three-phase sequence, and about Guntrip's and Fairbairn's belief that we start life with a unified self which sometimes splits later.

First then, we must clear up an ambiguity in the term 'regression'. Rycroft (1968) defines regression as 'a reversion to an earlier state of mode of functioning'. But what kind of a reversion? To an earlier state of feeling? Or to an earlier mode of personality organization? The answer is that there are two kinds of regression at least. One involves reversion to earlier feelings, and more generally *regression to an earlier way of experiencing self and others*. The other involves a *relaxation of integrating processes* and hence a reversion to an earlier and less integrated organization of structures, with more splits, more isolated regions, more 'islands'. Even in normal states of mind, as the following chapters show, some people have to make efforts to hold themselves together. When they relax in a therapeutic situation, they relax those efforts. This is the aspect of what is usually called regression which I shall call relaxation. Sometimes when

Guntrip believes people to be retreating to some earlier state of being, I believe them to be relaxing the connections which hold them together.

Secondly, we must note that Guntrip is here describing a sequence which, he implies, is a sequence of events in a child's life. We must not be misled by this; it is in fact a sequence of stages which some people go through in some kinds of psychotherapy. People do regress in an appropriately holding therapeutic environment. As they feel more and more secure with their therapist, they give up their self-protective devices more and more. This allows them to revive and express (and even act upon) more and more strongly protected thoughts, feelings, wishes, memories, phantasies. Many of these do indeed have their roots in childhood and infancy, and were part of our young minds, but they indicate more about how we felt then and feel now, than about the stages by which we got those feelings.

Thirdly, our troubles are aggravated by Fairbairn's and Guntrip's assumption that we start with a unified self which is destroyed by subsequent misfortunes, as for instance in the quotation below.

> 'Here, in this complex pattern of ego-splitting or loss of primary psychic unity, with all the weakness and internal conflict it involves, is the root cause of personality disorders in later life: and the most vulnerable part of the self is the most hidden part, cut off from all human relationships in the depths of the unconscious.'
>
> (Guntrip 1971: 172)

This is beautifully put, and I believe it to contain an accurate description of how it is with some people. But it also contains the misleading assumption that the self has a primary unity and then splits. I think that Guntrip was misled by what he learnt in the consulting room. In a relationship of trust, as self-protective devices are abandoned, some people relax and show themselves to be less integrated than they at first appeared to be. In my view, they are then as they have always been, at heart. Many many people have a hidden, tender, vulnerable side, and it would be good if this were more in touch with the rest of the personality. But this hidden 'regressed' withdrawn ego is not necessarily the result of splits in a region or a structure which was once whole. Although it is true that sometimes a more developed part of the self withdraws from involvement in everyday sensory life, it seems to me equally true that many people have parts which have never developed or which have never been allowed to come to the fore. These parts are hidden, but they have always been hidden – they have not retreated from a more visible position. I shall therefore not use Guntrip's terminology, but refer instead to the vulnerable tender part of the personality, having in mind something that is very sensitive, like a flower that shrinks at the slightest touch. Often this part has been split off or repressed, because it has been hurt. Shrinking, wincing, wounded, skinless, are the adjectives which best describe those regions then.

Guntrip, through his practice as a therapist, was familiar with these tender, vulnerable states of mind, none more so, but he was misled by what his adult patients said and did. He was not a paediatrician, like Winnicott, and this led him to over-reliance on the evidence he got from his adult patients. However, what he had to say on the structure of the personality, particularly as regards the vulnerable feelings, is absolutely valid if we disregard his developmental assumptions, and can be used to understand uniquely important aspects of the schizoid state of mind. This I hope to do in the next chapter.

·18·

Being schizoid

Recap on structures

To recapitulate. Basic units of experience are organized, in the course of development, into more complex structures. At first, they are like islands: isolated mental and physical functions preceding the stage of the cohesive self. These complex structures are dynamic from the start, involving motivation and action as well as imagery: they are structures of functions. At first, they are isolated from one another because there has not as yet been enough experience to create the links and interconnections which create more extensive structures.

In Hayek's terms, at the beginning of life we have only crude, very general, and very unstructured 'maps'. Then comes the process of constructing more detailed maps from incoming experiences. With more and more experiences, our maps get clearer and more defined, though each succeeding message has relatively less impact on our increasingly strong structures. On these maps are various subregions or partial maps, each of which holds an emotionally meaningful and internally coherent dynamic image of some aspect of the self in connection with some other person or thing.

Maps are relatively enduring structures. They are dynamic perceptual and cognitive processes by means of which we encounter life. They are the means by which we locate where we are: our experiences are shaped by them. As a rule, we are not

343

conscious of them, any more than we are conscious that it may be raining in Birmingham when we are on holiday in Penzance. As a rule, we are conscious only in terms of what Hayek called 'models', constructed partly from our maps, partly from what our senses tell us is happening at that moment. What we are conscious of *now* is our *model* of the world just now. Generally, we are not aware that we have turned ourselves into a perceptual apparatus through which we experience our world, and so we are not often aware that we are experiencing selectively. However, what we are experiencing is governed by a working model based on particular regions of the map – regions which for that moment carry our consciousness and our self-consciousness.

Our maps and models reflect the landscape of our lives, developing more features as life goes on. 'Splits' are part of the landscape from the start. There are spaces between the 'islands' formed by the first associations between basic units of experience; these spaces are the first 'splits'. They are due simply to lack of connecting experiences – they are woven over when subsequent experiences make the necessary connections. Other splits start simply as lack of connections but are subsequently maintained in spite of experiences which would normally connect them. They are maintained because closer connection would make a person anxious about the consequences or implications of making the connection, as when a person denies that what is sauce for the goose is sauce for the gander because to accept the goose/gander connection would affect other inequalities so far left unchallenged. Even the mere possibility of closer connection may create alarm – 'signal anxiety'. Anxiety operates also in a third kind of split – actual active splitting caused when a structure loses some of the interconnections which at one time kept it integrated. This is a split which had been covered up but which may open again at any time: a hidden fault underlies the landscape – a 'Basic Fault'.

All this is not idle playful logic-chopping. It provides a way of thinking about important psychological processes. In previous chapters we considered a frightened person's decision 'I will try not to notice what is happening to me'. Because of fear, this person's 'I' was not mapped with 'me' but had been split from that region, and the model of 'I-as-a-person-who-acts-in-this-situation' lacked connection with the information, mapped elsewhere but not available on the same model, about 'me-suffering'. That person's model of 'I-in-the-world' lacked 'me'. Guntrip's patient who said she was doing the hitting (p. 314) presented an extreme example of this process.

In the current chapter our interest lies in the schizoid process by which some regions of the personality are hardly experienced. Their connection with other regions (and hence our consciousness of them) can only be tenuous, because of the disappointment and distress we suffered when those regions of the personality were first mapped. We keep those regions isolated lest we revive the pain registered there, which we are bound to be in touch with when they are integrated. Thus they may never find expression in action or be illuminated by consciousness. Our working models of certain situations will never adequately include the intensity of feeling locked up in those areas of our personality.

The previous chapter made it clear that splits may occur for a variety of reasons, and may affect the structure of the personality in a variety of ways. I think it important to remember that each person has his or her own unique splits. However, the present chapter will look at some personality-organizations which have often been remarked upon.

Splits between the vulnerable and the coping regions of the personality

When things go well, the infant's experience of its needs comes to be associated with its experience of a good-enough world of other people and things, in which those needs find expression and satisfaction. There does not then have to be any great split between the infant's experience of its needs and its experience of satisfaction. It is people whose vulnerability and need are deeply split from their coping ego-functioning regions, who show the characteristic schizoid traits of which Guntrip has written with so much depth, insight, and feeling: introversion (interest turned away from the world of other people and things), withdrawal and detachment, narcissism (he meant by this, no interest in others), self-sufficiency, a sense of superiority, lack of feeling, loneliness, and depersonalization (see 1969: 44ff.).

In this subsection we consider the schizoid experience from a perspective profoundly influenced by Guntrip but with some conceptual difficulties left out for reasons explained at the end of the previous chapter.

When Guntrip refers to the split between the Central Ego and the Withdrawn Ego, he may be understood to be making a statement about a person's maps (the central organizations in terms of which everything that happens is experienced) and also about the models which may be operating at particular times.

Let us suppose that my maps are loaded with memories of needs which were left unfulfilled for intolerable lengths of time. I will then have regions of memories of anguish, rage, and terror, memories of extreme vulnerability and openness to attack, when I lacked the necessary boundaries and defences. Here would be the origins of my belief that I am little, weak, helpless, and vulnerable. Paradoxically the regions are *now* heavily defended: they cannot now be easily reached and modified by later information about the world. But being mapped, they influence my models of the situations in which I find myself and so they affect my experiences in the world today.

When protection of the tender and perhaps needy, hurt, and vulnerable-feeling self-regions has taken the form of isolation, we have the 'Withdrawn Ego' of schizoid experience. The withdrawn-ego regions are isolated from other regions which map other aspects of the world of other people and things. Implicit in those other maps are the details of our dealings with that world. They are part of the self that copes: the 'Central Ego'. Unless some good things happen, people structured in this way cope with the world without drawing on whatever is available in the tender, vulnerable, needy self-regions; these have been withdrawn from contact with ongoing processes and thus become something like 'autistic pockets'.

Guntrip also spells out how, in the schizoid personality-structure, these two kinds of regions stand in a particular relation to one another. The tender vulnerable-feeling needy parts are kept away from direct contact with the object world. Awareness of the object world, and the skill to survive there, resides in the coping regions of the self, out of touch with the region of importunate needs and hopes and wishes.

My vulnerable self-regions are plagued by my fear that discovery will destroy them. They are preserved by being split off.

And this is unfortunate, for this is the reason why these regions get more and more isolated and hence more and more in need of protection and concealment. Thus, for instance, Winnicott:

'The False Self has one positive and very important function: to hide the True Self (which it does by compliance with environmental demands). In the extreme examples of False Self development, the True Self is so well hidden that spontaneity is not a feature in the infant's living experiences.

. . .

In this way it is now possible to trace the point of origin of the False Self, which can now be seen to be a defence, a defence against that which is unthinkable; the exploitation of the True Self, which would result in annihilation.'

(1965[1960]: 146–47)

My tender vulnerable self is preserved. But since it is preserved from relating to the object world and to other parts of my self, it is kept incommunicado. Sensory messages reach it but are not integrated, and so they do not affect the terrors which may beset me. If the isolation is deep enough, *all* messages are intercepted, whether their news is good or bad. My coping self intercepts them and processes the information, and acts, and copes, but at a price: though my vulnerable self is protected, it cannot be reassured. Hurt feelings permeate the person with a sense that danger lurks everywhere. From the point of view of the whole person, such preoccupations with danger may be over-sensitive and unrealistic. Certainly the less the vulnerable regions of my self are in touch with the regions that cope, the greater my sense of being vulnerable and unable to cope. Those regions have neither the strength nor the skills which are needed, nor a realistic appreciation of danger. Perhaps this is why people plagued with this kind of personality sometimes take risks which appal less easily frightened people. Those who confine themselves to what they feel able to cope with are more realistically in touch with their surroundings.

'Schizoid' can thus be thought of in terms of isolated, vulnerable, needy regions, covered by more or less obvious protective coping regions mainly organized in terms of their contact with other people and things.

The process which isolates my vulnerable regions also isolates my coping self – I may lose touch with those self-regions from which my needs and feelings and simple bodily satisfactions arise. My coping self then only operates as needed for survival, and not for enjoyment, fulfilment, or happiness.

Of course, at an early age my map is still in the making, less rigid and unchanging than it later becomes. At this stage, splits between regions can be mended by subsequent good experiences – the separate regions can merge again and so obliterate the gap which hindered easy communications between them. As this happens, both regions would again be available to new input and both would once more contribute to my consciousness of myself-in-the-situation. With more communication between need and satisfaction and general well-being, the sense of 'I need some-thing' and the sense that 'I can get it' may be reconnected, though my map might always have a weakness at the join – a basic fault.

Ego-relatedness, or rather us-relatedness – knowing myself to be safely held by a protecting presence – helps the tender vulnerable regions of my self to be less panicked and in more realistic contact with my more coping regions and hence with the world of other people and things. It also helps my coping self to be less preoccupied with survival. This creates the conditions in which my vulnerable and perhaps needy self may find ex-pression and gratification. In ordinary life, love and friendship provide the necessary holding. When they fail, some kinds of psychotherapy may do so.

Splits impair the development of my ego-functions, that is of the skills which enable me to act appropriately in the situations in which I find myself. It may cause them to develop in isolation, out of touch with the biological needs which have become as-sociated with need, hurt, and vulnerability. This produces the people who correspond to the stereotypes of games-playing oafs, mad scientists, grey bureaucrats. To make matters worse, if we do not regularly exercise the skills which we need to act successfully in the world of other people and things, the world brought to us by our senses, then their development is impaired. Like an industry that does not invest in research, we become inflexible and cannot adapt to changes in circumstances – not enough information has been integrated that could be used to create fresh solutions when needed. If I prefer to stay with my phantasy satisfactions, my skills do not develop as far as they could with practice and the experiences of trial and error and success.

Summing up so far, we can distinguish two or three different kinds of people or moods.

one extreme	*another extreme*
an isolated region	in touch with other regions
withdrawn and vulnerable	outgoing, resilient
with very hurt feelings	self-reliant, confident
and poor ego functioning	skilled and compctcnt

Some people would smile at the suggestion that they could be described as vulnerable and needy. This is not surprising. People may not be even faintly aware of the great quantities of pain and fear they are continuously guarding against.

> *a third extreme*
> unconscious, hurt, needy, vulnerable feelings
> isolated from the rest of the self
> conscious confidence in being able to cope
> justified by high levels of skill and competence

How would we behave in the mood which matches the third alternative? We would have an 'observing ego', a set of cognitive skills with which to watch the world around us with a wary eye. We would be aware of this observing ego; we might even call it our 'self'. We would not feel very dependent on other people, and we would not have much sense of contact with other people, nor a sense of solidarity or fellow-feeling or empathy or understanding, but we would feel we understood 'enough', meaning that we understood enough not to feel endangered or handicapped: enough to cope. We would not be very communicative about ourselves, and have no strong wish to talk things over with others. We would not think of ourselves as having strong feelings, and other people would not think so either. We would have one unmistakably strong conviction, however, not necessarily recognized as a feeling, against people who do show their feelings — we would think of them as showing weakness. How male, how carefully not female, point by point!

Not surprisingly, such personalities are quite common in our culture. But there are some extreme forms. It is of these that Guntrip wrote that the core of the personality is fear, in contrast with the guilt which characterizes those who were the first to be understood in classical psycho-analysis. They take refuge in what Guntrip called the 'moral diagnosis': 'We do these bad things because we have these strong (bad) impulses which must be curbed.' But this covers what they actually wish to curb the expression of: the needy, dependent, vulnerable self.

The split-off phantasy world and the split-off life of the senses

In Chapter 14 we considered arguments which suggested that our strength and confidence are derived from our early days when, if we were lucky, our phantasies were confirmed by sensory events. Our baby phantasies that something nice would soon happen coincided regularly with the onset of the nice thing happening. Sensory events (of food, warmth, love, and so on) then confirmed our central (phantasy) processes.

We are weakened when there is a discontinuity between these two: in later days, the life of the senses will not be so deeply involved with thoughts of what we could enjoy.

When infant satisfactions are not closely related to the arousal of infant needs, the baby misses opportunities to acquire the sense that it has control over getting pleasant things for itself. Moreover, if the arousal of need is very unconnected with the arrival of whatever might in other circumstancs be greeted as a pleasant, satisfying thing, the baby is left feeling that there is little it can do for itself. To that extent, it will feel it cannot cope with the world. Disappointed babies and adults in this mood may prefer to remain in the world of their phantasies, and keep away from the world their senses convey to them. In the life of phantasy we can try to continue to have phantasy satisfactions, or at least some measure of control over our phantasy creations. The incentive to stay with our phantasies will be the greater, the more we have suffered from the world our senses bring to us — the world of other people and things over which we have no control. Alarm may flood us whenever that painful world threatens to intrude, and signal-anxiety may keep us clinging to our phantasies. Day-dreams are preferred to what the senses may bring.

> 'External relationships seem to have been emptied by a massive withdrawal of the real libidinal self. Effective mental activity has disappeared into a hidden inner world; the patient's conscious ego is emptied of vital feeling and action, and seems to have become unreal. You may catch glimpses of intense activity going on in the inner world, through dream and phantasy, but the patient's conscious ego merely reports these as if it were a neutral observer not personally involved in the inner drama. The attitude to the outer world is the same: non-involvement and observation at a distance without any feeling, like that of a press reporter describing a social gathering of which he is not a part, in which he has no personal interest, and by which he is bored. Such activity as is carried on may appear to be mechanical.'
>
> (Guntrip 1969: 18)

On the other hand, it is possible for people to retreat into the life of the senses, and to cut off their consciousness from more central processes. Babies and adults in this mood give an impression of responsiveness and lively feelings. But the responsiveness is to the momentary stimulus – it does not touch the more central regions in any coherent way. There is no coherence at the back of this apparent vitality and vivacity, no reliability of mood or direction – not even a strong self-preservative purpose. Such people sometimes appear to be at the mercy of their moods. Women who behave like this have often been prized by those with a strong need to nurture and protect; they are regarded as good fun, and their silliness is gratifying to others. But if no such protector can be found, their fate is tragic. Romantic literature is full of them.

So here is a split or weakness in the connections between the phantasy world and the coping self, and also between the sensory life and the coping self. Once there are such splits, people can choose to retreat into either, to diminish their pain.

Spacebats and homebodies: personality-structures and the structure of our personal relationships

In Chapter 7 we considered philobat (spacebatting) and ocnophil (home-loving) types of relating. Essentially the contrast was between two kinds of reactions to the infant's discovery of its separateness from the (m)other. Some infants, as they become more aware of 'objects' – aspects of the environment which they cannot control – turn more strongly to their own powers to care for themselves. Ever after, their trust and sense of well-being rests on the assurance that they can cope; other people and things are regarded with distanced interest, and perhaps wariness and mistrust. With this kind of start, I think I would be more likely to continue to experience the world in terms of the dichotomy of self versus not-self. I would avoid situations which threaten to bring me too close to others and so make me lose my individuality; I would tend to be on the defensive towards the intrusive impinging world of others, on whom I would not wish to be dependent. By contrast, people relating in a more ocnophil way are more inclined toward situations which recreate something of the primitive oneness they love, and tend to put their trust in close relationships with other people.

How might this difference affect the development of splits in the personality, and particularly the relation of the coping regions with other self-regions? This is a fascinating theme for speculation, for it allows us to consider how the structure of a person might be reflected in the structure of his or her relationships.

The loss of merged oneness, the experience of separateness, and the discovery of the other may be felt as a terror and an impingement, or as a matter of indifference, or as bringing convenient new resources. If I were a spacebat, I would be considering how to get others to serve my purposes. The more determined my spacebat element, the stronger my attitudes of wariness, manipulation, competition, and exploitation toward other people – the greater also my incentive to develop the skills (including ego-functioning skills) which facilitate my separateness and independence. My vulnerable side would have to be hidden. There would have to be quite a split, which would deepen if circumstances made it expedient.

By contrast, if I were a homebody I would react to the onset of individuation by clinging to my mother and to others all the more. With this element strong in my personality I would tend to mistrust my own abilities and powers, gladly depending on those who care for me. I have an incentive to show others my needy and vulnerable side, for they may perhaps be disarmed by this and co-operate in caring for the disarmingly vulnerable self. Here are incentives to develop those skills which facilitate dependence. Generally preferring co-operation to individual enterprise and initiative, my experience will tend to be in terms of 'us' and to avoid the harsher opposition of 'I' to 'them'. In general I would have much more nurturing mutual relationships with others. I would care about others and not see them primarily as objects to be negotiated (though in my own way I may draw on them as resources to be made use of). I cannot easily cut myself off: I am not 'schizoid'. When others are unkind I cannot easily dismiss them from my mind and drop the friendship: I will be hurt, angry, depressed. When others are distressed, I feel it. I can 'identify'. I feel about other people more as though they were part of me. More people matter to me, have significance and meaning for me as extensions of my own self.

This ready capacity to feel identified with others acts as an integrating principle of a particular kind. Structurally it creates connections on my map, between my self mapped there, and other people mapped there. To organize much of (what more splitting people might regard as) the world of others, into close association with my self, makes for a more tightly integrated personality. More of others is mapped with my self in important self-regions, regions where fulfilment and gratification and being loved and being welcomed – and being unfulfilled and deprived and unloved and rejected – are mapped. There is thus an intertwining of self and others; as regards well-being or as regards distress.

At the other extreme, to the extent that others are liable to be experienced as impinging rather than supplying good things, such mapping will not occur. The other will be mainly mapped as 'not me' and far from 'me'. The great difference, after all, between self-imagery in general and object-imagery in general, is that the self has a biological unity to start with (see pp. 62–6) and pp. 181–82). My body (and whatever self is connected with my body) is the common factor in all my experience, the place where I experience all events. The world of others is manifold and stays so, the more particularly if the manifold objects' most remarkable characteristic is that it is 'not-me but other'. The more I experience the world of others painfully as 'not-me impinging on me', the less I will identify with it.

We may be looking here at the roots of a very early and major difference between personality-structures, parallel with differences in our need for others. At one extreme we can imagine a tightly-integrated, highly-organized and interconnected set of regions forming the personality, with self and others strongly connected. At another extreme we can envisage a more 'schizoid' structure, altogether more loosely organized.

I shall call these two types 'loosely organized' and 'tightly integrated' respectively. Of the two, the more loosely organized people are nearer the splitty 'schizoid' end. This end of the range has recently had a bad press, in my view unfairly, in that the more extreme splitters have been compared with moderately-integrated people. Tightly-integrated is not better than loosely-organized, as we shall see below, where we compare differences in the experiences which might be expected to accompany these structural differences, represented by *Figure 46* (reproduced from *Figure 36* on p. 183).

Three relatively loosely organized regions

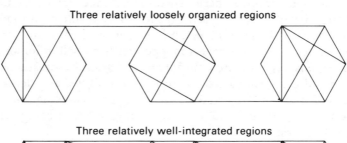

Three relatively well-integrated regions

Loosely-organized and tightly-integrated structures

How might people with these different personality-structures differ in their response to life?

When messages come to the more loosely-organized person, they are likely to be incorporated in the immediately relevant region in an appropriate way. But the messages would have to be relatively strong and exciting to reach the more remote regions, those which are linked only rather tenuously with the region where they were first received. Their effect is localized. Such people can 'shrug things off'. By contrast, when messages come to the more tightly-integrated person, they will eventually reach all the self-regions since there are fewer tenuous splits or tenuous links.

The strength of loosely-organized people lies in their ability to concentrate on one thing at a time, undistracted by consider-ations they consider irrelevant – headaches, fears, sorrows, whatever. On the other hand, the strength of tightly-integrated people lies in the wholeness of the response of their entire personality to the totality of the situation – they have no cut-off regions. While a loosely-organized person is, therefore, likely to be quicker off the mark in a more focused way, and to respond more quickly and more definitely – often regarded as a mark of high intelligence – the response might not be as solidly based as that of a person in whose experience everything ties in with everything else.

What an experience means to us depends on the context in which it happens, the context being the regions which surround the one where it is happening. This is the more true in an integrated structure. In a tightly-integrated personality, a dis-tressed region is closely connected with other regions because all regions are closely connected. If a painful thing happens to a tightly-integrated and on the whole happy person, the pain will be absorbed to some extent by the relative well-being of the surrounding self-regions. Tightly-integrated and on the whole unhappy people will be very vulnerable. When a painful thing happens to them the pain will spread throughout the already unhappy regions which are the context for the latest increment of hurt.

Tightly-integrated people are likely to feel loss very acutely.

They are attached more deeply and wholeheartedly, both to people and to particular things. The pain of a loss would permeate the whole self. They might be permanently mildly depressed, unable to recover from one blow before the next falls – life is not easy. The attachments of more loosely-organized people may be as strong and deep but there are fewer tendrils, so to speak: fewer regions of the personality are involved. The pain of loss, though as intensely experienced, would be more localized and more easily set aside for a while. On the other hand, tightly-integrated people would find more comfort in the attachments which were still in being, whose comforting effect would permeate the whole as much as, and at the same time as, the hurt. The context makes the pain more bearable.

Split-off centres of consciousness mark the extremely loosely organized, extremely schizoid personality (see also pp. 195–97). This has practical consequences for those who have an interest in evaluating or diagnosing or categorizing people whose difficulties in living are largely attributable to their personality. Such categories as 'narcissistic', 'schizophrenic', 'withdrawn', and 'paranoid' can be regarded as referring to the states of mind in which consciousness has been restricted to particular regions, while other regions are kept split off. The problem for the therapist is to find ways which make it possible for a person's consciousness to hold and carry what seem to be mutually exclusive states of mind, to make connections, for instance, between arrogant selfish 'narcissistic' expressions of the personality, and more depressed and vulnerable regions.

PART 6

HOLDING AND HEALING

HOLDING AND INTEGRATING
NEW BEGINNINGS: IMPLICATIONS FOR
PSYCHOTHERAPISTS

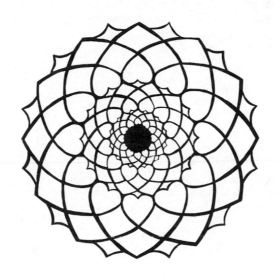

·19·
Holding and integrating

What are the forces which prevent people from 'falling apart'? 'Falling apart' and 'disintegrating' — ceasing to be integrated — are appropriate metaphors, suggesting that different regions of the personality lose contact with one another. Great anxiety, as well as high fevers and toxic states, can have this effect. We don't know where we are. We are 'at a loss'.

Many different kinds of regions and organizations make up the personality, and previous chapters have shown that people can disintegrate in different ways. We have seen that basic faults may split regions along a variety of lines, different writers tending to be interested in different lines. 'Falling apart' may refer to the dissociation of simple organizations of memory-traces as they lose touch with one another and we forget what we read in a book, or auntie's birthday, or what we had for dinner last Wednesday. It can also refer to the progressive isolation of more complex organizations such as particular self-images or particular relationships with other people and things. Or even more central processes may cease to function. Our ego-functions may desert us. Then there is the kind of isolation of different regions of the personality for which Kohut coined the phrase 'vertical split' — we do not feel we are ourselves. 'I don't know what came over me', 'I don't know what made me do it', 'It's not like me', 'It's the drink talking', 'I didn't mean it'. And there is the 'schizoid' feeling of disembodiment when constant attention

359

seems to be needed to keep the too loosely organized structures from flying apart.

What, on the other hand, holds us together? In a way the whole book has been about this, and in that sense the current chapter is no more than a recapitulation. We need to recapitulate because it helps pave the way for the final chapter, which is about how people can help each other not to fall apart and about how to mend a split.

Three homely metaphors pick out three aspects of the holding-together process: we can think of being held together by some kind of bonding or gluing, or held together by something like a wrapping container or skin, or held together by some central unifying force that rules the other parts and holds them together as the force of gravity does or the focus around which perspectives organize themselves — such a power, central and hierarchically organized, is postulated by Plato and has been the most generally accepted metaphor in Western thought from its beginnings.

No doubt there are minds almost entirely held together in one or other of these ways. As a rule, however, which metaphor is most useful at any time depends on a number of factors: the kind of person under discussion, the kind of structures which are falling apart, and so on.

Being 'held' by 'bonding'

When we think of neural connections, and when we think of the association of ideas, we tend to think of structures held together by connecting bonds. Neural connections exemplify this kind of cohesion. Sense-impressions build up into perceptions, which integrate into concepts and ever more complex structures. In Chapters 10 and 18 these ideas were explored further: variations in integration and coherence were seen to determine structure so that the very nature of structure could be defined in terms of bonds — there are more neural associations *within* a structure than *between* structures. Regions of the personality are bonded together more or less strongly depending on the number of associations between them. The number of associations determines the extent of integration. A relative absence of associations defines a gap or fissure – the fewer the associations, the wider the split.

Being 'contained' by a skin

As anyone knows who has glued things, the things to be stuck together need to be held firmly in a kind of frame until the glue holds. Then the frame is no longer needed. Davis and Wallbridge (1981) make clear, in a fine chapter on Winnicott's use of the concepts of boundary and space, that boundaries are frames of this kind. Frames provide restrictions or limitations which can be used to further the integration within. A picture must be painted on a certain size of canvas; a poem must be written in sonnet form. Within the frame there is space for creative life.

When there is a frame that gives space and protection, all the resonances and echoes and reverberations of an infant's experiences have time to work themselves out. They do not get lost; they are not cut off prematurely. Ego-relatedness normally provides this frame. It provides the safety within which various experiences may come to be connected and associated, although they occurred at different times and in different contexts (see pp. 129–34, 137f., and 233f.). Good parenting provides the frame within which psychological associations can ramify and become strong. In this way, good parenting leads to personalities which have strong and well-integrated structures. With less ego-relatedness, the infant has less space and time to get this inter-connecting process going, and so it retains more dissociated experiences.

The children described by Tustin seemed to experience themselves as lacking such containment. Something was rushing through them – a noise, a sensation, an impression – which they could not hold on to. This sense, of something rushing through, may be how we experience unintegrated sensory streams of unprocessed uncontained stimulation. It is what falling apart sometimes feels like: what is going on does not make sense to us. Not making sense is the same as not being organized into a meaningful pattern. Or we may be unable to find a framework of meaning into which to organize what is happening. Boundaries seem to facilitate organization; insecure boundaries seem often to hinder it.

Tustin made an interesting connection between the

uncontained state and the autistic child's desperate clutching of hard objects. She thought that, in some states of mind, *holding on to something with firm contours* might feel much like *being something with firm contours*. The common element would be 'There is something firm for holding something formless'. Firm contours seem to be needed, whether they belong to the infant (in us) or whether they belong to whatever the infant feels held and contained by. Whether the something firm is my skin or yours seems less important than the fact that it prevents me feeling a rushing shapeless flowing away.

The functions of the boundary frame are reminiscent of Pribram's 'bag of skin', and Winnicott's 'membrane'. Our skins provide a compelling metaphor for such holding functions, more flexible and organic than the idea of a frame. The skin protects: Guntrip reveals many instances of the plight of the vulnerable self in need of a skin. The vulnerable skinless self and its care at different stages of development has been a theme in this book.

Something or someone is needed to give infants space and protection against impingement from without, and also from within – from loneliness, pain, rage.

> 'Failure in the holding environment, perhaps because of illness in the mother, can mean that the infant's line of life is interrupted and its development hindered by the need for defence against primitive anxiety. But it can also be seen that failure of the father to protect the mother in the crucial weeks after the infant's birth can contribute to this state of affairs. If the circle made by the father, or by some person fulfilling the father's function is broken, the mother cannot abandon herself without anxiety to her infant's needs.'
>
> (Davis and Wallbridge 1981: 151)

The parents, who are normally the child's holding environment, may at times be fiercely tested, especially at times when feelings are strong.

Once again, we have reached a set of ideas where parallels can be perceived between what good parents do and what good psychotherapists do. The reader has probably become practised at recognizing these passages by now.

It is important that whoever holds the infant (or the older child or the adolescent or the adult) is strong enough to hold on to, either to prevent explosion and fragmentation, or to form the framework for such disintegration and for subsequent integration.

'The survival of the mother who does not retaliate, together with the father who comes to represent the indestructible environment, allows for freedom of the instinctual life – the source of spontaneity – within the family circle.'

(p. 147)

In the earliest days, it is the caring adult whose insightful and coping skills protect, as with a shielding skin, the helpless and defenceless infant. In favourable circumstances, however, these functions will gradually be taken over by the competent developing infant.

Being 'organized' by a 'centre'

The mother is the child's first skin. In general, the mother is also the first person to participate in processing and organizing and integrating the child's experiences, deeply influencing the meaning which events have for the child. At first, she does this by facilitating the selfobject state, in which the child's needs and wishes are taken care of in such a way that the child has an experience of what it feels like to take care of yourself and be an organized person doing things for yourself. Good parenting is the foundation and centre of this experience.

'The mother's capacity to identify with her baby allows her to fulfil the function summed up by Winnicott in the word "holding". Holding is "the basis for what gradually becomes a self-experiencing being".'

(p. 106)

'The conscious ego is the ego of separation, of doing, of acting and being acted upon . . . it must derive its strength from the deepest unconscious core of the self that has never lost the feeling of being-at-one-with the maternal source of its life.'

(Guntrip 1969: 265)

The establishment of a strong personality-structure depends in the first place on the extent to which there has been what

Winnicott called 'indwelling': the close integration of the most primitive bodily self-regions (the homunculi) and later psychic developments. This integration forms a central core which is potentially dynamic since the biological drives are incorporated there, as are other needs with a bodily base. If a child's needs are met when it expresses them, then the connections between need and consciousness of need and expression of need and need-satisfaction will all be strengthened thereby. Self-imagery will then also be rooted in this central core, and the True Self will be involved in the earliest homunculus-based self-representations. From this point on, the self-image and the True Self can become influential in how later experiences shall be met and organized.

The best chance of maintaining a personality capable of happiness, altruism, and energy comes from having a central core which has not had to split off unacceptable experiences, and which can therefore integrate distress without too much distortion or denial. Such personalities will be able to integrate later distresses without inevitably involving them in the distortions and denials which earlier splits would impose on experience. Lucky people – for them, later experiences connect straightforwardly with earlier ones, right back to the days when the very earliest body-imagery was being established. There is the central core, the centre of True Self.

People lucky in these respects must not be assumed to be lucky in every other way. We may imagine a range of people, all able to draw on the strength of a True-Self central core which organizes their experiences. At one extreme are those who had quite simple straightforward relations between their needs and their satisfactions. At the other extreme are those with much more stressful experiences, whose needs got satisfied only after long delays, or only in part, or after great distress. There is quite a range, from bliss to pain, of what people can bear without major distortion, or denial, or splitting. Of course, if there are many painful associations to this early core, quite a lot of good things would also have to happen if a person is to preserve some sense of inner goodness and not be overwhelmed by a sense of misery and worthlessness.

It is also possible for a False Self to act as a core. A child may have been disappointed when its expression of what it wanted was not followed by fulfilment. Yet its needs were eventually met. The question is, to what extent were its needs met on *its* terms and to what extent was it subject to other people's? On this criterion depend differences in the extent to which a person's core holds True and False components.

> 'When the mother cannot adapt well enough, the infant gets seduced into a compliance, and a compliant False Self reacts to environmental demands and the infant seems to accept them. Through this False Self, the infant builds up a false set of relationships, and by means of introjections even attains a show of being real so that the child may grow up to be just like mother, aunt, brother or whoever at the time dominates the scene.'
>
> (Winnicott 1965[1960]: 146)

Self-imagery as an organizing process

Whether a True or a False Self be the centre from which a person acts, self-imagery operates gyroscopically once it is established. Once there are coherent self-representations on the map, feedback processes will ensure that people feel discomfort or pain when expectations arise which go against that imagery. As foreshadowed in Chapter 4 (pp. 60 and 66ff.), the self can be regarded as a set of interlinking feedback systems. More central systems monitor the more peripheral ones, rather as, in hierarchical human organizations, managers higher up (nearer the centre) delegate quite complex operations to others down the line, on whom they keep an eye in case things go wrong. Self-imagery controls the plans that are made at each level in somewhat the same way.

> 'Our image of ourselves, and our preferred self-imagery, influence what we do. "I am a person who gets up early." "I am a person who runs towards trouble and not away from it." This is continually confirmed when I behave "like myself". The more I can do so, the more pleased I am to think of myself in particular ways. Whenever there is incongruity between what I am doing and the person I imagine myself to be (or prefer myself to be), I am under tension to reduce the incongruity.'
>
> (see Chapter 4: 66)

Self-imagery has a strong organizing function, keeping us coherent, consistent, and unfragmented, *provided* that we are able to call on it at need. Fortunate people have relatively strong self-images which reverberate easily and are therefore easily part of the working models of self-in-the-world, the models by which their actions are governed. Less fortunate people have more tenuous self-imagery, or are more tenuously in touch with it. Or they may lack the sense that their identity is rooted in solid experiences and memory-traces of experiences – they do not feel defined by a bodily self at the core. Something may have gone wrong at the mirroring stage. They do not retain an image of themselves for any length of time, let alone an image of themselves as good and lovable, and worth living up to. They are often not in touch with how they feel or what suits them. They can be told by others, defined by them as it were, but the image easily disappears again because remembering what you have been told about yourself is different from actually remembering the experiences in which you have been involved and which made you what you are. Characteristically, though, such people's imagery of themselves needs to be held for a while by others if they are ever to have the strength to hold it for themselves.

To the extent that people have a False Self, they have false imagery of themselves. They may be quite normally self-aware and self-conscious and verbal about their thoughts and feelings, memories and plans, but they lack some of the strong roots which connect their life now to the beginnings of their world. If so, they will at times feel a falsity or unreality in what they do. They sense that they are sometimes living up to an image of themselves which is not connected to the experiences which would make this image a basic neurological reality.

Some people have practically no coherent self-imagery at all, true or false, to which they can refer at need to keep a check on themselves. Not surprisingly, they are liable to behave irrationally and impulsively; they lack some important monitoring or steering or organizing structures. They also have little help in putting up with frustration, even in order to gain a benefit they know they desire. They cannot postpone gratification now for the sake of a later good. Unable to go to the zoo because of the rain, they cannot enjoy a visit to the Natural History Museum. It is 'not the same'. Substitutes will not gratify. The imagery which would hold these things together in the same frame is not there. The frame is not there.

Valued self-imagery as an organizing process

Self-imagery holds us together by a sort of self-fulfilling prophecy. We confirm that we are as we imagine ourselves to be, by acting in a way which confirms it. In this, we may be guided by realistic self-imagery: 'This-is-what-I-am', or we may be guided by more idealized imagery: 'This-is-how-I-would-wish-to-be'. There may not always be a lot of difference between these two: fortunate people are guided by ideas about themselves which please them, not crippled by aspects of themselves which shame or hurt them.

How do we come to value our selves? More to the point, how do we come to value the ideas about ourselves which we do value? Surely our sense of worth comes initially from (m)others, though of course that is not how the infant part of us experiences it. The infant has a right to feel grand. But in fact our sense of worth depends on a good mirroring facilitating environment.

In *The Restoration of the Self* (1977) Kohut considers one special area of experience in detail, to illustrate this process at one particular developmental phase: a mother who encourages her child to develop a valuable sense of self is contrasted to a mother who encourages her child to develop in terms of drives and 'fragments of body-self'. Children's experiences of grown-ups' reactions to faeces provide an especially useful example, because faeces are so very typical of the mix-up of self and other, being both 'me' and 'not me'.

> 'If a mother accepts the faecal gift proudly – or if she rejects it or is uninterested in it – she is not only responding to a drive. She is also responding to the child's forming self. Her attitude, in other words, influences a set of inner experiences that play a crucial role in the child's future development. She responds – accepting, rejecting, disregarding – to a self that, in giving and offering, seeks confirmation by the mirroring self-object. The child therefore experiences the joyful prideful parental attitude, or the parent's lack of interest . . . as the acceptance

or rejection of his tentatively established, yet still vulnerable, creative-productive-active self.'

(pp. 75–6)

However,

'If the mother rejects this self just as it begins to assert itself as a centre of creative-productive initiative (especially of course if her rejection or lack of interest is only one link in a long chain of rebuffs and disappointments emanating from her pathogenically unempathic personality) or if her inability to respond to her child's total self leads her to a fragmentation-producing preoccupation with its faeces – to the detriment of the cohesion-establishing involvement with her total child, her faeces-producing, learning, controlling, maturing, total child – then the child's self will be depleted and it will abandon the attempt to obtain the joys of self-assertion. It will, for reassurance, turn to the pleasures it can derive from the fragments of its body self.'

(pp. 75–6)

This search for good feelings then not only fails to consolidate a valued self-image, but also leads to further fragmentation.

'In order to escape from depression, the child runs from the unempathic or absent self-object to oral, anal and phallic sensations, which it experiences with great intensity.'

(pp. 75–6)

For Kohut (1971: 152) disintegration – de-differentiation – is the fear at the heart of the narcissistically injured, that is of those whose self-imagery is a source of frequent misery to them. They lack that which gives more fortunate people a constant sense of their own well-being and worthwhileness.

Both Kohut and Winnicott emphasize that, while the satisfaction of its needs gives the child a sense of well-being and strength, what eventually gives it its integration and its identity is being treated as a whole person when it is not as yet feeling whole. For this to happen, people must relate to the baby as a person, and not as a series of chores or achievements. When the baby is treated as a collection of 'part-objects', there is likely to be less integration and less sense of integrity. (Masud Khan bases his theory of perversion on considerations such as these – see 1979: 13ff.). A very different experience, with very different consequences, awaits the child whose oral, anal, and phallic sensations are welcomed as valid expressions of that child's whole self (even before the child *has* a whole self). The empathic, mirroring, reflecting function of the adult then ensures pride in these functions without giving any of them eminence above the child as a living and loving human being – the whole person is validated.

For people to value themselves, so that they can run their lives according to what they value, they have first to have been valued as persons. And they must have been loved for being, not for doing this or that – it is this which gives them the sense that they are valuable people rather than a jumble of bits. Initially, other people give the fortunate infant this identity by showing love and respect. In due course, this sense of value, given by (m)others, becomes self-respect, and becomes capable of acting as an integrating and guiding principle. Winnicott somewhere calls this process 'personalizing', because it is the opposite of 'depersonalising' (1965[1962]: 59).

Respect, recognition, understanding, and validation

We need recognition. Erikson (1950) considers that the sense of identity is nothing other than this recognition by others that I am what I am. Being recognized as a person capable of organizing my world and myself helps to make me feel good about myself. Lack of respect stunts and cripples.

Although the processes with which we are here concerned are among the very earliest ones, they are not so difficult to understand because they remain with us in adult life. Many of us, for instance, find it difficult to move on in conversation until we have received recognition that what we have just said has been understood and been given some consideration. Without this we feel devalued and stuck. Harold Pinter's dialogues are so devastating to listen to and so true to life, just because his remote and damaged characters inflict further damage on each other by talking in each other's presence without acknowledging that presence in a living way. When we do not take each other seriously, with joy and interest, we deprive each other of recognition and validation, and destroy our assurance of a worthwhile identity.

Many infants seem to be naturally joyous, interested, and sociable, many of them tremendously so. Their willingness to take notice of others and involve them in play is at the centre of Winnicott's therapy as well as his diagnosis: 'Babies *initiate* object relations' (1965: 59). They are always making advances which make us want to reciprocate. This is attachment behaviour, and if Bowlby is right about it, it is a biological trait working for the survival of the species. Many older babies, and toddlers too, show a natural talent in getting relationships going with those around them. Even many schoolchildren like to be with adults. It seems to me that infants and children try quite hard to stay in relationships, often against the odds. Even adolescents try, given a fair chance. Alas, the proportion of those who look with confidence and trust to adults declines in each successive age-group. There must be a lot of discouragement coming from somewhere.

Either the biological urge declines – and I do not think this is so – or the effect is due to lack of appropriate response. If more adults were able to take more natural pleasure in children as children, the world would be a happier place, I think. But we are caught in a vicious circle – we adults were children once, and what happened then to our natural joy and interest in being with the grown-ups? And where is the recognition in political and economic terms that this parental function is a worthwhile one?

If the infant is not given recognition in terms of the appropriate response for its age, it cannot feel held and contained. And it may not yet have learned to hold and contain itself. In that case, there are a lot of uncontained feelings going nowhere – they have been felt, and perhaps expressed, but they have not been communicated (that is recognized and understood by another person). Feelings experienced without containment tend to be overwhelming and frightening.

We know this quite well in the world of adults. In many circles it is not the done thing to show much feeling. When we do, others do not respond as though we had communicated anything that has meaning, or else they do not respond as though they had understood what we meant. They do not respond appropriately to what we would have said if we could have said it. Vice versa, when other people's expressions of rage or pain or even love come our way, we often fail to receive and hold them. It is often more polite to ignore them, and even when it is not, we may be at a loss how to respond appropriately to a sob or a spat of temper. In many circumstances, we have learnt to be impassive and not react to other people's expressions of feeling, except when they inconvenience us. We tend to react manipulatively, to stop or minimize them. Many a psychotherapist, having learnt to interpret them, has offended by doing this *instead* of receiving them, even in everyday life.

Adults are often very disrespectful toward children's expressions of feeling, showing amusement and ridicule or, when the expressions go beyond a certain limit, reactive rage. Or they may placate. It is distressingly rare, in much of Britain at any rate, for any but the mildest expressions of feeling to be regarded as a basis for mutual recognition. Such a response would involve listening to the other, and actually hearing what is meant, and receiving it, and acknowledging it. At the very least, the other person would get some validation and, perhaps respect, maybe love, certainly a kind of holding.

Some of our authors, incidentally, rather tend to write as though the feelings which we need others to hold for us and to respect and recognize, are necessarily negative ones. Certainly it is true that we need others to share our pain and to put up with our conflicts, our angers, ambivalences, and doubts. We need support in pain, rage, uncertainty, and fear of going to pieces. But it seems to me a very incomplete holding which does only this. We also need support in our happiness, excitement, and rapture, without fear of going to pieces.

Ego-functioning as an organizing process

The first holding which infants know about is an embrace which is physical. For the lucky ones this develops almost imperceptibly into understanding, respect, and validation, in the process of being taken care of – a more psychological sort of embrace. Embrace turns into recognition. At first, someone else has to hold me. Gradually I am able to do my share in taking care of my self. Fortunate people can embrace themselves: they can understand and accept themselves, respect and love themselves, and see to it they get their share of good things. But still someone else has had to do it for them first. The same is true for ego-functioning – thinking, understanding, making connections, planning ahead, thinking back, comparing, taking into consideration, giving an account of, making sense of life. Ego-functioning is only one aspect of holding, but it is an important part. And I must have had a mother or someone who *was* my self and did my ego-functioning for me, before I can have a self of my own and do my own ego-functioning.

Some people have had the blessings of natural integration more or less from their beginnings, and hold together effortlessly. Others will always have to give some attention to staying integrated. In conditions of stress, their integration will also be under stress. They always have to devote at least some small amount of energy to keeping the connections between parts of themselves intact, lest they find themselves acting on the basis of only part of who they are or what they know or what they want.

How may this more effortful integration be maintained? For this we need the rationality which comes from highly developed ego-functioning. I do not mean that this must be a cold and unfeeling reasonableness. I mean the ability to take care of things intelligently and to take enough factors into account so that we need not regret our impulsive actions afterwards. But even cold unfeeling rationality has a lot to commend it, when we contrast it with hot emotional irrationality. Ego-functioning, even when divested of attractive social values, can integrate and hold together what would otherwise be a jumble of impulses and responses ungoverned by any principle. We need only look at the lives of those whose ego-functioning is suppressed by disease, distress, or the misuse of drugs, to be persuaded of this. We should not belittle the uses of the intellect.

Ego-functioning can strengthen the integrating processes. It is ego-functioning which strengthens the bonds between a valued self-imagery and other aspects of living. There are times when we need to remind ourselves who we are and how we wish to be. It is ego-functioning that enables us to hold on to the knowledge that though we feel terrible now, this will pass. It is ego-functioning that enables us to say: 'Although these people treat me like dirt, I know who I am and I am not dirt.' A number of writers have noticed how many of those who survived in extreme conditions, as Japanese prisoners of war, in German concentration camps, or during natural disasters, said afterwards that they had had important values or ideas which they exerted themselves to hold on to (Bettelheim 1960, 1979, *inter alia*). Those of us who have fortunately not had to survive in such extreme circumstances, also know how to hold on to ideas which in turn hold us: 'I don't want to be embarrassed or ashamed, as I would be if I were untrue to myself and did not keep this promise, which turns out hard to keep, so I had better get on and do what I said I would do'.

In other ways, too, ego-functioning enriches our lives. Many of us have held on to the lovely idea of being able to paint or sing, as an incentive for doing boring practice-chores. Or, if not naturally gifted in what our senses bring us or our muscles do for us, we may have been able to increase our enjoyment of the arts by taking trouble to increase our understanding of brushwork in painting or voice production in singing – another triumph of ego-functioning. In much the same way, we can learn to extend our imaginative sympathy and empathy toward people of whom we have been ignorant or shy, by learning to understand the way they live (J. Klein 1985).

An adult who can help a child with this confers a major benefit. At the most primitive level it is a question of making sure that the infant does not feel overwhelmed by distress. But right from the start, the more fortunate infant has people talking to it, so that its world is made meaningful not only at the level of physical and emotional contentment but also at the level of things feeling right intellectually, cognitively one might say, in terms of the ego-functions. Bion (1962a and b) would say that the mother transforms the child's fragmentary 'beta-elements' into meaningfully integrated 'alpha-elements'.

The adult world organizes meanings for the child. Children of phobic parents are timid: they have had their world made meaningful in terms of the dangers it can hold. Children of parents who find food a comfort find food a comfort; children of parents who think that to be seen eating is only barely less disgusting than to be seen defecating will behave accordingly. Parents who enjoy explaining and making connections (in a spirit of enjoyment, exploration, and curiosity) have children who take an interest in how things work. Children of parents who habitually put words to feelings (in a kind way which does not make the child feel guilty or found out) will feel more at ease with their feelings. These are not conditioning processes; these are the normal processes by which parents organize or 'metabolize' or 'transmute' or 'pattern' the child's experiences and give them a particular meaning.

Children of parents who are able to maintain their emotional balance while the child loses control of itself and lets fly, have children less frightened by what they may find at the back of their minds. This seems to me a prototype of how the balanced adult mind works (or at least, one kind). The feelings come and go, excited by various events, internal and external. We accept, recognize, understand, and thereby validate them. In the short run we allow them expression as we judge appropriate in the circumstances; in the longer run, we give them further thought.

Rereading the previous sentences, let us say 'child' where the text reads 'feelings'.

> 'The children come and go, excited by various events, internal and external. We accept, recognize, understand and thereby validate them. In the short run we allow them expression as we judge appropriate in the circumstances; in the longer run we give them further thought.'

The adult here is in charge of the ego-functions. Our good-parent adult ego-functioning regions accept, recognize, understand, and validate our feelings, and allow them appropriate expression, but also reflect on the implications of it all, talking it over with the impulsive child (part of us) and co-operating in making sense of it all.

Ego-functioning = adult; feelings = child. These equations also work nicely when applied to two almost infallible rules of thumb in relationships: Do not retaliate, and do not retreat. Retaliation punishes people for being themselves – the opposite of recognition, acceptance, and validation. On the other hand, retreat in the face of dangerous feelings leaves them shapeless and unbounded when what they need is recognition and meaningful, acceptable, limited expression. Fortunate the child whose parents are on good terms with their feelings and their children. Even more fortunate the child whose parents can also use words intelligently, not only about feelings, but also about other things which strengthen ego-functioning. Practically all speech, other than expletives, is ego-functioning.

> '*Thursday 13 May, 1976*
>
> | | |
> |---|---|
> | *Natasha:* | Daddy? |
> | *Daddy:* | Yes Natasha. |
> | *Natasha:* | Do people tell the truth on television? |
> | *Daddy:* | Sometimes they do and sometimes they don't. |
> | *Natasha:* | When do they tell the truth? |
> | *Daddy:* | There is no way of knowing that for sure. |
> | *Natasha:* | Do they tell the truth when it's *The News*? |
> | *Daddy:* | Sometimes they do and sometimes they don't. |
> | *Natasha:* | Sometimes they tell lies and sometimes they just tell the truth? |
> | *Daddy:* | Yep.' |
>
> (Laing 1978)

As the child grows up and becomes more able to converse, good parenting allows for a lot of talk. But perhaps we should not leave this section without reminding ourselves that parental help in ego-functioning will help to strengthen the child only to the extent that there is affection and pleasure in the adult's recognition of the child (and later, in the adult's recognition of his or her own nature). Here is the same vicious circle again, for we cannot usually take more pleasure and interest in feelings (and in children) than we ourselves received.

As the child grows up, conversation with others also becomes an ever more important factor. Reading too. The rules of logic and of evidence can be taught. Through all these channels the person becomes strengthened and more able to make sense of things and give meaning to the world. New connections throw new light on our nature and on the world around us. We can learn from others. We can seek to be taught. We can grow further.

Talking as an organizing process

> 'I feel terrible now, but it will pass.'
> 'Although these people treat me like dirt, I know who I am and I am not dirt.'

'I don't want to be embarrassed or ashamed, so I had better do what I promised.'

Saying such things has an organizing function, in that it reminds us of imagery which we can hold on to at need – it keeps the reverberations alive. The very action of saying things has consequences of a steadying kind.

Speech can accomplish much more than this, for it enables people to reassess what has happened to them, to reconsider past events in the light of later experience and even, at a very deep level, to reorganize their understanding of themselves and of their world. In the next chapter I shall argue that it can even help to change the very structure of the personality.

Talking puts experiences into words. Sometimes talking allows us to connect experiences with words for the first time. This means that, sometimes for the first time ever, we are able to 'give an account' of those experiences – we are conscious of them for the first time.

Once the experiences are conscious, *there* are the experiences, and *there* is a narrator who is talking about them. Here we see a benign aspect of the process of depersonalizing and distancing. 'I' am for the first time consciously distanced from what happened to me. I can get some perspective: 'I then did this' or 'Such and such happened to me next'. Moreover, the 'I' and the 'me' in these accounts have a curious status. There is continuity and identity: these experiences were not someone else's but 'mine' (the speaker's), they belong to my self-regions. But at the same time, the 'I' who is doing the talking now is ten or twenty or more years older than the 'I' in the account. There is a distance between the self-structures-from-then and the self-structures-of-now, a gap of time. This allows for a new perspective and a new meaning. Meaning depends on context. I am now in a different context from then. If my self-structures today are more mature, more complex, with better ego-functions and capacities for respect and recognition, they may be able to hold and integrate the self-structures from then.

Talking, and being understood, changes the nature of the connections between 'I then' and 'I now', weakening them in some respects ('Because this happened to me thirty years ago I need not be afraid of thunderstorms now') and strengthening them in other respects ('I do not need to despise myself for having feared thunderstorms thirty years ago. I can stop despising myself and I can love myself'). If I try to talk honestly to others about my past life, it comes up for review. The relation between my semantic self and my episodic self may also be challenged and changed when they confront one another. Sympathetic listening, and the knowledge that what happened when I was little, weak, and ignorant cannot happen to me now, give me the strength to try and remember how it was with me then. Between us, we can hold 'me then'. Held, I dare give an account of hitherto hidden parts of my self. I can integrate them.

Friends who talk with us and hold us and help us integrate

This is one reason why friends are so important for our well-being, and why people who for some reason have been unable to make friends or to keep them may find psychotherapeutic groups useful. In the chapter which follows, the final one in this book, we consider specifically the role of professionals in helping people whose misfortune has led them into difficulties where friends cannot help. But in more fortunate circumstances, our friends can do a good deal of our organizing and ego-functioning with and for us. They do so anyway in the normal course of life, as we pass the time of day with them, gossip about others, or explore the meaning of the universe. They let us talk and blow off steam. They are patient while we talk nonsense. They talk a load of rubbish themselves. They relax us when we get too desperately tense, and amuse us. But more particularly, good friends strengthen and diversify our ego-functioning: they produce speculations, explanations, and suggestions of their own for us to consider, and much else. Thus the passage which follows may be read in terms of *friends* or in terms of *ego-functioning* or in terms of *organizing processes*.

They help us toward increasing knowledge of our selves: they produce new ideas, and they surprise us by changing and developing and expecting us to welcome the changes. Though they may be tolerant they will not put up with our nonsense indefinitely without protest. They love us and accept us and warm us and make us feel worth while. They help us stand firm under pressure. In times of crisis they are especially important, sustaining us while we encounter and explore new things, encouraging us to carry on, holding us when we temporarily lose our footing in the stress of reorganizing our concepts. They take care of us and step in when, in the course of the temporary disorganization which new developments may bring, we are about to do something permanently detrimental to our interests.

The task as an organizing process

Some people are able to give sense and direction to their lives by commitment to a cause or a task. That people can put something non-personal into the centre of their lives was foreshadowed in our discussion of Kohut (pp. 218ff.): I may have got no foundation for self-love from the love of others, but by being part of something admirable, I can make my life worthwhile. Some people who take this second chance will come to have a deep and rich identity, in terms of which they organize their lives. But others will not integrate in this organized way, and yet feel held by a sense of purpose and coherence because they know what they are doing and that it is worth while. Such people present quite a range. At one end are those who are contained within an ordered social system such as traditional societies are said to afford, or religious orders or other ideologically committed groups; these will be exercising individual judgement only in narrowly restricted areas. At the other extreme are people in the fragmented societies with which most readers will be familiar. Yet even here, those of us who have no solid sense of who we are, independent of what we do, may find significance in what we are doing and feel held by it. Many creative people belong in this category. As one creation is accomplished, they suffer a kind of 'post-coital depression', but this lifts when the next project begins to define itself. At a less elevated level are many of us who can always cheer ourselves up by the accomplishment of small tasks well done: shoes shined, cakes baked, lawns mown, letters written.

Summary and conclusions

What gives a person the sense of being well and 'together'?

There are many indications that if I am to have a deep, easy, and steady sense of well-being and identity, I must not have had any experiences so bad that they have cut me off from my bodily self. If they have, I must make a new beginning.

Secondly, I must have been experienced as a whole person to be able to feel that I am a whole person. This is of course a highly unconscious matter, but it is not mystical. It is neurological. Neurologically the infant forms a set of conceptual structures which are either closely interconnected or not, depending on whether those who relate to the infant regard it as a baby or as a set of tasks requiring to be done. The baby who is regarded as a loud yell at one end and a bad smell at the other will carry that knowledge through life.

Experiencing myself as lovable strengthens the basis for a sense of well-being and self-esteem yet further. This lovability must depend on having been valued for being myself rather than for anything I do (Fromm 1976). As Winnicott wrote of the breast, its value must lie exactly in not being exciting and not having to work or be worked for.

A 'poorly cathected' self is one which has experienced relatively little love, relatively little respect for its manifestations, relatively little empathy; lacking feelings of value and power, there are no deep roots for later self-esteem to develop from.

The baby who is recognized as a person from the start is able to use this experience of recognition as a validation of itself, and can let the consequent imagery of itself perform holding functions. This in turn creates the right conditions for further integrating processes.

·20·
New beginnings – implications for psychotherapists

Psyche-therapy: ministering to a person's breath, soul, life

What gives a person the sense of being well and 'together'? How does a person become strong, in the sense of having good self-esteem, a good ability to understand situations and use them creatively, a good personality-organization which allows feelings and needs to find expression in actions and in gratifications which in turn feed self-esteem? Bluntly, we do not know for sure. We may have some guesses based on what good parents, good friends, and good therapists have in common. It has been interesting to note, at various points in this book, what different authors thought to be parallels between the behaviour of good parents and good therapists. The present chapter looks specifically at these parallels and their implications. (I shall use the word 'psychotherapist' – 'therapist' for short – for all professionals who work in the psycho-analytic tradition. Though they may be called psycho-analysts, psychotherapists, counsellors, psychiatrists, or whatever, it is the way they think and behave that we are concerned with.)

Literally, psychotherapy means 'ministering to a person's breath, soul, life'. (The *Shorter Oxford English Dictionary* does not have the word in its main text; I have used the references to 'therapy' and to 'psyche'.) Parents do this, and psychotherapists

380

do this, but they are not the only ones. Friends and lovers are also notable in this respect.

Friends and lovers have certain advantages in ministering to each other. But in some particulars the professionals have the advantage. First of all, we must remember the many people who have no friends and yet need to have their psyche ministered to. Equally important, there are some things which are incompatible with friendship but which need to happen if a person's psyche is to be restored, and so this must be left to the professionals. What these things are will become clearer in the course of this chapter; they have to do with the circumstances in which a person can make a new beginning. In psychotherapy a person may find the secure boundaries which are essential for this work (see pp. 246–49, 371–78, and 391ff.). Psychotherapists can impose the boundaries within which work with transferences and re-gressions can safely be carried on. They can set rules and insist on them: only fifty minutes per session, only one session per day, no physical violence. Also, their other close relationships are not endangered by this relationship. And so on.

What friends are able and willing to do for each other depends on many factors and I see no good in trying to lay down the law about that. My own views are sometimes made clear in the text and sometimes not – in the latter case often because I am in fact not clear about them myself.

Psychotherapy is a developmental process, as growing-up is, and the two have features in common. A difference is that psychotherapy is remedial: it is intended to make people better, to make good some deficiency or disturbance whose roots may go back to the days of childhood. This necessarily raises questions it has been convenient to evade until now: what do I mean by 'good' development and by a 'fortunate baby'? And if something goes 'wrong', what do I mean? And what do I mean by 'better'? My own values necessarily permeate this book, and it is time to look at these explicitly, however briefly.

Values: ministering to what end?

Three interrelated clusters of values seem important to me: I think it is better for children (and for those who come into psychotherapy) if, in the course of development, they gain in

self-knowledge including knowledge of unwanted regions of
the self,
self-acceptance including acceptance of at least some unwanted
regions of the self,
self-direction including the ability to choose one's own goals
and values,

self-love,
love of other people and knowledge and acceptance of some of
their unwanted regions,
ability to relate to and yet be separate from others,

tolerance of frustration when goals, values or affection require,
a varied set of values,
freedom to develop further.

The first cluster of values has to do with the geography and
logistics of the self. It seems important to me that people should
have the opportunity to discover who they are – what is good
and bad in them, what hurts, what delights, and so on – as well
as the opportunity to decide what to do about it.

The second cluster has to do with relationships. It seems
important to me that people should enjoy themselves and each
other, and that they should know the difference.

The third cluster is about favourable conditions for work,
growth, and change.

People with split-off memories of need and hurt

In psychotherapy, as in helping children grow up, the ideal
development is one in which each new stage is accepted in such a
way that the satisfactions of the previous stage are still accessible, neither associated with such pain that thoughts of it must
be avoided at all costs, nor so delicious that developing to the
next stage seems a trouble from which we recoil. Ideally we
should only have to overcome our natural reluctance, conscious
or unconscious, to think about painful as well as about pleasant
things.

However, bad things may have happened to us before we had
sufficiently well-organized self-regions to absorb them. What are
the consequences? In some circumstances, the memory-traces of

the bad experiences are kept apart, and so are not subject to modification by later events. These split-off memory-traces can later be responsible for overwhelming feelings of misery, emptiness, inertia, and fear. By 'overwhelming' I mean literally that we feel we have ceased to be people and are just clumps of dreadful feelings. We may try to rationalize those feelings – we feel so terrible because we failed an examination, lost a lover or a job, or are worried about the state of the world. But in fact, we feel terrible because we are in touch with memories from when we did not yet exist as persons and yet were in a state of suffering; it would be more accurate to say 'There is a sense of dreadful misery' than to say 'I feel very miserable' (see also pp. 141–42): the misery of those earlier days has never been integrated. It we are ever to feel better, the bad memory-traces of those days have to be integrated later in less painful contexts (see also pp. 375–78, 402). During that process of integration, a process of dissolution also takes place (see also pp. 137–40). These reorganizations enable us to see things as they are, more or less closely connected with us and, by the same token, more or less distant from us. Thus we get a self which has feelings but is not dissolved in them. In therapy or in everyday life, processes have to happen at the end of which a person can say 'I feel miserable': there is an 'I' to feel it. The misery no longer feels overwhelming, eternal, and immovable. After that, further healing can take place.

People lacking 'ego-strength'

We may have been unable to integrate certain experiences because they happened at a time when we lacked the strength to do so. In the present day, we are therefore 'unconscious' that they happened – they happened before we were organized enough to be either conscious or unconscious. They happened in our pre-history, certainly in pre-conceptual history, when we did not have a structure strong enough to hold in one frame the knowledge of both acceptable and unacceptable aspects of existence. The question is, are we now strong enough to do so?

The idea that the strength to integrate is not always available, and that something more is required than bringing into consciousness what has been kept unconscious, has interested psychoanalysts and psychotherapists increasingly in recent decades.

Balint, for instance, pointed out that with some people –
'melancholics' and 'obsessionals', he called them –

> 'one can always count on a reliable and intelligent ego that is
> able to take in words and then allow them to influence itself.
> The ego is able to perform what Freud called "working-
> through".'

(1968: 9)

Such people are strong enough already. They have a coherent
self; they have reasonably well-developed ego-functions; their
trouble is that they have repressed (by means of horizontal 'lids')
things that were unacceptable to their imagery of themselves or
of the world. If they need therapy, they need help mainly in
talking about, accepting, and recognizing what they are doing
and saying, until they are able to recognize themselves – the
hitherto unconscious bits included. But other people find it hard
or impossible to reflect on themselves and their world, not
because they cannot accept this or that, but because the
excluded feelings really do not belong to the self that is judging
whether to accept them or not: there have been vertical splits.

These are splits which weaken the structure of the personality
– a person's strength depends on the existence of organizing and
integrating processes. These need not be too tremendously
powerful or consistent, but they do need to be sufficient not to
leave out great areas of experience. To put this the other way
round, the strength of a person's personality depends on having
a sufficiently integrated structure to be able to see life as it is
without too much distortion or denial. A person with too many
splits – a person who really lacks integration – does not have
what Balint required: 'a reliable and intelligent ego that is able to
take in words and allow them to influence itself'.

> 'An infantile ego has been rejected and repressed. It remains
> therefore undeveloped and weak, and deep maturing comes to
> a standstill.'

(Guntrip 1969: 175)

Such strength also requires 'indwelling' – the sense of being
based in one's body. People dwelling in their body know what
feels good and what feels bad, and can seek the former and avoid
the latter without having to think about it. On the other hand, a

split between body and mind erodes one's sense of being.

'There are no fears worse or deeper than those which arise out of having to cope with life when one feels that one just is not a real person at all.'

(p. 174)

Without such strength, we do not have the integrity to live life as it is without distorting or denying – we dread and resist the possibility of re-experiencing the deep feelings which were too unacceptable to be integrated when we first experienced them. If our integrative processes are not strong enough, we need help to gain strength first, so that we can bear the process of integration.

The first task, then, is to become strong enough. And what is 'strong enough'? I intend it to mean the possession of enough well-being and self-esteem to be able to accept (integrate) and live with our own imperfections and those of the world (see pp. 216–18, 272–79, 400–08). A person who lacks this strength, and whom luck has failed in other ways, may have to work with a psychotherapist until the time when

'the nuclear self . . . is consolidated, and the talents and skills that are correlated to the nuclear self are revitalised.'

(Kohut 1977: 178)

In what regions of the personality is strength to be found?

We do not yet understand perfectly just what it is, when a therapist works with people with this kind of weakness, that helps them get stronger. But it is clear that the processes involved do not take place in what Balint called the three-person region of classical psycho-analysis, the area in which Oedipal relationships find a place and in which feelings (instinctual ones in the view of classical psycho-analytic theory) are in conflict with considerations of good sense or good conduct (see pp. 112–13).

'The area of the Oedipus conflict is characterised by the presence of all least two objects, apart from the person. The area of the Basic Fault is characterised by a very peculiar exclusively two-person relationship. A third area is characterised by the fact that there are no external objects in it. Here people are on their own and their main concern is to produce something out of themselves; this something to be produced may be an object, but is not necessarily so. I propose to call this the level or area of creation. The most often-discussed example is of course artistic creation, but other phenomena belong to the same group, among them mathematics and philosophy, gaining insight, understanding somebody or something.'

(Balint 1968: 24)

At this third level, there is no 'other'. It is the level at which something or someone is being recognized and given shape and form for the first time (see pp. 113 and 266–72). Something or someone is in the process of becoming conceptualized, but is not yet clearly 'mapped'. At this level, although there are no others, there is a sense of connectedness. We know that there are no 'objects' in the regions where creation takes place, writes Balint (1968: 25) 'but we know also that for some of the time at least, the person is not entirely alone there'. Balint is here reaching for the concept of ego-relatedness.

Our idea of what goes on at these levels is still very tentative, and was even more uncertain at the time Balint was writing. (There is a summary of Balint's sources up to 1968 on p. 167–68 of *The Basic Fault*.) The discussion of appropriate techniques of therapy at these levels has hardly progressed at all since then, though a recent (sceptical) evaluation of the state of the art may be found in Kernberg (1980: Chapters 9 and 10). But I think we do now have some more strong hints. It is only right to warn the lay reader, however, that in this chapter we are not concerned with a description of what psychotherapy is or should be, only with an elucidation of some relatively neglected aspects.

What do psychotherapists do?

What Balint wrote, nearly twenty years ago, still applies:

'One might expect to encounter three different sets of thera-peutic processes in the mind, and possibly also expect that analysts may need three different sets of technical measures, each directed so that it should influence the corresponding area of the mind.'

(1968: 87)

Winnicott thought so too, even earlier, writing of 'management' where I would write of being held.

'*First*, there are those patients who operate as whole persons and whose difficulties are in the realm of interpersonal relationships. The technique for the treatment of these patients belongs to psycho-analysis as it developed in the hands of Freud at the beginning of the century.

Then *secondly* there come the patients in whom the wholeness of the personality only just begins to be something that can be taken for granted; in fact one can say that analysis has to do with the first events that belong to and inherently and immediately follow not only the achievement of wholeness but also the coming together of love and hate and the dawning of recognition of dependence. This is the analysis of the stage of concern, or of what has come to be known as the "depressive position". These patients require the analysis of mood. The technique for this work is not different from that needed by patients in the first category; nevertheless some new management problems do arise on account of the increased range of clinical material tackled. Important from our point of view here is the idea of the survival of the analyst as a dynamic factor.

In the *third* grouping I place all those patients whose analyses must deal with the early stages of emotional development before and up to the establishment of the personality as an entity, before the achievement of space–time unit status. The personal structure is not yet securely founded. In regard to this third grouping, the accent is more surely on management, and sometimes over long periods with these patients ordinary analytic work has to be in abeyance, management being the whole thing.

To recapitulate in terms of environment, one can say that in the first grouping we are dealing with patients who develop difficulties in the ordinary course of their home life, assuming satisfactory development in the earlier stages. In the second category, the analysis of the depressive position, we are dealing with the mother–child relationship especially around the time that weaning becomes a meaningful term. The mother holds a situation in time. In the third category there comes primitive emotional development, that which needs the mother actually holding the infant.'

(Winnicott 1958[1954]: 279)

It is with people in Winnicott's third grouping that we are mainly concerned: people with bad feelings stemming from two-person or one-person levels of experience. Naturally, most psycho-analytically oriented therapists are more confident in their understanding of the two- and three-person situations which formed the staple part of their training. They had never been unwell enough to need more than that. (And if they had been, not enough might have been known to help them.) So they are more comfortable with the classical techniques: getting people to notice the instinctual roots and unconscious aspects of their current relationships, and getting them to notice their reluctance to notice. When understanding and insight bring changes in people's relationships, based on a natural wish to stop behaving in useless, painful, and/or unpopular ways, we are in the area of classical psycho-analysis. But what if the therapist's interpretations, aimed at increasing understanding and self-control, only bring misery, confusion, and ineptitude? Then we may be in other areas entirely. Balint describes in almost comical terms what happens when people seem unable to comply with the psycho-analyst's 'fundamental rule' of honestly saying what is on their minds.

'They seem unable to apprehend what is expected of them. . . . At such times it is practically useless to try to remind them of the original complaints that prompted them to seek analytic help, since they have become exclusively preoccupied with their relationship to their analyst, the gratifications and frustrations they may expect from it. All sense for continuing with the analytic work seems to have been lost. . . .

In another pattern, they repeat endlessly that they know that they ought to co-operate but that they must get better before they can do anything about that. . . . This vicious circle – in their sincere conviction – can only be broken if something that has gone wrong is replaced in them, or if they can get hold of something in them, which they had at one time but which they have since lost.'

(1968: 88–9)

No wonder. Not only are they in the grip of the old, dreadful, helpless memories, but something new is indeed needed – strength. The people whom Balint is here discussing cannot change because they are not strong enough yet. (There are of course exceptions to this generalization, especially among those who, though strong enough structurally, fear to grow up and would prefer to remain children because things have gone wrong somewhere in the three-person regions of their personality.)

The need for strength requires psychotherapists to rethink their approach. First of all, less emphasis on instinctual drives may be required. In Kohut's view, 'a life lived with the major emphasis on the satisfaction of biological drives is the consequence of a marked and fairly continuous lack of empathic responses in early and later childhood' (Kohut 1977: 122). If the baby had felt good about itself and about the world's response to it, it would not have had to fall back on simple drive-satisfactions. Feeling good about yourself and your world is the result of a good selfobject phase; feeling good about what you can grab for yourself is the result of failures in that phase. (This does not mean, of course, that drive-satisfactions are not important biological gratifications in the fortunate person's life also. It means that they are there *incorporated in* the experience of self and other – *not substitutes* for that experience.)

> 'The deepest level to be reached is not the drive, but the threat to the organisation of the self, the experience of the absence of the life-sustaining matrix of the empathic responsiveness of the self-object.'

> (Kohut 1977: 123)

Similarly Guntrip:

> 'Being, the sense of stable assured selfhood, is the basis of healthy doing, of spontaneous creative activity. Without it, doing can only be forced self-driving to keep oneself going, a state of mind that breeds aggression, in the first place against oneself; and then, to gain some relief from self-persecution, it is turned against other people.'

> (Guntrip 1971: 120)

In these circumstances:

> 'Let me emphasize again that rage and destructiveness . . . are not primary givens, but arise in reaction to the faulty empathic response of the selfobject. . . . An isolated striving to search for an outlet for rage and destructiveness is not part of our primary psychological equipment, and the guilt with regard to unconscious rage that we encounter in the clinical situation should not be regarded as a patient's reaction to a primal infantile viciousness.'
>
> (Kohut 1977: 123–24)

And, speaking to his fellow psycho-analysts:

> 'When analysands become enraged in consequence of our attack on their resistance, they do so, not because a correct interpretation has loosened defences and has activated the aggressive energy that was bound up in them [as maintained by Hartmann 1950] but because a specific genetically important traumatic situation from their early life has been repeated in the analytic situation: the experience of the faulty non-empathic response of the selfobject.'
>
> (Kohut 1977: 90)

What were these enraged patients expecting? Balint explains.

> 'In this harmonious relationship, only one partner may have wishes, interests, and demands. Without any further need for testing, it is taken for granted that the other partner, the object, or the friendly expanse, will automatically have the same wishes, interests, or expectations. This explains why this is so often called the state of omnipotence. This description is somewhat out of tune: there is no feeling of power, in fact, no need for either power or effort, as all things *are* in harmony.
>
> If any hitch or disharmony between subject and object occurs, the reaction to it will consist of loud and vehement symptoms suggesting processes either of a highly aggressive and destructive or of a profoundly disintegrated nature – as if the whole world including the self had been smashed up, or as if the subject had been flooded with pure and unmitigated aggressive-destructive impulses. On the other hand, if the harmony is allowed to persist without much disturbance from outside, the reaction amounts to a feeling of tranquil well-being, rather inconspicuous and difficult to observe.

This difference in mood, expressed in adult language, would run somewhat like this: I must be loved and looked after in every respect by everyone and everything important to me, without anyone demanding any effort or claiming any return for this. It is only my wishes, interests, and needs that matter; none of the people who are important to me must have any interests, wishes, needs different from mine, and if they have any at all, they must subordinate theirs to mine without any resentment or strain; in fact, it must be their pleasure and their enjoyment to fit in with my wishes. If this happens, I shall be good, pleased, and happy but that is all. If this does not happen, it will be horrifying both for the world and for me.'

(1968: 70–1)

'On the level of the basic fault, any difference is felt by the patient to be a major tragedy, reviving all the bitter disappointments that established the fault' (1968: 112). Winnicott also notices the absoluteness of this state of mind.

'With the regressed patient the word "wish" is incorrect: instead we use the word *need*. If a regressed patient *needs* quiet, then without it nothing can be done at all. If the need is not met the result is not anger, only a reproduction of the environmental failure which stopped the processes of self growth. The individual's capacity to "wish" has become interfered with, and we witness the reappearance of the original cause of a sense of futility.'

(1958[1954]: 288)

Therefore

'analysts must do everything in their power not to become, or to behave as, separate sharply-contoured objects. They must allow their patient to relate to them or exist with them as if they were one of the primary substances. This means they should be willing to carry the patient, not actively, but like water carries the swimmer or the earth carries the walker, that is, to be there for the patient, to be used without too much resistance against being used.'

(Balint 1968: 167)

This is the counselling ethic at its best: attentive listening, confirming, mirroring, reflecting, accepting without judging or condemning, concerned with feeling rather than fact, responding to what makes sense rather than to wrong or silly bits, celebrating rather than nit-picking, and so on. Small wonder that Truax and Carkhuff (1967) found that, regardless of the school of thought to which US psychiatrists, psycho-analysts, psycho-therapists, or counsellors belonged, their patients got better according to the extent to which they could give them (1) accurate empathy, (2) unconditional warmth, with (3) genuineness and authenticity. Friends do it effortlessly. People who have these resources easily available have an advantage in ministering to the distressed psyche. Some therapists find it easy only with relatively sensible people. Others find it easier with the very disturbed, strange, and apparently incoherent − if necessary for years (see Searles 1965; 1979). Others again had better not try.

> 'There are innumerable ways in which analysts may respond to their patients' subtle forms of regression . . . indifference, disapproval, some slight sign of annoyance. They may tolerate acting out but follow it immediately with a correct and timely interpretation which, in turn, will take the patient some steps further to learning the analysts' language and will inhibit further acting-out. They may sympathetically permit it as a kind of safety-valve; or they may take it in their stride, feeling no more, or for that matter no less, need for interpretation (i.e. for interfering with the acting-out), than with any other form of communication, say verbal associations. Evidently it is only in this last case that acting-out and verbal associations are equally accepted as communications addressed to the therapist.'
>
> (Balint 1968: 83−4)

What ought to happen in therapy, in Balint's view, is for analysts to let themselves be used as 'primary objects', objects of the absolute and primary love which existed before a basic fault cut the person off from that memory. This is not a task for loving friends to do on a non-professional basis. It needs a peculiar combination of freedom and firmness about boundaries, which is not compatible with everyday personal relationships.

The idea of regression, relaxation, and a new beginning

'The child that is to survive psychologically is born into an empathic-responsive human milieu just as it is born into an atmosphere that contains an optimal amount of oxygen. . . . And its nascent self "expects" an empathic environment to be in tune with its need-wishes, with the same unquestioning certitude as its lungs may be said to "expect" oxygen.'

(Kohut 1977: 85)

We have to have had some experience of security, acceptability, and well-being before we can even make a start on growing up into 'independent centres of initiative and perception' (Kohut 1977: 177). Presumably we, who have survived, all have some memory-traces of this good state, which would normally give us the strength to accept life as it comes. They are sources of strength. If we are cut off from them, we need to go back to recover and integrate them.

What about people whose early experiences of themselves-in-the-world included an amount of badness, emptiness, and uselessness that overwhelmed the newly emerging self? Their sense of futility and powerlessness derives from the fact that they are cut off from that part of their being where our bodily needs and satisfaction were first experienced: this has become a split-off hurt and needy region, part of the 'something lost' that must be recovered if a sense of wholeness is ever to be achieved. Such recoveries sometimes come about when people work with a therapist who, by his or her own behaviour, provides a context which resembles the empathic selfobject one-person level where there is unconditional permission to exist and be. But the process is not well understood, and is at present a lengthy and chancy one.

It does appear that some of us need to re-integrate the memory-traces of whatever happiness and well-being we may at one time have had, as well as the misery we could not at that time accept. These must be recalled and revived – if possible in words, not in action – and reflected upon, for we need to discover that both good and bad memories can be lived with once we are strong enough to do so. Therapeutic regression allows this revival (which may or may not be acceptable elsewhere) to be confined to the consulting room.

394 OUR NEED FOR OTHERS

However, some people are very tightly organized against any such relaxation, perhaps for fear of falling apart, perhaps for fear of threatening the present supremacy of their ('Central Ego') ego-functions. They can only do what they were driven to as children, and struggle against the temptation to relax,

> 'by developing a hard and hostile attitude to any "weakness" in themselves, i.e. to develop an anti-libidinal ego which is really the child's determined effort to keep going by being independent.'

(Guntrip 1969: 78)

The 'anti-libidinal ego' is the child's premature attempt at being organized and strong, at 'pulling itself together' as the phrase goes. Unfortunately, as Guntrip points out, it succeeds only in pulling itself further apart. The anti-libidinal forces hinder the growth of a more relaxed and resilient kind of strength, with roots in a natural sense of well-being.

Trying to relax this tight organization is a very painful process, which requires much courage. Anything a psychotherapist can do, to help people discover and hold on to the strength they have already found, is of course tremendously important. Such strength is difficult to find and hold on to, because the anti-libidinal forces will destroy a person's awareness of good things. ('It is presumptuous of me to believe that I do anything well, or to be happy when things go well for the moment.')

> 'Usually, it is a very long time before the patient can consistently accept and bring to the analyst the regressed, passively dependent ego. The analysis of anti-libidinal reactions, against not only active but passive needs, constitutes, I believe, the most important part of "analysing". I have seen real improvement appear and be retained when what Winnicott calls "therapeutic regression" at last comes to be understood and accepted. ... I have found encouraging results with several patients who, each in his or her own way, have been able to find security for their regressed ego in the psychotherapeutic relationship.
>
> There appear to be two aspects of the problem. The first is the slow growth out of their anti-libidinal (Freudian sadistic super-ego) persecution of themselves; they need to unlearn

their ruthless driving of themselves by ceaseless inner mental pressure to keep going as "forced pseudo-adults", and to acquire the courage to adopt a more understanding attitude toward the hidden hard-pressed and frightened child.

Simultaneously with this there goes a second process, the growth of a constructive faith that if the needs of the regressed ego are met, first in relation to the therapist who protects it in its need for an initial passive dependence, this will mean not collapse and loss of active powers, but a steady recuperation from deep strain, diminishing of deep fears, revitalising of the personality, and rebirth of an active ego that is spontaneous and does not have to be forced and driven; what Balint calls "primitive passive dependence" making possible "the new beginning".'

(Guntrip 1969: 85–6)

We are here considering people under such stress that they are in danger of being split apart by their own anti-libidinal forces. Their present psychological structures needs to some extent to be re-organized, because it is not viable in the long run anyway, and because it is at present preventing the development of a natural flow of strength and well-being. (This is another description of the phenomenon which Guntrip called 'the regressed ego'.) Yet people in this plight know that any change in their present state of equilibrium is liable to disturb the balance of forces which holds them together. If there is ever to be a change, it can take place only in a very safe environment which can give them some hope that they may be held together somehow. This puts a heavy responsibility on those who seek to help them. The normal classical procedures of psycho-analysis and psychotherapy, and the normal common-sense procedures of parents and friends, may not be appropriate in these circumstances.

'How can the need of the exhausted regressed ego, for recuperation in and rebirth from a reproduction of the womb-state, be met at all, and how can it be met without the risk of undermining the central ego of everyday living? That seems to be the ultimate problem for psychotherapy.

There is evidence that it can be done, although we have almost everything to learn about this process. At least it is safe to say that it cannot be done without the aid of a psycho-

therapist, i.e. the setting up of a psychotherapeutic relationship. . . .

The final aim of this therapy is to convert regression into
rebirth and regrowth. This must result from the regressed ego
finding for the first time a relationship of understanding
acceptance and safeguarding of its rights, with a therapist who
does not seek to force on the patient a preconceived view of
what must be done, but who realises that deep down patients
know their own business best, if we can but understand the
language.'

(Guntrip 1969: 78)

For, now,

'The rebirth and regrowth of the lost living heart of the
personality is the ultimate problem psychotherapy now seeks
to solve.'

(p. 12)

Creating security and space to hesitate, discover, and understand

Some people may need the kind of regression that is a relaxation
of structures. Their central ego-functioning 'coping' self is out of
gear, else they would not be in therapy. The time may have come
for them to relax and let go of their present personality-
integration, so that a new arrangement may come about in which
areas of their life may be integrated which have so far been
denied a place.

It is for this reason that therapists need to be careful to
distinguish the circumstances in which it is right to focus on
guilt-provoking emotions like rage or greed. Anyone in an
authoritative or helping capacity is easily experienced as on the
side of anti-libidinal forces. In the kind of regression and
relaxation we are now considering, people need all the strength
they can muster, in order to stay in touch and not evade their
feelings of emptiness and desolation, and pain and terror, about
which they already feel very guilty and ashamed. They must not
be further weakened by having their moral and intellectual
failings brought to their attention as a central issue. If, additionally, we consider that some people will need to recover those
split-off regions where their bodily experiences and their (per-

haps scant) memories of good times are mapped, the injunctions against promoting guilt and shame become even stronger. This is not the time to put people right — we have first to strengthen whatever strengths they already possess.

Even the voice of another person can at times be disturbing.

> 'It appals me to think how much deep change I have prevented or delayed in patients in a certain category by my personal need to interpret. If only we can wait, the patient arrives at understanding creatively and with immense joy, and I now enjoy this joy more than I used to enjoy the sense of having been clever.'
>
> (Winnicott 1974[1971]: 101)

It is important not to be in too much of a hurry when faced with error or delusion or distress or disintegration. People come to therapy unready for a direct encounter with their deeper anxieties. If they had been ready, they would have faced them and contained them. When, encouraged by an unwise therapist or friend, they are made to drop the defences they need before they are strong enough to integrate new insights, they will awake the terror which has always surrounded this split-off part, a terror which includes the terror of disintegrating altogether. They will then tighten up more than ever, yet feel obscurely shamed and weakened by a sense of having failed to perform as expected.

Too stark a confrontation with the deepest anxieties, especially if encouraged by someone on whom a person is very dependent for a sense of security and connectedness, encourages the formation of a False Self, in order to please the therapist. Much has been written about the dangers of *coaxing* a patient into what looks like a recovery — the so-called 'transference cure'. But disturbed people may also be *frightened* into what looks like recovery, taking their therapists' 'interpretations' as implicit advice and acting rigidly on it in order to contain their disintegration. The corrosive hidden sense of hollowness and badness cannot be reached in this way.

> 'A principle might be enunciated, that in the False Self area of our analytic practice we find we make more headway by recognition of the patient's non-existence than by a long-

continued working with the patient on the basis of ego-
defence mechanisms. The patient's False Self can collaborate
indefinitely with the analyst in the analysis of defences, being
so to speak on the analyst's side in the game. This unreward-
ing work is only cut short profitably when the analyst can
point to and specify an absence.'

(Winnicott 1965[1960]: 152)

And Kohut,

'It is not the aim of analysis to confront the patient with a now
supposedly fully uncovered drive. . . . The deepest level to be
reached is not the drive . . . but the experience of the absence
of the life-sustaining matrix.'

(Kohut 1977: 123)

To let people reach this terrifying level of experience in safety,
therapists must allow themselves to be a safe environment,
facilitating, unobtrusive, unwounding.

In general, it is a good thing when people are allowed space to
make their own discoveries. Winnicott set the example when he
let the baby play with the shiny spoon (p. 245). A period of
hesitation is necessary if people are to make their own discoveries about what the breast/spoon/insight is for and can do.
It is an impingement when things are shoved at you before you
know whether you want them and can use them. Those things
feel alien – to turn away from them is a healthy reaction: to
comply is the unhealthy response of the intimidated. So, we
must allow for periods of hesitation which precede the moment
when people start to make some new structure their own, truly
theirs, not half the therapist's. (See, especially, Casement 1985.)

What is at issue here is *how* true new insights are to be
integrated. They must not be integrated in a depersonalized form
(see pp. 151, 348). 'I-now' have to understand and hold and
accept 'me-then' and the situation as I experienced it then (see
pp. 376–77). I have to be the first to be making the connections
if I am truly to feel 'I discovered that', 'I made that', 'I did that',
even 'I exist', 'I existed then', 'I am' (see pp. 239–40, 266–76,
314). When things are at their best, therapist and other arrive
together at new meanings.

Once there is a certain amount of strength – by which I mean at least the beginnings of a true-self core as an organizing principle – and once good rapport and understanding have been established, the many occasions on which such perfect timing does not happen may also serve a useful purpose. They enable people to start to come to terms with the fact that being perfectly understood (and the perfect capacity for always having perfect insight) never were and never will be their lot. The reality of other people, in all their goodness and badness and *separateness* (see pp. 276–79), is thereby established, and hence also one's own reality. And this has to be established if the experience of being held is ever to become a reality – it takes two for one to be held. To this we now turn.

'Using' a psychotherapist as a preliminary to allowing oneself to relax and be held

As I have defined them, psychotherapists are professionals who allow people to relate to them in terms of earlier dreaded or desired experiences. They may be treated as selfobjects satisfactory or unsatisfactory, as a compliant or stubborn other, as a tyrant, a terror, a feeder, attacker, protector, omniscient, omnipotent, powerless, always getting it wrong, and so on – just like a parent. Therapists let themselves be used, first as 'inner objects', and later, as the patient improves, as objects in shared reality (Winnicott 1974[1971]: 106).

That is why psychotherapists deserve their pay (within limits), and why friends and family may in the long run not be the best people to help someone integrate who has gone to pieces. It is not right that they should try to put up with being the object of unrealistic phantasies for more than a little while. If they do, they deprive the sufferer of an important realistic relationship while themselves being no more than inexperienced, untrained psychotherapists. Professional psychotherapists are needed to be the climbing-frames of the consulting-room adventure-playground, where people can discover what they are made of and what the world of the other is made of. At such times, the therapist is 'used' in the sense in which Winnicott employed the word when he wrote of the use of an object. It is not an easy position to occupy!

'The expected control over the narcissistically-cathected object and its function is closer to the concept which grownups
have of the control they expect to have over their own body
and mind, than of their experience of others and of their
control over them.'

(Kohut 1971: 33)

The object of such affections will feel pretty oppressed! Yet
accepting that a person may need to behave in this way is the
only way we know of at present, to provide enough safety to let
people relax their defences and reach the sore regions.

In Chapter 14 we looked at the rage which the baby feels when
it has to give up its imagined omnipotence and to live in the
world of shared reality. Winnicott argued that in fortunate
circumstances, the rage has the effect of establishing the world of
shared reality, and also of establishing this world as a safe place.

'The subject says to the object "I destroyed you", and the
object is there to receive the communication. From now on the
subject says "Hullo object! I destroyed you. I love you. You
hace value for me because of your survival of my destruction
of you." . . . The subject can now *use* the object that has
survived.'

(Winnicott 1974[1971]: 105–06)

From the point of view of psychotherapy, for people to discover
that the imagined effects of even the most destructive rage, and
even the most chaotic confusion, in fact destroys neither them
nor the therapist, may be the major repair to be done. The world
is a safer place when you can stop thinking of yourself as
omnipotent, with a vengeful world retaliating. The (m)other may
not have survived in a person's phantasy – the therapist does:
'C'est son métier'. How does this help? It heals splits.

Healing and holding splits in context

Once another person's reality is safely established as independent of my confusion or rage, I become more capable of realistic
acceptance of myself and others, and of ambivalence. I become
saner. I can allow my model of myself-in-the-situation, and my
map of myself-in-the-world, to carry contradictory images. I can

accept that I am sometimes honest and sometimes not, and that you are sometimes kind to me and sometimes not. By contrast, when I was unsure of your independent reality, I tried to carry only one coherent internally consistent model at any time: 'the right one'.

In shared reality, I have to put up with the fact that others are to some extent exactly as I want them to be and to some extent remain stubbornly their own inconvenient selves. Very interestingly, Winnicott thought that babies whose mothers can tolerate their times of rage, soon show themselves as more sure of themselves than other babies. This must have a bearing, too, on sex differences, considering our culture's encouragement for boys to prove their assertiveness, and for girls to prove their good nature even to the point of submissiveness – even, sometimes, to the point of allowing themselves to be victimized.

> 'Babies that have been seen through this phase well are likely to be more aggressive *clinically* than the ones who have not been seen through the phase well, and for whom aggression is something that cannot be encompassed, or something that can be retained only in the form of a liability to be an object of attack.'
>
> (1974[1971]: 109)

It is easy to imagine that allowing a person to rage and make chaos is in itself therapeutic. In some circumstances this is so. But in the circumstances now under consideration, it is the (m)other's or the therapist's ability to 'survive' that is being tested and established. A person may need to get back to the bad feelings of the very early days, yes, but in my view the therapeutic experience is not just that of expressing the hurt or angry or terrified feelings. These have to be expressed in order that further healing may take place. The real healing comes also in part from being listened to and understood and recognized as a person while having these feelings. The real healing comes from being held while all this is going on, at first by another person, and later by one's own functioning personality.

In this process it may also happen that a person gets in touch with some totally unexpected good and quiet times of being. This is what must sometimes be the aim of regression and

relaxation, re-integrating the good and quiet times when someone else is looking after us.

In therapy, people can discover another person, the therapist,
who is affected by the baby (part of them) but whose fate is not
under that baby's control. Symmetrically, that baby can discover that it is part of a whole person. This starts the process of
growing up, of becoming an adult who can become angry but
who is not swallowed up by anger. The anger is integrated as a
part of the whole personality, but it is not the whole. The anger
can become depersonalized, in Jacobson's and Kernberg's sense
of the word.

We can come to distance and detach our selves from other
feelings, and cease to be overwhelmed by misery, fear, or
futility. The great achievement is to be able to say, 'I feel terrible,
but I am more than a terrible feeling'.

Meaning depends on context. The context holds things
together. Without a context there is no meaning, only unintegrated bits.

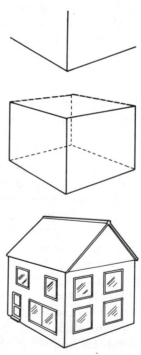

This is a bit
without a context

After a good deal
of holding, it begins
to make sense in
the context of the
cube of which it
has become a part.

After a good deal
more work, it has
become part of a
house to live in.

Being held

Many therapists believe that some people need to go to pieces, to become totally disorganized, in order to have a chance at better organization. I think this may be true as things stand at present. Our understanding of psychotherapy is not sufficiently developed for therapists to be able to help people disintegrate just in the right area and to the right extent, and in fifty-minute packages! Nor is enough known as yet about the circumstances in which the natural healing process (*vis medicatrix naturae*) will work best, and how we may encourage it. There is still much to learn.

What is clear, however, is that some people feel that they may be falling apart, or even flying apart. An absolutely terrifying state of mind, an unbearable agony, Winnicott (1974) called it, yet one which he assumed had already happened in infancy: 'the unbearable has already happened'. (See also pp. 327–28.) Yet it may be that this is a thing that may need to happen to them again before they can get to an integrated personality-structure which feels better at a fundamental level. It is also clear that they need to be held somehow during that falling-apart time. It is surely almost obvious that being held by a person is in principle more appropriate than being held by a hospital organization or a bed or a drug. In practice, however, there is still a lot that psychotherapists need to learn.

A little more is known about more controlled therapeutic regressions and relaxations of integration. At certain times in therapy, we may be in touch with a baby part of ourselves, and its terrible experiences, while at an adult level, too, all is confusion, disintegration, lack of connectedness, lack of context or meaning. This horrible experience is nothing new. What is new is the experience of feeling like this in the presence of someone who can take all this without losing his or her hold. At first, the adult part of us cannot hold on, never having been able to since babyhood. But the therapist holds it, is not swallowed up by it, does not deny it but continues to be in touch both with the disintegrated adult and the disintegrated baby parts. In due course, if things go well, the adult part of us co-operates with the therapist in holding the baby and, further along in time, the therapist's help is no longer needed. Then, the adult is able to feel the baby's disintegration without feeling overwhelmed by it – the disintegration is integrated as part of the personality: it is not the whole.

It is this that helps people get better. The facilitating environment is there to enable the maturational processes to proceed: safety, recognition, opportune reality-presentation. What else? A facilitating environment is in the end not enough. People are needed. Persons. Personal relationships between whole persons. Even when the relationship is not between two whole persons, because one of them is still a tenuous patchwork of disintegrated and suffering adult and baby bits, even then it is important that there is a person in the relationship who is adult and whole, and that is the therapist. Like a good parent, like a good friend, the therapist is there to maintain the consoling knowledge that there are still good things, and most basically, that the good relationship has survived. 'You are still you, I am still I, we are still together and sharing.' 'You and I are both at risk of natural disasters but the relationship is surviving.' 'You may be (I may be) more confused, more lost, more inept, more of a coward, more sadistic or dirtier than you wanted to believe, but we both know it now and the relationship is still there.' 'Your parent(s) may have been more confused, lost, inept, cowardly, sadistic, or dirty than you wanted to believe, but we both know it now, and the relationship is still intact.' That is what holding is. It is not easy to achieve.

This is what Kohut means when he warns that analysts waste their time if they concentrate on either the grandiose or the wretched part of the psyche (see p. 222). Both must be accepted, both held: when they are, then parts of the personality which were previously disowned will contribute strength and solidity to the whole.

> 'What is the nature of the analytic work which is performed at the "vertical" barriers? What are the activities of the analyst? ... It is to bring the central sector of the personality to an acknowledgment of the simultaneous existence (1) of unaltered conscious and preconscious narcissistic and/or perverse aims, and (2) of the realistic goal structures and the moral and aesthetic standards which reside in the central sector.'
>
> (Kohut 1971: 183)

This is not as cold or complex a process as the language implies. It is amazing how close to 'kissing it better' the whole business sometimes is. Or is it amazing that psychotherapists are only now finding a place for such processes in their theories?

What good parents do: implications for therapists

This chapter addresses itself to the question: how does a person become strong, in the sense of having good self-esteem, a good ability to understand situations and cope with them, a good personality organization which allows feelings and needs to find expression in actions and gratifications which in turn feed self-esteem? Bluntly, we do not know for sure. We may make some guesses based on what good parents and good therapists are thought by some to have in common.

Let us think of a simple, everyday pain: a child has hurt a finger. The finger gives pain. The pain must be recognized and accepted. Parents know this who put large plasters on tiny grazes. They give recognition to the fact that the child has had a shock. The pain was a shock. The child's illusions of omnipotence or safety may have shattered. It has certainly been reminded that it does not have perfect control over what happens to it. The suddenness of the shock may have been experienced as an impingement – this needs healing as much as the graze does, so that the boundaries of the self may feel secure again. Consolation is needed. So is mourning with the child, as in depression about other losses: mourning the fact that the world is not a better place, and mourning our limited power to be safe and keep our good things safe. In mourning there is a kind of recognition and acceptance which is consoling. As Bowlby pointed out, the process takes a while, and during that time we just have to sit about, being not doing.

'London February 1973
I'm sitting in my armchair reading.
Natasha walks in, stifling her sobs, clambers on my lap, positions herself upright, facing away, tilts her head fully back, and bursts into howls and howls and howls.
I make a move to cuddle her but she elbows my arms away, and when I tentatively touch the tips of her fingers, by way of

some gesture of consolation, she snatches them away, and her howls threaten to turn into shrieks, or even skreeks. As her howls continue, I have just time to check my impulse to ask her what's the matter, to hug her, stroke her, to offer words of comfort, before she is lowering her head and turning to look at me for the first time, her last howl fades. In one smile she says hello, bye-bye, perhaps thanks daddy. With a sigh of completion, she gets down from my lap, and without a word between us since she came in and without looking back, she ambles out of the door, ready for her next adventure.'

(Laing 1978)

This is why bed-rest is sometimes a good treatment (to accompany other help) in the case of psychologically wounded people. It would be great if hospitals could provide this. But alas, financial shortages, the wrong medical model of psychological troubles, and a demoralized management structure which cannot support and educate its nursing staff, militate against this as things are at present – as does the professional's passion to be doing or at least talking.

Just as the good-enough parent accepts the small child as it is, giving recognition and acceptance by 'mirroring' in an atmosphere which implies that what is seen in the mirror is good, so will therapists, accepting people who are hoping for a new beginning, find themselves impelled to mirror. Mirroring is not quite interpreting, though in some ways near it. The best simple example comes from Virginia Axline's account of her work with Dibs, the very anxious and confused little boy of four who had been very much overwhelmed by parents obsessed with doing at the expense of being. Dibs remembered his therapy as 'Everything I did, you did. Everything I said, you said.'

Good parents give the small child permission to be just whatever it happens to be at the time. And they not only give it room to be, but also recognize that it is a person in its own right, even before it is so, and praise it for what it is not yet. They also validate its needs and requirements. They also provide the conditions for ego-relatedness, allowing the child to feel safe and protected and yet not obligated by their presence. So the child feels safe enough to begin to discover something about itself in the world.

In much the same way, friends and therapists can provide an opportunity for people to discover that it is safe just to be, to be *arglos*, undefended, in a safe ego-related us-related state. In this state of mind people can let their thoughts drift in a free-association kind of way. It may be that, contentedly in touch with a person who matters to them and whom they have come to trust, they are unconsciously getting close to sharing something which cannot (yet) be put into words (Balint 1958: Part V, The Regressed Patient and the Analyst). They may be getting ready to be a person they have not yet dared to be, or to reveal a split-off part of self which had hitherto been disowned. Words are not very suitable for conveying your essential being. The new (organization of the) self is therefore sometimes acted out somehow, the person half-hoping that the right response from the friend or psychotherapist will do something that will somehow make something good happen. This is a route by which people can sometimes get back to a state of being when something was so unbearable that they had to stay split.

At such times there may be a lot of anger, or other behaviour it is as hard to put up with as it would be in three-person regions of relationships. But, as Guntrip pointed out (pp. 304–05), this can be a cover-up. In these regressions, anguish is much more common, and may be the norm. Can this be conveyed in words, except by a poet?

> I am gall, I am heartburn. God's most deep decree
> Bitter would have me taste: my taste was me;
> Bones built in me, flesh filled, blood brimmed the curse.
>   Selfyeast of spirit a dull dough scours. I see
> The lost are like this, and their scourge to be
> As I am mine, their sweating selves; but worse.

> (Gerard Manley Hopkins, *I wake and feel the fell of dark,*
> *not day*)

Therapists, parents, or friends, faced with these feelings, may find themselves in conflict. This person who has come for help seems so clearly to need comfort and reassurance, is so obviously in agony, ashamed, or frightened; the feelings are so hard to bear. How to react for the best? On the one hand, here is a person in pain. On the other hand, the pain could be very largely due to some very distorted ideas about how others would react if they really knew them. Those ideas need to be changed. Putting them right by reassurance or sensible arguments has not worked in the past and does not seem worth trying again. The old pain, the shame-making situation, the hidden person, have first to come into view and be seen and acknowledged and recognized and *shared*. *After* that it may become possible to repair the damage which had previously prevented the bad experiences from being fully integrated into the personality at the obvious moment, the moment when they were first aroused. But integration can be achieved only if they are now allowed to come into consciousness, now, while the sufferer is in a relationship with someone willing to have them come to light. The process must therefore not be impeded by too many expressions or reassurance and comfort, however well meant, lest the sufferer get the idea that we cannot bear (contain, accept, integrate) these feelings either. That might cause such an increase in anxiety that the splits would be deepened rather than mended. The whole point of reviving all that pain is to have someone there who is able to survive it, contain it, and integrate it.

Recognition is a basic need. To be recognized is part of the healing process, whether it be recognition of good or of bad things. What is recognized is that here is someone who has lived thus and has felt thus and not otherwise. Just the experience of going to pieces, of being lost, furious, disgusting, terrified, ignored, yet safe and known and accepted, may be what a person is after, just the experience of being so in someone else's presence and not having to do anything about it.

Getting stronger, helped by parents, friends, and/or psychotherapists

When does a person need the kind of recognition that goes with support and with praise for achievement, and when do people need us to stand back and let them be a little while longer?

It is clear that it is not supportive to prevent people from telling us their bad feelings when they are urgent to do so, and there is time, and we are ready to hear them. And it is not supportive to behave like blocks of stone while we are listening.

But how far to go? It has been interesting to see the newer therapies which are less firmly attached to psycho-analytic roots and which have recently gained in popularity – Transactional Analysis, Gestalt, Bio-energetics, Psychosynthesis, and so on – also grappling with this question. These newer techniques are much more emphatic about the need to provide safety, recognize 'being', and communicate acceptance. This emphasis derives from many sources; among others, there is the fact that they evolved in an era when people in fear of disintegration were seeking non-religious, non-medical, non-psycho-analytic help for their condition (and were often rightly avoided by more orthodox psychotherapies because they were considered unsuitable for psycho-analysis). Disintegrating people need holding, and the newer techniques are freer in encouraging comfort, praise, and warmth. Thus they help people to bear both the pain of their everyday lives and the pain of therapy, where painful new discoveries are made and painful old feelings revived: people get a supply of strength while they seek new ways of being. Groups are ideal for this purpose, different members offering different gifts of themselves, and support coming from many quarters at once.

The more orthodox psycho-analytically based therapies on the whole refrain from giving gratifying support of this kind, and this can be hard both on patient and on therapist – the many warnings against it prove how strong the temptation is. They impose restraint on the grounds that people must eventually find those gratifications for themselves in themselves and in others: the wrong kind of dependence may be created when a therapist gives realistic gratifications.

Abstinence from support, praise, warmth, or reassurance can serve another purpose also: it can serve to give recognition to our strivings to be strong, able, competent. Having given room for ocnophilic dependency-needs, room has equally to be made for the philobat's independence-strivings. So while many of the newer therapies at first made much of physically holding people, surrounding them with cuddling words and gestures, many are now also quite explicit on the importance of waiting for people to stop sobbing or shouting, letting them gain control over themselves, and allowing them to find within themselves the strength needed for self-control and self-esteem.

Older and newer agree on the importance of people finding out for themselves who they are and what they can do and what they like doing. But their methods of achieving this vary, particularly here, in the timing and indeed the nature of helpful interventions. There seem at present no hard and fast rules which make things right for everyone. We will, for a while longer, just have to guess what each particular person needs at a particular moment, to help him or her become strong enough to bear reality after having denied it for long or after having distorted it and secretly held on to all kinds of cherished delusions which must now be given up.

Getting words and understanding and the skills to look after oneself

We have been considering why and how parents and others might create an atmosphere in which it is safe for people to let themselves go, in which they can be defenceless and even go to pieces, and yet know that someone is looking after them. In a sense, the whole book has been about this. We are coming to the end.

A more realistic phase is now starting. Conversations are becoming possible. From the very early days, of people's life and of their therapy, there will have been phantasies about the world, about living, about parents and/or therapists, sometimes of a quite frightening kind. What is to happen to these phantasies? The time has come for them to be established as either true or untrue. In the early days, the parent/therapist's role was concentrated on providing an atmosphere which conveyed that it was all right to have phantasies, not wrong to have thoughts about *anything*. In therapy this often comes as a surprise, and the discovery has therapeutic effects. But when conversations become possible, further gains can be achieved. Words can now be provided, for use when thinking or talking about hazardous things – words in which the at-first blurry phantasies can be talked about, words like 'penis', words like 'hate', words like 'disagree' and 'conflict'.

The parent/therapist can now convey new things to the child (part of us) knowing that we are ready for it. The parent/therapist teaches, making meaning for us, or helping us to find meaning, still often ego-functioning for us as a form of support.

Verbal labels help us look for and remember things – symbolic thought becomes possible, reasoning. Explanations can now be made in words; there is less need to rely on direct experience to make the connections. 'If you put your fingers into those little holes, you will get a nasty shock from the electric current.' 'It may be that you are feeling disgruntled because you missed a session last week, and now you feel somehow sold short.'

Facts will be changing accordingly. The parent/therapist can say, or allow the discovery to be made, that a particular phantasy is true (or false, as the case may be): 'Yes, fathers and mothers have sex.' 'No, your mother is not a man.'

The child learns language. The child learns road safety, and crocheting, and other skills. Some of these are learned because someone sets out to teach them. I think there is an observable difference between those whose parents took trouble over such things, and those who were left too entirely to their own devices. In somewhat the same way there is a difference between people whose therapists' technique differed in this respect.

Words, skills, and the ability to look after yourself are related. At this time in development, the child part of us is now no longer so confined to creating its own realities as in the ego-related state. We become interested in our new opportunities – and discover new limitations. We begin to be interested in doing things for ourselves; now we need to be allowed freer opportunities to discover both the world and our place in it. At this time we need recognition that we can safely be strong enough to do things for ourselves. We need to be allowed to discover what we can do, within fairly wide limits, and not be inhibited too much in our play and our trial-and-error explorations, which necessarily involve a good deal of error, failure, and frustration.

Yet good parents are very much there: they are not uninvolved, or let the child discover things for itself in a *laissez-faire* sort of way. They give praise in recognition of the fact that it is strong and can do things. But they protect the child's growing self-confidence by keeping away problems which might prove too overwhelmingly difficult, which would necessarily defeat it and sap its growing self-esteem. The child needs protection against what it cannot yet handle. Support is needed for instance when we have to give up our omnipotent or endlessly greedy phantasies. Part of this support consists of help in recognizing limits: 'No, you can't have the moon, but you can have my love, and a hug, and a game with Tommy next door.' Support is needed, too, while learning to accept the reality of other people: 'Yes, you can play with Tommy but no, you must not kick him. He doesn't like it any more than you would.' We need to have boundaries pointed out to us and maintained, if necessary against our wishes at the time. In psychotherapy, the therapist's willingness to do this new kind of holding may be tried and tested over and over. At this time, a laid-back psychotherapist, *laissez-faire* because anxious not to intrude, may fail to provide a feeling of safety.

At this stage, when there is much frustration and disillusion-ment at what is not possible as well as much pleasure at what can now be done, the need for a reliable, comforting, sharing-the-mourning kind of holding is as crucial as ever. It is what gives us the strength and vitality to keep on trying. These periods of being-at-rest and being-at-one allow the new things to be securely integrated and valued. They bring us back to our central strength.

For we can be sure that we have the seeds of the goodness and strength we need, hidden and repressed or split-off though they may be. Locked in our memory are traces of the experiences which enabled us to survive. We know that this is so because we have in fact survived. We did not die. At least the minimum goodness was there, and just enough strength, at least. We are already possessed of what we need, if we can but get to it.

> 'Oh joy! that in our embers
> Is something that doth live,
> That nature yet remembers
> What was so fugitive!
> The thought of our past years in me doth breed
> Perpetual benediction: not indeed
> For that which is most worthy to be blest –
> Delight and liberty, the simple creed
> Of childhood, whether busy or at rest,
> With new-fledged hope still fluttering in his breast:–
> Not for these I raise
> The song of thanks and praise. . . .

But for those first affections,
Those shadowy recollections,
   Which, be they what they may,
Are yet the fountain-light of all our day,
Are yet a master-light of all our seeing;
Uphold us, cherish, and have power to make
Our noisy years seem moments in the being
Of the eternal Silence: truths that wake,
      To perish never:
Which neither listlessness, nor mad endeavour,
      Nor Man nor Boy,
Nor all that is at enmity with joy,
Can utterly abolish or destroy!

   Hence in a season of calm weather
      Though inland far we be,
Our souls have sight of that immortal sea
      Which brought us hither,
   Can in a moment travel thither,
And see the children sport upon the shore,
And hear the mighty waters rolling evermore.

Then sing, ye birds, sing, sing a joyous song!'

(William Wordsworth, *Ode on Intimations of Immortality
      from Recollections of Early Childhood*)

APPENDICES

Appendix to Chapter 2: notes

1   Much of this chapter up to this point has come from Carlson, N. (1977) *Physiology of Behaviour*. Boston and London: Allyn & Bacon, pp. 14–16 and 25.

2   Carlson (1977: 503):

'Mark, Ervin and Yakoviev (1962) made stereotaxically placed lesions in the thalamus in an attempt to relieve the pain of patients suffering from the advanced stages of cancer. Damage to the sensory relay nuclei produced a loss of cutaneous senses: touch, temperature, and cutaneous pain (the ability to detect pinpricks). However, patients obtained no relief from deep, chronic pain. Lesions in the parafascicular nucleus and intralaminar nucleus were successful: pain, but not cutaneous sensitivity were gone. Finally, destruction of the dorso-medial and anterior thalamic nuclei left cutaneous sensitivity and the perception of pain intact – however, the patients did not pay much attention to the pain: the lesions appeared to reduce or remove its emotional component.'

3   Carlson (1977: 504):

'It has been known for some years that electrical stimulation of the brain can attenuate pain. It seems likely that stimulation at some loci produces true analgesia (elimination of pain perception) and increased pain tolerance at others. Furthermore, there is very good evidence that stimulus-produced analgesia works by the same mechanisms that mediate analgesia produced by morphine.'

417

418 OUR NEED FOR OTHERS

4 Carlson (1977: 507):

'The puzzle as to why the brain contains opiate receptors has been solved – the brain produces its own opiates. Terenius and Wahlstrom (1975) reported the existence of a substance in human cerebro-spinal fluid that has a specific affinity for opiate receptors extracted from rat brain. They called this chemical a "morphine-like factor". Hughes, Smith, Kosterlitz, Fothergill, Morgan and Morris (1975) found that they were actually two morphine-like factors. ... They synthesised these substances and found that the artificial *enkephalin* acted as a potent opiate. ... It appears likely that one of the reasons that electrical brain stimulation produces analgesia is that the stimulation causes the release of enkephalin by the brain. The enkephalin then stimulates the opiate receptors and produces analgesia.'

Terenius, L. and Wahlstrom, A. (1975) A Morphine-Like Ligand for Opiate Receptors in Human CSF. *Life Sciences* 16: 479–82.

Hughes, J., Smith, T. W., Kosterlitz, H. W., Fothergill, L. A., Morgan, B. A., and Morris, H. R. (1975) Identification of Two Related Pentapeptides from the Brain with Potent Opiate Agonists Activity. *Nature* 258: 577–79.

5 Carlson (1977: 44).

Flynn, J., Vanegas, H., Foote, W., and Edwards, S. (1970) Neural Mechanisms Involved in a Cat's Attack on a Rat. In R. F. Whalen, M. Thompson, M. Verzeano, and N. Weinberger (eds) *The Neural Control of Behaviour*. New York: Academic Press.

Appendix to Chapter 9: from dependence to interdependence – Guntrip on Fairbairn

Kernberg looks at relationships as organized along dimensions of pleasure and pain; Fairbairn looks at them as organized primarily along dimensions of dependence, independence (isolation), and interdependence. This gives us a very modern way of looking at what upsets people and spoils their lives. It does seem as though many people now seeking psychotherapeutic help feel isolated, feel they don't belong anywhere, or feel trapped or abandoned or enslaved; all these are descriptions of how one person can be dependent on another and find the experience painful.

Fairbairn postulates three successive stages in the development from an infantile kind of dependence (which is essentially the symbiotic situation of infant and mother absorbed in each other), via a transitional stage which Fairbairn's great commentator Guntrip (1961: 375ff.) elaborated into a whole variety of possibilities, to a final state of mature dependence. The mature person has established separateness from 'the other', but not on a rejecting basis, and is able to love and work interdependently with others. It is pleasant to note that Fairbairn does not go in for independence as the typical mature characteristic, he goes for interdependence.

On the way to mature interdependence and accurate differentiation of self from others, there is a variety of intermediate kinds of relationships. In presenting these for us to read, Guntrip obviously had to put them in a sequence, but he does not suggest that everyone goes through the whole of the sequence, or that the sequence is invariably the same. Each variant shows something of what can happen in the process of differentiation, and Guntrip looks at what this can mean for

419

the self, for the other, and for the relationship. He brings out very strikingly the difficulty we all have at times in deciding quite which end of a relationship we are at: are we loving or loved? hating or hated? frightening or frightened? All we know is that there is a lot of love, or hate, or fear.

Also to be noted is the relatively greater variety of the more primitive relationships. Guntrip calls them pre-moral, as one might say, pre-Oedipal; he means those relationships which do not involve any elements of concern for the other – in these relationships the need for love or approbation from others is not as important as other satisfactions. It is pleasing that he sees this as not civilized. His standard of civilization is high: it excludes even the immature moral variants.

Guntrip's eight types of object-relationships, giving rise to fourteen relationship patterns

1   ORIGINAL LIBIDINAL: *Infantile symbiosis with mother.* A satisfying and non-aggressively dependent relationship of ego to object. Satisfaction experienced in oneness based on primary identification of ego with object. In the womb, a state of bliss, of direct enjoyment of the object in complete but unrealized dependence. Its attempted revival by secondary identification after birth, and regression in feeling and phantasy, leads to claustrophobic anxieties of being stifled, swallowed. The original bliss partly recaptured by the baby at the satisfying breast. The relationship is stable when satisfying since there is no inner motive for change.

(i)   The baby depending on the mature and satisfying mother.

(ii)   The mature and satisfying mother carrying, or nursing, the baby. Regressive escapes from later disturbed positions back to (i) give rise to the pattern of the helpless child and the protective comforter.

The schizoid level, pre-civilized disturbed patterns

2   PRE-MORAL LIBIDINAL: *Aggressively dependent.* The *Libidinal Ego* with natural needs stimulated by the unsatisfying *Exciting Object.* An unequal relationship between a needy child and a needed parent, a reversible parent–child pattern involving frustration and instability.

(iii) The infantile dependent person possessively longing for a mother-figure.

(iv)   The infantile dependent person possessively trying to be a mother-figure.

3   PRE-MORAL ANTI-LIBIDINAL: *Aggressively rejective.* The *Libidinal Ego* as a needy, frightened, rejected child masochistically suffering under the angry *Rejective Object*, the sadistic adult. An unequal relationship giving rise to a child–parent pattern involving great hostility and therefore unstable and reversible.

(v)   The infantile dependent person persecuted and rejected.

(vi)   The infantile dependent person persecuting and rejecting another.

4   PRE-MORAL MIXED: *Libidinal and aggressive.* The *Anti-Libidinal Ego*, the child, placating the *Rejecting Object* by giving up needs and identifying the parent's anti-libidinal attitudes. A frustrating relationship, unstable, and a reversible pattern.

(vii)   The weak fearfully admiring the ruthless strong.

(viii)   The pseudo-strong infantile dependent person demanding admiration from the submissive weak one.

There are only two ways out of difficulties of the disturbed immature relationships of (2), (3), and (4); the real solution is that of growth to maturity (8). A false solution is often attempted by the ego in the form of an escape (5).

5   SCHIZOID WITHDRAWAL: The escape from too great pressure by abolishing emotional relationships altogether in favour of an introverted and withdrawn personality which is unable to show any feeling.

(ix)   The cold detached person who acts mechanically with people.

The depressed level, the struggle to reach a civilized level

6   IMMATURE MORAL: *Dependent morality.* Relationships based on the childish conscience founded on fear, the child seeking security through approval, for the giving up of his libidinal needs and aggressions.

(x)   The infantile dependent person fearing disapproval of his libidinal (sexual) need.

(xi)   The infantile dependent person fearing disapproval of his anger.

7   IMMATURE MORAL: *Aggressive morality.* The former relationships are unstable because of the hostility involved, and the pattern can be reversed thus:

(xii)　The infantile dependent person condemning others' needs.

(xiii)　The infantile dependent person condemning others' angers.

The mature civilized level

8　MATURE BOTH LIBIDINALLY AND MORALLY: The fully adult relationships between emotional equals, characterized by mutuality, spontaneity, co-operation, preservation of individuality and valuable differences, and by stability. The relationship is irreversible and stable, having no motive for change. Its morality is implicit, not imposed, a natural acceptance of obligations to other people.

(xiv)　The relationship of mature dependence is equal partnership and friendship; love, that is capacity to give to another a relationship in which his [sic] personality can flourish.

Appendix to Chapter 13: introjection and projection

That great innovator, Melanie Klein, observed that the small children whom she psycho-analysed – itself a major innovation – could imagine that they ate up parts of their parents, so that these were then inside them – that is to say, they had been 'introjected'. The breast is the first internal object', writes Segal succinctly (1957). Reciprocally, the children could also imagine being inside their parents.

Besides imagining themselves greedily taking in things from their parents, children could also imagine their parents forcefully putting things inside them. Reciprocally, they could also imagine putting things inside their parents. They could imagine being entirely inside their parents, or putting things in them or doing things to them in there. They could imagine their parents inside them, putting things in there, doing things. Quite naturally a language developed of our putting things 'out' of ourselves and 'in' to others: projection. This is commonly thought of as a way of disowning parts of ourselves which we find unacceptable, and locating them inside someone else instead, where their unacceptable nature can be dealt with more painlessly, through blame, correction, avoidance, or whatever.

This way of thinking, in terms of each of us having an inner self in which people and things (objects) may be found, a self into which they may be put and from which they may be taken, was a brilliant and useful innovation in child psychotherapy. Here was a way in which children in a sandpit or a doll's house could demonstrate, and perhaps put into words, their phantasies, their hopes and fears and speculations. The child-therapist helped the children develop this way of thinking so that they could talk more easily about what was on their

424 OUR NEED FOR OTHERS

mind. This helped many children clear up painful fears and damaging confusions, gave them support, and in other ways brought relief.

Though I believe that phantasies like these are fairly common, they are not precisely what I have been writing about in this chapter.

1 The structures I have been writing about are much less clearly defined than those of children talking in terms of breast, penis, stomach, and other definite parts of the body.

2 The structures I have been writing about, being less clearly defined, are better thought of as merging into one another than as being put one inside the other.

3 One of the main premises of this book is that we only slowly and with much trial-and-error e-merge out of the confusion of self-and-other into more accurate clearly delimited perceptions of ourselves and other people. In view of this, it should occasion little surprise that we attribute some of our bad-feeling phantasies (or good-feeling ones) to other people, nor that we attribute some of our good-feeling phantasies about them (or bad-feeling ones) to ourselves. At the very primitive level where this confusion exists, unconscious minds are timeless and anarchic. As a patient of Margaret Little's said:

> 'What's yours is mine; what's mine is my own. What's yours is half mine, and half the other half's mine, so it's all mine.'
>
> (1981: Chapter 5)

These are infantile ways of thinking. There is a danger that when we are too concrete, too spatial, too pictorial in our language, we disable ourselves from empathizing with people in this state of mind.

Bibliographical references

Abercrombie, M. L. J. (1960) *The Anatomy of Judgment*. London: Hutchinson. (1969) Harmondsworth: Pelican.

Abraham, K. (1924) Short Study of the Development of the Libido, Viewed in the Light of Mental Disorders. In (1979) *Selected Papers*. London: Maresfield Reprints.

Auden, W. H. (1948) *Selected Poems*. London: Faber.

Axline, V. (1964) *Dibs: In Search of Self*. London: Gollancz. (1971) Harmondsworth: Pelican.

Balint, M. (1952) *Primary Love and Psychoanalytic Technique*. London: Hogarth.

—— (1957) *The Doctor, The Patient, and his Illness*. London: Pitman Medical Publishing.

—— (1959) *Thrills and Regressions*. London: Hogarth.

—— (1968) *The Basic Fault*. London: Hogarth.

Bartlett, F. (1932) *Remembering*. Cambridge: Cambridge University Press.

Bettelheim, B. (1960) *The Informed Heart*. New York: Free Press.

—— (1979) *Surviving and Other Essays*. London: Thames & Hudson; New York: Alfred Knopf. Many of these essays are republished (1986) *Surviving the Holocaust*. London: Fontana.

Bick, E. (1968) The Experience of the Skin in Early Object-Relations. *International Journal of Psycho-Analysis* 39: 484–86.

Bion, W. R. (1962a) The Psycho-Analytic Study of Thinking. *International Journal of Psycho-Analysis* 43: 306–10.

—— (1962b) *Learning from Experience*. London: Heinemann.

Blakemore, C. (1977) *Mechanisms of the Mind*. BBC Reith Lectures for 1976. Cambridge: Cambridge University Press.

Boring, E. B. (1946) Mind and Mechanism. *American Journal of Psychology* 59: 173–92.

Bowlby, J. (1969) *Attachment*. London: Hogarth. (1971) Harmondsworth: Pelican.

—— (1973) *Separation, Anxiety and Anger*. London: Hogarth. (1975) Harmondsworth: Pelican.

—— (1980) *Loss, Sadness and Depression*. London: Hogarth. (1981) Harmondsworth: Pelican.

Bruner, J., Goodnow, J., and Austin, G. (1956) *A Study of Thinking*. New York and London: John Wiley.

Carlson, N. (1977) *Physiology of Behaviour*. Boston, Mass. and London: Allyn & Bacon.

Casement, P. (1985) *On Listening to the Patient*. London: Tavistock.

Chalmers, N., Crawley, R., and Rose, S. P. R. (eds) (1971) *The Biological Bases of Behaviour*. Milton Keynes: Open University.

Coltart, N. (1985) Slouching toward Bethlehem. In G. Kohon (ed.) *The British School of Psychoanalysis: The Independent Tradition*. London: Free Association Press.

cummings, e. e. (1960) *selected poems 1923–1958*. London: Faber. (1963) Harmondsworth: Penguin Poets.

Davis, M. and Wallbridge, D. (1981) *Boundary and Space*. London: H. Karnac. (1983 revised edn) Harmondsworth: Penguin.

Ehrenzweig, A. (1967) *The Hidden Order of Art*. London: Weidenfeld & Nicolson.

Empson, W. (1955) *Collected Poems*. London: Chatto & Windus.

Erikson, E. (1950) *Childhood and Society*. New York: W. W. Norton.

—— (1959) Identity, Youth and Crisis. *Psychological Issues* 1. New York: International University Press. Subsequently (1968) New York: W. W. Norton.

Fairbairn, W. R. D. (1952) *Psycho-Analytic Studies of the Personality*. London: Tavistock with Routledge & Kegan Paul. Subsequently (1954) as *An Object-Relations Theory of the Personality*. New York: Basic Books.

Fenichel, O. (1945) *The Psychoanalytic Theory of Neurosis*. New York: W. W. Norton. Subsequently (1946) London: Routledge & Kegan Paul.

Ferenczi, S. (1916) Stages in the Development of the Sense of Reality. In *Contributions to Psychoanalysis*. Boston, Mass: Richard C. Bager.

Flynn, J., Vanegas, H., Foote, W., and Edwards, S. (1970) Neural Mechanisms Involved in a Cat's Attack on a Rat. In R. F. Whalen, M. Thompson, M. Verzeano, and N. Weinberger *The Neural Control of Behaviour*. New York: Academic Press.

Freud, A. (1936, trans. 1937) *The Ego and Mechanisms of Defence*. London: Hogarth.

—— (1960) A Discussion of Dr John Bowlby's Paper 'Grief and

Mourning in Infancy and Early Childhood'. *Psycho-Analytical Study of the Child* 15: 53–62.

Freud, S. (1895) Project for a Scientific Psychology. Posthumously translated and published in 1966. Standard Edition 1: 281–97.

—— (1915) Instincts and their Vicissitudes. Standard Edition 14: 117–40.

—— (1920) *Beyond the Pleasure Principle.* Standard Edition 18: 3–64.

—— (1923) *The Ego and the Id.* Standard Edition 19: 1–66.

—— (1926) *Inhibitions, Symptoms and Anxiety.* Standard Edition 20: 75–175.

—— (1927) *The Future of an Illusion.* Standard Edition 21: 5–56.

Fromm, E. (1946) *The Fear of Freedom.* London: Routledge & Kegan Paul. Also (1941) as *Escape from Freedom.* New York: Holt, Rinehart, & Winston.

—— (1976) *To Have or To Be?* (1978) London: Jonathan Cape. (1979) Tunbridge Wells: Abacus.

Fuller, P. (1980) *Art and Psychoanalysis.* London: Writers and Readers Publishing Coop.

Goldberg, A. (ed.) (1978) *The Psychology of the Self.* New York: International University Press.

Gooddy, W. (1949) Sensation and Volition. *Brain* 72: 312–39.

Green, H. (1964) *I Never Promised You a Rosegarden.* London: Gollancz. (1967) London: Pan.

Greenberg, J. R. and Mitchell, S. A. (1983) *Object Relations in Psychoanalytic Theory.* Cambridge, Mass. and London: Harvard University Press.

Grotstein, J. S. (1981) A Review of Tustin's *Autistic States in Children. International Review of Psycho-Analysis* 10: 4.

Guntrip, H. (1961) *Personality Structure and Human Interaction.* London: Hogarth.

—— (1964) *Healing the Sick Mind.* London: Allen & Unwin.

—— (1969) *Schizoid Phenomena, Object Relations and the Self.* London: Hogarth.

—— (1971) *Psychoanalytic Theory, Therapy and the Self.* New York: International University Press.

—— (1975) My Experience of Analysis with Fairbairn and Winnicott. *International Review of Psycho-Analysis* 2: 2.

Guthrie, E. R. (1935) *The Psychology of Learning.* New York: Harper.

Hartley, L. P. (1944) *The Shrimp and the Anemone.* London: Putnam.

Hartman, H. (1947) On Rational and Irrational Action. In (1964) *Essays on Ego Psychology.* New York: International University Press.

—— (1950) Comments on the Psychoanalysic Theory of the Ego. In

(1964) *Essays on Ego Psychology*. New York: International University Press.

—— (1958) *Ego Psychology and the Problem of Adaptation*. New York: International University Press.

von Hayek, F. (1952) *The Sensory Order*. London: Routledge & Kegan Paul.

Heathers, G. (1954) The Adjustment of Two-Year Olds in a Novel Situation. *Child Development* **25**: 147–58.

Hebb, D. O. (1949) *The Organisation of Behaviour*. New York: Wiley. London: Chapman & Hall.

—— (1958) *A Textbook of Psychology*. Philadelphia and London: W. B. Sanders.

Hopkins, G. M. (1953) *Selected Poems*. London: Heinemann (ed.) J. Reeves, who tentatively dates this poem as having been written in 1885.

Horney, K. (1950) *Neurosis and Human Growth*. New York: W. W. Norton. (1951) London: Routledge & Kegan Paul.

Hubel, D. H. (1963) The Visual Cortex of the Brain. In N. Chalmers, R. Crawley, and S. P. R. Rose (eds) (1971) *The Biological Bases of Behaviour*. Milton Keynes: Open University. First published in *Scientific American* November 1963.

Hudson, L. (1975) *Human Beings, an Introduction to the Psychology of Human Experience*. London: Jonathan Cape. (1978) St Albans: Paladin.

Hughes, J., Smith, T. W., Kosterlitz, H. W., Fothergill, L. A., Morgan, B. A., and Morris, H. R. (1975) Identification of Two Related Pentapeptides from the Brain with Potent Opiate Agonists Activity. *Nature* **258**: 577–79.

Jacobson, E. (1953) On the Psychoanalytic Theory of Affects. In (1971) *Depression*. New York: International University Press.

James, W. (1890) *Principles of Psychology*. New York: Holt.

Kafka, F. (1916) *Metamorphosis*. See e.g. the translation by W. and E. Muir (1976) Harmondsworth: Penguin Classics.

Katz, B. (1961) How Cells Communicate. In N. Chalmers, R. Crawley, and S. P. R. Rose (eds.) (1971) *The Biological Bases of Behaviour*. Milton Keynes: Open University. First published in *Scientific American* September 1961.

Kernberg, O. (1976) *Object Relations Theory and Clinical Psychoanalysis*. New York: Jason Aronson.

—— (1980) *Internal World and External Reality*. New York: Jason Aronson.

Khan, M. (1975) Introduction to D. W. Winnicott (1975) *Through Paediatrics to Psychoanalysis*. London: Hogarth.

—— (1979) *Alienation in Perversions*. London: Hogarth.
—— (1983) *Hidden Selves: Between Theory and Practice in Psychoanalysis*. London: Hogarth.
Klein, J. (1965) *Samples from English Cultures*. London: Routledge & Kegan Paul.
—— (1985) *Imagination in Adult Education*. Ian Gulland Memorial Lecture for 1984. London: Goldsmiths College.
Klein, M. (1957) *Envy and Gratitude*. London: Tavistock.
—— (1959) Our Adult World and its Roots in Infancy. *Human Relations* 12: 291–303. Also in (1960) *Our Adult World and Other Essays*. London: Heinemann Medical.
Klein, M. with Riviere, J. (1937) *Love, Hate and Reparation*. London: Hogarth.
Kohut, O. (1971) *The Analysis of the Self*. New York: International University Press.
—— (1977) *The Restoration of the Self*. New York: International University Press.
Kraepelin, E. (1905) *Lectures on Clinical Psychiatry*. 2nd rev. edn. in translation. London: Bailliere, Tindall.
Laing, R. D. (1960) *The Divided Self*. London: Tavistock. (1965) Harmondsworth: Pelican.
—— (1978) *Conversations with Children*. London: Allen Lane and Pelican.
Laing, R. D. and Esterson, A. (1964) *Sanity, Madness and the Family*, London: Tavistock. (1970) Harmondsworth: Pelican.
Langer, S. (1967) *Mind, an Essay on Human Feeling*. Baltimore, Md: Johns Hopkins.
Little, M. (1981) *Transference Neurosis and Transference Psychosis*. New York and London: Jason Aronson.
Lorenz, K. (1952) *King Solomon's Ring*. London: Methuen. (1957) London: Pan.
McKellar, P. (1968) *Experience and Behaviour*. Harmondsworth: Pelican.
MacNeice, L. (1966) *Collected Poems*. London: Faber (ed.) E. R. Dodds. The poem *Prayer Before Birth* is dated 1944.
Mark, V. H., Ervin, F. R., and Yakoviev, P. I. (1962) The Treatment of Pain by Stereotaxic Methods. *Confina Neurologica* 22: 238–45.
Matte Blanco, I. (1975) *The Unconscious and Infinite Sets*. London: Duckworth.
Miller, G. A., Galanter, A., and Pribram, K. (1969) *Plans and the Structure of Behaviour*. New York: Holt.
Milner, M. (1955) The Role of Illusion in Symbol Formation. In *New Directions in Psychoanalysis*. London: Tavistock.
Milner, M. (1969) *The Hands of the Living God*. London: Hogarth.

Norman, D. A. (1976) *Memory and Attention: Introduction to Human Information Processing*. New York: John Wiley.

Pascal, B. (*c.* 1660) *Pensées*. See e.g. the translation by J. M. Cohen (1961) Harmondsworth: Penguin.

Penfield, W. and Rasmussen, T. (1957) *The Cerebral Cortex of Man. A Clinical Study of Localisation*. New York: Macmillan.

Pinter, H. (1957) *The Dumb-Waiter*. In (1960) *The Birthday Party and Other Plays*. London: Hudson. (1961) Harmondsworth: Penguin Plays.

Plato (*c.* 400 BC) *The Republic*. See e.g. the translation by H. D. P. Lee (1955) Harmondsworth: Penguin Classics.

Pribram, K. (1971) *Languages of the Brain*. Englewood Cliffs. NJ: Prentice Hall.

Pribram, K. and Gill, M. (1976) *Freud's Project Reassessed*. London: Hutchinson.

Reich, W. (1935) *The Mass Psychology of Fascism*. See e.g. the translation by Mary Boyd Higgins (1975) Harmondsworth: Penguin.

—— (1945) *Listen, Little Man*. See e.g. the translation by T. P. Wolfe (1945) Harmondsworth: Penguin.

Ricks, D. (1975) Vocal Communication in Pre-Verbal, Normal and Autistic Children. In N. O'Connor (ed.) *Language, Cognitive Defects and Retardation*. London: Butterworth.

Riesen, A. H. (1947) The Development of Visual Perception in Man and Chimpanzee. *Science* 106: 107–08.

Robertson, J. (1952) Film: *A Two-Year-Old Goes to Hospital*, London: Tavistock Child Development Unit. For a full bibliography, and other films, see references in J. Bowlby (1973) *Separation, Anxiety and Anger*. London: Hogarth.

Romer, A. S. (1970) The Eye. In N. Chalmers, R. Crawley, and S. P. R. Rose (eds) (1971) *The Biological Bases of Behaviour*. Milton Keynes: Open University. First published in (1970) *The Vertebrate Body*. Philadelphia, Pa. and London: Saunders.

Routenberg, A. and Lindy, J. (1965) Effects of the Availability of Rewarding Septal and Hypothalamic Stimulation on Bar-Pressing for Food under Conditions of Deprivation. *Journal of Comparative and Physiological Psychology* 60: 158–61.

Rycroft, C. (1968) *A Critical Dictionary of Psychoanalysis*. London: Nelson. (1972) Harmondsworth: Penguin.

Schafer, R. (1968) *Aspects of Internalisation*. New York: International University Press.

—— (1976) *A New Language for Psycho-analysis*. Newhaven, Conn. and London: Yale University Press.

—— (1978) *Language and Insight*. Newhaven, Conn. and London: Yale University Press.

—— (1983) *The Analytic Attitude*. London: Hogarth.
Searles, R. R. (1965) *Collected Papers on Schizophrenia and Related Subjects*. New York: International University Press.
—— (1979) *Countertransference and Related Subjects*. New York: International University Press.
Sechehaye, M. A. (1931) trans. B. and H. Würsten (1951) *Symbolic Realisation*. New York: International University Press. Also trans. R. Rabson (1956) *A New Psychotherapy in Schizophrenia, Relief of Frustrations by Symbolic Realisations*. New York: Grune & Stratton.
Segal, H. (1957) Notes on Symbol-Formation. *International Journal of Psycho-Analysis* 38: 391–97.
—— (1964) *Introduction to the Work of Melanie Klein*. London: Hogarth.
—— (1979) *Klein*. Brighton: Harvester Press. London: Fontana.
Senden, M. V. (1932) *Raum and Gestalt Auffassung bei operierten Blindgeborenen vor und nach der Operation*. Leipzig: Barth.
Spitz, R. (1985) The Primal Cavity: a Contribution to the Genesis of Perception and its Role in Psychoanalytic Theory. *Psychoanalytical Study of the Child* 10: 215–40.
Terenius, L. and Wahlstrom, A. (1975) A Morphine-like Ligand for Opiate Receptors in Human CSF. *Life Sciences* 16: 479–82.
Tolman, E. C. (1948) Cognitive Maps in Rats and Men. *Psychological Review* 55: 189–208.
Truax, C. B. and Carkhuff, R. R. (1967) *Towards Effective Counselling and Psychotherapy*. Chicago, Ill: Aldine Press.
Tulving, E. (1972) Episodic and Semantic Memory. In E. Tulving and W. Donaldson (eds) *Organisation of Memory*. New York: Academic Press.
Tustin, F. (1972) *Autism and Childhood Psychosis*. London: Hogarth. (1973) New York: Jason Aronson.
—— (1980) Autistic Objects. *International Review of Psycho-Analysis* 7: 27–37.
—— (1981) *Autistic States in Children*. London: Routledge & Kegan Paul. For an interesting review, see Grotstein (1981).
—— (1982) I-ness. *Bulletin XIII of the British Association of Psychotherapists*.
—— (1984) Autistic Shapes. *International Review of Psycho-Analysis* II: 279–88.
—— (1986) *Autistic Barriers in Neurotic Patients*. London: Karnac. New Haven, Conn: Yale University Press.
Valenstein, E. S. and Beer, R. (1964) Continuous Opportunity for Reinforcing Brain Stimulation. *Journal of the Experimental Analysis of Behaviour* 7: 183–84.
Vernon, M. D. *The Psychology of Behaviour*. Harmondsworth: Penguin.

Winnicott, D. W. (1949) Mind and its Relation to the Psyche-soma. Chapter 19 in (1958).
—— (1951) Transitional Objects and Transitional Phenomena. Chapter 18 in (1958a).
—— (1954) Metapsychological and Clinical Aspects of Regression. Chapter 22 in (1958a).
—— (1958a) *Collected Papers: Through Paediatrics to Psychoanalysis.* London: Tavistock. (1975) London: Hogarth; the first part of the title was then dropped.
—— (1958b) The Capacity to be Alone. Chapter 2 in (1965).
—— (1960) Ego Distortion in Terms of True and False Self. Chapter 12 in (1965).
—— (1962) Ego Integration in Child Development. Chapter 4 in (1965).
—— (1963) The Development of the Capacity for Concern. Chapter 6 in (1965).
—— (1964) *The Child, the Family and the Outside World.* Harmondsworth: Pelican. A large section of this material was originally published in two other volumes: *The Child and the Family* and *The Child and the Outside World* (1957) London: Tavistock.
—— (1965) *The Maturational Processes and the Facilitating Environment.* London: Hogarth.
—— (1971) *Playing and Reality.* London: Hogarth. (1974) Harmondsworth: Penguin.
—— (1974) The Fear of Breakdown. *International Review of Psycho-Analysis* 1: 1.
—— (1978) *The Piggle.* London: Hogarth.
Yeats, W. B. (1921) *Michael Robartes and the Dancer.* Dublin: Cuulu Press.

Index

296, 312, 353, 367–69, 374,
420–21
relating and the capacity to relate to
others xv, xvi, 6, 91–2, 94–6,
106, 129, 138, 141, 143–45, 179,
240–41, 281, 286–87, 304, 310,
317–18, 328, 349, 352–53,
355–56, 368, 370, 374, 382
renunciation 165–71, 206, 215,
309–11, 315–17, 338
repression (*see also* disowning) 112,
126, 187–88, 198–99, 224–25,
339, 352, 384, 412
reverberation 34–6, 41, 58, 60, 83,
127, 135, 189, 281, 283, 285, 361,
366, 371, 378
reversible phenomena 46–7, 332
Ricks, D. 93
Riesen, A. H. 33
Robertson, J. 106, 309, 323
roles 67, 143–44, 183–84, 241–42,
244, 264, 317, 333
Romer, A. S. 16
Routenberg, A. 21
Ruby 334–35
Rycroft, C. 340

safety and security 98–100, 101–02,
116–21, 207, 208, 231, 236, 241,
283–84, 300, 307–08, 328, 361,
391–408, 411
Schafer, R. 65, 68–9, 125
schizoid processes and traits 155,
157, 172, 187, 233, 293, chs 16,
17, 18 *passim*, 359, 420–21
schizophrenic processes and traits
101, 157, 172, 295–300, 331–32,
334–38, 356
scientific discovery and invention
287
Searles, R. R. 378
Sechehaye, M. A. 295–303
second chances 218–22, 378
Segal, H. 156, 291, 295, 404
selective perception 42f., 58,
131–34, 138, 165–68, 170,
189–92, 311, 315, 344–45

self and ego 116, 132, 147, 169, 194,
229
self as agent, object, and/or place
65, 69, 76, 182, 183, 234, 354
self-awareness 65–6, 68f., 138–39,
156–76, 185–86, 195–200, 348,
366, 379, 382, 409
self-confidence, self-esteem, self-
respect (cf. narcissism) 2–3, 93,
116–21, 164–67, 171–72, chs 11
and 12 *passim*, 269, 274–77, 286,
296, 308–10, 314–17, 324,
348–56, 364, 366–67, 377–79,
380, 382, 385, 401, 411–13
self-imagery ch. 1 *passim*, 63–6,
68–9, 78, 85, 88–92, 132–35, 138,
144, 156, 158, 160, 162, 165, 170,
182–84, 195–200, 208, 235–38,
242, ch. 13 *passim*, 274–75, 302,
314, 316, 322, 323–25, 334–35,
336–38, 343, 345, 353, 359,
364–69, 372–73, 376–79, 382,
394, 407
self-object states 76, 113–14,
126–28, 204–16, 223, 224, 230,
232–36, 248, 249, 250, 260, 261,
276, 280–82, 307, 363, 367,
389–90, 393, 399
self-structures: bipolar selves
220–22; episodic and semantic
selves 184, 187, 376–77; part-
selves, substructures, and
subsystems 60–3, 67–8, 161–73,
181–86, 189, 198–200, 221–25,
242, 260–65, 274–77, 286,
311–18, 324, 326, 333–37,
338–42, 343–50, 352–53, 360,
366–69, 376, 382, 391–96, 398,
402, 404, 406–08
Senden, M. V. 32
senses, the life of the 20, 26–8,
59–60, 64–5, 76, 78, 81–4, 89,
123, 167, 182, 184, 187, 254–58,
267–69, 271, 276, 289, 296, 314,
338, 344, 346–48, 350–51
set theory 256, 262
sexuality and sex differences 101,